Redesigning Animation

United Productions of America

The Focus Animation Series aims to provide unique, accessible content that may not otherwise be published. We allow researchers, academics, and professionals the ability to quickly publish high impact, current literature in the field of animation for a global audience. This series is a fine complement to the existing, robust animation titles available through CRC Press/Focal Press.

Series Editor Giannalberto Bendazzi, currently an independent scholar, is a former Visiting Professor of History of Animation at the Nanyang Technological University in Singapore and a former professor at the Università degli Studi di Milano. We welcome any submissions to help grow the wonderful content we are striving to provide to the animation community: giannalbertobendazzi@gmail.com.

Published:

Giannalberto Bendazzi; *Twice the First: Quirino Cristiani and the Animated Feature Film*

Maria Roberta Novielli; *Floating Worlds: A Short History of Japanese Animation*

Forthcoming:

Pamela Taylor Turner; *Infinite Animation: The Life and Work of Adam Beckett*

Lina X. Aguirre; *Experimental Animation in Contemporary Latin America*

Marco Bellano; *Václav Trojan: Music Composition in Czech Animated Films*

Rolf Giesen; *Puppetry, Puppet Animation and the Digital Age*

Redesigning Animation
United Productions of America

Cinzia Bottini

CRC Press
Taylor & Francis Group
Boca Raton London New York

CRC Press is an imprint of the
Taylor & Francis Group, an **informa** business

A FOCAL PRESS BOOK

CRC Press
Taylor & Francis Group
6000 Broken Sound Parkway NW, Suite 300
Boca Raton, FL 33487-2742

International Standard Book Number-13: 978-0-8153-8178-5 (Paperback)
International Standard Book Number-13: 978-0-8153-8179-2 (Hardback)

Library of Congress Cataloging-in-Publication Data

Names: Bottini, Cinzia, author.
Title: Redesigning animation : United Productions of America / Cinzia Bottini.
Other titles: UPA
Description: Boca Raton : Taylor & Francis, 2018. | Includes bibliographical references. | Revision of the author's thesis (doctoral--Nanyang Technological University, 2016) under the title: UPA : redesigning animation.
Identifiers: LCCN 2018011862| ISBN 9780815381785 (pbk. : alk. paper) | ISBN 9780815381792 (hardback : alk. paper)
Subjects: LCSH: United Productions of America. | Animated films--United States.
Classification: LCC NC1766.U52 U7335 2018 | DDC 791.43/34--dc23
LC record available at https://lccn.loc.gov/2018011862

Visit the Taylor & Francis Web site at
http://www.taylorandfrancis.com

and the CRC Press Web site at
http://www.crcpress.com

Art does not reproduce the visible; rather, it makes visible.

Paul Klee,
"Creative Credo"

Contents

Foreword

UPA: THE EXERCISE OF SYNTHESIS

It is commonplace to call the rise of United Productions of America—UPA—a revolutionary turning point in animation history. There are many reasons for that. Within the American animation industry, at that time, artists had to follow the standards of the studios that employed them. The animators had to copy the artistic guidelines of few main creators, being faithful to the studios styles and characters.

UPA animations were low-budget, short productions with a plurality of styles expressing the free inspiration of their authors. Each film was an independent artistic proposal without commitments to the previous productions (except the Mr. Magoo and Gerald McBoing-Boing characters, who were the most relevant subjects of a few attempts at creating animated series).

The UPA team had a lot of previous experience inside the animation industry, as many of the professionals had cut their teeth in studios like Disney or Warner Bros. During World War II they were involved in many animated war propaganda films, learning how to be direct, fast and economical in their work. The popularity of TV in the early 1950s made room for many animated commercials and UPA had the leadership in that particular production.

Many UPA animators, while employed at Disney, were involved in the well-known polemic strike in the 1940s. Later some names were blacklisted after Walt Disney testified before the House Committee on Un-American Activities (HUAC).

UPA was created during a political conflict inside animation industry. It is natural to label its production as a counterpoint and resistance to the Disney legacy.

The book that we have in our hands now helps to follow this dichotomy. The author carefully traces the influences of the artistic movements from the first half of 20th century during the creation of UPA, including the Disney legacy. Although UPA was not identified with the Disney emphasis on photorealism, UPA filtered from Disney production those strategies that could be positive in establishing a powerful visuality in popular media.

The author is sensitive to, and comprehensively presents, the main common historical points of that particular time, but this book does not frame the importance of UPA considering only those factors.

One of the highlights is the UPA legacy in the career and filmography of many directors and studios. One example is the reference to the Zagreb Animation production and its contribution to sound design in animation, giving one step ahead of what UPA initially proposed.

The reference to the Japanese animator Osamu Tezuka is very precise, as he was a confessed admirer of Disney style and also highly influenced by UPA visuality.

Even Disney Studios was influenced by UPA and the author analyzes some of Disney productions from the 1950s, detecting those influences carefully.

Another important contribution from this book is the comprehensive analysis of many UPA films considering their creative artistic background, dialoguing with the best of fine arts, graphic design and advertising heritages.

This book establishes a better understanding of UPA's legacy. Beyond making a revolutionary contribution, UPA proposed an exercise of synthesis, revealing that, besides the differences of vision, style and political statement, UPA and Disney legacies can also be understood today as two opposite sides of the same coin.

Animation would never be the same after that experience. It was a moment of maturity.

Welcome to this journey. We could not be guided by better hands.

Heitor Capuzzo
Universidade Federal de Minas Gerais,
Escola de Belas Artes

Acknowledgments

When I started this project, I could never have imagined what a formative learning experience it would be, both professionally and personally. As it happens with every doctoral dissertation turned into a book, I owe many people a debt of gratitude for all their help throughout this long journey.

I deeply thank my supervisor, Professor Heitor Capuzzo; my cosupervisor, Giannalberto Bendazzi; and Professor Vibeke Sorensen, chair of the School of Art, Design and Media at Nanyang Technological University, Singapore for showing sincere compassion and offering unwavering moral support during a personally difficult stage of my doctoral studies. I am also grateful for all their suggestions, critiques and observations that guided me in this research project, as well as their dedication and patience.

My gratitude goes to Tee Bosustow, who graciously shared memorabilia his father had collected. I also thank all the enthusiastic staff of the American archives and libraries that I visited: Howard Prouty and Jenny Romero, archivists of the Margaret Herrick Library, Academy of Motion Picture Arts and Sciences in Beverly Hills; Mark Quigley, archivist of the UCLA Film & Television Archive; Michelle Harvey, archivist of the MoMA archives in New York City; and Brent Phillips, media specialist and processing archivist at the Fales Library and Special Collections of New York University.

Special appreciation also goes to those who shared their observations and comments on the general topic: Adam Abraham, who provided invaluable information and sent me a copy of *The Boing-Boing Show* animated shorts; Professor Emerita Marsha Kinder; Professor Ben Alvin Shedd; Associate Professor Jaroslaw Kapuscinski; Associate Professor Hans-Martin Rall; Assistant Professor Kathrin Albers; and the many experts on animated cinema and UPA who kindly agreed to be interviewed and shared their memories and opinions with me. Among them, I would like to mention

UPA animators Alan Zaslove, Willis Pyle, Howard Beckerman and Fred Crippen; UPA sound designer Joe Siracusa; animators Ishu Patel and Eric Goldberg; artist Hans Bacher; and animation historians Maureen Furniss and Karl F. Cohen.

I thank the School of Art, Design and Media and Nanyang Technological University for their support and generosity in granting the necessary funds for this research. I am especially grateful to Associate Professor Michael J. K. Walsh, Associate Chair (Research) at ADM; Hong Bee Kuen, manager of the Ph.D. program at ADM; and all the ADM librarians, particularly Phoebe Lim Choon Lan and V. Somasundram.

I would not have been able to complete this undertaking without the kindness and generosity of many dear friends. Carlos Jaramillo helped me enjoy Singapore city life, as well as providing enlightening conversations that offered new perspectives on life's twists. Darlene Espeña revealed to me the importance of being optimistic. My colleagues Mohammad Javad Khajavi, Catherine Yang Jing, Juan Camilo González and Christine Veras De Souza contributed to my learning process at different stages and in different ways. Andrijana Ruzic translated interviews from Croatian to Italian for me. Dr. Jodi Finkel welcomed me in Los Angeles during my research field trip, taught me how Angelenos live and generously gave me many rides to diverse parts of the city. My dearest friend, Federica Travaglianti, constantly motivated me during the lonely months I spent in Italy, writing this study, and accompanied me on a visit to the Bauhaus Archive/Museum of Design in Berlin.

I thank Katherine Barnhart, who shared her opinions on this work, edited it and patiently answered all my queries during the process; and I am sincerely grateful to Sean Connelly, Executive Editor of CRC Press, who enthusiastically decided to publish my research, as well as Jessica Vega, Editorial Assistant, who helped me along the way.

I finally thank my genuinely sincere friends, supporters and motivators Valentina Guzzardo and Michela Vuga. No words are enough to acknowledge all the love and patience that my husband, Andrea Fusi, has shown me during this challenging period of our life together. I dedicate this study to him and our beloved daughter, Matilde Antonietta.

Summary

United Productions of America (UPA) was a small American animation studio founded in 1943 by three former Disney employees who had previously taken part in the infamous Disney strike. UPA succeeded in challenging Disney's supremacy in the entertainment market by creating cutting-edge animated cartoons. UPA films express a simplified audiovisual language that consists of stylized layout designs, asymmetrical compositions, colors applied flatly and in strong contrast with each other, limited animation, abstract sound and minimal scores. How did UPA artists develop these original visual and aural solutions? The innovative style was developed via the assimilation of aesthetic features already expressed by Modern painters, graphic designers, advertising men and musicians. The minimalism that characterizes Modern paintings was transferred into the advertising business and the animation industry. Graphic design and animation cross-fertilized starting in the 1940s, and UPA artists absorbed the theoretical principles applied first by Modern painters and then by Modern graphic designers. At the core of this work there is the assumption that UPA is a Modern animation studio and that UPA animated cartoons are Modern animations, because they synthesize a common minimalist tendency that was occurring in U.S. animation during the 1940s and later exploded internationally in the 1950s and 1960s. Therefore, this work proposes to consider UPA animated films as case studies of a simplified audiovisual language that influenced international productions.

This study comprises five parts. First, UPA studio is framed within its historical, sociological and cultural background in order to illustrate the conditions under which UPA studio was founded, flourished and declined. An examination of the contradictory figure of Stephen (Steve) Bosustow, executive producer of the company, and the UPA production system as possible concurrent causes of UPA films' inventiveness follows in Chapter 2. In Chapter 3, Modernist stylistic features of painting, graphic design and poster advertising are explored, and their influence on UPA animations is traced. The fourth chapter analyzes UPA animated films, highlighting those stylistic elements that were groundbreaking in animated cinema at that time. Then, in order to demonstrate the impact of UPA Modernism on animation, examples of international films that show direct or indirect influences from the UPA aesthetic are considered in Chapter 5. Finally, the Conclusion considers the UPA legacy and clarifies the way in which graphic Modernism determined UPA's new attitude toward animation. This study also suggests the relevance of UPA in the search for a theoretical definition of animated cinema, as carried on by animation historians since the 1950s. Ultimately, it firmly situates UPA within the history of animation, attributing it a crucial role in the origins of Modern animation.

Notes

The source *Steve Bosustow's UPA collection, in the care of his son, Tee Bosustow* (abbreviated form: *Steve Bosustow's UPA collection*) refers to materials that were produced by the animation studio United Productions of America (UPA), collected by UPA executive producer Stephen Bosustow and preserved to the present by Stephen Bosustow's son, Tee. During my research trip to the U.S. (May–July 2014), I visited Tee Bosustow in Burbank, California. His apartment was full of boxes piled up and just waiting to be opened. He was in the process of donating all the materials that his father had stored during his life to the Margaret Herrick Library, Academy of Motion Picture Arts and Sciences, in Beverly Hills for the benefit of future researchers. I remember how gentle Tee was, as he opened his father's boxes in my presence. We traveled back in time to the days when UPA cartoons drew crowds to LA and NYC movie theaters, UPA artists gave full rein to their creativity and the animation studio was booming. We found all types of memorabilia: UPA publicity documents, sketches, cels, photographs, interoffice memos, financial statements. Among the many artifacts were handwritten and typewritten notes compiled by Stephen Bosustow, several of his appointment books starting from 1944 and even detailed drawn UPA timelines, copies of which can be found in the Appendix. In his later years, after UPA was just a memory, Stephen Bosustow had the idea of writing a book about his experience as an executive producer in the animation business. Whenever he could, and despite the cancer that was consuming him, he wrote. Stephen Bosustow's personal memories as well as the precious UPA materials he left behind are the most relevant primary sources for this work. I am deeply grateful to Tee Bosustow for his generosity, his willingness to preserve UPA items and documents and his devotion to showing UPA animated cartoons to young generations. At the time of this writing (March 2018), Tee is working on an animated documentary about UPA, a project he started several years ago.

***

The term *animated cinema*, used to address animated films, mainly refers to hand-drawn animated cartoons when not otherwise specified.

The reader is encouraged to watch the UPA animated films referred to in this book as accompaniment to the text.

Author

Cinzia Bottini received her Ph.D. from the School of Art, Design and Media at Nanyang Technological University in Singapore (2016). She graduated in Philosophy (2004) and earned a Master's degree in Philosophical Studies with an emphasis on fine art and cinema from the University of Milan (2010). She has worked as a journalist for radio, magazine, and television, and she has written about the history and theory of animation for the following journals and books: *ITINERA—Rivista di Filosofia e di Teoria delle Arti, Animation—A World History* by Giannalberto Bendazzi, *Animation Studies Online Journal,* and *Cabiria—Studi di Cinema.*

Introduction

1. "ALMOST TOO GOOD TO BE TRUE"

The animated films produced by United Productions of America (UPA) from 1943 to 1959 marked a turning point in the history of animation. When *Gerald McBoing Boing*[1] premiered in 1951, film critic Arthur Knight welcomed it as the new *Three Little Pigs*.[2] Walt Disney Company's *Three Little Pigs* (1933) had been a milestone for character animation primarily in the U.S., but also internationally: it was one of the first color short films in the *Silly Symphony* series produced by Disney, featuring three anthropomorphic pigs and one wolf animated according to the principles of Disney's "realism."[3] It appeared five years after *Steamboat Willie*,[4] the first fully synchronized sound cartoon, released by Disney in black and white in 1928 and marking the debut of Mickey Mouse and Minnie.[5]

During the 1930s, Mickey Mouse's popularity reached its apex,[6] and by the 1940s, Disney had become a well-established production company in the U.S., especially after the release of its first animated feature film, *Snow White and the Seven Dwarfs*.[7] From this moment on, more animated feature films would follow, thus confirming Disney as the leading animation company in the U.S. market. Due to its success and popularity, Disney became *the* studio, the point of reference at home and abroad. Disney's "realism" became the standard formula in animation. Early in the *Silly Symphony* series, this was based on the concept of "plausible impossibility": characters are animals that act like human beings and behave according to their specific personality (impossibility) and according to the situations they are placed in and the difficulties they face (plausible).[8] Disney's "realism" was further developed with the adoption of the multiplane camera in 1937, a device that provides the illusion of depth. It is composed of seven layers of artwork shot under a vertical and movable camera. The final result is sequences in which characters are animated on a three-dimensional background. A quite effective example of the use of the multiplane camera is *Bambi*,[9] in which the little deer is set before a deep three-dimensional forest and subsequently animated.

When UPA animated films appeared in theaters,[10] film critics enthusiastically admired their innovative audiovisual style. Something new was happening in U.S. animation. The public and critics were mesmerized. The comparison inevitably was to Disney: the small studio dared to challenge Disney's production patterns by proposing animated cartoons that departed from Disney's increasing naturalism and favored instead a stylized approach in the layouts, the animation and the sound effects. In 1952, Arthur Knight praised UPA artists for their ability to express the basis of animation, which consists of departing "from pure representation into pure imagination."[11] Bosley Crowther saw in UPA animated shorts an "introduction of maturity and sophistication into the cartoon,"[12] while George Seldes enthusiastically affirmed that:

> [T]he best way to identify the quality of their product is to say that every time you see one of their animated cartoons you are likely to recapture the sensation you had when you first saw Steamboat Willie, the early Silly Symphonies, The Band Concert—the feeling that something new and wonderful has happened, something almost too good to be true.[13]

Accolades and praise echoed also from Europe: as early as 1951, an article lauding *Gerald McBoing Boing* and the accomplishments of Mr. Bosustow's team[14] was published in the French *Cahiers du Cinéma*.[15]

Two animated characters are most associated with the UPA studio: Gerald of *Gerald McBoing Boing* and the nearsighted Mr. Magoo. Little Gerald appeared for the first time in theaters in 1951 and allowed the studio to break into the animation industry with something highly original in terms of both story and audiovisual style. Mr. Magoo, featured for the first time in 1949, in the animated cartoon *The Ragtime Bear*,[16] consolidated UPA's reputation as a creative and innovative animation studio. In the following decade, Mr. Magoo was employed in 53 animated short subjects and one feature film. The character was so successful that he arguably became as popular in the 1950s as Mickey Mouse was in the 1930s.

Stylistically, UPA excelled in the one-shot animated cartoons belonging to the *Jolly Frolics* series, whose production commenced after the signing of the Columbia agreement. The first film produced was *Robin Hoodlum*.[17] Another 37 animated cartoons followed. Some of these one-shot cartoons brought fame and glory to UPA and can be considered UPA masterpieces, such us the aforementioned *Gerald McBoing Boing, Rooty Toot*,[18] *The Unicorn in the Garden*,[19] *The Tell-Tale Heart*[20] and *Fudget's Budget*.[21]

Why were UPA films so successful? Certainly, it was a matter of style, but it was also a matter of story. If UPA animated films were "on the road to revolutionizing the cartoon world,"[22] the reason lies in the "marriage of form *and* content."[23] Every UPA animated cartoon tells a story that is expressed in a unique audiovisual style, and the audiovisual style was developed by UPA artists according to the subject matter; in other words, the style fits the story. This might seem obvious today, but it was not so in the 1940s when the U.S. animation market consisted principally of Warner Bros., Disney and Metro-Goldwyn-Mayer (MGM) films, three companies whose trademarks were based on styles—three very different audiovisual styles—that were applied and repeated in every animated films as consolidated formulas. Hence, what came to be distinctive of UPA animated films was this bond between form and content. In Leonard Maltin's opinion, UPA's assets were the visual style, the story selection and the treatment of it,[24] while Charles Solomon states that all UPA films had a different graphic style yet shared three characteristic elements: "unconventional stories, often with modern settings, contemporary graphics and a more stylized approach to the animation itself."[25]

UPA unconventional stories range from a boy who cannot speak words but utters only sounds (*Gerald McBoing Boing*) to a popular ballad centering on the theme of infidelity and murder (*Rooty Toot Toot*) up to the economic difficulties of a family that struggles with its monthly resources (*Fudget's Budget*). And, these are but a few examples. At UPA, the content of the shorts came from heterogeneous sources: almost everyone could contribute to the production of a cartoon by proposing a story or suggesting ideas for visual or sound developments.[26] It is known, for example, that *Gerald McBoing Boing* is based on a story originally written by Theodor Geisel (Dr. Seuss) and adapted by UPA story men Bill Scott and Phil Eastman, or that *Madeline*,[27] based on the namesake fable written by Ludwig Bemelmans, was suggested for production by executive producer Stephen Bosustow, who had read the book and found the story interesting.[28] *Madeline* was not the only animated cartoon based on an already published story. Overall, UPA artists favored stories that came from literature and best expressed themselves in those animated cartoon adaptations. This led to a revolutionary shift in U.S. animation: for virtually the first time, UPA cartoons featured human beings as protagonists instead of anthropomorphic pigs and bunnies. This choice had a twofold outcome. First, UPA animated shorts proposed themes that were closer to everyday life and personal and familial issues than were Warner Bros.' or MGM's animated cartoons, which were mostly based on chases and gags in the vaudevillian tradition, or Disney's animated feature films, which brought the spectator into an imaginary realm of beautiful and innocent princesses, jealous queens and handsome princes. Second, since every story was different, and stories were the subjects to start with, it came as a natural consequence that the styles were developed around the story and that every film had its unique audiovisual treatment.

In other words, UPA films were truer to life. The public could empathize with the themes presented and sometimes even identify with some of the problems proposed. As much as the subject matter was innovative for U.S. animation, the audiovisual styles developed could not be anything but original. This "revolutionary" approach in U.S. animation did not happen by chance but rather evolved as a natural consequence of the historical, sociological and cultural setting of the U.S. in the 1940s and 1950s.

2.   UPA IN HISTORY AND THE HISTORY OF UPA

In the late 1930s, the major American animation studios were facing a novelty: the rise of labor unions. With the exception of top animators, the bulk of the animation workforce—from inkers, painters, and background artists up to assistant animators—received low salaries. At Disney, for example, differences between the artists were remarkably stark: a top animator like Art Babbitt or Vladimir "Bill" Tytla earned $300 a week, while an inker or a painter earned $18 per week.[29] The Disney strike of 1941 is considered the event that "changed the world of animation forever."[30] It also paved the way for the foundation of UPA. Protests had taken place during the release periods of animated feature films: *Fantasia*[31] and *Pinocchio*[32] were released in 1940; *Dumbo*,[33] in 1941; and *Bambi*, in 1942. Considering himself a good employer, Walt Disney felt betrayed by those who were opposing him. The actual strike lasted five months.[34] Toward the end of it, Walt left the country for South America, embracing the "Good Neighbor Program,"[35] and left his brother Roy to settle the situation. Just a few weeks after his return in October 1941, a different scenario would unfold: the attack on Pearl Harbor, the declaration of war on Japan and the war effort.

World War II had a significant impact on the animation industry and forced a stylistic change. From 1942 on, about half of the cartoons produced were made as war propaganda and to train soldiers, sea captains and flight commanders.[36] Many motion-picture branches were set up, such as the First Motion Picture Unit (FMPU), the Marine Corps Film Unit, the Navy Photographic Unit and the Army Signal Corps, among others.[37] When the Disney strike was over, many of the artists who had taken part in it ended up stationed at the FMPU, the film production unit of the U.S. Army. This proved to be a unique and productive lesson since artists were forced by economic restrictions to experiment with the graphics: characters and backgrounds became stylized, as well as the animation. Others spread out to different animation studios such as MGM, Leon Schlesinger, Walter Lantz and Screen Gems,[38] where they also designed more stylized characters and backgrounds and tried a more stylized way of animating the characters.[39]

By the end of World War II, a new American society was born from the ashes of the war. Faith in the future and optimism described the early postwar period, but toward the end of the 1940s and the beginning of the 1950s, national and international settings were characterized by a certain degree of instability. Although the U.S. economy was prosperous, the 1950s were affected by mistrust, suspicion and uncertainty that amounted to paranoia, fear, hysteria and to some extent a general national neurosis. The patriarchal family of the 1950s, shaped from preexisting historical and sociological conditions, sought stability inside the walls of a secure suburban house.[40]

It is in this framework that UPA was born. In 1943, Stephen Bosustow, Zachary Schwartz and David Hilberman, three of those rebels who had picketed during the Disney strike, founded Industrial Films and Poster Service. The company was renamed United Productions of America in 1945. With the Columbia agreement (1948), UPA entered the entertainment business and started production of animated shorts that were intended for theatrical distribution. The studio flourished during the first half of the 1950s. The "Cold War," a term in use since at least 1947,[41] had repercussions on the existence and the evolution of the small animation studio and also on the contents and especially the satirical verve of its films. When the House Un-American Activities Committee (HUAC) turned its attention toward the small animation studio, at least eight artists were forced to leave in 1952.[42] Among them were designer-director John Hubley and writers Phil Eastman and Bill Scott, three people whose artistic contribution had been fundamental in early UPA productions. After 1956 UPA began its artistic decline, and in 1960 the company was sold by its executive producer, Stephen Bosustow.

Many were the directors who worked at UPA, and each of them brought a different artistic sensitivity and aesthetic. After concluding his masterpiece, *Rooty Toot Toot*, John Hubley left the studio, an event that allowed animator Robert (Bobe) Cannon to rise to prominence and become the most prolific director in the company. Indeed, some of Cannon's films were the biggest contributors to defining UPA's revolutionary attitude toward animation, films such as *Willie the Kid*,[43] *Madeline, Christopher Crumpet*,[44] *Fudget's Budget* and *The Jaywalker*.[45] Bobe Cannon's creativity had already reached great heights with *Gerald McBoing Boing* (1951), a quintessential UPA film awarded with an Oscar for Best Cartoon, Short Subject[46] in 1950, but the departure of Hubley allowed it to flourish. To be sure, Hubley and Cannon were not the only directors at UPA, although they have been recognized as the most relevant creative forces behind the studio, especially in its initial phase. Other animators and designers had the chance to direct and leave a mark not only in the history of UPA but in the history of animation, such as William T. Hurtz and Ted Parmelee, who directed *The Unicorn in the Garden* and *The Tell-Tale Heart*, respectively. Still other artists expressed their personal directing style in the animated segments of *The Boing-Boing Show*, a 30-minute program commissioned by CBS that premiered in 1956 and whose existence was possible thanks to the rise of television networks during the 1950s.

Another relevant UPA director was Pete Burness, who devoted himself to Mr. Magoo. After Hubley got tired of working on the same character and decided to relinquish the direction of Mr. Magoo theatrical releases to other UPA artists, animator Pete Burness was put in charge of the task.[47] His major achievement was *When Magoo Flew*,[48] the first UPA animated cartoon featuring Mr. Magoo to win an Oscar from the Academy of Motion Picture Arts and Sciences for Best Cartoon, Short Subject, in 1954. Burness was a key figure in ensuring UPA a continuing character designed for an animated series. From an economic perspective, without the Mr. Magoo theatrical releases, whose steady production was imposed by Columbia, UPA would not have had the opportunity to produce the one-shot animated cartoons that were so aesthetically groundbreaking. On a greater scale, the existence of the studio itself was bound to the Mr. Magoo theatrical releases. Significantly, if Burness had not succeeded in maintaining the popularity of the character, Columbia could have feasibly ended the distribution deal long before it was actually terminated (1958), which would have resulted in such animated cartoons as *Christopher Crumpet, The Unicorn in the Garden, The Tell-Tale Heart, Fudget's Budget* and *The Jaywalker* never having been produced.[49]

Every cultural expression, as is, for example, an animated film, mirrors the historical period in which it is produced. UPA animated shorts encapsulate the spirit of the 1940s and 1950s and can be interpreted as "cultural artifacts" of this transitional historical period. What was happening in the arts affected the way UPA films were designed and animated, and determined the birth of UPA's new attitude toward animation. Contributions came from almost every field of art, and UPA was part of a major stylistic change.

UPA artists were extremely receptive to contemporary artistic expressions. They looked for stories with subject matter intended for adults and not only children thus addressing more controversial issues, but they also incorporated Modern[50] stylistic tendencies of the historical period: from painting to jazz music to graphic design. The reconfiguration of these Modern expressions in the service of animation led to a new way of interpreting animation as an art form. UPA thus marked the transition toward Modern animation in the U.S.

The UPA aesthetic "revolution" was carried out by artists who came from the most traditional training in animation, which at the time meant only one studio: Disney. After they left Disney, those who were destined to become future UPA artists were aware that Disney had reached a stylistic apex in animated cinema, especially in terms of the visual effects achievements that allowed a high degree of photo-realism. Experimentation, therefore, could only follow a course outside the Disney stylistic domain, directing it toward developing a completely new approach to the animation medium. Who were these people?

3. UPA STUDIO AND ITS PEOPLE

UPA artists were among the most skilled designers, animators and story writers of their time. Some of them, such as Zachary Schwartz, David Hilberman, Art Babbitt, John Hubley, Stephen Bosustow and Bill

Melendez came from the Disney studio and were eager to prove themselves in new artistic adventures. When Industrial Films and Poster Service was founded, many of the renegades who had participated in the Disney strike and were consequently excluded from the company enthusiastically joined what would later become UPA.

In the late 1940s and early 1950s, a significant number of talented people concentrated at UPA. These artists included animators and directors Bobe Cannon, Art Babbitt, Pete Burness and Rudy Larriva; designers and directors John Hubley and Ted Parmelee; storyboard artist William T. Hurtz; story writers Phil Eastman and Bill Scott; animators Bill Melendez, Alan Zaslove, Willis Pyle and Pat Matthews; colorists Herbert Klynn, Bob McIntosh and Jules Engel; sound designer Joe Siracusa; and background artist Paul Julian. Some of them had already exhibited as independent painters,[51] had had their training at the Leon Schlesinger studio[52] or Disney, or had already worked in professional contexts, such as sound designer Joe Siracusa, who had collaborated with musician Spike Jones.[53] All of them brought to UPA their experience and skills, thus making the studio a highly creative place.

These artists were aware of those features that characterized American animation up to that moment and sensed the possibility of experimenting and transforming them into something different and new. Designer John Hubley, who wrote a paper in collaboration with Zachary Schwartz titled "Animation Learns a New Language" in 1946,[54] especially wanted to depart from the traditional representation of pigs and bunnies in animation and develop a new type of audiovisual language that could express meaningful stories. By turning to Modern artistic expressions for inspiration, UPA artists purposefully sought to elevate animation from craft to art form.

UPA animated shorts, especially the theatrical releases, were intended as works of art. Still, UPA animated shorts were produced for the market, thereby fulfilling economic and commercial needs of the entertainment industry. If the one-shot animated cartoons belonging to the *Jolly Frolics* series allowed the artists to experiment with different styles, it was the Mr. Magoo series that granted a steady continuity in the production. Cartoons cannot be sold on an individual basis,[55] and Columbia Pictures clearly demanded animated shorts that featured the nearsighted character instead of the more creative, less profitable one-shot animated cartoons.[56] The conditions were dictated by the distribution company, which bore significant weight in creative decisions, such as who could be hired by executive producer Stephen Bosustow and what type of cartoons could be made. In 1953, for example, Columbia Pictures stated in the renewal of the agreement that UPA artists had to seek approval from Columbia for any non-Magoo subjects.[57] The studio could only adjust to this decision. The entire UPA filmic production can be interpreted as an attempt at finding a compromise between highly artistic aspirations and economic needs dictated by the market.

In fact, although its artists and even its executive producer, Stephen Bosustow, had high artistic ambitions, UPA was a for-profit organization. In order to compete in the animation industry, the studio diversified its production into industrial, educational and commercial cartoons, aside from the animated shorts made for theatrical release. The studio indeed survived a difficult early stage by focusing solely on the production of industrial films. Commercials came a bit later, in 1947, when UPA's first animated TV commercial was produced for Southern Select Beer of Galveston.[58] In 1950, the company opened a branch in New York City, and in 1956, another in London, with the intention of expanding in the advertising industry. UPA commercials were so successful that between 1951 and 1954 they received awards at least seven times from the New York Art Directors Club, one time from the Los Angeles Art Directors Club, and another time from the Art Directors Club of Chicago.[59] They also had a relevant impact on the history of animated commercials not only in the U.S. but internationally. A comprehensive study of UPA animated commercials and their international influence is yet to be conducted. It would shed light on a trend that occurred internationally during the 1950s and 1960s: animated TV commercials expressed a common tendency toward a minimalist approach in animation that owed much to UPA innovations. It is the opinion of the author that UPA anticipated this trend and effectively synthesized it.

In the 1950s, many U.S. animation studios making TV commercials were using stylized layouts and simplified animation.[60] UPA was one of them, but the only one lucky enough to also produce theatrical releases. In 1956, the studio ventured into TV programming with *The Boing-Boing Show*, the first animated program specially made for network television. UPA's innovative attitude toward animation also applied to the way commercials and *The Boing-Boing Show* were made, thus placing UPA at the cutting edge in every production.

UPA animated cartoons were simultaneously "profitable" and "art." This union between profitability and art culminated in the perfect marriage with the UPA animated TV commercials, so much so that, according to Spigel,[61] abstract animated commercials—among which she included UPA productions—might be considered the missing link between abstract expressionism and pop art in the history of Modern art. In short, the UPA studio was ahead of its time.

UPA introduced another novel element in U.S. animation history: a production system based on non-fixed units of interchangeable artists that allowed the spontaneous creation of small teams of artists working on the same film. The lack of a strictly hierarchical structure determined the way films were produced and their quality: each film expresses a unique audiovisual style because it was created and developed by a unique group of artists working on an animated cartoon for the entire duration of its production.

Along with the artists, a key figure at UPA was the executive producer, Stephen Bosustow. His drive pushed him to be on a par with Walt Disney, sharing with him the idea that animation should be a form of art. He did not have a creative role and tended to give the artists complete freedom to work on films without his interfering in their artistic decisions. This led to a certain state of anarchy[62] that was creatively effective and managerially disruptive at the same time. Nevertheless, Bosustow's management was one of the conditions that allowed UPA to succeed, albeit only for a short period of time.

UPA was also unique for the type of artists who were working there. According to one of its founder, David Hilberman, UPA was "the first studio to be run by design people."[63] In contrast to Disney, the layout men were as important as the animators. This determined the visual styles of the animated cartoons: graphic design became important enough to affect the way layouts were designed and characters were animated. Together with Modern art, graphic design came to be at the core of UPA animations. And graphic design at the end of the 1940s and the early 1950s was synonymous with minimalism and reductionism, two tendencies that characterized the concept of Modernism in the arts.

4. UPA MODERNISM

UPA artists applied to animation that common vision toward minimalism and reductionism embraced by many visual artists and musicians during the 20th century. Indeed, throughout the last century, painting, graphic design, and advertising illustration mutually influenced each other. In the U.S., specifically, animation turned "Modern" at the end of the 1940s and beginning of the 1950s by assimilating those Modern features and adopting a minimalist approach in the layout designs and in the animation. Visually, it meant the rejection of mimetic forms of representation and the use of more expressive lines and colors, asymmetrical layouts, non-objective imagery and flatness. Aurally, it was mainly improvisation, abstract sounds and a freer rhythmical structure. Simplicity became the distinctive characteristic of a functional design that was employed in painting, advertising and animation. It derived from a graphic functionalism whose theoretical principles were developed and applied to the arts at the Bauhaus school.[64] Simplicity and functionalism are key characteristics of Modernism in the visual arts:

> Modernism emerged after 1900 as a radical rejection of the traditional values of the Victorians. Everything Victorian was discarded in a dramatic move among progressive thinkers towards a simpler way that was seen as more fitting to the new twentieth century. ... Just as the Victorians had embraced complexity and embellishment, the Modernists advocated simplicity. The painter Hans Hofmann said, "The ability to simplify means to eliminate the unnecessary so that the necessary may speak." These visionaries also looked for a new kind of functionalism in what Hofmann called "the necessary."[65]

Beginning in the 1940s, American graphic design was in the process of developing its cultural identity within a greater movement that came to be called the New York School. A key figure in this process of modernization was Hungarian-born designer György Kepes, whose book *The Language of Vision*, published in 1944, became a source of inspiration for American designers, and also those artists and animators who were stationed at the FMPU during World War II.[66] Kepes praised all those Modern painters such as Paul Cézanne, cubists, neoplasticists, suprematists, constructivists and contemporary photographers and advertisers who abandoned the fixed perspective typical of Renaissance paintings in favor of multiple perspectives that could express the object in its *spatial essence*.[67]

UPA artists did not copy the masters of the fine arts but learned from them. Paul Cézanne, Pablo Picasso, Georges Braque, Francis Picabia, Joan Miró, Paul Klee, Wassily Kandinsky, Raoul Dufy, Kazimir Malevich, Salvador Dalí, Henri Matisse, Henri Rousseau, Amedeo Modigliani, the expressionists and the fauves, among others, were studied by UPA artists as expressions of a new, simplified visual language. Their examples, together with the functionalist design inherited from the Bauhaus tradition and brought to full maturity by American advertising, the aesthetic principles taught by György Kepes, and traditional animation learned at the Disney studio from teacher Donald Graham provided that inspirational impulse to experiment in animation. A new language of vision was also explored.

In the 1940s and 1950s, a "sound revolution" was occurring hand in hand with this "design revolution" in U.S. animation. These tendencies followed similar paths that were inextricably interconnected due to the audiovisual nature of the animation medium. In animation, the use of dialogue, sound effects and music showed remarkable influences from jazz, radio shows and early TV shows. A "freer rhythm" of the animated line characterized UPA design and animation: it was assimilated from the study and interpretation of Modern painting, graphic design and advertising. Similarly, "improvisation" of the sound effects, talking sequences and even voice-narrated stories, especially in adaptations of already published short stories, characterized UPA scores. These aural features were assimilated through study and interpretation of Modern music, especially jazz, but were also the consequence of in-progress experimentation with sound occurring in animation during the 1940s and 1950s. In UPA animated films, sound effects do not simply illustrate the visuals but provide additional information, for example, on the psychology of the characters, as is the case of *Gerald McBoing Boing*, where they are *expressive* of psychological subtleties as much as colors in the backgrounds.[68]

Therefore, in UPA films, sounds and images function as complementary elements: they rarely correspond or overlap, thus providing two different types of information simultaneously. Imaginative abstract sounds quite often compensate the simplicity of UPA images—sometimes even their "economy"—thereby adding sophisticated meaning and expressive quality to the audiovisual artwork. Imagination in UPA animated films plays a relevant role, since the viewer is engaged in conferring meaning to the cross-references between images and sounds. As animated cinema is a medium based on the interrelationship of sound and images in movement, post-World War II stylistic research was oriented toward creating a *simplified audiovisual language*. In the U.S., UPA artists expressed this aesthetic need by rejecting the photo-realistic approach pursued by Disney's films in favor of a more stylized approach both in the visuals and the audio.

Every form of art has its own definition, and animation is a relatively young art. *Fantasmagorie*,[69] the first animated cartoon screened in public, was created and released by French animator Émile Cohl in 1908. By the end of World War II, a debate on the nature of animation as opposed to live-action cinema occurred internationally among film critics and scholars. The search for a definition of animated cinema commenced in Europe, where a group of film critics explored the nature of the animated cartoon medium by comparing different international visual styles. These film critics were Giuseppe Maria Lo Duca, Robert Benayoun, Denys Chevalier, Ralph Stephenson, Walter Alberti, Gianni Rondolino, and, above all, André Martin, who organized the first Rencontres Internationales du Cinéma d'Animation in 1956, within the 9th Cannes Film Festival.[70]

They tried to outline the principles of animation: its aesthetic components, the techniques involved in the creative process and especially those characteristics that a film must have in order to be defined as "animated." The major question was, what differentiated animated cinema from all other artworks? Less than 30 years passed from the first European book on animation, written by Lo Duca in 1948, to Rondolino's book (1974), which can be considered the first world history of animation. During this period, an animated film history had been developed and an animated film criticism had arisen.

With the exception of Lo Duca, all these film critics agreed that Disney's naturalism was a reductive use of the animated cartoon medium, as it proposed a photo-realistic approach that put animation in close approximation to live-action cinema. Animated cinema, instead, was born from an extension of graphic narrative, and its plasticity distinguished it from live-action cinema. This consideration fertilized the idea that certain types of animation better expressed the essence of animated cinema.

UPA animated cartoons were used by film critics as examples of what animated cinema could and should be, together with films made by directors Jiří Trnka and Norman McLaren.[71] This was possible because UPA films did not attempt to reproduce reality but rather proposed an expressive use of the animated line that had been majestically employed by other animators and directors before UPA, first among all Émile Cohl. In contrast to live-action cinema, animated cinema does not reproduce reality by interpreting it; it re-creates reality. Early animators like Émile Cohl and Winsor McCay showed that animation is based on the principle of *metamorphosis*: the succession of drawings in time is perceived by the spectator's brain as an uninterrupted stream of images.

By refusing to work in a studio (Disney) where decent working conditions were inconsistently granted to employees and, consequently, organizing a strike, future UPA artists were also opposing the studio's strict hierarchical structure that disregarded the contributions of those artists who constituted the great majority of the Disney studio staff: considered of "minor" importance in comparison to the top animators, these artists were kept from playing an active role in creative meetings and decisions. In other words, those former Disney employees who were destined to become future UPA artists were also fighting for freedom of expression during the strike. Thus, the "creative anarchy" that characterized UPA's internal organization was a consequence of the refusal to follow strict artistic rules imposed from the top. In this regard, the principle of *metamorphosis* as put into practice by early animators, as well as an expressive use of the animated line—the "anarchic" line—may have seemed to UPA artists a more familiar ground to which they could anchor their minimalist experimentations on audiovisual styles. By returning to the basic principles of animation and refusing the Disneyesque photo-realistic approach that brought the animated medium too close to live-action cinema, UPA artists were performing an act of artistic rebellion that reflected the political background that led to the strike and reinforced the idea of animation as an independent form of art that does not reproduce reality but creates it. Therefore, UPA films are animations of purely graphic elements that express a synthesis of reality. The UPA approach in animation recombined the plasticity typical of early animations with the minimalism of Modern art, graphic design and advertising illustration. As a result, the animated line was freer, the style became linear and the animation stylized. Nevertheless, it is important to point out that UPA artists were not going back to the animated line of the pre-sound era but were creating a new way to describe the animated space, the frame, which became subjective.[72]

UPA animated shorts found their place within the artistic trends that characterized the 20th century: reductionist experimentations, deconstructive approaches, and processes of simplification that ultimately resulted in pure abstraction and that could be synthesized with the motto "less is more." In redesigning animation as a simplified audiovisual language, UPA artists exemplified and anticipated a trend that was occurring internationally.

5. UPA AND THE INTERNATIONAL SCENE

During the 1950s and 1960s, a general trend characterized animation worldwide: backgrounds and characters became stylized, colors were used more expressively, more non-objective imagery and abstract sounds were employed, and animation was mostly *limited* rather than *full*.[73] The tendency was to depart from the Disney naturalism in favor of a minimalist design. Since UPA inaugurated a stylistic renovation in comparison to the Disney style, it came to represent the example to follow. Therefore, the UPA attempt at redesigning animation as a simplified audiovisual language was emulated. Nevertheless, the UPA lesson was assimilated differently from country to country, according to local traditions and cultural expressions. To summarize this general tendency, it can be stated that the UPA aesthetic "revolution" exercised a direct impact on U.S. animation and an indirect influence on international animation.

In the U.S., animation studios, artists and directors inevitably had to vie with Disney. American animation reached its "golden age" in the 1930s and 1940s with Disney productions. The studio was considered synonymous with excellence in the industry, both for the quality of the films and the efficiency of the production system. With the success of UPA, it became clear that it was not necessary to be as big as Disney to make good films: small production companies could also produce animated shorts that expressed a personal style, and, above all, that were financed with small budgets. UPA paved the way for the creation of small studios that aimed at making high-quality films.

Among the artists who applied the UPA formula were, firstly, former UPA employees. During the 1950s, many artists left the company for different reasons. Especially toward the end of the decade, some of them sensed that the studio was creatively declining, and that economic collapse was near. Overall, among those who had passed through UPA were David Hilberman, John Hubley, Ade Woolery, Herb Klynn, Jules Engel, Bobe Cannon, Frank Smith, Sterling Sturtevant, Mary Cain, Bill Melendez, Gene Deitch, Ernest Pintoff, Jimmy Murakami, John Whitney, Pete Burness, William T. Hurtz, Ted Parmelee, Roy Morita, Fred Crippen,

Sam Clayberger and many others. All of them had different skills and a different sensibility, but they all applied what they had learned at UPA to their future projects. In some cases, the UPA lesson was the starting point for the development of a more personal style, as happened to designer and director John Hubley.[74]

The UPA simplified audiovisual language also affected animators and artists who had already developed a personal style, such as Tex Avery, Friz Freleng and even artists working at Disney. These people applied some of the UPA stylistic visual solutions, such as the stylized backgrounds and characters or the use of limited animation, to their films, maintaining at the same time a personal touch.

It is more complex to ascertain UPA's indirect influence on international animation. In Europe, for example, animation was born from isolated experiments made by avant-gardist painters and filmmakers. Early European animations were already based on the idea of a simplified design and already expressed a personal style. According to the countries in which they were made, they also showed features that derived from local artistic trends. Character-based animation was later developed with Disney in mind, after Disney films had a huge impact on Europe during the 1940s. Disney's films dominated the global market and started to be imitated worldwide. Nevertheless, even during the 1940s, there were European studios, such as the British Halas & Batchelor Cartoon Films, whose style was not influenced by Disney.

Those directors and animators who did not relate to Disney's naturalistic approach found in UPA minimalism an example to follow. The UPA simplified audiovisual language became as much a global source of inspiration as Disney was. UPA stylistic solutions, such as stylized backgrounds and characters, abstract sounds, limited animation, expressive colors and a subjective use of the frame, were praised, studied and incorporated into local productions. These features shaped Western European animations to different degrees. Indirect UPA influence can be found in the animated films of John Halas and Joy Batchelor, George Dunning and Bruno Bozzetto. Also, at the National Film Board of Canada, the UPA minimalistic approach had a certain impact, especially on directors Gerald Potterton and Ron Tunis.[75]

After World War II, Eastern European animators were also exploring a minimalist approach based on the incorporation of graphic design and the use of limited animation. Some of the animated films produced in

Yugoslavia by the Zagreb Film School and in Romania by Ion Popescu-Gopo expressed stylistic features similar to the ones explored by UPA artists. It is difficult to verify a UPA influence on them, since there is no historical proof that UPA cartoons were screened in countries belonging to the Eastern bloc. Still, it is evident that minimalism, simplicity and reductionism in animation were global stylistic tendencies that paralleled what had already occurred in European Modern art and was occurring in American advertising in the 1940s and 1950s. Therefore, the animation directors mentioned above are simply examples of a major global trend characterized by influences, alterations, mixtures and fusions between the UPA attitude toward animation and local productions. Arguably, UPA audiovisual styles were also studied in the Soviet Union and Japan.[76]

UPA stylistic solutions came to help all those designers and animators who were looking for an audiovisual style different from Disney's. The simplified design proposed by UPA found a counterpart in the stylized and non-mimetic representation of painting and advertising. UPA audiovisual innovations echoed in other countries and influenced local productions.

6. RESEARCH PURPOSE, SIGNIFICANCE OF RESEARCH AND GOALS

During the 1940s and 1950s, animation was redesigned in the Modernist tradition of the arts. UPA played a significant role in this process, since it embraced Modernism in all its cultural manifestations. As animation historian Maureen Furniss has affirmed, "UPA aligned itself with everything modern—in its art style, in its adaptation of contemporary literature, and in its progressive social views."[77] And also, one might add, in its music and sound effects. This thesis contends that UPA films are *Modern* animated cartoons because they express a *simplified audiovisual language* for animation. The purpose of this research is to evaluate UPA studio and its animated cartoons as case studies of a Modern animation studio and Modern animations.

The history of UPA and its aesthetic contribution to the history of animation have been recounted by animation historians Leonard Maltin, Charles Solomon, Michael Barrier and Giannalberto Bendazzi.[78] A comprehensive history of the studio was covered by scholar Adam Abraham.[79] In *Cartoon Modern: Style and Design in Fifties Animation*, Amid Amidi discussed UPA Modern cartoons within the broader framework of 1950s American animation: major 1950s American animation studios are described, as well as the relevance of design and stylization in their animated TV commercials. Amidi's book established "the place of the 1950s animation design in the great Modernist tradition of the arts."[80]

This work starts from where Amid Amidi's contribution ended by studying UPA animated cartoons as Modern audiovisual cultural expressions. It does not intend to rewrite the history of UPA or to highlight the aesthetic contributions of UPA within the worldwide or U.S. history of the animated cinema, since this has already been done by remarkable scholars. Historical references are taken into consideration when needed to understand why and how UPA animated films lost their superior quality starting in the second half of the 1950s. Instead, this work aims to analyze UPA films' stylistic features as the outcome of an aesthetic "revolution" that occurred in U.S. animation during the 1940s and 1950s.

The UPA role in redesigning animation was possible and happened only because specific historical, sociocultural and artistic conditions converged. The rise of labor unions in the animation industry and the resulting Disney strike had the dual effect of pushing former Disney artists to reject a hierarchical structure that did not guarantee adequate working conditions and salaries and to look for an animation studio where they could freely express themselves and push the boundaries of animation further than what had been explored up to that moment. When former Disney artists gathered at the newly born UPA studio—not by coincidence a studio founded by three unionists—they found the opportunity to challenge Disney's patterns of production and, above all, its excellent stylistic standards in the animated cartoon medium. And when Stephen Bosustow became sole executive producer of the company, his political views, personal artistic ambitions and limits in running the studio determined a creative freedom that no other U.S. animation studio offered at that time, spurred in part by the need to specialize in animation techniques that were less expensive than the ones perfected, for example, at the Disney studio.

Simultaneously, the UPA embrace of a minimalist approach in animation was validated by the diffusion, in the U.S., of Modernism in the arts and in graphic design: their impact on animation generated that *simplified audiovisual language* that reaffirms animation as an independent art form. The new UPA attitude toward animation was also the result of the complex political scenario of Cold War America and the consequent HUAC focus on Hollywood, which ultimately determined who worked or kept on working at UPA and, to a lesser degree, what stories were accepted for production by Columbia. These deciding factors caused certain directors and artists to rise to prominence instead of others, such as, for example, Bobe Cannon or Pete Burness, and consequently certain stylistic decisions to be approved. The interrelationship of these many and different contexts permitted the development of the innovative UPA aesthetic approach to animation.

This work proposes a new interpretation of UPA as a Modern animation studio by focusing on those peculiar conditions that were decisive in the evolution of the UPA studio and its artistic success, such as the historical, cultural and sociological framework in which UPA was born and flourished (Chapter 1); the role of UPA executive producer Stephen Bosustow and its production system (Chapter 2); those stylistic and narrative features that derived from Modern audiovisual expressions and were then adapted to the animated cartoon medium by UPA artists (Chapter 3); UPA animated cartoons as expressions of a simplified audiovisual language in animation (Chapter 4); and those international animated films produced during the 1950s and 1960s that reveal a direct or indirect influence from the UPA aesthetic and contextualize UPA Modernism as part of a broad international tendency toward minimalism in animation (Chapter 5). The aim of this work, therefore, is to present UPA animated cartoons as pivotal Modern audiovisual expressions in the history of animation.

This work puts greater emphasis on the visual features of UPA animated cartoons and their interconnections with painting, graphic design and advertising than on their aural features. Therefore, it will not present a comprehensive analysis of the sound achievements of UPA, as the topic could be the subject of another thesis, although it will refer to audio occasionally. The focus, rather, is on the graphic contribution of UPA to animation history; therefore, the aural features of UPA animated cartoons and their interconnections with jazz music, radio and TV shows, modern American composers and musicians, and the inherited tradition of voice actors in U.S. animated cartoons are only briefly taken into consideration. Exceptions are made mainly for those UPA animated films that are analyzed as case studies in Chapter 4 and other UPA animated films that show a remarkable innovative use of sounds.

Animation is a *graphic cinematic medium*: what happens in the frame is graphic; what occurs between the frames is cinematic since movement is implied.[81] Animator Norman McLaren has noted:

> Animation is not the art of drawings that move but the art of movements that are drawn; what happens between each frame is much more important than what exists on each frame; animation is therefore the art of manipulating the invisible interstices that lie between the frames.[82]

UPA stylization characterized the layouts *and* the animation. Compared to Disney's films, in UPA animated shorts the design prevails over the animation because, as Charles Solomon explains:

> An angular, two-dimensional cartoon figure couldn't move like a rounded Disney character—realistic movement in three dimensions would clash with its design. To accommodate the new, flatter style, the artists … avoided moving the characters in depth, restricting the action to the picture plane. They timed motions as carefully as before, but used fewer in-betweens and emphasized strong poses.[83]

The analysis of UPA animated cartoons aims to investigate also the combination of flat characters and simplified[84] animation in UPA animated cartoons. Therefore, The questions raised in this book are

1. How did graphic Modernism influence the way characters are drawn *on* the frames in UPA animated cartoons?

2. How did graphic Modernism influence the way characters are animated *between* the frames in UPA animated cartoons?

Regarding the analysis of UPA animated cartoons, animated TV commercials are excluded. The examination of UPA audiovisual styles focuses on those films that were produced from 1943 to 1959. In 1960, the company was sold by Stephen Bosustow to Henry G. Saperstein, who started the production of a Mr. Magoo television series that definitively abandoned the high-quality standard of previous UPA productions. For this reason, UPA animated films produced after 1960 are excluded from this study.

ENDNOTES

1. *Gerald McBoing Boing*, directed by Robert Cannon (1951; DVD, *UPA: The Jolly Frolics Collection*, Culver City, CA: Sony Pictures Home Entertainment, 2012).

2. *Three Little Pigs*, directed by Burt Gillett (1933; DVD, *Walt Disney Treasures: Silly Symphonies*, Burbank, CA: Walt Disney Home Video, 2001). Arthur Knight, "The New Look in Cartooning," *Saturday Review of Literature*, April 21, 1951.

3. The first color *Silly Symphony* was *Flowers and Trees*, directed by Burt Gillett (1932; DVD, *Walt Disney Treasures: Silly Symphonies*, Burbank, CA: Walt Disney Home Video, 2001).

   According to animation historian and theoretician Paul Wells, "any definition of 'reality' is necessarily subjective. Any definition of 'realism' as it operates within any image-making practice is also open to interpretation. Certain traditions of film-making practice, however, have provided models by which it is possible to move towards some consensus of what is recognisably an authentic representation of reality." He adds: 'realism', it seems, is a relative thing, but the kind of film which seems to most accurately represent 'reality' is the kind of film which attempts to rid itself of obvious cinematic conventions in the prioritization of recording the people, objects, environments and events which characterise the common understanding of lived experience."

   Paul Wells, *Understanding Animation* (London, UK: Routledge, 2008), 24. Therefore, it is possible to affirm that "realism" is implied in any animation that expresses a certain degree of verisimilitude with the real world by means of mimetic representation. Wells explains that there are different degrees of realism that could be implied in animated films. In the case of Disney's animations, for example, he notes that

   "Disney moved further away from the plasmatic flexibility of many of the early *Silly Symphonies*, and coerced the animated form into a neo-realist practice … insist[ing] on verisimilitude in his characters, contexts, and narratives. He wanted animated figures to move like real figures and be informed by a plausible motivation." Ibid, 23.

4. *Steamboat Willie*, directed by Ub Iwerks and Walt Disney (1928; DVD, *Mickey Mouse in Black and White*, Burbank, CA: Walt Disney Home Video, 2002).

5. Giannalberto Bendazzi, *Cartoons: 100 Years of Cinema Animation* (London, UK: John Libbey Cinema and Animation; Bloomington, IN: Indiana University Press, 1994).

6. Film theorist Esther Leslie affirms that "by 1930, Disney's Mouse was an international phenomenon." Mickey Mouse became especially popular in Germany and France, where countless imitations began to appear during the 1930s. She also explains that "in 1929, the rights to use Mickey on school writing tablets were sold to a company in New York. In February 1930, Walt Disney agreed to a contract with the George Borgfeldt Company for the

international licensing, production and distribution of Mickey Mouse merchandise." Esther Leslie, *Hollywood Flatlands* (London, UK, and New York, NY: Verso, 2002), 30–31.

7. *Snow White and the Seven Dwarfs*, directed by David Hand (1937; DVD, Burbank, CA: Walt Disney Home Video, 2009).

8. Bendazzi, *Cartoons: 100 Years of Cinema Animation*.

9. *Bambi*, directed by David Hand (1942; DVD, Burbank, CA: Walt Disney Home Video, 2004).

10. UPA animated films were theatrically released by Columbia Pictures from 1948 to 1959. The Columbia agreement was signed in 1948 between UPA studio and the distribution company. It was renewed in 1953 and expired in 1958. For more information, see Chapter 2, Section 1.

11. Arthur Knight, "UPA, Magoo & McBoing-Boing," *Art Digest*, February 1, 1952, 22.

12. Bosley Crowther, "McBoing Boing, Magoo and Bosustow," *New York Times Magazine*, December 21, 1952, 15.

13. George Seldes, "Delight in Seven Minutes," *Saturday Review*, May 31, 1952, 27.

14. Stephen Bosustow was the executive producer of UPA from 1945 to 1960. For further information, see Chapter 2, Section 1.

15. François Chalais, "Le fil à couper Disney," *Cahiers du Cinéma*, no. 6 (1951).

16. *The Ragtime Bear*, directed by John Hubley (1949; DVD, *UPA: The Jolly Frolics Collection*, Culver City, CA: Sony Pictures Home Entertainment, 2012).

17. *Robin Hoodlum*, directed by John Hubley (1948; DVD, *UPA: The Jolly Frolics Collection*, Culver City, CA: Sony Pictures Home Entertainment, 2012).

18. *Rooty Toot Toot*, directed by John Hubley (1952; *UPA:* DVD, *The Jolly Frolics Collection*, Culver City, CA: Sony Pictures Home Entertainment, 2012).

19. *The Unicorn in the Garden*, directed by William T. Hurtz (1953; DVD, *UPA: The Jolly Frolics Collection*, Culver City, CA: Sony Pictures Home Entertainment, 2012).

20. *The Tell-Tale Heart*, directed by Ted Parmelee (1953; DVD, *UPA: The Jolly Frolics Collection*, Culver City, CA: Sony Pictures Home Entertainment, 2012).

21. *Fudget's Budget*, directed by Robert Cannon (1954; DVD, *UPA: The Jolly Frolics Collection*, Culver City, CA: Sony Pictures Home Entertainment, 2012).

22. David Bongard, "Animated Cartoons Find Higher Purpose: Film Cartoonists Try to Be More Than Just Quaint," *Los Angeles Daily News*, February 2, 1953, 22.

23. Leonard Maltin, *Of Mice and Magic: A History of American Animated Cartoons* (New York, NY: New American Library, 1987), 332.

24. Ibid.

25. Charles Solomon, *Enchanted Drawings: The History of Animation* (New York, NY: Alfred A. Knopf, 1989), 220.

26. For more information, see Chapter 2, Section 4.2.

27. *Madeline*, directed by Robert Cannon (1952; DVD, *UPA: The Jolly Frolics Collection*, Culver City, CA: Sony Pictures Home Entertainment, 2012).

28. Typewritten notes by Stephen Bosustow; Steve Bosustow's UPA collection, in the care of his son, Tee Bosustow.

29. Adam Abraham, *When Magoo Flew: The Rise and Fall of Animation Studio UPA* (Middletown, CT: Wesleyan University Press, 2012); Norman M. Klein, *Seven Minutes: The Life and Death of the American Animated Cartoon* (London, UK, and New York, NY: Verso, 1997); Tom Sito, *Drawing the Line: The Untold Story of the Animation Unions from Bosko to Bart Simpson* (Lexington, KY: University Press of Kentucky, 2006).

30. Sito, *Drawing the Line: The Untold Story of the Animation Unions from Bosko to Bart Simpson*, 101.

31. *Fantasia*, directed by Ben Sharpsteen (1940; DVD, Burbank, CA: Walt Disney Home Video, 2010).

32. *Pinocchio*, directed by Ben Sharpsteen and Hamilton Luske (1940; DVD, Burbank, CA: Walt Disney Home Video, 2009).

33. *Dumbo*, directed by Ben Sharpsteen (1941; DVD, Burbank, CA: Walt Disney Home Video, 2006).

34. For a better understanding of causes, development and ending of the Disney strike, see Abraham, *When Magoo Flew: The Rise and Fall of Animation Studio UPA*, Chapter I.

35. The trip to South America is recounted in the documentary *Walt and El Grupo*, directed by Theodore Thomas (2008; DVD, Burbank, CA: Walt Disney Studios Home Entertainment 2010). In it is explained U.S. government interest in the "ABC countries"—Argentina, Brazil and Chile—as possible allies in the upcoming world war. In service to his country, Walt Disney agreed to produce a film presenting the cultures of these countries with all the typical Disney appeal but for an audience that included all the Americas. The agreement stated that even if the film was not a success, the U.S. government would reimburse the investment. The creative result of this trip were two animated feature films: *Saludos Amigos*, directed by Wilfred Jackson, Jack Kinney, Hamilton Luske and William Roberts (1942; DVD, Burbank, CA: Walt Disney Studios Home Entertainment, 2000) and *The Three Caballeros*, directed by Norman Ferguson (1944; DVD, Burbank, CA: Buena Vista Home Video, 2000).

36. Michael S. Shull and David E. Wilt, *Doing Their Bit: Wartime American Animated Short Films, 1939–1945* (Jefferson, NC: McFarland, 2004).

37. In 1943, Leon Schlesinger began production of the series *Private Snafu*. Another series was *A Few Quick Facts*. They were both shown to military audiences as part of a pseudo-newsreel called *Army-Navy Screen Magazine*. Live-action director Frank Capra also made propaganda films. Theodor Seuss Geisel, who joined the FMPU in 1943, headed the Capra unit's animation and graphic section. J. Michael Barrier, *Hollywood Cartoons: American Animation in Its Golden Age* (Oxford, UK: Oxford University Press, 1999); Solomon, *Enchanted Drawings: The History of Animation*.

38. In 1937, Columbia Pictures purchased Charles Mintz studio and renamed it Screen Gems. Frank Tashlin, head of production from 1941, chose former Disney strikers to build his staff.
39. For more information, see Chapter 1, Section 5.
40. For more information, see Chapter 1, Section 3.1.
41. Marty Jezer, *The Dark Ages: Life in the United States, 1945–1960* (Boston, MA: South End Press, 1982). According to the 10th edition of *Merriam-Webster's Collegiate Dictionary*, the term first appeared in print in 1945.
42. Karl F. Cohen, *Forbidden Animation: Censored Cartoons and Blacklisted Animators in America* (Jefferson, NC: McFarland, 1997).
43. *Willie the Kid*, directed by Robert Cannon (1952; DVD, *UPA: The Jolly Frolics Collection*. Culver City, CA: Sony Pictures Home Entertainment, 2012).
44. *Christopher Crumpet*, directed by Robert Cannon (1953; DVD, *UPA: The Jolly Frolics Collection*, Culver City, CA: Sony Pictures Home Entertainment, 2012).
45. *The Jaywalker*, directed by Robert Cannon (1956; DVD, *UPA: The Jolly Frolics Collection*, Culver City, CA: Sony Pictures Home Entertainment, 2012).
46. An Academy Award for animated film was first established by the Academy of Motion Picture Arts and Sciences in 1932. Specifically, the category was called "Short Subject, Cartoon" from 1932 to 1970. It changed to "Short Subject, Animated Film" for the period 1970 to 1973. In 1974, it changed to its current form, "Best Animated Short Film." For more information, consult the Academy Award database available at the official website of the Academy of Motion Picture Arts and Sciences (www.oscars.org). Whenever the award is mentioned in the thesis, it is referred to by the category name in use at the time.
47. For more information, see Chapter 4, Section 3.
48. *When Magoo Flew*, directed by Pete Burness (1954; DVD, *Mr. Magoo: The Theatrical Collection*, Culver City, CA: Sony Pictures Home Entertainment, 2014).
49. This consideration refers to the most aesthetically relevant one-shot UPA animated cartoons produced after the renewal of the Columbia agreement in 1953.
50. In this study, the term *Modern* refers to styles, practices or genres in the visual arts, music, and literature that intentionally, or less consciously, broke with previous traditions in their respective fields. These innovative aesthetic trends echoed historical, sociological, economic, cultural and even ideological transformations that occurred at specific times, and in different countries, during the 20th century. In painting, for example, Modern styles are those expressed by European avant-gardists such as the cubists, fauves, dadaists, neoplasticists, suprematists, and so on. In graphic design and in advertising, the theoretical principles expressed at the Bauhaus School of Arts and Crafts and their artistic outputs, as well as the visual expressions of the New York School, are considered Modern. Modern genres in music are rock 'n' roll, jazz, blues and soul, among others. In reference to the history of U.S. animated cinema, the term *Modern* is used as inclusive for all those animations that are historically situated within the transitional period of

the "Golden Age of Animation" (from 1928 to approximately 1960) and express aesthetic features that depart from the consolidated styles of the animation studios. Lastly, the term *UPA Modernism* is used to describe the UPA tendency to incorporate aesthetic features from various Modern artistic expressions. It also indicates a historical category by implying that UPA animated cartoons can be ascribed to Modern U.S. animation. This work will explore the historical and aesthetic reasons for this categorization.

51. Ed Penney, "U.P.A. Animated Art," *The Arts*, March 1953; Knight, "UPA, Magoo & McBoing-Boing."

52. Among them was animator Bobe Cannon.

53. Joe Siracusa, interview by author, May 23, 2014.

54. For more information, see Chapter 3, Section 3.

55. Stephen Bosustow explained sales methods for animated cartoons:

"In motion picture selling the salesman goes in with a feature contract and works very hard to get top dollar for it. Attached to the feature contract is a rider for newsreels and short subjects. ... When they get down to negotiating for the short it is a flat deal. You either get $2.50, $1.25, or $5.00 per booking and that is it. A cartoon just can't be sold on an individual basis." Quoted in Howard Edward Rieder, "The Development of the Satire of Mr. Magoo" (master's thesis, Graduate School of the University of Southern California, August 1961), 51.

56. In 1953, Columbia Pictures requested that every film had to carry the name Magoo in the title and starting from 1955, Columbia released only the Magoo films. As Bosustow recalled,

"The bookers for theaters want to buy only a series. ... Columbia felt on an overall basis there wasn't enough money in off-beat films. Ultimately, the same circumstances which forced us to make the Magoo series forced out the off-beat films which had won us our fame." Quoted in Howard Edward Rieder, "The Development of the Satire of Mr. Magoo," 108.

57. Abraham, *When Magoo Flew: The Rise and Fall of Animation Studio UPA*.

58. "Creativity Basic," *Television Age*, December 1, 1958; Steve Bosustow's UPA collection.

59. René d'Harnoncourt Papers, III.26.b, The Museum of Modern Art Archives, New York.

60. For more information, see: Amid Amidi, *Cartoon Modern: Style and Design in Fifties Animation* (San Francisco, CA: Chronicle Books, 2006).

61. Lynn Spigel, *TV by Design: Modern Art and the Rise of Network Television* (Chicago, IL: University of Chicago Press, 2008).

62. Gene Deitch, "10. Steve Bosustow," *genedeitchcredits: The 65 Greats behind the Scenes!* (blog), April 9, 2012, http://genedeitchcredits.com/roll-the-credits/10-steve-bosustow/, accessed May 5, 2015.

63. David Hilberman, interview by John Canemaker, June 16, 1979; The John Canemaker Animation Collection; MSS 040; box 1; folder 40.0039; Fales Library and Special Collections, NYU.

64. For more information, see Chapter 3, Sections 2 and 4.
65. Roger Remington and Lisa Bodenstedt, *American Modernism: Graphic Design, 1920 to 1960* (London, UK: Laurence King Publishing, 2003), 16.
66. Barrier, *Hollywood Cartoons: American Animation in Its Golden Age*; Amidi, *Cartoon Modern: Style and Design in Fifties Animation*.
67. György Kepes, *Language of Vision*, 2nd ed. (New York, NY: Dover, 1995).
68. For more information, see Chapter 4, Section 2.2.1.
69. *Fantasmagorie*, directed by Émile Cohl (1908; Paris, FR: Société des Etablissements L. Gaumont). www.youtube.com/watch?v=aEAObel8yIE, accessed September 25, 2015.
70. Bernard Clarens, ed. André Martin 1925–1994. *Écrits Sur L'animation*, vol. I (Paris, FR: Dreamland, 2000).
71. For more information, see Chapter 3, Section 3.2.
72. For more information, see: Klein, *Seven Minutes: The Life and Death of the American Animated Cartoon*. See also Chapter 3, Section 1.
73. Limited animation is defined in relation to full animation: "In true full animation, every drawing in a production is used only once … and shapes are altered to reflect something about the character's feelings or reactions"; while "in limited animation … there is much less shape-shifting of characters and more reliance on only x- and y-axis movement." In full animation, drawings are not reused, and every second of animation is achieved by creating 24 drawings, each drawing per frame (24 frames per second [fps] is the standard running time set by motion picture film). Limited animation implies the use of 12 or eight images per seconds, with repetitions of the same image for two or three frames. Maureen Furniss, *Art in Motion: Animation Aesthetics* (Sydney, AU: John Libbey Publishing, 1998), 133–134.
74. For more information, see Chapter 5, Section 2.
75. For more information, see Chapter 5, Section 2.
76. For more information, see Chapter 5, Section 4 and Section 5.
77. Furniss, *Art in Motion: Animation Aesthetics*, 141.
78. Maltin, *Of Mice and Magic: A History of American Animated Cartoons*; Solomon, *Enchanted Drawings: The History of Animation*; Barrier, *Hollywood Cartoons: American Animation in Its Golden Age*; Bendazzi, *Cartoons: 100 Years of Cinema Animation*.
79. Abraham, *When Magoo Flew: The Rise and Fall of Animation Studio UPA*.
80. Amidi, *Cartoon Modern: Style and Design in Fifties Animation*, 7.
81. The researcher acknowledges animator and colleague Juan Camilo González for this observation (personal communication, August 2014).
82. Quoted in Furniss, *Art in Motion: Animation Aesthetics*, 5.
83. Solomon, *Enchanted Drawings: The History of Animation*, 220.
84. The term *simplified* is used as a synonymous of *limited*. It was used by animator Bobe Cannon to describe the animation technique UPA artists were using. Designer-director John Hubley referred to it as "stylized" animation. Abraham, *When Magoo Flew: The Rise and Fall of Animation Studio UPA*.

CHAPTER 1

UPA within the Historical and Cultural Framework of Cold War America

They are all good men, men of the "movement," as it was called, not the Communist movement but the surge of hope and confidence and determination that took over from the Great Depression, the anti-monopoly-capital movement, the common-man movement, the anti-colonialist movement of the thirties and forties.

ELIA KAZAN[1]

United Productions of America (UPA) is a historical, cultural and sociological artifact of its time. It is a product born from the ashes of the 1941 Disney strike. It took form during World War II, culminated in the first half of the 1950s and declined during the second half of the decade.

Historically, UPA studio reflects general occurrences in the animation industry, since it was formed in the wake of the Disney strike and adjusted its existence to war propaganda production and the crisis of the entertainment industry. Moreover, UPA artists were not immune to investigation by the HUAC, whose prying forced eight employees to leave the studio[2] and induced a dull intellectual conformity on UPA animated shorts, especially the Mr. Magoo cartoons, which lost some of their satirical spirit after *When Magoo Flew* (1955).[3]

Culturally, UPA animated shorts encapsulate the spirit of the 1940s and 1950s both for their subject themes and for their audiovisual styles, which incorporate Modern graphic design and art. UPA was so successful in the U.S. and internationally that it attracted the attention of film critics such as George Seldes,[4] Arthur Knight,[5] and François Chalais[6] of the *Cahiers du Cinéma*, among others. In 1955, UPA animated shorts were so well-known and loved by the public that the Museum of Modern Art hosted an exhibition.

Sociologically, UPA stands out as a studio of its time, a transitional period in which theaters were losing their power and TV was gaining prominence. In response, the studio diversified its production into educational and training films (during World War II), TV commercials, theatrical releases (from 1948 to 1959), a 30-minute TV show and an animated feature film.

This chapter aims to frame UPA within its historical, cultural and sociological background. It considers the historical period that spans from 1929 to 1960 (with the exclusion of the years 1939–1945), then offers a description of American society and some of its cultural expressions, so as to conclude with an analysis of UPA as a cultural artifact of its time and with the 1955 Museum of Modern Art (MoMA) exhibition.

1.1   THE 1930s: FROM THE GREAT DEPRESSION TO THE NEW DEAL

The 1929 stock market crash and the Great Depression of the 1930s forced the U.S. to face possibly one of its most challenging economic and social crises. When Democrat Franklin D. Roosevelt became president of the U.S. in 1933, a quarter of the nation's workers—15 million people—had no jobs: "in a nation of 130 million, perhaps 34 million were literally without support: no money for rent, no food to feed their children, no coats against the wintry cold."[7]

From the start of his presidential campaign in 1932, Roosevelt opposed Herbert Hoover's "willingness to ignore reality."[8] Hoover had taken office in 1929, and as a Republican, an engineer and a Quaker, he firmly believed in social responsibility. In spite of the rising unemployment rate, in 1931 he affirmed that the depression was "a passing incident in our national life" and that "the number who are threatened with privation is a minor percentage."[9] He embraced the philosophy of "rugged individualism" and economic laissez-faire, which could be synthesized in his refusal to set up any federal program that might address the problem of unemployment: "No governmental action, no economic doctrine,—he stated in 1931—no economic plan or project can replace that God-imposed responsibility of the individual man and woman to their neighbors."[10] A year later, Roosevelt was campaigning for a federally funded program of public works jobs and federal relief for the unemployed. His speeches to the nation excited the population, who, finally, were hearing their problems recognized by a politician. Roosevelt started to address "the forgotten man":

> These unhappy times call for the building of plans that rest upon the forgotten, the unorganized but the indispensable units of economic power; for plans ... that put build from the bottom up and not from the top down, that put their faith once more in the forgotten man at the bottom of the economic pyramid.[11]

He advocated a call to action, affirming: "The country needs and, unless I mistake its temper, the country demands bold, persistent experimentation. It is common sense to take a method and try it: If it fails, admit it frankly and try another. But above all, try *something*."[12] He called for public works to provide jobs and introduced the now-famous "new deal" expression:

> I pledge you, I pledge myself, to a new deal for the American people ... This is more than a political campaign. It is a call to arms. Give me your help, not to win votes alone, but to win in this crusade to restore America to its own people.[13]

One of Roosevelt's first actions as president was to get the Federal Emergency Relief Act approved by Congress in 1933. Harry Hopkins, who had been the executive director of New York's Temporary Emergency Relief Administration (TERA) from 1931,[14] was appointed as administrator. Hopkins, however, firmly believed that what people needed were jobs, not handouts provided as economic relief. In 1933 Congress also passed the National Industrial Recovery Act,[15] legislation that regulated production by grouping industries into voluntary trade associations exempt from antitrust laws and by adopting common standards for wages, hours, working conditions and minimum age for workers.[16]

Among the many programs that Roosevelt's administration put into effect, the most relevant is the Works Progress Administration (WPA). Aiming to be a permanent federal jobs program that could put as many people as possible to work—at least 3.5 million of the unemployed—it was approved in 1934 and consisted of several employment projects totaling $100 million.[17] WPA projects ranged from building roads, public buildings, airports, schools, hospitals, courthouses and city halls to sidewalks and sewer systems, playgrounds, parks and zoos, thus involving both unskilled laborers and white-collar professionals such as clerks, stenographers and researchers. Women were generally employed as teachers, nurses and seamstresses. WPA projects also created paying jobs for providing a great variety of other public services, such as copying old records and saving them from dust, repairing toys for poor children at Christmastime, rebinding books for libraries, indexing newspapers, compiling lists of historic buildings, recording folk songs and carrying books to rural areas by horse or mule.[18] At the beginning of 1936, the unemployment rate was still staggering, but "three and a half million people were on the government's work-relief rolls," and "the vast majority, 2.8 million, were WPA workers."[19]

In 1936, Franklin D. Roosevelt was reelected to a second term. While he and the Democrats tried to keep the WPA out of the campaign, the Republicans attacked it, to the point that Republican candidate Alfred M. Landon "railed against New Deal attempts at economic planning as Communist-inspired."[20] Still, Roosevelt successfully won the election, with 523 electoral votes to Landon's eight, marking the greatest presidential victory since George Washington's and James Monroe's in the early years of the republic.

Among his next moves was to gain approval of specific arts programs that would employ sculptors, painters, photographers, actors, writers and designers, among other professional artistic profiles. By April 1936 the Federal Theatre Project, under the direction of Hallie Flanagan, for example, "had put 10,700 theatrical workers back to work across the United States, 5,000 in New York alone,"[21] while the Federal Music Project, headed by Nikolai Sokoloff, "became the largest of the arts project employers, with 15,842 workers on the rolls,"[22] simultaneously expanding music education through both concerts and classes in schools. Meanwhile, the Federal Writers' Project, directed by Henry Alsberg, put 6,500 people to work, for example, on the *American Guide* series, and by the middle of 1936, the Federal Art Project, headed by Holger Cahill,[23] "was employing some 5,000 mural and easel artists, printmakers, sculptors, poster artists, and art teachers."[24] Related to the Federal Art Project was the Index of American Design, which aimed to locate and preserve examples of American design, such as costumes, dolls, ballet slippers, pottery and glass, furniture, door knockers, tin boxes and other objects.

Regarding the aesthetic of the WPA art projects, most of them would belong to that representational school known as American scene painting. As Taylor points out, "While European artists had embraced modernism as a departure from the past, at this time American artists believed that depictions of real people in real settings would help them reveal American democracy and create a uniquely American art form."[25] Modernism had yet to reach America.[26]

At this time, there were principally painters who focused on the country's virtues and its positive aspects, such as Grant Wood and Thomas Hart Benton, expressing in their artwork the simplicity and beauty of the rural life and landscape, and the so-called social realists, who portrayed the effects of the depression on urban and industrial America, artists such as Joseph Hirsch, Ben Shahn and Jack Levine.[27] These social realists focused on the slums, corruption and the desperate people who lived in extreme poverty and labored in poor working conditions, thus conveying also a political message through their artworks. In this setting, and among the many types of art projects, murals came to be considered typically American and "New Deal art." Murals were painted on the large walls of federal and public buildings, such as schools, libraries, city halls, hospitals, airports and colleges: "In an America that was striving to make sense of itself, to review its origins and trials and mark its progress, these WPA creations would evolve into a form all their own."[28] There were also graphic artists whose job was to advertise WPA art exhibitions and theater and musical performances, as well as to inform on the importance of preventing diseases such as syphilis, gonorrhea and pneumonia or to encourage the population to lead a healthy and fulfilling social and cultural life. To the many artists facing the depression's effects, the WPA provided them full-time work on art projects for the first time in their lives, without having to supplement their minimal income from art with another type of job.

Moreover, Cahill firmly believed that the art projects were not only a means to employ artists but also a way to bring art to the people. Therefore, he authorized the creation of art centers in communities that had little or no access to art and art education: "by the end of 1936, more than 1 million people had participated in free programs at these WPA centers."[29]

That general feeling of optimism, faith and confidence that the New Deal and the WPA instilled in the population during the 1930s can be recognized also in future UPA artists' attitude toward social, political and cultural issues. Their involvement in labor movements and strikes, as well as their liberal beliefs, were founded in a clear awareness of the common person's economic and social needs, but especially the artists' needs. Future UPA artists found in the artworks of some WPA painters and graphic artists a political message: the often outrageous, sarcastic and caricatural paintings and prints of the social realists[30] strove to raise consciousness of the extreme poverty affecting a large portion of society, while the advertising and informational posters were effectively providing a useful social service to the population. The works of some WPA art projects thus represented examples of the possibility to convey social, political and cultural messages through pictorial representations, a concept in alignment with future UPA artists' beliefs and intentions to the point that one could argue it might have influenced their aesthetic choices and innovative attitudes toward the animation medium.[31]

Nevertheless, detractors of the New Deal and particularly of the WPA who had been active during the first half of the 1930s became more insistent toward the end of the decade, especially among the conservatives. Typical complaints were that the president was using jobs to buy votes, social workers rather than businessmen were in charge of the vast spending program, corruption and malingering were rampant among WPA workers, and WPA projects, especially the art projects, were frivolous abuses of public-spending power. For the latter, the anti-New Dealers often used the verb *boondoggle*. Moreover, these conservative thinkers, allied with Republicans, opposed the unions and wage-and-hour legislation, as well as the rumors that Roosevelt would run for a third term in the upcoming elections.[32]

In 1938, the House Un-American Activities Committee (HUAC) was reborn under the direction of Texas Democratic Martin Dies. Its previous incarnation had emerged in 1930–1931, when Republican representative Hamilton Fish "toured the country as chair of a committee investigating

Communist activities in the United States."[33] It was next chaired by Massachusetts Democrat John W. McCormack, who investigated Nazi and other forms of propaganda. As Taylor points out, "McCormack's had been the first committee to have a title that specified its task as investigating 'un-American activities.'"[34] The Dies committee[35] shifted its attention from right-wing sedition to Communism and labor organizing, focusing especially on the art projects: the arts and artists in general with their Bohemian lifestyle, need for artistic freedom and often liberal beliefs came to be considered as possibly dangerous and anti- and un-American. Consequently, conservative thinkers and Republicans exploited the association of the WPA and the New Deal to Communism for political reasons.[36] That same year, in 1938, the director of the Women's and Professional Projects, Ellen Woodward; the head of the Federal Theatre Project, Hallie Flanagan; and the director of the Federal Writers' Project, Henry Alsberg, were called to testify before the HUAC. A year later, Congress approved a ban that prevented WPA employees from being involved in any political activites, such as working in or managing a political campaign or influencing the outcome of a campaign, as well as a requirement that WPA workers take a loyalty oath to the U.S. in which they affirmed their commitment not to advocate the overthrow of the government by force or violence. Those WPA workers who refused to sign it were dismissed.[37]

This was as early as 1939, after the New Deal and the WPA had shown to the population how much a large-scale work program reduced the unemployment rate and improved the working conditions of millions of people. In the next decade, owing to political changes in the international and national scene, those who had been involved or were involved in labor strikes and other forms of agitation were often and easily accused of being radicals and/or un-American. Among those who inevitably fell under the inquisitorial HUAC focus were some of the UPA artists, as well as the entire studio.

In 1938, Hopkins resigned as WPA administrator, and with the rise of the conservatives in Congress, the New Deal was close to its end as a means to reform through legislation. It gradually shifted to becoming an agency that contributed to national defense with projects sponsored mainly by the War and Navy departments and focused on the construction and rebuilding of military infrastructure. The art projects also redirected efforts to the service of war preparation: writers penned orientation packets for new military camps or pamphlets on the dangers of malaria, unsafe drinking water and unprotected sex; musicians were tasked with entertaining the draftees undergoing military training; and graphic artists designed civil defense and other informational posters urging Americans to show their patriotism. In 1941, the WPA Federal Writers' Program officially became the Writers' Unit of the War Services Division of the WPA; and the Federal Art Project, the Graphic Section of the War Services Division.[38]

The demands of war production decreased unemployment even further: "It would drop below 10 percent for 1941, the first time since 1929 that it had reached single digits. The number of jobless was 3.5 million, down from 13 to 15 million when Roosevelt took office."[39] At the end of 1941, it was under 5 percent and would reach 1.9 percent in 1943. The WPA was no longer needed. In a 1941 letter addressed to Philip Fleming, administrator of the Federal Works Agency, Roosevelt noted: "By employing eight millions of Americans, with thirty millions of dependents, it [the WPA] has brought to these people renewed hope and courage."[40]

1.2   THE AMERICAN POSTWAR STAGE

Victory over Japan Day, better known as V-J Day, occurred on August 15, 1945. Not only did it mark the definitive end of World War II; it symbolically marked the end of 15 years of economic privation and inaugurated a period of prosperity. With the war over, the U.S. became a world power; and New York, its cultural capital. In a world devastated by war, the U.S. had the healthiest economy:

> In the late 1940s, with 7 percent of the world's population, the United States had 42 percent of the world's income; produced 57 percent of the world's steel, 62 percent of the world's oil, and 80 percent of the world's automobiles; and owned three-quarters of the world's gold. Per-capita income was almost double the incomes in the next most well off nations, and Americans consumed 50 percent more calories a day than most people in Western Europe did. ... unemployment was less than 4 percent.[41]

The postwar prosperity brought hope, optimism and faith in the future. An increase in the national birth rate became known as the "baby boom" phenomenon, which spanned nearly two decades, from 1946 to 1964. Despite postwar inflation, "the masses of ordinary Americans were living at a higher material standard than their groups had ever known and with a much greater sense of status in the community."[42] But, at the same time, fear of a possible new war and uncertainty characterize the 1950s. Two main concerns preoccupied Americans: how to guarantee a continuous and steady wealth that avoided falling into another depression[43] and how to guarantee democracy internationally. The national debate over postwar U.S. policy revolves around these worries and wove an interrelationship between domestic and international affairs.

Harry S. Truman became the 33rd president of the United States of America on April 12, 1945. As vice president, Truman succeeded President Franklin D. Roosevelt when the latter died after months of illness. Truman served two presidential terms; he was reelected in November 1948, winning against the Republican candidate, Thomas E. Dewey.

Truman was a supporter of the New Deal that he inherited from Roosevelt to the point that he called his campaign "the Fair Deal." As a Democrat, he wanted to favor lower-income groups, but he also felt that price controls in peacetime were somehow un-American. On the domestic front, the end of World War II ushered in a period of intense striking, of which perhaps the most representative was led by the United Automobile Workers (UAW), the country's biggest union. In 1946, all the strikes in the U.S. were "piling up a record loss of 107,475.000 man-days of work, hobbling production and pushing prices towards still higher levels."[44]

In the animation industry, strikes for better working conditions and salaries began even before World War II: they started in 1937 at the Fleischer Studios in New York City and culminated at Disney on May 29, 1941. In the same period, near-strikes also occurred at the Leon Schlesinger studio[45] and at MGM.[46] UPA was an overtly liberal studio founded by former Disney strikers who firmly believed and supported unionization. In fact, two of the early UPA films, *Hell-Bent for Election*[47] and *Brotherhood of Man*,[48] were commissioned by the UAW.

Foreign politics from the U.S. perspective were characterized by the trials of captured Nazi generals, images from concentration camps and of starving people around the world, the famous 1946 Churchill speech about a Europe divided by an "iron curtain" that goes "from Stettin in the Baltic to Trieste in the Adriatic" and the increasing number of countries governed by Communist regimes in Eastern Europe and beyond, such as China and Indochina. This scene heightened the dichotomy between American and anti-American, liberalism and communism and, ultimately, good and evil. When Henry Wallace, commerce secretary and former vice president under Roosevelt, declared just six months after Churchill's speech that "the danger of war is much less from Communism than it is from Imperialism,"[49] he was dismissed from the president's cabinet for being considered "pro-Soviet."[50]

In an attempt to control the expansion of the Soviet Union, Truman's administration opted for a policy of "containment," which aimed to contain communism internationally and keep the U.S. secure inside and out. The Truman doctrine, created to ward off both Republican opposition and Soviet Union expansion, implied this policy of containment, as explained by Truman himself: "I believe that it must be the policy of the United States to support free peoples who are resisting attempted subjugation by armed minorities or by outside pressures."[51] The stance was marked by two major events: the Greek-Turkish crisis of 1947, in which Truman decided that U.S. intervention in support of the Greeks was necessary to avoid a civil war in which Red guerrillas might prevail, and the reconstruction of European countries via the Marshall Plan,[52] which became law in 1948. By 1947, the term *Cold War* was in common usage to define the relationship between the U.S. and the USSR.

By the late 1940s, the association of the New Deal with Communism revived,[53] and those who embraced Taft Republicanism also believed that New Deal policies were bankrupting the U.S. Senator Robert A. Taft[54] called for a counterrevolution against the "half-century of Revolution" [read: New Deal-Fair Deal], with the goal of limiting American commitments in foreign countries and putting more attention on internal issues. Senator Taft firmly believed that the solution was to return to the "traditional American heart of things, liberty."[55] The debate intensified in 1949, when three main events occurred in the same year: the Communists took China and Chiang Kai-shek's Nationalist government fled to Formosa,[56] the Soviet Union announced development of the atomic bomb and the domestic case of Alger Hiss, accused of espionage, gripped the public. Hiss,[57] a highly respected governmental official, soon became suspected of treason in an era susceptible to treason because of "years of Democratic softness towards Communism."[58] The Hiss and anti-Hiss supporters came to symbolize the conflict between the New Deal and Taft Republicanism in domestic affairs. The combination of these events at home and abroad soon morphed into a "theory of conspiracy" in U.S. political verbiage. At the bottom of the conspiracy theory was the idea, diffused by Taft Republicans, that "it was not really the Russian and Chinese Communists but Reds in the United States who had brought the crisis and who now directly threatened America."[59]

In order to understand what communism meant to American people, it is necessary to reflect on the origins of the U.S. The Declaration of Independence, signed in 1776, declared that "all men are created equal, that they are endowed by their Creator with certain unalienable Rights, that among these are Life, Liberty and the pursuit of Happiness."[60] Emphasis should be put on the word *liberty*. In 1823, the Monroe Doctrine laid the foundations of future U.S. foreign policy by declaring that "the American continents, by the free and independent condition which they have assumed and maintain, are henceforth not to be considered as subjects for future colonization by any European powers."[61] This notion of nationalistic sovereignty would also be echoed in the artistic desire and search for a definition of American art as opposed to European art during the Cold War era.[62] In this context, animation came to play a relevant role, especially after American animation became well-known, appreciated and even imitated in Europe and worldwide, first via Disney in the late 1930s and early 1940s[63] and later via UPA in the 1950s. American animated films by these studios set the standard internationally for an entertainment animation industry that could compete with the live-action production system (thanks to Disney) and proposed abroad stylistic experimentation that helped re-affirm animation as an independent art form (thanks to UPA).

Liberalism and individualism[64] have been part of U.S. identity since its creation as a nation. Therefore, Marxism, communism and other radical ideas are often perceived as anti-American, or even un-American, since they are "incompatible with national identity."[65] Post-World War II anti-communism echoed the Red Scare in the years following World War I (1919–1921), and the association of the New Deal with Communism is made more understandable once one realizes that "in the United States, the policies of the CP [Communist Party] had very little to do with socialism, communism, or any other radical idea; indeed, on most pressing issues, the Party differed little from the New Deal Democrats."[66]

Regarding democracy and conformism, physicist Albert Einstein gave an interesting analysis of American society:

Modern conformism ... is alarming everywhere, and naturally here it is growing worse every day, but, you see, American conformism has always existed to some extent, because American society, being based on the community itself and not on the authority of a strong central state, needs the cooperation of every individual to function well. Therefore, the individual has always considered it his duty to act as a kind of spiritual policeman for himself and his neighbor. The lack of tolerance is also connected with this, but much more with the fact that American communities were religious in their origin, and religion is by its very nature intolerant. This will also help you understand another seemingly strange contradiction. For example, you will find a far greater amount of tolerance in England than over here, where to be "different" is almost a disgrace, for everyone, starting with schoolboys and up to the inhabitants of small towns. But you will find far more democracy over here than in England. That, also, is a fact.[67]

The anti-Communist crusade of the postwar years, with its culmination during the period 1950–1954[68] (what is commonly known as the McCarthy era, named after the demagogic senator from Wisconsin, Joseph McCarthy), spread to every sector of society: from the government to the army, from Hollywood to the press, from primary and secondary schools to university campuses—and even to the animation industry. Between 1946 and 1948, 26 investigations of purported Communism were carried out, and over the next six years, another 109.[69] No one was immune. Teachers and journalists, among others, became victims. In 1947, the Federal Office of Education introduced the "Zeal for Democracy" program with the goal of balancing anti-Communism ideology and democratic idealism. Columnists were blacklisted and left-wing newspapers were harassed by the government. Moreover, distorted news and a lack of objective information affected media reports: like government officials, media people "lived in a world of Cold War fantasy in which ideological orthodoxy was considered an adequate substitute for actual facts."[70]

The power to investigate alleged subversion gave John Edgar Hoover's Federal Bureau of Investigation (FBI) the ability to destroy the reputation of any person selected for investigation, and the "HUAC [seemed] more interested in destroying public officials who had supported the New Deal than in investigating subversion in the postwar years."[71]

The election of veteran General Dwight D. Eisenhower to the U.S. presidency in 1953 brought in a period of conservatism in internal and external affairs. In 1953, Eisenhower put an end to the Korean War[72] and started a massive retaliation policy based on less dependence on local defense and more on-air power and atomic weapons. Just one year later, in 1954, the U.S. accomplished the first explosion of the H-bomb.[73] In domestic affairs, Eisenhower encouraged a free market and abolished the rigid price-support practice. Reelected in 1956, he continued his foreign policy based less on containment and more on a "coexistence"[74] that provided an equilibrium between the two superpowers, the USSR and the U.S., until the end of his mandate, in 1961.

1.3 A CHANGING SOCIETY, A DIFFERENT LIFE

1.3.1 The Patriarchal Family

In the Private Snafu[75] cartoon *Payday*[76] (1944), Snafu is encouraged to save money and invest in the future instead of spending his army salary at a local bazaar in the Middle East, or in a bar in the Caribbean, or in a dice game in a Quonset hut in the Artic. His bright future is depicted in a poster with a new suburban home, a streamlined car parked in the driveway, a wife, Snafu Jr. in a stroller and even a doghouse on the lawn. But as soon as Snafu incautiously spends his money, everything disappears from the poster until only the phone is left, with a mouse singing "Snafu doesn't live here anymore."

World War II shaped a new and different society, much as UPA, born from the ashes of the Disney strike, shaped a new and different attitude toward animation. The wartime experience disrupted old living patterns and paved the way for those social changes that allowed the UPA animation studio and its cartoons to succeed. In the postwar years, more and more families migrated from the cities and agricultural areas to the suburbs; between World War II and 1970, rural America had an out-immigration of 25 million people.[77] Family farms were in crisis and suburban areas became the new landscape of the upper middle class. The exodus was encouraged by federally guaranteed mortgage loans promoted under the 1949 National Housing Act,[78] bank policies and the development of mass production techniques in the building industry. The neighborhoods in the cities were occupied by new immigrants who fueled a population shift: in Washington D.C., for example, from 1950 to 1960, the nonwhite population rose from 35 percent to 55 percent; in Chicago, from 14 percent to 24 percent; in Boston, from 5 percent to 10 percent.[79]

The unstable international setting and a persistent fear of mass destruction increased isolation and insecurity. Families stopped relying on extended relationships and became isolated, consuming units consisting of three or four people: the father, who embraced the corporate world for values, tended to move from one suburb to another with his wife, usually a homemaker and a mother of one to two children. The "suburban myth" promoted an image of the suburbs as a classless and homogeneous microcosm of white, Anglo-Saxon, Protestant (WASP) families, but mistrust, suspicion and uncertainty amounted to paranoia and fear. Closed inside the wall of a secure suburban house, the patriarchal family avoided venturing out into the world. Less cooperation and more individualism were leading to a competitive capitalist culture in which "the isolated nuclear family, viewing the world with abnormal distrust, became the perfect counterpart of a materialistic society."[80]

UPA animated cartoons reflect these social changes to some extent. *Mr. Tingley's Tangle*[81] portrays the apparently monotonous life of Mr. Tingley, a man who commutes every day by train from suburbia to the city: he leaves his family in the early morning and comes back home at the evening. [82] Suburban families are also portrayed in other UPA animated shorts, such as *Willie the Kid*, *Christopher Crumpet's Playmate*[83] and *Fudget's Budget*. In *Willie the Kid*, kids are playing cowboys and Indians in suburban courtyards that turn into canyons and valleys according to their imagination: they do not need to exit the secure environment of their courtyards to play with their imagination.

In *Christopher Crumpet's Playmate*, Christopher's dysfunctional belief of having an elephant as an imaginary friend is supported by Christopher's father's boss, who had a hyena as an imaginary friend when he was a child. In *Fudget's Budget*, a family is struggling with its monthly budget and the economic ups and downs of ordinary life.

As the U.S economy was expanding, it was necessary to both invest in overseas markets and avoid inflated consumer spending by pushing people to buy as much as possible. The credit boom of the postwar years goes hand in hand with the explosion of advertising, especially television advertising. Television had become pervasive: whereas in 1947 there were only 17 TV stations in the whole country, after 1952 there were more than 2,000; in 1947, the number of cities with reception were eight but grew to more than 1,200 after 1952.[84] Furthermore, "by 1956, two out of every three American families had at least one TV, and by 1960 the figure was up to 87 percent."[85] The explosion of advertising during these years has prompted a new interest in sociological and psychological studies.

Although the family model portrayed on TV series such as *Father Knows Best* and *The Honeymooners* was still WASP, society was, in fact, changing. Minority ethnic groups such as African Americans and religious groups such as Catholics and Jews were beginning to demand and sometimes receive recognition. The year 1954, for example, marked one of the first steps in desegregation with the Supreme Court's decision that no child could be banned from a public school simply because of his or her skin color.[86]

Women, too, were asserting themselves. Continuing the trend established during World War II, women stayed on in the workforce "making up about 21.000.000 out of a total working force of roughly 64.000.000" in 1954–1955.[87] Still, if the image sold by TV and advertising was that of a happy family made up of a cheerful mother whose main work was in the kitchen and a busy father who had time to talk with kids only during the weekend, the reality was far different. Women, under this structure, were the first to be left behind, at home, excluded from work. "More so than at any time since the Victorian Age, women were to define themselves through a patriarchal vision intended to uphold male privilege."[88] Finding it difficult to identify with the image they were trying to conform to, women were unsatisfied.[89] Yet, "the imposed order of the postwar era was beginning to crack,"[90] and by 1960, there was evidence of growing social discontent. Some of the women rebelled and refused the role of wives or mothers embracing, for example, the Beat movement and demanding rights equal to those granted to men.

At the same time, women who already were in the workforce were becoming more independent both in public and private roles. In the late 1950s, a debate over the "womanization" of America and the crisis in American masculine identity arose.[91] The paternal figure was losing his authoritarian role, and "peer-oriented"[92] teenagers were expressing certain hostility toward the father. Moreover, during the early Cold War period, feminism, homosexuality and youth culture became linked to authoritarianism, totalitarianism and Communist ideology.[93]

The elderly were excluded from active society, while youth was idealized and new advertised products were considered better. Simultaneously, juvenile delinquency was rising to a "national crisis"[94] level. As opposed to their parents, young people lacked confidence and optimism in the future. A friction between the two generations developed: the adults wanted their daughters and sons to be educated according to current values, but the young could not identify themselves in the type of society whose image was promoted by their elders.[95] Young people started to read books that were meant for adults, began to date at an earlier age than the previous generation and tended to mock the man in the suit by promoting the rock 'n' roll or "greaser" style. In general, "the young were trained for nothing in life but what the adult world assigned them."[96] Therefore, rebels and outcasts became subjects of sympathetic films, books or theatrical pieces.

1.3.2   The Debate Among Intellectuals

Among intellectuals, scientists and artists, a broader discussion based on the threat of totalitarian ideologies in the age of mass culture was taking place. The question was how to redeem a world in crisis. High Modernists such as philosophers Max Horkheimer and Theodor Adorno, and literary critic Lionel Trilling clamored for a defense of the humanities to counterbalance modern science and modern technology, which were becoming too aggressive and uncontrollable with the advent of weapons of mass destruction. This debate found in psychoanalysis the fertile ground to be nurtured. Psychoanalysis was in its golden age during the 1940s and 1950s; it became pervasive, especially Freudianism and behaviorism. Psychoanalytic theories were often integrated and used by academics and intellectuals to further support their studies. Intellectuals were debating over the characteristics that an authoritarian personality had in contrast to a democratic personality.[97] Developed with an interdisciplinary perspective, research broadened to politics and anthropology in order to define "the type of psychological makeup appropriate for the healthy functioning of democratic institutions and the type of personality adaptable to the demands that freedom entailed."[98] Believing that fascism and communism were slight variations of the same disease, High Modernists proposed a well-integrated ego as the only foundation for the democratic personality, which is to say an ego with a strong oedipal identity, able to resist those pathological deviations that can lead to a totalitarian society. Art, in their vision, served to temper the domineering tendencies of the ego.[99] Romantic Modernists like painters Jackson Pollock and Barnett Newman and writer Jack Kerouac, instead, believed that modern man was castrated by the repressive and bureaucratic nature of society and that the threat of totalitarianism was no more external than internal, meaning psychological as well. The ego itself was excessively controlled and could be liberated only by an intense emotional release.

It merits note that there were intellectuals, scientists and artists who tried to rethink gender, sexual identities and the interpretation of the self-identity by criticizing the hyper-masculine artist proposed by the abstract expressionists and the Beats, or the High Modernist assumption that a strong oedipal ego was the only nonpathological form of identity. These individuals are classified as the Late Modernists by Genter: classicist Norman Brown, artist Jasper Johns, novelist James Baldwin, sociologists Ervin Goffman and Charles Wright Mills, literary theorist Kenneth Burke, novelist Ralph Ellison, and to this list could be added biologist and sexologist Alfred Kinsey. They all tried to offer an image of the self as an open, never-fixed but flexible ego that develops in the social realm and through its connection with the human body. Their sexual and psychological interpretations went beyond the oppositional categories of femininity and masculinity and anticipated ideas that would be further developed by the counterculture movement during the 1960s.[100]

1.4 YEARS OF ENDLESS EXPERIMENTATION

Manifestations of this different and evolving society can also be found in some of its cultural expressions. During the 1940s and 1950s, literature, poetry, music, painting, graphic design, cinema and television were going through a period of intense experimentation.

1.4.1 Literature, Poetry, Music and Painting

Forms of rebellion toward the conformity of American middle-class life took shape during the late 1940s and the 1950s. The Bohemian lifestyle flourished in a few isolated artistic communities. Improvisation became the leitmotif of many artistic trends: in the poetry and literature of writers William S. Burroughs and Jack Kerouac, poet Allen Ginsberg and other members of the Beat generation; in the painting of abstract expressionists Jackson Pollock, Mark Rothko, Barnett Newman, Clyfford Still and Willem de Kooning; and in the musical genres of rock 'n' roll, bebop and jazz.

Instinctual and impulsive artistic productions were valued as expressions of personal freedom resulting from an immediate creative need. Romantic Modernists turned inward for inspiration. Abstract expressionists transformed painting from being "a reflection on external reality to being a reflection of the interior landscape of the artist"[101] through the gesture of painting itself: action painting. The Beat poets reestablished a lost connection with their unconscious selves by "taking literature out of the ivory tower … and made it a tool for understanding everyday existence."[102] Both critical of a culture in decay and against formal aesthetic, the Beat generation and abstract expressionists were intimately connected with jazz. For example, the verses of Beat poems were written to be spoken before a public; Kerouac and Ginsberg were creating musical rhythmic constructions by looking at the written line as an "improvisation with the phrasing reflecting the rhythm and structure of a jazz solo."[103]

The UPA animated film *Rooty Toot Toot* is based on the popular ballad "Frankie and Johnny." It is a story of jealousy, betrayal and murder told in the rhythm of a jazz lyric. Improvisation can be seen in the way the music is used as part of the storytelling as, for example, when tunes underline the personality of the characters or stress topical moments within the animation's narration.

Jazz musicians at the time were trying to convey emotions and feelings that would describe the inner-self experience. By 1947, the *New Yorker* would affirm that "the most serious and furious arguments about music nowadays all seem to involve jazz,"[104] and by the mid-1950s, rock 'n' roll and jazz had both reached a wider public. Both these musical genres brought to the attention of white American audiences some themes belonging to the African American culture and the American folk tradition of blues, bluegrass, work songs and traditional ballads. At the same time, typical of the decade were minimalistic experimentations with abstract sounds, especially in TV commercials, or silence. Gail Kubik, American composer, music director and violinist, won the Pulitzer Prize in music in 1952. Two years before, he had composed the music for *Gerald McBoing Boing*, which was awarded an Oscar in 1950 (Figure 1.1). In it, the sounds became the emotive language through which Gerald tries to communicate his feelings.

Other recurrent artistic themes of the 1950s were a certain attraction to primitivism and mystical and esoteric claims. Painter Barnett Newman, who incorporated biological themes by addressing the origin of life in his works, promoted the association between avant-garde painting and primitivism.[105] He encouraged other Modern artists to look at the original man, that artist liberated from cultural, sociological and psychological restraints. Romantic Modernists turned to Oceanic and Native American traditions, the European Modern canvas[106] as painted by André Masson, Joan Miró and Wassily Kandinsky, ancient mythology and Jungian theory.[107] A series of exhibitions helped American Modernists become acquainted with the

FIGURE 1.1   Stephen Bosustow Receives the Oscar for Gerald McBoing Boing. Reprinted with permission from Tee Bosustow (*Steve Bosustow's UPA collection, in the care of his son, Tee Bosustow*).

subjects: *Pre-Columbian Stone Sculpture* (1944) and the *Northwest Coast Indian Painting* were both organized by Newman. Also, the MoMA held such exhibitions as *African Negro Art* (1935), *Prehistoric Rock Pictures in Europe and Africa* (1937), *Twenty Centuries of Mexican Art* (1940), *Indian Art of the United States* (1941) and *Ancestral Sources of Modern Painting* (1941).[108]

1.4.2   Graphic Design

During the 1920s and 1930s, American graphic design was dominated by traditional illustration for book design, editorial design for fashion and business magazines, and promotional and corporate graphics. In Europe, the principles taught at the Bauhaus School of Arts and Crafts initiated modern graphic design by departing from spiritual values and expressionistic inclinations in favor of a functionalist aesthetic. The school was founded in Weimar, Germany, in 1919 and operated until 1933, when it was forced to close by the Nazi government. Among its faculty members were artists Paul Klee, Wassily Kandinsky, El Lissitzsky, Jan Tschichold, Johannes Itten and László Moholy-Nagy, with his assistant György Kepes. During the 1930s, due to the anti-Semitic laws under Nazi Germany, many designers left Europe for the U.S., including Herbert Bayer, László Moholy-Nagy, György Kepes and Herbert Matter.[109] Moholy-Nagy arrived in Chicago in 1937 and established the New Bauhaus, which closed just after one year. He later opened the School of Design in 1939. An exhibition under the title *Bauhaus 1919–1928*, curated by Bayer, was held at the MoMA in New York City in 1938, while Kepes became an influential teacher for many graphic designers, such as Saul Bass, mentored by Kepes at Brooklyn College,[110] and the generation of artists who left Disney and founded UPA.[111]

Other immigrants who introduced European Modernism to American graphic design were Romaine de Tirtoff (Erté), Mehemed Fehmy Agha, Alexey Brodovitch and Alexander Liberman, who, respectively, designed the first *Harper's Bazaar* cover in 1921, became director of *Vogue* in 1928, directed *Harper's Bazaar* from 1934 to 1958 and became art director of *Vogue in* 1943.[112] Another major figure in the development of American graphic design was Walter P. Paepcke, who founded the Container Corporation of America (CCA) in 1926, which specialized in producing packaging materials. Among those who worked at the CCA's department of design were Egbert Jacobson, Adolphe Jean-Marie Mouron (Cassandre), and Herbert Bayer, chairman from 1956 to 1965. Others included Fernand Léger, Man Ray and Herbert Matter.

During World War II, informational and scientific graphics simplified the graphic visual language as much as the experience at the FMPU provided opportunities for experimenting in animation. Informational design expressed a synthesis of function, flow and form. Advertising expanded during the 1940s, and a new professional figure able to design any type of industrial packaging, posters, booklets, brochures and so on was in demand. The graphic designer gained relevance in the advertising industry. A new profession was taking shape: "It was only in the 1940s that the *graphic designer* superseded the advertising artist and that humble drudge the layout man, to become an amalgam of the two."[113] Designers were taking a more prominent role in the creative process, moving away from being just the layout men.

Graphic design was the penultimate art to be conquered by Modernism. The last was animation. It was the New York School that defined the American Modern graphic design: it had strong roots in European Modernism during the 1940s, gained prominence in the 1950s and lasted until the 1990s. Reflecting on American Modern graphic design and the influence of the Bauhaus principles, Bartram states: "Bauhaus graphic design was especially suited to advertising, which happily chime with American interests,"[114] while the then-new Swiss typography, intellectual and analytical, was less "adaptable to American taste."[115] Nevertheless, the Swiss style of design, which emerged in Switzerland after World War II, became popular in Europe and the U.S. in the 1950s and 1960s. Having its roots in Russian constructivism and German Bauhaus, it promoted "legibility, objectivity, and clean simple design"[116] and was characterized by "sans-serif typefaces, asymmetrical layouts, an adherence to a grid system for page layouts and a tendency towards ranged-left, ragged-right text placement."[117]

Paul Rand, who embraced the European thinking, especially Jan Tschichold's new typography, proposed an integration of form and function favoring an asymmetrical balance in which there are strong contrasts of shape, color and texture. He was the one who paved the way from commercial art to graphic design.[118] Rand affirmed: "When I designed a cover of *Direction*, I was really trying to compete with the Bauhaus. Not with Norman Rockwell."[119] *Direction* was an arts and culture magazine that featured articles written by architect Le Corbusier, writer Jean Cocteau and other avant-gardists.

In his opening titles for many feature films, Saul Bass used simple effective images for expressing the essence of the films' subject, as in the well-known *The Man with the Golden Arm*.[120] Bass, who was introduced to Moholy-Nagy's Bauhaus visions as well as to the work of Russian constructivists like Alexander Rodchenko, and whose career as designer and filmmaker was based on the idea of graphic functionalism, valued "a simplicity which also has a certain metaphysical implication that makes that simplicity vital."[121]

Another relevant artist who marked a significant step in the evolution of American postwar visual culture is cartoonist Saul Steinberg, whose graphic art deeply influenced UPA artists, especially in *Brotherhood of Man* and *Flat Hatting*.[122] Born in Romania, he immigrated to Italy in 1933, where he studied architecture in Milan. By 1941 Steinberg's drawings were appearing in *Life* magazine and *Harper's Bazaar*. His collaboration with the *New Yorker* lasted almost 60 years: he produced nearly 90 covers and more than 1,200 drawings "that elevate the language of popular graphics to the realm of fine art."[123] Animator George Griffin explains the significance of Steinberg for a generation of artists:

> I think Steinberg is basically a writer and what he draws could fill a book. He would refer to history, philosophy, existentialism, nationalism, national characters. There is a very rich kind of reference well that he dips into. And he did it: he captured America. He is the quintessential immigrant. ... He brings this stranger sensibility, the stranger's eyes, and he is able to see things that we can't see ourselves. He is able to see cowboys, politicians, women.[124]

1.4.3   Cinema

American cinema was experiencing the crisis of the motion picture studio system. The "consent decrees," signed by the five integrated major studios in 1940, outlawed block booking and reduced blind selling to groups of five pictures. The antitrust law was mildly abided by during the 1940's while business were successful. But during the 1950's the impact of law's enforcement came into effect. In 1948, the Supreme Court issued the so-called Paramount decree,[125] which established the abandonment of block booking, blind bidding, price-fixing and all privileged arrangements between the studios and theaters for the distribution and exhibition of movies. It also removed theater holdings from the integrated major studios, which now were forced to function only as production-distribution companies. All of this had the effect of opening doors for smaller, independent companies and led to an industry in which movies were produced, marketed and sold on a picture-by-picture and theater-by-theater basis. The studio-based production system, with its "contract personnel, steady cash flow, and regulated output"[126] was fading. Other concurrent events intensified the crisis: the growing independence of top talents, a diminution of interest in the movies and the rise of commercial television, the most serious threat. If during the war, movies were symbols of unity for the country, in the postwar years Americans were less attracted by cinema. The migration to suburban areas distanced people from theaters, which were located in the cities. Drive-ins, meanwhile, became a big hit, and TV programs gathered families in their living rooms.

This scenario is illustrated in the film *The Last Picture Show*,[127] set in Anarene, Texas, between World War II and the Korean conflict. It focuses on the lives of the residents of this small town, where boredom is omnipresent, and the young generations are tempted to leave for a better future elsewhere. The title, imbued with nostalgia, symbolizes a world that is disappearing: the small local theater is forced to close because no one is going to see movies anymore; rather people are turning to other types of entertainment, primarily TV.

Postwar audiences demanded different pictures, as well, ones that were truer to life. In American movies of the 1950s, "the subtext became as important as the apparent subject matter or even more important."[128] In particular, a sympathy for outcasts was expressed, for example, in *Rebel without a Cause*,[129] *The Man with the Golden Arm* and *Sweet Smell of Success*.[130]

Director Elia Kazan, with his filmic adaptation of *A Streetcar Named Desire*,[131] was one of the first to challenge the studio rules. The Catholic Legion of Decency condemned the film for the sensuality of some scenes. In particular, Marlon Brando's acting, confirmed in 1954's *On the Waterfront*,[132] was a style breakthrough for its ability to realistically reveal the natural behaviors of people, and the content received attention for centering on the corruption of the unions. Martin Scorsese believes that Kazan paved the way for the iconoclasts of the 1950s and 1960s, those directors who worked outside of the studio system rules, such as writer-directors and writer-producers Robert Aldrich, Richard Brooks, Robert Rossen, Billy Wilder and, among the younger generations, Arthur Penn and Sam Peckinpah:

> They all defied the guardians of public morality by daring to tackle controversial issues like racism [*Apache*], inner-city violence [*Blackboard Jungle*], juvenile delinquency [*The Wild One*], homosexuality [*Advise and Consent*], war atrocities [*Paths of Glory*], the death penalty [*I Want to Live*].[133]

1.4.4 Television

Television was the perfect vehicle to bring art to the masses. In her book *TV by Design*, Spigel illustrates the popular enthusiasm for visual art during the 1950s and 1960s and explains how much television and art were intertwined.[134] Modern art was incorporated at various levels in

TV programs, and graphic design was incorporated in TV commercials. Among the artists, designers and photographers hired by the three U.S. TV networks were Ben Shahn, Feliks Topolski, Leo Lionni, René Bouché, John Groth, Georg Olden, Andy Warhol, Paul Strand, Saul Bass, Paul Rand and Richard Avedon. The popular embrace of art during the Cold War era went hand in hand with the process of defining American art and defining the U.S., at home and abroad, as a "nation of good taste." As opposed to Europe, where art was synonymous with "the Masters," American art was abstract expressionist, abstract and primitive.[135]

During the 1950s, ad agencies began to set up art departments specifically for television, whose commercials entered the homes of ordinary people and accustomed them to a certain amount of abstract imagery. From there, "America developed a taste for taste."[136] Many TV commercials were made for ad agencies by UPA through its Burbank and New York offices. Another influential commercial production company was Tempo Productions in New York, run by former UPA animators. It was TV that brought certain aesthetic concepts to the American mass mind: when people watched television or read a newspaper, they were also looking at Modern design. And, corporate advertising ended up creating a Modern visual look for TV, the new medium.[137] By 1954, "CBS was the leading US television network and the largest advertising medium in the world."[138]

It is in this context that the MoMA developed a TV format for art education. MoMA's Television Project aimed to make art as accessible as possible via television, bring it into people's homes, and especially to the female audience. A series called *They Became Artists* was initially commissioned to UPA but never realized.[139] Nevertheless, UPA did make *The Boing-Boing Show*, a 30-minute TV program aired by CBS and the first animated program specially made for network TV,[140] and several TV commercials.

UPA animated cartoons and the artists behind them also helped to accustom audiences to the Modern aesthetic. As Arthur Knight observed in 1952, "Their reception [of UPA cartoons] strongly suggests that the American public, increasingly apathetic in the presence of the conventional cartoon, fully appreciates the stimulus of the UPA approach, an approach that is at once modern and basic."[141] Moreover, he affirmed: "Does this mean that American movie audiences have suddenly acquired a taste for modern art? It would almost seem so—at least, for modern art presented in this manner."[142]

The success and peculiarity of UPA animated cartoons owes to the ability of UPA artists to include Modern art in the animated cinema, a medium that in the U.S. was intended for the masses, not for the elites: "Thus 'Gerald' [of *Gerald McBoing Boing*] performs that rarest of tricks: It combines art with mass popularity."[143] Animation is a "commercial art" as much as TV advertising is, and UPA animated cartoons contributed to the modernization process by popularizing Modern art through animated cartoons; therefore, Modern art reached the masses in part thanks to UPA animations. Critic Ed Penney has stated:

> It is even possible to present satire to the American public, as long as you don't tell them that it's satire, just as Menotti gives the American people opera, disguising the fact by calling it "musical-drama." In brief, good taste has proved to have commercial value.[144]

Furthermore, UPA animated cartoons contributed to the characterization of a precise visual "look," a well-defined aesthetic: "Gradually this simplicity will create a standard of acceptance in American minds and this acceptance will be felt by UPA's competitors."[145] Significantly, the UPA Modern aesthetic was also harmonious with television advertising, which explains the success of UPA animated TV commercials: "UPA is just too good to be kicked into another medium because the middlemen don't know how to get their products to the public. The public itself has no doubt. They go for UPA whenever they get a chance."[146]

1.5 AMERICAN ANIMATION GOES MODERN

1.5.1 Animation during and after World War II

With the production of animated feature films, Disney had set the standard for the animation industry. By 1941, its rivals, like Fleischer Studios or Hugh Harman of MGM, were gone, but the strike of that year[147] led to a new and unexpected scenario.

The Disney strike was a pivotal event in the history of U.S. animation. A division occurred in the animation industry between those who rejected Walt Disney's labor system and those who were loyal to him. Resentment toward Walt Disney the businessman among former Disney employees only boosted the rejection of the classic Disney aesthetic and the urge to experiment with the medium. Therefore, the strike marked the beginning of a period of experimentation carried on by those artists who had worked at Disney but aspired to expand the medium of animation once they were dismissed. This stylistic research passed through many unplanned trials and errors and took place at different and various studios. Michael Barrier calls it "the Disney diaspora": the "rapid spread of artists with Disney training, and Disney-bred attitudes, to studios where neither had been common before."[148] The great majority of them ended up at Walter Lantz and Screen Gems, places of low prestige in the industry. The Screen Gems studio can be considered a UPA embryo, for some of the people who worked there, such as John Hubley and Zachary Schwartz, later moved to UPA, bringing with them the desire to experiment, as Barrier seems to imply:

> As at Lantz, the new Columbia cartoons actually looked less like Disney cartoons than many that had come from Screen Gems before, but the new cartoons *felt* more like Disney cartoons because there was behind them the same urge to expand the vocabulary of the medium.[149]

Designer-animator John Hubley recalled the impulse to experiment with the medium at Screen Gems studio:

> Under Tashlin we tried some very experimental things; none of them quite got off the ground, but there was a lot of ground broken. We were doing crazy things that were anti the classic Disney approach. That was in 1942.[150]

During that same year, after Frank Tashlin left and Dave Fleischer took over, Hubley codirected with animator Paul Sommer five cartoons before entering the army. Schwartz, meanwhile, designed at least three films before he left in 1944:[151] *Song of Victory,*[152] *Willoughby's Magic Hat*[153] and *Magic Strength.*[154]

Experimentation that purposely departed from Disney-like animation also took place at the Schlesinger studio and MGM. Two key figures were Chuck Jones, who directed *The Dover Boys at Pimento University*[155] in 1942, and Tex Avery, who directed *Red Hot Riding Hood*[156] in 1943.

The Dover Boys at Pimento University was the collaborative effort of Jones as director, John McGrew as a layout man, Gene Fleury as a background painter and Bobe Cannon as an animator. In it, some poses are kept longer than usual in order to focus the viewer's attention on characters' psychological reactions, thus demonstrating that "if strong poses were used for a definite purpose, and were not stiff and blank but had life, they could actually encourage audiences to accept the reality of cartoons characters."[157] Although the characters are still three-dimensional, the design of the backgrounds and the characters and the movement are stylized. In *Red Hot Riding Hood*, the exaggerated physical reactions of the wolf demonstrate a predilection for comedy and gags rather than Disney realism, thus putting an emphasis on timing.

In subsequent years, both Jones and Avery experimented with stylization. Flatter backgrounds are present in later animated shorts directed by Jones: *The Case of the Missing Hare*,[158] *The Aristo-Cat*,[159] *The Unbearable Bear*[160] and *Wackiki Wabbit*.[161] Stylized movements characterized these later shorts by Avery: *Northwest Hounded Police*,[162] *Uncle Tom Cabaña*,[163] *King-Size Canary*[164] and *Señor Droopy*.[165]

The Disney strike also affected those artists who were loyal to Walt Disney and did not leave the company. Toward the end of the 1940s, some of them experimented with stylized background, such as Mary Blair, for example, who designed *Once upon a Winter Time*, an animated short within the animated feature film *Melody Time*,[166] released in 1948. In *Once upon a Winter Time*, the streamlined design is achieved through stylized backgrounds and characters.[167]

World War II challenged old stylistic patterns. The demand for animated war propaganda shorts increased to the point that from 1942 to 1945, 47 percent of all cartoons produced were war related, and by 1943, Disney, Schlesinger, MGM and Lantz had signed contracts with the army.[168]

Many animators were stationed at the FMPU, the film production unit of the U.S. Army, in particular in the animation and graphic section of Frank Capra's unit, headed by Theodor Geisel, aka Dr. Seuss. Here, animators had the chance to experience new positions, accomplish different tasks and find solutions other than the Disney ones. The experience was extremely productive: with small budgets, animators were suddenly dealing more with human beings than animals, more graphic and stylized drawings and an alternative to expensive full animation.[169]

In the postwar years, as television and advertising exploded, small studios in the mid-1940s started making animated TV commercials and entertainment cartoons especially for early TV, and by the 1950s, "the studios that made theatrical cartoons began metamorphosing into television-cartoon studios."[170] Animation in TV now exploded: "During peak years in the 1950s, ... one out of every four ads on television was animated,"[171] and by 1951, "as much as 30 percent of UPA's total output was dedicated to television and advertising."[172] The general trend was to use few drawings for economic reasons (limited animation), highly stylized backgrounds and characters, and a Modern graphic design look expressed by bold colors and few essential lines and shapes.[173]

MGM closed its units in 1953 with the exception of Hanna-Barbera. Avery, who left the same year, went to work at Lantz studio. After Disney's golden period of animated feature films, Walt Disney shifted his attention to live-action films and theme parks, although never abandoning the production of both animated feature films and short subjects, the latter showing a certain level of experimentation and freedom from the classic Disney standards. Disney made its first TV program, *One Hour in Wonderland*, in 1950 to promote the forthcoming release of *Alice in Wonderland*[174] and the first animated TV commercial in 1952 for Mohawk Carpet Company. In 1954, the company signed an agreement with ABC for a television series called *Disneyland* along with financial help for the theme park.[175] Increasingly less time was being devoted to motion picture and animated features.

In 1948, UPA negotiated a contract with Columbia Pictures for the distribution of its animated shorts in theaters provided that the animated shorts featured the Columbia characters the Fox and the Crow. The need to sell something tangible to theatrical exhibitors pushed Columbia to ask for a new "recognizable character," and in 1949, UPA responded with the nearsighted Mr. Magoo, who became a successful series character during the 1950s.

1.5.2 UPA as a Cultural Product of Its Time

Animated cinema is a young art; it arrived at that synthesis of minimalism typical of the 20th century later than all other art forms and was heavily influenced by them, being especially intertwined with graphic design. UPA animated shorts anticipated this tendency toward reductionism in animated cinema that occurred internationally during the 1950s and 1960s. The industry was ready for a change, and as Maltin has put it: "If there hadn't been a UPA, someone [else] would have had to invent it."[176]

Initially founded as Industrial Films and Poster Service in 1943 by former Disney employees Zachary Schwartz, David Hilberman and

Stephen Bosustow,[177] UPA survived the competitive market by producing educational and training films during World War II. This practical business move simultaneously provided the opportunity to experiment with stylized images and stylized animation for economic reasons, consequently incorporating more graphic design into animation.

From the training and educational films made during the war to the ones created for the UAW, the years 1944–1946 were crucial in the development of those characteristics that would mark UPA animated shorts during the Columbia era. These films can be considered experimental, expressions of unconventional artistic research. The two Private Snafu cartoons made by UPA, *A Few Quick Facts*[178] and *A Few Quick Facts about Fear*,[179] for example, are "distinguished from those made by Warner Bros. by [their] total lack of humor"[180] and already express stylized images, backgrounds and animation. Analysis of these two films reveals the relevance of wartime production of educational and training films in relation to experimentation for the purpose of finding alternative graphic solutions.

A Few Quick Facts is less than two minutes long and is about inflation. It opens with a city full of neon signs; the background is flat, and the camera moves from left to right. A few scenes later, we see an overseas serviceman going to a small local store to purchase an item. The store has a stylized design and, inside of it, rectangles of equal size represent the item in stock. In the background is only the white store, with nothing around it other than the man. The animation is limited rather than full. The more items purchased, the more the price goes up, and when the situation is multiplied over and over, inflation occurs: more and more people run to buy stuff in local stores, and money loses its buying power. The effect is *inflation*, the word appearing on the screen while the voice explains what it is.

In a similar vein, *A Few Quick Facts about Fear* opens with a mounted knight who, after being introduced by silhouettes of heralds playing horns in unison, exits the castle, a highly stylized flat castle, and fearlessly ventures into the forest. Soon, beneath the armor appears Private Snafu experiencing fear much as the medieval knight did. The physical symptoms of fear follow in effective, simplified animations: ready to recognize the danger, "you see more clearly, you hear more keenly, muscles tense, the body is ready to act, and act fast," the narrator explains. Here appears a sketched white eye on a black background, white lines moving out of a rectangular plane that symbolizes the ear, in an almost abstract animation, and an oblique line that tenses the biceps of Snafu. The opening of the film presages the animated shorts *The Fifty First Dragon*[181] and *The Invisible Moustache of Raoul Dufy*[182] of *The Boing-Boing Show*. Moreover, when the medieval knight is attacked by the dragon early in the segment, the decoration of the flat black dragon resembles the pattern of a Greek vase, something Schwartz was familiar with.[183]

Experimentation naturally took place in a company where freedom of expression was encouraged by the executive producer, Stephen Bosustow, and by a group of progressive artists. New stylistic solutions included stories dealing with adult subject matters, a "flat" graphic design style, expressive sound effects and references to Modern and primitive art. UPA animators applied to animation that common vision toward minimalism and reductionism embraced by many visual artists. In their attempt to simplify animation's visual language, they came up with a *subjective* frame, a space defined by the psychology of the characters that inhabited it, their interior landscapes. Their style eventually defined an *attitude* toward animation.

UPA animated shorts also reproduced the postwar anxiety and expanding consumerist world of the 1950s. Norman M. Klein argues that the most important shift in animation brought about by UPA was the fact that characters were part of this abstract space, which is the *Modern space* defined by Modern architecture[184] and urban planning, the suburbia. He also emphasizes the nature of Mr. Magoo and of Gerald McBoing Boing, whose physical deficiencies are revealed to be necessary to survive in an absurd Ionesco world, the hysterical world of the 1950s.[185]

Mr. Magoo also grabbed the attention of Milton J. Rosenberg, Yale University professor of psychology, who analyzed the Mr. Magoo shorts as comic devices for the arousal and reduction of anxiety. In his opinion, Magoo is:

> [A] personification of a part, though only a part, of every man's inner image of himself. … The dangers he faces symbolize the less dramatic dangers to which we all are sensitive in our own lives. Perhaps all ages have been ages of anxiety, but certainly ours is as full of fright as any other. The fear of war, the fear of loss of identity, the fear of boredom, the fear of isolation, the fear of our own impulses—all these are rearoused in us as Magoo faces his more concrete horrors … and it is Magoo's function to still our fears.[186]

From slapstick comedians such as Charlie Chaplin, Buster Keaton and Harold Lloyd to the animated characters of Donald Duck, Daffy Duck and Wile E. Coyote, all comic heroes share a common destiny: to be "a handicapped man, only saved from annihilation by incessant stratagems typical of the oppressed and paradoxically great luck."[187] But different from all other comic heroes, Magoo seems to be saved only by himself, or, better yet, "by complete allegiance to a set of social values and moral conceptions."[188] His values are those of the old American society: the individualism of the self-made man.

> He wants what he wants when he wants it—but only because he is convinced that the rules of society justify his wants and have put him clearly "in the right." He speaks his mind always and expects as much from other men. He plays fair and expects to be treated fairly.[189]

Ultimately, Magoo is still an "inner-directed" person in an increasingly "other-directed" world, and "the underlying serious and unconscious message of these cartoons is ... simply this: to stand secure in an insecure world, a man must stand for something."[190]

Mr. Magoo reveals the strong desire for satire on the part of his creators John Hubley and voice actor Jim Backus, especially a desire "to satirize the symbols of family authority that each of us knew."[191] But, after more than 10 years of production of 53 Mr. Magoo short subjects, many changes had taken place. Political pressures in the wake of the HUAC investigations led to a fear of satire, especially any public satire of authority. Pete Burness, a sweeter person than Hubley in the opinion of Bosustow,[192] added a warm, sentimental side to old Magoo when he took charge of the character.

There were also now economic pressures. As production costs rose, footage of the films was cut, forcing creators to squeeze a story into the reduced footage.

UPA one-shot animated cartoons, although acclaimed by critics, meant nothing to distributors or theatrical exhibitors since a single cartoon cannot be sold. In 1955, Columbia Pictures favored the release of only Mr. Magoo films, and in 1957, asked for an accelerated production. In 1959, Columbia terminated its releasing contract, and the following year, UPA began production of a Mr. Magoo TV series under new owner and executive producer Henry G. Saperstein. After 1955's *When Magoo Flew*, UPA films were of inferior quality and lost most of their satirical edge. Magoo was commercialized first in theaters and later on TV, and by the late 1950s, "the freedom to express an individual point of view gradually disappeared at UPA."[193]

1.5.3   The 1955 MoMA Exhibition

The Museum of Modern Art curated its first show devoted entirely to animated film 25 years after the New York City institution opened its doors. *UPA: Form in the Animated Cartoon*[194] premiered on June 21, 1955 and closed on September 25 of the same year.[195] Under the direction of Douglas McAgy, the exhibit strove to be "aesthetic rather than historical or technological."[196]

The 1955 UPA MoMA exhibition was significant in the history of UPA studio because it asserted that UPA animated films were Modern artworks. Furthermore, the duration of the exhibit confirmed that UPA films were highly appreciated by the public and that UPA was now considered a leading studio in the entertainment animation industry. Finally, the fact that the MoMA's first show entirely devoted to animation featured the aesthetic of UPA films indicated not only that animation was a recognized art form which deserved to be exhibited in museums but that UPA played a significant role in this process.

The exhibition was structured into four parts. The first focused on the "creative atmosphere of UPA activity,"[197] with three murals that illustrated with photographs and drawings "the lively and varied interests of the individuals in the UPA community in Burbank and their enjoyment of early films, famous comedians of the silent screen, modern art, motor cars, and jazz."[198] The second part, divided into two sections, was about the animated movie form. Three types of devices where used to show its metamorphosis through time: "an authentic old mutoscope,"[199] three zoetropes and two phenakistiscopes.[200] The mutoscope had been used to animate Christopher Crumpet as he turns into a chicken; one of the phenakistiscope demonstrated a walking sequence of Mr. Fudget of *Fudget's Budget*; and one of the zoetropes animated "a series of single drawings."[201] Other featured animations included *Rooty Toot Toot* and *Madeline*, and additional elements used in this second part of the exhibition were "film strips in light boxes, enlarged drawings, actual storyboards and the cels used in making the films."[202] The third part studied the different types of films that UPA made: as entertainment, for educational purposes, television commercials, and industrial and military films. The fourth was a program of selected UPA films that ran daily in the museum's theater for the entire duration of the exhibition, which included the world premiere of new UPA films *Christopher Crumpet's Playmate, Magoo Express,*[203] *The Jaywalker* and *Baby Boogie.*[204]

Together with storyboards and rough sketches that illustrated sequences of drawings, there were also exposure sheets from *Little Boy with a Big Horn*[205] and *How Now Boing Boing*[206] that showed how dialogue, sound effects and action were related in the film.[207] Particular attention was given to color: for example, in order to show how UPA artists selected a color to represent the mood for an entire film, the same sketch was displayed multiple times in several color combinations alongside the final one that was used in the film.[208] In addition, to demonstrate the changing characteristics of Mr. Magoo over time, an entire panel was devoted to the popular character, with a series of drawings taken from nine different cartoons that illustrated the changes in his personality, "as he developed from an irritable old man into a rather lovable, though fumbling, old man."[209] Some of the drawings were taken from the following cartoons: *Ragtime Bear, Trouble Indemnity,*[210] *Hotsy Footsy,*[211] *Magoo's Masterpiece,*[212] *Magoo Goes Skiing*[213] and *Magoo Express.*

The 1955 UPA exhibit at the MoMA is interesting for three reasons. First, the curators were aware that UPA departed from the Disney style, as stated in a press release:

> UPA, under Stephen Bosustow, went back to the original meaning of cartoon—a flat line drawing. No attempt is made to simulate real people or real movement but instead the drawings caricature people and their movement. Furthermore in such films as *The Tell-Tale Heart*, UPA has demonstrated that cartoon films do not have to be humorous, but can be dramatic.[214]

Second, they believed that UPA's founding ushered in a new trend in the animation industry and that its artists:

> [H]ave made UPA more than a trademark—it is also the brand of a style. Like Dada and each of the isms in 20th century art, UPA stands for an attitude that is common to many pictures because it is common to many artists.[215]

Finally, they consciously connected UPA animation to Modern art by affirming, for example, that

> Pothook profiles from "Fudget's Budget" are cartoon versions of Klee uncluttered script. An interior in "Christopher Crumpet's Playmate" shows units of furniture detached in a space that first was plotted by Matisse. Imaginary machinery invented by Picabia has its counterpart in the electronic nonsense of "How Now Boing Boing." The work of these artists, of Picasso, Grosz and many others form a capital of imagery on which UPA draws.[216]

As the MoMA exhibit confirms, by the mid-1950s, the UPA trademark was well known and appreciated by the general public, and UPA's creative work was recognized in the art world.

ENDNOTES

1. Elia Kazan, *A Life* (London, UK, Sydney, AU, and Auckland, NZ: Pan Books, 1988), 142–143.
2. Cohen, *Forbidden Animation: Censored Cartoons and Blacklisted Animators in America*; Abraham, *When Magoo Flew: The Rise and Fall of Animation Studio UPA*.
3. Pete Burness commented on the effects of political pressure on the content of the animated shorts:

    "Satire was a hoped for ingredient of all UPA cartoons in the beginning. We tried for it as much as we could. There came a time, a few years later, when the political climate was such that there was a fear of satire, that we might do something in the spirit of fun which would be misinterpreted. Columbia said don't make fun of policemen or judges. We tried not to, but we still tried to put satirical comments in whenever we could."

    Burness, quoted in Howard Edward Rieder, "The Development of the Satire of Mr. Magoo," 107.
4. Seldes, "Delight in Seven Minutes."
5. Knight, "The New Look in Cartooning"; "UPA, Magoo & McBoing-Boing"; "Up from Disney," *Theatre Arts*, August 1951; "U.P.A. Goes Boing-Boing," *Esquire*, February 1953.
6. Chalais, "Le fil à couper Disney."
7. Nick Taylor, *American-Made—The Enduring Legacy of the WPA: When FDR Put the Nation to Work* (New York, NY: Bantam Dell, 2008), 1.
8. Ibid., 15.
9. Quoted in Taylor, *American-Made—The Enduring Legacy of the WPA: When FDR Put the Nation to Work*, 25.
10. Ibid.

11. Quoted in Taylor, *American-Made—The Enduring Legacy of the WPA: When FDR Put the Nation to Work*, 59.
12. Ibid., 62.
13. Ibid., 67.
14. By March 1932 the TERA program, with Hopkins as its head, had managed to put 80,000 people to work and had prevented the starvation of 130,000 families. Taylor, *American-Made—The Enduring Legacy of the WPA: When FDR Put the Nation to Work*.
15. According to Taylor, its fifteen major pieces of legislation brought new protections to homeowners, farmers, and investors, provided necessities of life to those without them, established the Tennessee Valley Authority (TVA) as the instrument that would electrify the rural south, created new work programs, and attempted to force restraint on the inhumane world of industrial and agricultural laissez-faire. Ibid., 109.
16. Ibid.
17. Ibid.
18. This last activity was related to the so-called packhorse libraries. Ibid.
19. Ibid., 220.
20. Ibid., 231.
21. Ibid., 263.
22. Ibid., 289.
23. Holger Cahill was an art critic and curator. As the acting director of the Museum of Modern Art, in 1932 he curated an exhibition in which he showed how the work and popular culture of early American folk artists fertilized fine art and high culture. He also curated shows that linked primitive art with the work of Modern masters. Ibid.
24. Ibid., 270.
25. Ibid., 273.
26. For more information, see Chapter 3, Section 2.1 and Section 4.
27. Taylor specifies that Benton taught WPA artists, including a 23-year-old Jackson Pollock, and that Hirsch, Shahn and Levine all worked for the WPA. Ibid.
28. Ibid., 273.
29. Ibid., 280.
30. On the influence of the work of Ben Shahn on future UPA animator John Hubley, for example, see Chapter 4, Section 2.2.2.
31. See also on Chapter 3 the influence of the Bauhaus principles on American modernism and, consequently, on UPA artists, Sections 2 and 3.
32. Taylor, *American-Made—The Enduring Legacy of the WPA: When FDR Put the Nation to Work*.
33. Ibid., 393.
34. Ibid.
35. According to Taylor, the Dies committee became "a national phenomenon" and "during its short life, no institution in the country had ever received as much press coverage. The reams of newsprint that it generated defied any

sober assessment of its methods, and the obvious biases of its report. A Gallup poll showed that 60 percent of the country was now [in 1939] familiar with the committee, and three-quarters of those wanted it to continue." Ibid., 426.

36. For example, in a 1938 radio broadcast, Republican Representative J. Parnell Thomas of New Jersey affirmed that the New Deal progressive reforms were a plan "to sabotage the capitalist system" and that the theater project "was 'a patronage vehicle for Communists,' in which 'practically every play presented ... is sheer propaganda for Communism or the New Deal.'" Ibid., 409.

37. Ibid.

38. Ibid.

39. Ibid., p. 513.

40. Quoted in Taylor, *American-Made—The Enduring Legacy of the WPA: When FDR Put the Nation to Work*, 518. Taylor sums up the legacy of the WPA in statistics:

"650,000 miles of roads, 78,000 bridges, 125,000 civilian and military buildings, 800 airports built, improved or enlarged, 700 miles of airport runways. It served almost 900 million hot lunches to schoolchildren and operated 1,500 nursery schools. It presented 225,000 concerts to audiences totaling 150 million, performed plays, vaudeville acts, puppet shows, and circuses before 30 million people, and produced almost 475,000 works of art and at least 276 full-length books and 701 pamphlets." Ibid., 523–524.

41. *New Yorker* magazine, *The 40s: The Story of a Decade* (New York, NY: Random House, 2014), 232.

42. Eric Frederick Goldman, *The Crucial Decade—and After. America, 1945–1960* (New York, NY: Random House, 1969), 47.

43. The Great Depression of the 1930s had taught the U.S. that in order to be a healthy country, it needed to grow national production of consumption goods, as well as overseas economic expansion. Depression, mass unemployment and consequential social upheaval are caused when capitalism decreases, markets shrink and profits fall. Yet, if a nation produces more products than it can actually sell, depression occurs as well. Until the 1890s, westward expansion continually assured jobs for a growing population busy in building the infrastructure and cities of the country, but after the 1890s, the United States went into periodic economic depressions. Jezer, *The Dark Ages: Life in the United States, 1945–1960*.

44. Goldman, *The Crucial Decade—and After. America, 1945–1960*, 25.

45. Leon Schlesinger Productions was an independent company. Leon Schlesinger sold the studio to Warner Bros. in 1944. The studio then continued to operate under the name of Warner Bros. Cartoons, Inc.

46. Sito, *Drawing the Line: The Untold Story of the Animation Unions from Bosko to Bart Simpson*.

47. *Hell-Bent for Election*, directed by Chuck Jones (1944; Los Angeles, CA: Industrial Film). www.youtube.com/watch?v=2NLDih_5jAI, accessed May 11, 2015.

48. *Brotherhood of Man*, directed by Robert Cannon (1945; Los Angeles, CA: Industrial Film). www.youtube.com/watch?v=Fnrxbkajy9M, accessed May 11, 2015.
49. Goldman, *The Crucial Decade—and After. America, 1945–1960*, 40.
50. Toward the end of World War II, conservatives, whose thoughts were best expressed by Senator Robert A. Taft, already feared an alliance with the Soviets. Ibid.
51. Quoted in Goldman, *The Crucial Decade—and After. America, 1945–1960*, 59.
52. Under the Marshall Plan, officially called the European Recovery Program (ERP), the United States offered economic support to countries devastated by the war in order to help rebuild their economies. Total aid distributed came to US$17 billion. Interestingly, the offer of aid was extended to the Soviet Union, which declined it. Ibid. Behind the generous initiative there was the firm belief that the plan could prevent the spread of communism. Moreover, European countries were regarded as places of potential investment for American business. Foreign trade was recognized as an important element in postwar U.S. policy. Jezer, *The Dark Ages: Life in the United States, 1945–1960*.
53. In 1945, a book called *The Road to Serfdom*, written by the Austrian-born philosopher Friedrich von Hayek was published in the United States. In it, Nazism, communism, socialism and the New Deal-type liberalism were considered to have the same roots, which can lead to totalitarian serfdom. Goldman, *The Crucial Decade—and After. America, 1945–1960*.
54. Robert Alphonso Taft was the elder son of William H. Taft, 27th president of the United States and chief justice of the Supreme Court. He opposed Roosevelt's New Deal economy and the labor unions. On the international front, he advocated for noninterventionism during World War II and noninvolvement in European or Asian wars. Taft was praised by Senator John F. Kennedy in his book *Profiles in Courage* for his condemnation of the Nuremberg Trials on the basis that when the crimes were committed, there wasn't any law that could define those types of crimes. Taft's disapproval of the trials was harshly criticized by Republicans and Democrats, while Senator Kennedy believed that it was a proof of Taft's principles. Taft's opposition to the trials is also considered the main cause for his failure to receive the nomination as the Republican candidate for president in the 1948 election. John F. Kennedy, *Profiles in Courage*, 1955, 1st ed. (New York, NY: HarperCollins Publishers, 2004).
55. Goldman, *The Crucial Decade – and After. America, 1945–1960*, 55.
56. It was later internationally called Taiwan.
57. Alger Hiss, a lawyer and government official, was accused of being a Soviet spy by Whittaker Chambers, a former Communist Party member, who testified before the HUAC in 1948. Hiss was condemned of perjury during his second trial, in 1950. Chambers was a writer and an editor, who had translated into English Felix Salten's 1923 novel *Bambi, a Life in the Woods*.
58. Goldman, *The Crucial Decade—and After. America, 1945–1960*, 105.
59. Ibid., 122.

60. "Declaration of Independence," National Archives and Records Administration. www.archives.gov/exhibits/charters/declaration_transcript.html, accessed November 27, 2014.

61. "The Monroe Doctrine: Also, Jefferson's Letter to Monroe," University of California. www.archive.org/stream/monroedoctrineal00unit/monroe doctrineal00unit_djvu.txt, accessed November 27, 2014.

62. For deeper insight, see: Spigel, *TV by Design: Modern Art and the Rise of Network Television*.

63. Soviet film director and film theorist Sergei Mikhailovich Eisenstein said about Walt Disney, for example: "The work of this master is the greatest contribution of the American people to art." Sergei Eisenstein, *Eisenstein on Disney* (Calcutta, IN: Seagull Books, 1986), 1.

64. American individualism was rooted in the Puritan work ethic. It emphasizes the moral worth of the individual and values independence and self-reliance.

65. Jezer, *The Dark Ages: Life in the United States, 1945–1960*, 81.

66. Ibid., 82.

67. *New Yorker* magazine, *The 40s: The Story of a Decade*, 425.

68. During the years 1951–1952, when the assault on communism was reaching fever pitch, Senator Robert A. Taft was aligned with Senator Joseph McCarthy. On March 9, 1954, CBS aired journalist Edward R. Murrow's now-historic anti-McCarthy episode, part of his documentary TV show *See It Now*. A transcript of the episode is available online: "Edward R. Murrow: A Report on Senator Joseph R. McCarthy. See it Now (CBS-TV, March 9, 1954)," Media Resources Center, Moffitt Library, University of California, Berkeley, CA. www.lib.berkeley.edu/MRC/murrowmccarthy.html, accessed October 9, 2015. The event is also portrayed in the movie *Good Night, and Good Luck*, directed by George Clooney (2005; DVD, Montreal, QC: TVA Films, 2006). In 1954, the Senate conducted an investigation of McCarthy, who was consequently censured.

69. Jezer, *The Dark Ages: Life in the United States, 1945–1960*.

70. Ibid., 105.

71. Ibid., 96.

72. The Korean War began in 1950. It was never a popular war among the American public. It cost the U.S. "25 thousand deaths, 115 thousand other casualties and 22 billion dollars." Goldman, *The Crucial Decade—and After. America, 1945–1960*, 247.

73. The hydrogen bomb, or H-bomb, was tested in March 1954, at Bikini Atoll, in the Marshall Islands. The bomb was subsequently never used by the U.S. The Soviet Union had tested the H-bomb one year earlier.

74. Goldman, *The Crucial Decade—and After. America, 1945–1960*.

75. In wartime slang, *snafu* was an acronym for "Situation Normal—All Fucked Up." The *Private Snafu* cartoon series was government-commissioned and produced mostly by Warner Bros. For more information, see: Shull and Wilt, *Doing Their Bit: Wartime American Animated Short Films, 1939–1945*.

76. *Payday*, directed by Friz Freleng (1944; DVD, *Private Snafu Golden Classics*, Ann Arbor, MI: Thunderbean Animation, 2010).
77. Jezer, *The Dark Ages: Life in the United States, 1945–1960*, 155.
78. The National Housing Act of 1949 was part of Truman's Fair Deal. The public policy aimed at providing a "decent home and a suitable living environment for every American family" (ibid., 179). It failed at improving the conditions of people living in the cities because it led to a higher crime rate. By removing small local business in the neighborhoods in favor of decentralized corporate shopping chains, more delinquency spread in the cities, especially among the young generation.
79. Ibid.
80. Ibid., 221.
81. *Mr. Tingley's Tangle*, directed by T. Hee (circa 1955; Burbank, CA: United Productions of America).
82. For more information, see Chapter 4, Section 4.1.
83. *Christopher Crumpet's Playmate*, directed by Robert Cannon (1955; DVD, *UPA: The Jolly Frolics Collection*, Culver City, CA: Sony Pictures Home Entertainment, 2012).
84. Jezer, *The Dark Ages: Life in the United States, 1945–1960*.
85. Ibid., 130.
86. Goldman, *The Crucial Decade— and After. America, 1945–1960*.
87. Ibid., 266.
88. Jezer, *The Dark Ages: Life in the United States, 1945–1960*, 226.
89. The representation of 1950s U.S. society in the media can be useful in understanding the complex reality addressed here. Although media products, such as movies, TV series, animated cartoons, songs, novels and so on, cannot be used to describe historical facts, they provide an interpretation of reality that casts light and shadow on the many sociological aspects portrayed. For example, the fiction movie *Pleasantville*, directed by Gary Ross (1998; DVD, Los Angeles, CA: New Line Home Video, 1999), describes the 1950s as a conformist society in which women were mainly housewives, while men had a more active and decisional role in society. The fictional world of the 1950s reigned over by apparent perfection is presented in black and white as opposed to color, which is used instead to express the complexity of reality determined by the passions that make men and women imperfect.
90. Jezer, *The Dark Ages: Life in the United States, 1945–1960*, 234.
91. The "womanization" of America was discussed by Philip Wylie in a 1958 issue of *Playboy*; in a 1958 article, "The American Male: Why Do Women Dominate Him?" written by J. Robert Moskin for *Look* magazine; and even by psychiatrists Ferdinand Lundberg and Marynia Farnham, psychoanalyst Helene Deutsch and others. For deeper insight, see: Robert Genter, *Late Modernism: Art, Culture, and Politics in Cold War America* (Philadelphia, PA: University of Pennsylvania Press, 2010).

92. The term refers to David Riesman's sociological theory, illustrated in his 1950 book *The Lonely Crowd*. "Inner-directed" personalities tend to listen to the voice of the parents as behavioral models to follow, whereas "other-directed" personalities value and conform to peer group behaviors. With the disappearance of rural America and the traditional bourgeois family, American youth turned from being inner-directed (parent-oriented) to other-directed (peer-oriented). This phenomenon also marked the beginning of suburban conformism. Ibid.

93. As an example of this ideological tendency to link feminism, homosexuality and youth culture to authoritarianism, totalitarianism and communism, Jezer (*The Dark Ages: Life in the United States, 1945–1960*) mentions the novel *cityCityCITY*, written by Jack Kerouac (1954), which portrays a population controlled by an authoritarian regime made up of women.

94. Jezer, *The Dark Ages: Life in the United States, 1945–1960*, 238.

95. The play *Death of a Salesman* best expresses this generational conflict. Written by playwright Arthur Miller and directed by Elia Kazan, it premiered in theaters in 1949. It has been described by Wolcott Gibbs, theater critic for the *New Yorker*, as "the portrait of a failure" about "a man who has finally broken under the pressures of an economic system that he is fatally incapable of understanding" (*New Yorker* magazine, *The 40s: The Story of a Decade*, 514). Willy, who is 63 years old, is at the end of his life career as a salesman. The company has cut off his salary, and he is now paid on commission. His two sons have not been able to provide him the vicarious satisfaction of a bright career: the elder is a stock clerk interested in women, and the younger is an itinerant farmhand. After realizing that he is just a man who earns a dollar per hour, Willy turns to suicide, believing that at least this way his family will obtain some money from his insurance. For deeper insight, see: Arthur Miller, *Death of a Salesman*, 1949, 1st ed. (New York, NY: Penguin Books, 1998).

96. Jezer, *The Dark Ages: Life in the United States, 1945–1960*, 250.

97. *The Authoritarian Personality* was a comprehensive study commissioned by the American Jewish Committee and authored by Theodor Adorno, Else Frenkel-Brunswik, Daniel Levinson and R. Nevitt Sanford. It attempted to analyze the irrational nature of the modern individual and to identify the authoritarian potential of individuals according to specific personality traits. Genter, *Late Modernism: Art, Culture, and Politics in Cold War America*.

98. Ibid., 95.

99. Ibid.

100. Ibid.

101. Ibid., 165.

102. Jezer, *The Dark Ages: Life in the United States, 1945–1960*, 260–261.

103. Ibid., 261.

104. *New Yorker* magazine, *The 40s: The Story of a Decade*, 539.

105. In his essay "The First Man Was an Artist," Newman affirms:

"The earliest written history of human desires proves that the meaning of the world cannot be found in the social act. An examination of the first chapter of Genesis offers a better key to the human dream. It was inconceivable to the archaic writer that original man, that Adam, was put on earth to be a toiler, to be a social animal. The writer's creative impulses told him that man's origin was that of an artist and he set him up in a Garden of Eden close to the Tree of Knowledge, of right and wrong, in the highest sense of divine revelation. The fall of man was understood by the writer and his audience not as a fall from Utopia to struggle, as the sociologicians would have it, nor, as the religionists would have us believe, as a fall from Grace to Sin, but rather that Adam, by eating from the Tree of Knowledge, sought the creative life to be, like God, "a creator of worlds," to use Rashi's phrase, and was reduced to the life of toil only as a result of a jealous punishment."

"The First Man Was an Artist," *Tiger's Eye* 1, no. 1 (October 1947): 59–60.

106. The fascination toward primitivism also characterized European Modern painters who studied African artifacts. For more information, see Chapter 3, Section 4.2.

107. As much as the High Modernists defended the aesthetic experience to counterbalance the excessive threatening faith in technology, Romantic Modernists thought that primitivism's concepts could reconnect modern man with a redemptive magical and natural world. See: Genter, *Late Modernism: Art, Culture, and Politics in Cold War America.*

108. Ibid.

109. Not only designers left Europe for the U.S. during the 1920s and 1930s but also many artists, writers and intellectuals. Among them, there were filmmakers Josef von Sternberg, Billy Wilder and Oskar Fischinger; composers Igor Stravinsky and Arnold Schoenberg and writer Aldous Huxley. The group would be joined by artist Man Ray, writer Thomas Mann and philosopher Theodor Adorno in the early 1940s. As Roger Remington, professor of graphic design, notes: "The new aesthetic in America extended far beyond just graphic design. Architects, painters, sculptors, writers, poets, composers, musicians, dancers and actors immigrated to New York, and their talent blended into the fabric of America, becoming the lifeblood of Modernism." Remington and Bodenstedt, *American Modernism: Graphic Design, 1920 to 1960*, 67.

110. Jennifer Bass and Pat Kirkham, *Saul Bass: A Life in Film & Design* (London, UK: Laurence King Publishing, 2011).

111. Amidi, *Cartoon Modern: Style and Design in Fifties Animation*; Barrier, *Hollywood Cartoons: American Animation in Its Golden Age.*

112. Philip B. Meggs, *Meggs' History of Graphic Design* (Hoboken, NJ: John Wiley & Sons, 2006).

113. Alan Bartram, *Bauhaus Modernism and the Illustrated Book* (London, UK: British Library, 2004), 81.

114. Ibid., 96.

115. Ibid.

116. Anna Gerber, *Graphic Design: The 50 Most Influential Graphic Designers in The World* (London, UK: A&C Black Publishers, 2010), 32.
117. Ibid.
118. Remington and Bodenstedt, *American Modernism: Graphic Design, 1920 to 1960*.
119. Paul Rand, quoted in Steven Heller, *Design Literacy: Understanding Graphic Design* (New York, NY: Allworth Press, 2014), 54.
120. *The Man with the Golden Arm*, directed by Otto Preminger (1955; DVD, Los Angeles, CA: Passport International Entertainment, 2002).
121. Bass and Kirkham, *Saul Bass: A Life in Film & Design*, 107.
122. *Flat Hatting*, directed by John Hubley (1946; Burbank, CA: United Productions of America). www.youtube.com/watch?v=bzIhwXKZdYc, accessed December 17, 2014.
123. "Life and Work," Saul Steinberg Foundation, www.saulsteinbergfoundation.org/life_work.html, accessed June 18, 2015.
124. George Griffin, interview by author, February 24, 2014.
125. For deeper insight, see: Thomas Schatz, *The Genius of the System: Hollywood Filmmaking in the Studio Era* (New York, NY: Pantheon Books, 1988).
126. Ibid., 435.
127. *The Last Picture Show*, DVD, directed by Peter Bogdanovich (1971; Los Angeles, CA: Sony Pictures Home Entertainment, 2009).
128. Martin Scorsese in *A Personal Journey with Martin Scorsese through American Movies*, directed by Martin Scorsese and Michael Henry Wilson (Santa Monica, CA: Voyager Co. and Buena Vista Home Entertainment, 1995), DVD 3.
129. *Rebel without a Cause*, directed by Nicholas Ray (1955; DVD, Burbank, CA: Warner Home Video, 1999).
130. *Sweet Smell of Success*, directed by Alexander Mackendrick (1957; DVD, New York, NY: The Criterion Collection, 2011).
131. *A Streetcar Named Desire*, DVD, directed by Elia Kazan (1951; Burbank, CA: Warner Home Video, 2006).
132. *On the Waterfront*, DVD, directed by Eliza Kazan (1954; Culver City, CA: Columbia Tristar Home Entertainment, 2001).
133. Scorsese and Wilson, *A Personal Journey with Martin Scorsese through American Movies*, DVD 3.
134. Spigel, *TV by Design: Modern Art and the Rise of Network Television*.
135. Ibid., 22.
136. Ibid.
137. Ibid.
138. Ibid., 73.
139. Ibid.
140. Maltin, *Of Mice and Magic: A History of American Animated Cartoons*.
141. Knight, "UPA, Magoo & McBoing-Boing," 22.
142. Ibid.

143. Luther Nichols, "A Star Is Drawn: Meet Gerald McBoing-Boing," *San Francisco Chronicle*, January 21, 1951.
144. Penney, "U.P.A. Animated Art," 13.
145. Ibid.
146. Archer Winsten, "The Problem of Quality," *New York Post*, August 23, 1955, 38; Steve Bosustow's UPA collection.
147. For more information, see: Abraham, *When Magoo Flew: The Rise and Fall of Animation Studio UPA*; Sito, *Drawing the Line: The Untold Story of the Animation Unions from Bosko to Bart Simpson.*
148. Barrier, *Hollywood Cartoons: American Animation in Its Golden Age*, 374. In 1939, Disney employees numbered more than 1,000; in 1946, the staff consisted of 614 people.
149. Ibid., 380.
150. John Hubley and Faith Hubley, "Animation: A Creative Challenge—by John and Faith Hubley (interview)," interview by John D. Ford, September 24–25, 1973 (Kansas City, MO: Kansas City Art Institute), Book—Periodical Annex, Margaret Herrick Library, Academy of Motion Picture Arts and Sciences.
151. Barrier, *Hollywood Cartoons: American Animation in Its Golden Age.*
152. *Song of Victory*, directed by Bob Wickersham (1942; Culver City, CA: Screen Gems). www.youtube.com/watch?v=Bmd-UuP0-H8, accessed September 25, 2015.
153. *Willoughby's Magic Hat*, directed by Bob Wickersham (1943; Culver City, CA: Screen Gems). www.youtube.com/watch?v=-vb5QTQSj5Y, accessed September 25, 2015.
154. *Magic Strength*, directed by Bob Wickersham (1944; Culver City, CA: Screen Gems).
155. *The Dover Boys at Pimento University*, directed by Chuck Jones (1942; Burbank, CA: Leon Schlesinger Studios.) www.youtube.com/watch?v=dpOPyjmB8SI, accessed December 17, 2014.
156. *Red Hot Riding Hood*, directed by Tex Avery (1943; DVD, *Tex Avery*, Burbank, CA: Turner Entertainment, 2003).
157. Barrier, *Hollywood Cartoons: American Animation in Its Golden Age*, 448.
158. *The Case of the Missing Hare*, directed by Chuck Jones (1942; DVD, *Looney Tunes Golden Collection*, vol. 3, Burbank, CA: Warner Home Video, 2005).
159. *The Aristo-Cat*, directed by Chuck Jones (1942; DVD, *Looney Tunes Golden Collection*, vol. 4, Burbank, CA: Warner Home Video, 2006).
160. *The Unbearable Bear*, directed by Chuck Jones (1943; DVD, *Looney Tunes Mouse Chronicles: The Chuck Jones Collection*, Burbank, CA: Warner Home Video, 2012).
161. *Wackiki Wabbit*, directed by Chuck Jones (1943; DVD, *Looney Tunes Golden Collection*, vol. 3, Burbank, CA: Warner Home Video, 2005).
162. *Northwest Hounded Police*, directed by Tex Avery (1946; DVD, *Tex Avery*, Burbank, CA: Turner Entertainment, 2003).

163. *Uncle Tom's Cabaña*, directed by Tex Avery (1947; DVD, *Tex Avery*, Burbank, CA: Turner Entertainment, 2003).

164. *King-Size Canary*, directed by Tex Avery (1947; DVD, *Tex Avery*, Burbank, CA: Turner Entertainment, 2003).

165. *Señor Droopy*, directed by Tex Avery (1949; DVD, *Tex Avery*, Burbank, CA: Turner Entertainment, 2003).

166. *Once upon a Winter Time*, directed by Hamilton Luske (1948; DVD, *Melody Time*, Burbank, CA: Buena Vista Home Entertainment, 2000).

167. The suggestion comes from animator Eric Goldberg, interview by author, May 28, 2014.

168. Shull and Wilt, *Doing Their Bit: Wartime American Animated Short Films, 1939–1945*.

169. Barrier, *Hollywood Cartoons: American Animation in Its Golden Age*; Abraham, *When Magoo Flew: The Rise and Fall of Animation Studio UPA*.

170. Barrier, *Hollywood Cartoons: American Animation in Its Golden Age*, 559.

171. Amidi, *Cartoon Modern: Style and Design in Fifties Animation*, 12.

172. Abraham, *When Magoo Flew: The Rise and Fall of Animation Studio UPA*, 166.

173. For deeper insight, see: Amidi, *Cartoon Modern: Style and Design in Fifties Animation*.

174. *Alice in Wonderland*, directed by Clyde Geronimi, Wilfred Jackson and Hamilton Luske (1951; DVD, Burbank, CA: Buena Vista Home Entertainment and Walt Disney Studios Home Entertainment, 2010).

175. For deeper insight, see: Amidi, *Cartoon Modern: Style and Design in Fifties Animation*.

176. Maltin, *Of Mice and Magic: A History of American Animated Cartoons*, 342.

177. Another former Disney employee, Les Novros, founded Graphic Films in 1941. David Hilberman had previously collaborated with Novros. See: *Abel Gance Lifetime Achievement Award Presented to Lester Novros*, directed by Ammiel G. Najar and Michael Bober (DVD, Los Angeles, CA: Graphic Films and Large Format Cinema Association, 1999). The author would like to acknowledge Ben Alvin Shedd, Professor at ADM-NTU, for having suggested this audiovisual material as a reference source.
    The foundation of the company and its beginning as an informal startup are recalled by David Hilberman: during the time he was working at Graphic Films, he also rented a room with his friend Zachary Schwartz at the Otto K. Olesen Building in Hollywood. One day, Bosustow proposed to Les Novros the production of a sound slide film, but Novros was not interested. Hilberman heard about it and invited Bosustow to join him and Schwartz in their little studio. The sound slide film was *Sparks and Chips Get the Blitz*, director unknown (1943; Los Angeles, CA: Industrial Film). See: David Hilberman, interview by John Canemaker, June 16, 1979.

178. *A Few Quick Facts*, directed by Osmond Evans (1944; Burbank, CA: United Productions of America). www.youtube.com/watch?v=JYvembTqKKU, accessed December 18, 2014.

179. *A Few Quick Facts about Fear,* directed by Zachary Schwartz (1945; Burbank, CA: United Productions of America). www.youtube.com/watch?v=sjijPC0X9hM, accessed December 18, 2014.

180. Shull and Wilt, *Doing Their Bit: Wartime American Animated Short Films, 1939–1945,* 200.

181. *The Fifty-First Dragon,* directed by Pete Burness (1954; Burbank, CA: United Productions of America), animated short of *The Boing-Boing Show.*

182. *The Invisible Moustache of Raoul Dufy,* directed by Aurelius Battaglia (1955; Burbank, CA: United Productions of America).

183. Schwartz recalled that while he was working at the Disney studio, he became fascinated with Greek vase paintings and Persian miniature paintings. He bought a book on Persian miniature paintings and wanted to use these graphic stylizations in the films he was working on, believing that it was not necessary to be always realistic. With the intention of proposing this idea and supporting it with references, he gave the book to Walt Disney. After some time, it was returned to him with no signs on it. Zachary Schwartz, interview by John Canemaker, September 12, 1979; The John Canemaker Animation Collection; MSS 040; box 2; folder 40.0065; Fales Library and Special Collections, NYU.

184. Not only UPA characters, but even UPA artists were part of this *Modern space* defined by Modern architecture. In 1947, Bosustow hired architect John Lautner to design a Modern building that would reflect UPA aesthetic. In 1949, the building was ready and UPA employees moved to this new studio, located in Burbank at 4440 Lakeside Drive. Filmmaker John Whitney vividly remembers its "novel architecture":

"The striking design had high roofs vaulted with corrugated metal, and the rooms were laid out along several corridors around a courtyard, so that every office, inside and outside, had a glass wall looking out on trees and flowers—some even had a country-club view. How pleasant those walkways were—and such a different ambience from Disney or the other animation studios I knew, which offered factory cubicles with artificial light and no view."

John Whitney, in William Moritz, "UPA, Reminiscing 30 Years Later," *ASIFA Canada* 12, no. 3 (1984), p. 18; The John Canemaker Animation Collection; MSS 040; box 2; folder 5; Fales Library and Special Collections, NYU.

185. Klein, *Seven Minutes: The Life and Death of the American Animated Cartoon.*

186. Milton J. Rosenberg, "Mr. Magoo as Public Dream," *Quarterly of Film Radio and Television* 11, no. 4 (Summer 1957): 340.

187. Jean-Pierre Coursodon, *Keaton et Cie: Les burlesques Américains du "Muet,"* Cinéma d'aujourd'hui (Paris, FR: Éditions Seghers, 1964), 53. "Un handicapé que seules sauvent de l'anéantissement d'incessantes astuces de brimé et une veine paradoxalement énorme" (translated by Giannalberto Bendazzi).

188. Rosenberg, "Mr. Magoo as Public Dream," 341.

189. Ibid.

190. Ibid., 342.

191. John Hubley, quoted in Howard Edward Rieder, "The Development of the Satire of Mr. Magoo," 65.

192. Ibid.

193. Ibid., 124.

194. Department of Film Exhibition Files, 60, The Museum of Modern Art Archives, New York. Installation views of the exhibition can be seen on the website of the Museum of Modern Art: www.moma.org/calendar/exhibitions /2434?locale=enhttps:/, accessed February 7, 2018.

195. The exhibition was originally on view from June 22 through August 21. Owing to its popularity and success, it was extended until September 25, 1955. Ibid.

196. René d'Harnoncourt Papers, III.26.b, The Museum of Modern Art Archives, New York.

197. Ibid.

198. Film, 60. MoMA Archives, NY.

199. Ibid.

200. The six optical tools displayed in the exhibit were described as follows in a MoMA press release:
    "an authentic old mutoscope, which flips still pictures when the handle is turned, three zoetropes in which strips of still pictures become animated when seen through small slits in the side of a large drum on a revolving turntable, and two phenakistiscopes which use mirrors and revolving disks to achieve the same effect of animation." Ibid.

201. Ibid.

202. Ibid.

203. *Magoo Express*, directed by Pete Burness (1955; DVD, *Mr. Magoo: The Theatrical Collection*, Culver City, CA: Sony Pictures Home Entertainment, 2014).

204. *Baby Boogie*, directed by Paul Julian (1955; DVD, *UPA: The Jolly Frolics Collection*, Culver City, CA: Sony Pictures Home Entertainment, 2012).

205. *Little Boy with a Big Horn*, directed by Robert Cannon (1953; DVD, *UPA: The Jolly Frolics Collection*, Culver City, CA: Sony Pictures Home Entertainment, 2012).

206. *How Now Boing Boing*, directed by Robert Cannon (1954; DVD, *UPA: The Jolly Frolics Collection*, Culver City, CA: Sony Pictures Home Entertainment, 2012).

207. Film, 60, MoMA Archives, NY.

208. Ibid.

209. Ibid.

210. *Trouble Indemnity*, directed by Pete Burness (1950; DVD, *Mr. Magoo: The Theatrical Collection*, Culver City, CA: Sony Pictures Home Entertainment, 2014).

211. *Hotsy Footsy*, directed by William T. Hurtz (1952; DVD, *Mr. Magoo: The Theatrical Collection*, Culver City, CA: Sony Pictures Home Entertainment, 2014).

212. *Magoo's Masterpiece*, directed by Pete Burness (1953; DVD, *Mr. Magoo: The Theatrical Collection*, Culver City, CA: Sony Pictures Home Entertainment, 2014).
213. *Magoo Goes Skiing*, directed by Pete Burness (1954; DVD, *Mr. Magoo: The Theatrical Collection*, Culver City, CA: Sony Pictures Home Entertainment, 2014).
214. Film, 60, MoMA Archives, NY.
215. Ibid.
216. René d'Harnoncourt Papers, III.26.b, The Museum of Modern Art Archives, New York.

CHAPTER 2

Stephen Bosustow
*Life, Merits, Limits, Gaps and
the UPA Production System*

There is plenty of evidence that the success of an industrial product, simultaneously in the cultural, technical and economic fields,
depends entirely on a balanced teamwork between the designer,
the scientist, the engineer, the market analyst and the salesman.

WALTER GROPIUS[1]

Stephen Bosustow was the sole executive producer of UPA from 1945 to
1960. His role was to ensure the smooth day-to-day operations of the company and to find clients for the production of TV commercials, educational films and industrial films, as well as handling the distribution of
the theatrical shorts by negotiating and renegotiating the Columbia agreement. He was the financial brain of UPA, he had a sincere passion for art
and animation, and he shared a vision for the medium with Walt Disney,
a person in the industry he admired. He gave his employees free rein to
experiment with alternative audiovisual styles different from the standards of the moment and encouraged them to express themselves. What
were his skills? What were his merits and limitations in administering the
company? What was the opinion of his employees and the press?

This chapter begins with an essential biography of Stephen Bosustow, a
contradictory person. It follows with a description of what has been said

about him by the press and by his employees, in juxtaposition to how Bosustow perceived himself and how he evaluated his professional life, in order to show the many, often opposed opinions about a figure who was crucial to the existence of UPA studio and its artistic achievements. It ends by illustrating the UPA production system.

This chapter is mainly based on the memories and recollections of former UPA employees and of Bosustow. The latter wrote undated handwritten and typewritten notes, as well as personal diaries and agendas. While acknowledging that memories can be questioned, even subjective, especially when they are delivered in a personal diary, this work includes them as a reference source because of the unique type of information they contain and the relation they have to the main objective of this section, to delineate Bosustow's merits, limits and gaps in managing the UPA animation studio. Similarly, it is worth noting that the opinions of former UPA employees about Stephen Bosustow's management are subjective, even personal, and must be considered as such. Nevertheless, they, too, are included in this work as a reference source, since they are useful in framing Bosustow's personality, behavior and attitude in relation to the UPA studio.

2.1 STEPHEN BOSUSTOW: AN ESSENTIAL PROFESSIONAL BIOGRAPHY

Stephen Reginald Bosustow was born on November 6, 1911, in Victoria, British Columbia, Canada. In 1920, he won a watercolor contest at the Victoria County Fair.[2] He moved to California with his family when he was 11 years old.[3]

He graduated from Lincoln High School with a specialization in art. His desire was to become a newspaper cartoonist, but he also played in orchestras on the weekends. Once out of school, he held several kinds of jobs, such as working in a furniture factory, driving a truck and working in a soap factory.[4] It was thanks to music, however, that he got a foot in the animation industry's door, as he later recalled:

> In addition to art, I had picked up trumpet and playing among my skills. I hadn't intended it to be more than a means to earn extra money as I tried to succeed with my art.

I was able to get a job in a small band. One night we were playing an engagement in Balboa. I glanced down from the bandstand and saw I [sic] girl I knew at school, Xenia Beckwith.

At the next break that evening, I talked to her and discovered that she had gotten a job in a cartoon studio.

Again, my old excitement in succeeding in art engulfed me. As we sat there, I got more and more entrigued [sic] about what my own chances might be.

I wasn't very enthralled with the orchestra business. As we talked, I began to imagine myself at work in a studio. Her own voice, as she talked about the routine in her new job and how much she liked it, faded away as my own meandering thoughts propelled themselves in my consciousness.

I was so busy imagining Stephen Bosustow as *enfante* [sic] *terrible* in animated short subjects that I nearly missed her change in conversation.

She was finished talking about her own job and she was urging me to contact her boss and see if I might get a job too.

It didn't take me long to decide to take the plunge.

Frank Webb was operating on less than a shoe string in some rooms over a store on Santa Monica Blvd, in Hollywood. He was making an animated cartoon, true. But his whole operation was on a scale that was less than ample.

His main financing came from people he would talk into investing in the project, in return for a percentage to be paid at an unspecified time in the future. I remember one policeman who invested $25, for example.

But I didn't care. It was experience and a chance to make the old dreams come true. I didn't even mind the group of prostitutes who had set up operations across the hall. It was part of "the business" as far as I was concerned.

I found out later that all his employees were not salaried. About half got a small sum of money each week and the other half were given lunch. I was one of the later [sic] group.

I started out painting the back of cels that were later traced by someone else onto celluloid.

"Goofy Gus and His Omnibus" was easily the worst cartoon ever made. In artistic concept, it was of the most primitive era, even pre-Mickey Mouse.[5]

Although far from glamorous or lucrative, it was experience, first as a painter and then as an inbetweener.[6] And, it was helpful in getting hired at the Ub Iwerks studio in 1932, through connections of his friend Cal Howard. There, Bosustow contributed to the Flip the Frog cartoons as an inbetweener, earning $10 per week.[7] A year later, again through the help of Cal Howard, he got a job at Walter Lantz studio. The circumstances of the event are worthy of note: Chuck Jones had been working as an inbetweener at Universal but quit his job to join Ub Iwerks studio. Meanwhile, Howard had introduced Bosustow to Walter Lantz, and Bosustow ended up getting Jones' job[8] working as an assistant and animation artist on the Oswald the Lucky Rabbit and Woody Woodpecker cartoons under the supervision of Tex Avery. He lost his job when Lantz fired Avery's whole unit in 1934, a few days before Christmas.[9]

Thanks to Lantz's recommendation, Bosustow was able to find a job at Disney in 1935,[10] working first as an inbetweener on Mickey Mouse's *Silly Symphonies*. Then, he had the chance to work as an assistant to Freddy Moore on *Snow White and the Seven Dwarfs*, before being accepted in the Story Department, where he proposed story ideas for *Bambi*. He spent his last year at Disney working in the Effects Department on *Dumbo* and *Fantasia*, until he was laid off[11] on May 20, 1941, eight days before the strike began.

Bosustow was on the picket line as a captain.[12] When the strike ended, he was approached by Cy Young, formerly in charge of the Effects Department at Disney. They founded a company called Associated CineArtists together with a third partner, Tom Armstrong.[13] Bosustow assumed the role of salesman: he travelled to New York City and Washington, D.C., trying to sell ideas for savings-bonds storyboards to the government, but the partnership soon fell apart and the company dissolved.[14]

With a wife and two sons to support, Bosustow needed to find a job. In 1942, after having gone to night classes for a period of at least ten weeks, he was hired at Hughes Aircraft Company in Culver City, California, to teach production illustration. He turned out sketches to be used as work guides by personnel who were unable to read blueprints. Within a year, he was promoted head of the Production Scheduling and

Control Department. In 1943, he started to teach design sketching to engineers at the California Institute of Technology.[15] In the same period, he, Dave Hilberman and Zack Schwartz created Industrial Films and Poster Service.

The new company's first works were posters commissioned by Hughes Aircraft. Next followed *Sparks and Chips Get the Blitz*, an educational sound slide film that had been brought to Bosustow's attention by one of his students, who, it turned out, worked at the Consolidated Steel shipyards in Long Beach.[16] The film taught safety rules to its welders. Other industrial films were produced, such as one for the Boeing Aircraft Company in Seattle, as well as training films for the Office of War Information (OWI), the U.S. Navy, the U.S. Army, and the State Department.[17] The company started to generate some income.

The lucky year was 1944. Through Bill Pomerance of the Screen Cartoonist's Guild, Bosustow got in touch with Bill Levit, head of the educational committee for the UAW.[18] Levit was looking for a company to produce a campaign picture in support of Franklin D. Roosevelt for the upcoming presidential election. The storyboard was designed by Bill Hurtz, under the supervision of John Hubley. The film was *Hell-Bent for Election*, but it had to be delivered in 90 days. Other companies such as Graphic Films, run by Les Novros, had turned the project down owing to the close due date.[19] Luck in the form of coincidence came into play, as Bosustow recalled:

> Wild things happened, or perhaps you could call them miracles like one day when the UAW committee came into the office to see our first black and white rough reel that had been done in sixteen millimeter for their local chapters across the country[.] They were so excited about how great the film looked they wanted to know if we could do it in thirty-five millimeters. So that they could run it in theatres. I was already nine thousand dollars over the budget and during those times of the war it was next to impossible to beg[,] borrow or steal a thirty five millimeter camera as all the animation studios were up to their necks in Government training films. Now believe this or not but just as I was discussing this with them sitting across the desk from them the phone rang and Bud Fuer (?) [*sic*] who had designed and built the cameras for Disney and also supplied the army training units called me and asked if I would like to lease a camera as the Navy had just returned one of them? With out

[*sic*] hesitating I said yes turned back to the UAW committee and with a nine thousand dollar lose [*sic*] to date I told them as calmly as I could that for nine thousand dollars I could reshoot it in thirty five millimeter and deliver to them a thirty five millimeter print.[20]

The next film commissioned by the UAW to follow was *Brotherhood of Man*, which was directed by Bobe Cannon. In the following years, disagreements with the other two partners arose, and Bosustow bought them out, thereby owning the majority of stock.[21] On December 30, 1945, the company was renamed United Productions of America, later simply called UPA.[22]

Another lucky year was 1948, when the Columbia agreement was signed. In the words of Bosustow:

> This contract was to serve as the backbone of UPA for ten years, and really got us off the ground. We did six or eight a year. Even though I was now the boss with the final say in how things were done, I felt I had taken two steps forward and one back because I didn't really want to do the animated shorts they wanted me to do.[23]

The terms of the contract were the following: Columbia asked for two Fox and Crow entertainment cartoons, reserving the right to possibly acquire two more. UPA retained 25 percent ownership of the shorts. The studio was obligated to produce six cartoons per year, and the contract was valid for the subsequent five years.[24] After *The Magic Fluke*[25] (1949) was nominated for an Academy Award, Bosustow and his employees earned the liberty to make a cartoon based on a human character under the strict contractual stipulations. This human character would be the nearsighted Mr. Magoo.

With *Gerald McBoing Boing*, which won an Academy Award for Cartoon Short Subject in 1950, national and international success arrived. UPA became famous for its audiovisual style. It may have occurred as an economic necessity, but still, it defined a new attitude in animation, which was reflected in Bosustow's recollections:

> More than anything else, what came to be known as the UPA style came out of a limited amount of money. We put good drawings in

key positions but had a limited amount of action. This required less animation and was cheaper to produce.

We always strived for a good looking production. It may have been a new look but it was inexpensive.

Walk cycles, for example, had a limited amount of movement. Disney, on the other hand, would milk every movement out of a walk.[26]

From this came two other Academy Awards: first for *When Magoo Flew* in 1954 and then for *Magoo's Puddle Jumper* in 1956.[27]

In 1955, William Paley from CBS TV network asked Bosustow to produce *The Boing-Boing Show*, the first "all cartoon half-hour TV show ever made."[28] It was broadcast for less than two years, from December 1956 to October 1958, with even a gap in its run:[29] it survived as a "token of good taste,"[30] appealing more to television critics than to children.

The year 1955 marked the peak of UPA's commercial and artistic success:

> In 1955, UPA earned over one million dollars in revenue; in 1956, its assets were valued over five hundred thousand dollars. With 250 employees worldwide, UPA produced *The Boing-Boing Show*, television commercials, the Mr. Magoo shorts, and the opening titles for *The Twilight Zone*. In 1957, all three films nominated for the Academy Award for animated short subject were produced by UPA—a feat even Walt Disney never accomplished.[31]

By 1958, however, the studio was already in decline, with the New York branch in the process of closing its doors and the London studio already shut down.[32] The animated feature-length film *1001 Arabian Nights*[33] received mixed reviews from the press. In 1958, Columbia did not renew the contract, and the studio faced serious financial problems. On June 27, 1960, Bosustow sold UPA to Henry G. Saperstein.[34] Bosustow sat on the board of the new company until October,[35] but payment of his salary stopped in July.[36] A legal battle followed: Bosustow claimed that the contract had been breached on the grounds that Saperstein did not complete the stock purchase, did not pay the agreed-upon salary without interruption and did not make the agreed-upon life-insurance and car payments.

Saperstein responded by suing Bosustow "for stealing fourteen awards and certificates, including three Academy Awards, a British Oscar, and prizes from the Edinburgh and Venice film festivals."[37] More allegations followed from Saperstein in 1965, and in 1966 a trial took place: the court found in Bosustow's favor, and Saperstein was instructed to pay him $125,000.[38]

After the UPA adventure, Bosustow accepted an offer to reorganize the animation department of the China Paint Manufacturing Company in Hong Kong. He stayed there six months, until June 7, 1963.[39] Following are the memories of Dick Wong, an artist who worked there at the time:

> He [Steve Bosustow] had legal troubles in the US and for some reasons [sic] ended up in Hong Kong. At first we were not used to his kind of animation: the character's body was still, with only his limps [sic] moving. This was originated from Bosustow. In 1964, we had a big team that used the entire third floor of the paint factory and hire [sic] about thirty people. We wanted to make an animated TV series, and recruited even more people, including the best illustrators in Hong Kong. ... We had a lot of advertising jobs at the time, but cost was also high. We had thirty something people in our organization. The income had to be used for salaries, and purchasing equipment. We hardly made any profit. After about a year, the boss gave Bosustow some pressure—and in the end, he left us to go back to the US."[40]

Back home, he set up a company called Stephen Bosustow Productions,[41] mainly run by his son Nick. Among the animated films produced, *Is It Always Right to be Right?*[42] won the Oscar for Best Cartoon Short Subject in 1971, and *The Legend of John Henry*[43] was nominated for an Academy Award in 1974.

During the 1970s, Stephen Bosustow planned to write a book about animation and the UPA studio. Among his typewritten notes, there is what amounts to a draft of the introduction, probably as part of a letter he received as feedback on his ideas:

It seems to me that our work should serve two purposes:

1. As an interesting guide for the general public through the mysteries of animation—a kind of how-to-do-it approach vividly illustrated which would detail your theories of the craft.

2. As a story about your own experiences in the industry as you put these ideas to work: observations on the art, the famous people in it and, finally, what happened to you in your studio, UPA.

We could call this "'Stephen Bosustow's Complete Guide to Animation."

… The alternative is to do two books: the how-to-do-it book (which I know you have partially outlined already) and another giving a biography-like treatment to your life in animation, the people you have known, what happened at UPA.

A third choice would be to fictionalize the whole thing, but I lean to a factual account. It will have more credence and be more interesting.[44]

The book was never finished. Stephen Bosustow died on July 4, 1981.

2.2 STEPHEN BOSUSTOW: COMMENTS FROM THE PRESS

2.2.1 National Press

As the executive producer of UPA, Steve Bosustow was the de facto representative of the company and therefore spoke in the name of the company. Apart from a few early articles in which Bobe Cannon[45] or John Hubley[46] are mentioned as key figures in the studio, Bosustow is generally the person who is recognized by the press as the "father of this [aesthetic] revolution."[47] For example, Arthur Knight stated in *Art Digest*: "The keynote of the UPA films is simplicity, a technique which Bosustow relearned from the poster and the training illustration, and which he then returned to the cartoon film."[48]

Bosley Crowther, meanwhile, referred to Bosustow, in 1952, as the "center of this hive of activity" and "an energetic, 41-year-old chap … who started UPA on a shoestring during the war years and is now its serenely competent head."[49] Neither David Hilberman nor Zack Schwartz are mentioned as the cofounders of the company.[50] Crowther further suggested of Bosustow's role: "At UPA, Bosustow makes it a point to allow his directors a free hand in the conception and development of their pictures, once he has approved their selections of stories and settled the matter of budgets with them."[51] Quite the same is affirmed one year later by David Bongard, "Bosustow, once he approves a story for production, leaves the execution up to his staff of young, imaginative directors,"[52] and by Arthur Knight,

"Bosustow gives his artists both the credit for his success and great freedom in working out their own ideas."[53]

Other points made in contemporary pieces worth noting are a physical resemblance between Bosustow and a young Walt Disney[54] and the fact that the UPA style influenced Walt Disney Productions, especially in *Toot, Whistle, Plunk and Boom*.[55] It was also pointed out that unlike Disney, Steve's door was always open for his employees, and it was easy to approach him.[56]

Also interesting is how Bosustow talked about himself to the press. Regarding the relationship with his employees, he affirmed: "Everybody has good men. ... But we give them more chance to exercise their talents."[57] He communicated the same message to Barbara Moon:

> I don't want to make cartoons myself: I just want to keep a studio running that can turn out cartoons. ... There is no single company style, imposed from above. If anyone gets a good idea he is free to develop it. A good deal of the time I don't even see the stuff to okay it.[58]

And, if Moon affirmed that "He [Bosustow] still thinks of himself as an artist,"[59] Knight argued: "He is no frustrated artist, however."[60]

In 1953, Bosustow first confessed his desire: "I always wanted to be a producer."[61] In 1955, he admitted the difficulties of his position:

> Yes, it took me a long time to learn how important distribution and promotion were to a film company. And being an artist myself, it took me time to learn how to do it. But I think we are on the way now.[62]

In 1957, he joked about it: "I am an executive. ... At least I sit behind a desk now, so I suppose I'm an executive. I worry about money and that sort of thing."[63]

Bosustow also had opinions on the medium, although we do not know how much his thoughts were also the expressions of his employees. Following are some of his comments on animation:

> It's simple enough; ... animation ought to stand in relation to the motion picture as drawn art stands to the still photographs. It's a whole interpretive art form.[64]

We believe the animated cartoon is a medium of art—just like the ballet, the theatre, and music. … We've done comedies, mysteries, vignettes, satires, musicals and pure abstraction.[65]

2.2.2 International Press

Gerald McBoing Boing, which first opened in New York City on December 12, 1950,[66] and was officially released on January 25, 1951,[67] was screened abroad at the Cannes International Film Festival and the Venice Film Festival and received an award at the Edinburgh International Film Festival.[68] Multiple UPA animated films were also awarded by the New York Art Directors Club, British Film Academy, Venice Film Festival, Brazilian Film Festival, Belgian Film Festival, Golden Reel Film Festival and U.S. Navy.[69] During the 1950s, UPA became popular internationally, and European film critics began to praise the new UPA audiovisual style.

In 1951, in the *Cahiers du Cinéma*, for example, François Chalais affirmed: "Mr. Bosustow … succeeded in what Mr. Disney had failed: the animation of drawn men or women could never, in any case, have had the perfection of a photography."[70] Bobe Cannon is also praised in the article as the director of *Gerald McBoing Boing*. In 1953, UPA style is discussed in the international magazine *Graphis*: "Under the direction of its founder, Stephen Bosustow, the UPA has developed its own style in this genre, and since the invention of 'Gerald McBoing Boing' (1950) has gained national fame and several prize honours."[71]

In 1954, animation film critic André Martin referenced Bosustow and his team in comparison to Walt Disney:

The major contribution of Stephen Bosustow is to have ceased, for the first time, to animate in the Disney way or similarly. … This team has opened the door to every style, every story, thus giving them a historic place within the evolution of animated cartoon in America.[72]

Martin's writings record that in April 1956 the Premières Rencontres Internationales du Cinema d'Animation (First international meeting on animated cinema) took place at the 9th Cannes International Film Festival. According to Martin, Bosustow was invited to present a new animated film to the public. Martin praised the work of Bosustow's team. He mentioned John Hubley, Robert Cannon, Pete Burness, Ted Parmelee and Bill Hurtz as those who renewed "the conception of the drawing, the rhythm and the subject of the cartoon."[73] Moreover, he stated that thanks to Stephen Bosustow, Norman McLaren and Jiří Trnka, animated film was solid enough to be considered a cinematographic "genre" in its own right, completely independent of live-action film: "It seems that the animated cinema finds again all those elements that formed its specific enchantment among the primitives: predominance of a more symbolic than descriptive line, and of a more poetic and immediate than comic or moralistic gag."[74]

The comparison with Walt Disney was also explored in the international press. Walter Alberti wrote in 1957: "It would seem that Bosustow's 'troupe' has skipped over the experience of Walt Disney and instead directly reconnected with the American masters of caricature and humor."[75] In 1961, Robert Benayoun spoke about Bosustow as the creative mind behind the UPA film, referring to a "Bosustow style" as the "*I style*," in comparison with the Disneyesque "*O style*."[76] Denys Chevalier corrected his colleague in 1962, stating that there is no "style Bosustow" but "on the contrary, an infinite number of graphic expressions, each of them corresponding to a dual balance between the type of inspirational story chosen and the personality of the animator."[77]

The international press even went so far as to call Bosustow Walt Disney's antagonist. Unfortunately, as elsewhere, some film critics acknowledged him as the main creator of UPA animated films, disregarding others' contributions, while other critics, correctly, also credited the principal directors. Still, confusion occurred: in 1966, Piero Zanotto referred to Bosustow as UPA's "main animator,"[78] and one year later, Ralph Stephenson informed that "Bosustow as producer and head of the studio gave up directing after *Swab Your Choppers* (1947)."[79]

2.3 STEPHEN BOSUSTOW AT THE UPA STUDIO

2.3.1 Opinions from His Employees

According to his employees, Steve Bosustow was the businessman of the company. He was running the studio, not contributing to the creation of the animated shorts. Gene Deitch joined UPA when he was 22 years old and the company was still operating at the Otto K. Olesen building in Hollywood. It was 1946. The three partners had recently split, and Bosustow was the sole executive producer:

> It was now Steve Bosustow who was head honcho, apparently by
> dint of some inherited money. He was not on the creative level of
> the collection of former Disney stars who were the bones of the

staff. Steve had been an obscure assistant animator at Disney's, and was one of the most radical strike leaders during the struggle for Union recognition. What Steve had was charisma. He looked good; dapper, with his 1930s moustache, and most fortuitous, a remarkable resemblance to Walt Disney! What's more, he had Walt Disney-size ambitions, feeling sure that UPA would one day rule the world of animation. Of course, we all were believers. UPA was a religious center for us, deeply convinced that we had the key to cartoon Gloryland; that we possessed the animation mojo.[80]

At UPA, salaries were low, but the artists felt it was a privilege to work there, affording them the opportunity to experiment with the medium. Moreover, an environment of politically left-oriented people characterized the general atmosphere. Deitch remembered an episode about Bosustow that provides a clue to how much the studio was union-based and politically left-oriented. Referring to the period that followed the winning of the Oscar for *Gerald McBoing Boing*, Deitch said:

He [Steve] was getting the credit. He was actually believing he was greater than Disney! He used his smooth tongue on me at many key moments, all of it designed to keep me satisfied with low pay. … He laid his hand once again on my somewhat fleshier shoulder, and said, "Gene, you're a good Marxist, aren't you?" This was code; that we all toiled for brotherhood rather than mere money.[81]

Deitch also worked at the New York City branch as production director of animated TV commercials. His opinion of Bosustow is harsh. He believed Bosustow an incompetent leader:

I never spoke to a single staff member of UPA who respected Steve as a leader. He was in fact a company joke. … He never had creative control, and he allowed the chaotic free-wheeling that was on the one hand UPA's glory, but on the other hand led to its destruction. There was no reasonable guidance.[82]

Furthermore, it would seem that not only did Bosustow not have the creative control necessary to run the company, but he was not the creative brain behind UPA, according to its original cofounders, David Hilberman and Zachary Schwartz. Hilberman recalled that their roles were divided in this way: Schwartz was the designer, Hilberman was the director, and Bosustow was the businessman.[83] Schwartz also emphasized that Bosustow was not the creative head of UPA; he did not attend the story meetings and did not have the creative weight of John Hubley or Bobe Cannon: "Steve's function was not a creative function; he was only running the studio."[84] In the same interview, Schwartz referred to a French book in which Steve is praised as the creator of UPA style and denied this.[85] The book was *Le Dessin Animé après Walt Disney*, written by Robert Benayoun.

Hilberman later considered it a mistake to have sold his stocks to Bosustow,[86] since Bosustow got complete control of the studio. Instead, he believed, if the stocks had been sold to the artists, they could have been running UPA and making different decisions. Bill Hurtz made a similar assertion: "The studio was sold to a businessman and it became a schlock outfit very, very quickly."[87]

On the creative side, story man Bill Scott remembered Bosustow as lacking the ability to select a story that could be transformed into an animated cartoon. Instead, he tended to trust other people to do so. Scott referred to one day when Bosustow bought on the spot from his close friend Ted Geisel (Dr. Seuss) what he believed was a story, but was instead only a gag:

> They were having lunch together, and Geisel says, "I have a great idea for a film about eyebrows. You start with some guy's face, and see how his eyebrows move up and down, and furrow and knit and all the things eyebrows usually do, and then suddenly the eyebrows manage to move away from the face and just keep on dancing on their own."
>
> Steve thought it was great, and bought it. I mean, he pulled out his checkbook right there at the table, and bought it on the spot. Then he passed it on to Phil [Eastman] and me, and said, "Here's a new film we're going to do."
>
> We looked it over, and said right away, "Wait a minute. Where's the story? What happens?"
>
> Steve said, "Well, can't you figure something out?"
>
> So we worked on it for a while, but basically it isn't the idea for a film; it's a gag that has to fit into some other context. When Steve finally realized that, he went back to Geisel and asked for his money back. And he got it.[88]

Scott also recalled that:

> Steve did have the tendency to say the wrong things on the spur of the moment—my favorite example: when he brought the "Oscar" for GERALD McBOING BOING to the studio the day after the ceremony, everybody was assembled, and Steve makes a speech that started: "This Oscar may seem little, but it's going to do great things for us. Now we can afford to hire some really first rate animators!"[89]

The way Scott remembers this event might suggest a negative attitude on the part of Bosustow, who "did have the tendency to say the wrong things on the spur of the moment." Another interpretation of this anecdote might be that Bosustow wanted to praise the animators by making a humble self-deprecating joke that somehow expressed the embarrassment of the moment.

2.3.2 Stephen Bosustow According to Himself: A Mr. Magoo Personality

In his notes, handwritten and typewritten probably in his later years, Bosustow often talked about luck and miraculous events, as if his personal abilities and skills were not enough to run a motion picture company. He also indirectly admitted to being an innocent and naive enthusiast who did not know what he was doing to the point of comparing himself to the very character that brought glory and money to UPA, Mr. Magoo:

> Mr. Magoo and I have a lot in common. He bumbles around in life and comes out unscathed. I bumbled around in life and wound up doing what I hadn't intended to do, and probably what I wasn't altogether a good enough businessman to do: operate a motion picture company.
>
> My theory of life has always been one in which one-third of what happens to you is the result of where you are at a particular moment in your life, that is timing.
>
> Another third is the result of who you happen to meet and how they change your life.
>
> That last third is your background, environment and ability.[90]

According to Bosustow, his background was formed not only by a passion for art but also by his union activities and his Democratic beliefs:

> I had always been on the left side of the picture. My father and mother and my wife and her family had always been Democrats. Around the mid-1030s [sic], I had turned into an ultra-liberal, although I never became a Communist.[91]

He grew up observing his father as a worker who believed in organized labor. At Disney, Bosustow took part in union activities, although he feared being discovered by Walt Disney:

> Just as I was beginning to make progress in animation, my old background caught up with me. I had always been a believer in organized labor. My father had been a steelworkers [sic] organizer in Vancouver.
>
> Cartoonists were not organized then in Hollywood but a movement was just beginning to to [sic] that end.
>
> One day I asked Freddy Moore about joining the union. He did not answer me, but went to Walt Disney to see if he thought he should join.
>
> Disney's reply was to take me out of animation and put me back in the in-betweener department. ...
>
> I became the studio representative in the first discussions about forming a local at the Disney studio.
>
> In those days, to consider belonging to a union in the cartoon industry, let alone be an organizer or an officer, was like being a Communist today in the eyes of Walt Disney. Had my activities been know [sic], I would have been instantly fired.[92]

Still, when the strike broke out, Bosustow volunteered as a picket captain, although he felt he was not talented enough for that position:

> Maybe it was because my father used to tell me stories of how terribly the union organizing period of his life had been when he was president of the machinist workers of Canada. He couldn't get the majority of workers to pick [sic] and help. And then, because he had been the leader, he couldn't get a job afterwards. ... I was supposed to make my way down front to get some instructions about being the picket captain and I wasn't the guy at all for this job.

There were hundreds there that had more talent and respect from the other artists than I had and nobody would march around with a picked [*sic*] sign for me. It was madness.[93]

Furthermore, being a unionist also meant risk: "Mysteriously, I was given my notice at Hughes. I was never able to confirm it, but I imagine it was because of my union background."[94] And, undoubtedly, it attracted the attention of the HUAC to the studio and his employees in 1951, something scarcely discussed in Bosustow's notes.[95]

According to Bosustow, the early years of Industrial Films and Poster Service were characterized by much enthusiasm and an almost-desperate search for funding to support the company. While lack of experience could bring failure, it could also sometimes, due to serendipitous events, bring luck: "Not having too much experience in production schedules and dead lines [*sic*] I readily accepted the job to complete a sixteen minute animated film with full animation in color to deliver in ninty [*sic*] days." *Hell-Bent for Election* turned out to be a successful film: many animators and layout men worked on it, mostly freely, through nights and weekends, and the film led to other commissioned works for the newly renamed UPA studio.

Money, nevertheless, was still needed, and again, luck came to the rescue. One day, a credit arrived:

> As the clients began to mount up so did our bills such as art materials and it was then that Mr. Flax that owned the Flax Art Supplies Store on 8th street down from Art Center offered to give us a two thousand dollars line of credit.[96]

Administering a company, however, is not an easy task and requires entrepreneurial skills as well as some basic financial and accounting knowledge, qualities that the young enthusiastic Bosustow was lacking:

> Another incident before we leave 1944 concern [*sic*] a friend of mine from Hughes Air Craft Company, he was project supervisor of a department that I had worked in. He was also a good personal friend so I discussed our financial problems with him. He instructed me in the basic business elements that when you need money you go to a bank and borrow it. Not having this kind of experience before we went to his bank … [he drew up for me] a

financial statement [and I] borrowed twenty five thousand dollars. My joy however was short lived. The bank called me one day and asked me to come down and bring my friend Frank Clark, as they had some serious questions about our financial statement. When we got there the bank manager notified us that we would soon be going to jail because we had falsified our financial statement. It turned out that not only was I a neophyte in the business world of borrowing money but so was my friend Frank. ... He gave us ten days to raise the money or they would file charges of bank fraud.[97]

Through trial and error, lucky events and the work of brilliant directors, animators and artists, UPA survived for more than ten years, bringing glory to Bosustow and ushering in an aesthetic revolution within the animated cartoon medium. Bosustow naturally considered himself to be part of the creative process that was going on at the studio, and it is without doubt that his decisions influenced what was produced, or not, by UPA. Bosustow wrote of the first Columbia agreement:

The "Fox and Crow" we made for them was like none they had seen before. We simplified caricatures and backgrounds and made the painting and drawing more contemporary. It won an academy nomination for Columbia, the first their cartoons had ever received. We were in solidly with Columbia. I felt I would be able to approach them now with my ideas and get what I wanted. Although I had had to compromise, it was worth it.[98]

After Hubley left the company, Bosustow relied heavily on Cannon's opinion of which stories could be turned into animated cartoons. Among the still-unarchived materials of Steve Bosustow's UPA collection are inter-office memoranda between the two in which Bosustow solicited Cannon's opinion of stories he believed could be turned into animated cartoons. More than once Cannon rejected the subjects submitted by Bosustow. Surely Bosustow had the final decision on what subject was going to be produced, but Cannon had more than a relevant role in it (Figure 2.1).

Still, it was specifically Bosustow who believed that the story proposed by Geisel—*Gerald McBoing Boing*—could be turned into an animated film, although he probably never imagined that it would have such an impact. Bosustow's memories of the episode follow:

FIGURE 2.1 Director Robert Cannon. Reprinted with permission from Tee Bosustow (*Steve Bosustow's UPA collection, in the care of his son, Tee Bosustow*).

"Ted. What a surprise. What are you doing here?"

I had just walked into the studio one day in 1950 and literally ran into Theodor Suess Geisl [*sic*] who was coming out.

He explained that he had just had a meeting in our story department about a new character he thought might interest us. He had been turned down.

Intrigued, I asked him to come into my office and discuss it further.

Ted Geisel and I had worked together before. He was in Frank Capra's motion picture unit at OWI's Hollywood office during the war and this was one of our first big customers.

Since then, he had gone into advertising business and started to write children's book under the name Dr. Seuss.

Although I hadn't seen him for years, I was familiar with his work. At that time, his most well-known book had been "500 Hats of Bartholomew Cubbins."

The minute he told me about his idea I knew it was something I could get Columbia to finance. They were more favorably disposed to new ideas since the "Fox and Crow" cartoon had gotten the academy nomination.[99]

Within the general topic of creative ideas, Bosustow's notes also reveal some of his own thoughts on the person he so esteemed and to whom he was so often compared by the press, Walt Disney. He admired "Disney's story mind and his sense of what the public wanted"[100] but, at the same time, thought that "Disney's iron hand eventually erodes the espirit [*sic*] among his employees."[101] Bosustow believed that Disney transmitted his "parochial attitude"[102] to his films, since they all became personal projects to the point that they no longer looked like Rudyard Kipling's *The Jungle Book* or James M. Barrie's *Peter Pan* but rather Walt Disney's personal stories. Whether Bosustow believed this to be good or bad is not revealed. For sure, it was an approach far different from UPA's, where the directors and animators tried to be as faithful as possible to the original story by finding an audiovisual style that fitted the content, such as in *Gerald McBoing Boing, Madeline, The Tell-Tale Heart* or *The Unicorn in the Garden*.

In his recollections, Bosustow certainly thought of himself as part of that group of creative people who looked for a new style in animation. "I was happy," he admitted, reflecting on the period after the creation of Mr. Magoo, "because I had accomplished two things: given Columbia a successful continuing character, but without compromising my own beliefs in style, story and format."[103]

After *The Boing-Boing Show*, UPA started to decline. The contract with Henry G. Saperstein is another example of misjudgment on Bosustow's part. Erroneously, Bosustow felt that Saperstein "was certainly a businessman who had been around."[104] This and other mistakes led to the eventual selling of the company. Bosustow recognized his errors:

> When the low periods come, most studios cut back to a skeleton crew. I had so much of a union background, I couldn't do it. We kept a full crew on at all times.
>   This is just one example of my bad business judgment.
> Another mistake I made was in not putting my own name on every project. That was Disney's greatest asset. He sold the studio's product as his own, in his own image. All his characters—Kipling, Lewis Carroll, fairytales—wound up as Walt Disney Characters.[105]

Walt Disney left an empire to his family; Stephen Bosustow unfortunately did not, UPA did not survive the market, but it did have an impact on the animation history.

Bosustow had always wanted to be an artist and was lucky enough to get into the business and run a company. His leadership led to that creative chaos in the studio that allowed the formation of non-fixed units. Nothing was regimented from above, and Bosustow probably behaved as one of the crew instead of imposing his leadership.

Which is the luckiest UPA character? Mr. Magoo.

"In my innocence and enthusiasm, I thought anything could be done,"[106] admitted Bosustow. And, the impossible became possible, at least for a short time (Figure 2.2).

FIGURE 2.2 Stephen Bosustow Draws Mr. Magoo. Reprinted with permission from Tee Bosustow (*Steve Bosustow's UPA collection, in the care of his son, Tee Bosustow*).

2.3.3 Stephen Bosustow: Merits, Limits and Gaps

Opinions on Stephen Bosustow portray a contradictory figure: highly praised for his artistic achievement as the executive producer of UPA studio and sometimes even as the creative brain behind the UPA aesthetic "revolution" by the national and international press; a leader who had no creative control over the company he had founded, although he had sufficient charisma, ambition and courage to run the studio and to believe he could compete with Walt Disney, according to his employees; a person too naive to be an efficient fundraiser or lacking the skills necessary to run a motion picture company, as he himself admitted. All these contradictions are reflected in the way Bosustow managed the UPA studio, the way his employees could freely express themselves artistically and subsequently share their outspoken opinions on Bosustow's administration, and ultimately, the way UPA animated cartoons successfully express a simplified audiovisual language. An analysis of Bosustow's merits, limits, and gaps helps to assess him as UPA executive producer and UPA as an artistically successful animation studio.

Stephen Bosustow's major limit was that he was unable to run the company without being over budget. "The studio was constantly on the verge of financial collapse,"[107] and Bosustow had to borrow capital from Columbia by selling a portion of its 25 percent ownership of each film. Alas, by the end of the 1950s, all the animated shorts produced by UPA for Columbia were owned by the distribution company.[108]

Economic troubles were present from the very beginning, as Schwartz recalled:

> When we started UPA, none of us—that's Dave Hilberman, myself, and Steve Bosustow, who was the third partner—had the slightest notion about how you run a business. We just thought you went in and did the best you could. … It was a great shock to us to find out that you also needed money—what they call capital.[109]

And if Walt Disney had his brother Roy as the financial brain behind the company, Bosustow seemed to be the only one who dealt with the administration of the business. The New York and London branches, subsidiaries of the Burbank studio, became especially necessary as they provided a steady income through the production of TV commercials:

We rode high in New York, but yet slid the financial slopes. Steve continuously siphoned our TV commercial profits to support the artistic efforts of the Hollywood studio, and we were entirely dependent on UPA-Hollywood for our rent and pay checks. We had to lock ourselves in the office every payday, hoping to God we'd receive the checks before the staff would beat the door down. What we did receive were almost daily pep-talks from Steve on the flexible Dictaphone belts which came in the mail. No e-mail in those days either, but we got lots of vocal advice from Steve on those belts![110]

Often referred to as a mistake is Bosustow's compliant behavior toward the HUAC. In 1952, Columbia came up with a list of eight employees—Jules Engel, Fred Grable, John Hubley, Bill Hurtz, Paul Julian, Herb Klynn, Bill Melendez and Myer Shaffer—who were asked to write a letter admitting or denying a connection with Communism. Seven letters were written and signed; Hubley refused to do it.[111] "Steve did little to save him,"[112] and Hubley left the company. The other seven were not dismissed, although people such as Bill Scott, Phil Eastman, Charles Dagget and John McGrew were forced to leave the studio in the early 1950s.[113] Hubley and Eastman were called to testify before the HUAC, and both refused to answer questions or mention names. Melendez, Scott and McGrew never had to testify.[114] Schwartz,[115] Charles Dagget, a UPA publicity man, and David Raksin, a musician who collaborated at UPA, became friendly witnesses. Raksin named 11 people—minor figures, such as assistant animators and others—who had to leave the studio, too.[116] Hilberman, who had left UPA in 1946, was named by Walt Disney[117] and Eugene Fleury[118] and subsequently blacklisted.

Bosustow's behavior could be partially explained by Columbia's hold over UPA. After all, Columbia had the last decision on who UPA's executive producer could hire,[119] and demanded Bosustow enforce the blacklist.[120] Furthermore, Columbia not only owned 25 percent of UPA stock but also could easily end the distribution deal.[121] It is very possible that Bosustow was afraid of losing the studio by being associated with Communism and that for this reason, after reporting to the HUAC, he chose to become a member of the conservative Hollywood Producers Association.[122] Needless to say, after this episode occurred in 1951, the studio was never the same, and Bosustow's morale was broken.[123]

Still, as Adrian Woolery has stated, "UPA would never have come into existence had it not been for Steve."[124] Even Deitch agreed: "Though Steve was not the actual UPA creator, he was its greatest proselytizer. He had, as they used to say, the gift of gab, a smooth talker, and thus the perfect front man for the studio."[125]

As in a Mr. Magoo cartoon, where shortcomings become advantages and the situation is reversed, Bosustow wanted to be an artist but ended up working as executive producer of an animation studio. Probably aware of his own limitations as an artist, he unpretentiously stepped aside from the more creative production phases, relying on Bobe Cannon's opinions, for example. As the executive producer and fundraiser for the studio, he could not avoid coming to depend on the Columbia agreement, acquiescing to requests and decisions, and even making mistakes in judgment, such as when he put his trust in the wrong person and was nearly sent to jail for a falsified financial statement or when he continued to sell the ownership of UPA films to Columbia. Nevertheless, in spite of his lack of knowledge about and confidence in the economic rules of the business market, he was able to negotiate an agreement with Columbia that allowed UPA to steadily produce theatrical animated cartoons. Moreover, the economic constraints he had to face from the very beginning pushed him and UPA artists to endorse a minimalist approach in animation that was less expensive.

Yet, he demanded quality: although UPA films' animation was stylized, the shorts were remarkably designed, to the point that the use of limited animation became functional to the two-dimensional innovative stylized look of UPA animated cartoons. It became not just an economic expedient but a hallmark. This was possible because he strove for films that were first and foremost works of art. Similar to Walt Disney, he hired the most talented and skillful artists available at the time in order to accomplish this goal, but in contrast to Disney, he conceived the studio as a more familiar and informal place to work, a place where everyone had a voice and Bosustow, although executive producer, could easily be approached for any concern, as a journalist pointed out.[58] This might have led to a state of disruptive anarchy in the way he ran the company, according to his employees, but it was also what led UPA to its creative and artistic success.

Too highly influenced by his love for the medium and the idea of producing something that had artistic value not to feel part of the creative process, Bosustow probably evaluated situations and made decisions as the chief of UPA but according to his artistic desires as well as his politically left-oriented background. Sometimes he described himself as someone who did not really know what he was doing, taking too little credit for UPA artistic achievements; other times he very consciously debated about animation, firmly stating that the animated cartoon is a medium of art and thus showing a sharp awareness of the artistic direction he wanted to impress upon his company; yet other times it seemed he was overwhelmed by national and international UPA success, praise and acknowledgment to the point of taking too much artistic credit for them.

His contradictory personality is also evident in his much-discussed behavior toward the HUAC.[126] Whereas his union activities and Democratic beliefs helped create that "primordial ideological soup" that acted as a propellant when the studio was founded and pioneering managerial and artistic decisions needed to be taken, they became a threat in later years due to the changed political setting and the HUAC's focus on Hollywood and eventually a heavy burden that may have contributed to UPA's artistic decline. Although Bosustow's decision to be compliant with the HUAC and its blacklist practice possibly accelerated the company's demise, it also granted the survival of the studio for about eight more years. Again, Bosustow's contradictory personality and behavior perhaps can be explained by his love for the animated medium and his eagerness to excel and leave a mark in the history of animation, much as Walt Disney did.

Within the studio, he left his employees to work in the most creative of conditions, without imposing his presence. This may be interpreted as a lack of leadership, but UPA films still speak for themselves today. By dealing with the clients and financial troubles, he freed artists like Cannon to focus only on the creative side of the work. At the same time, Bosustow acted as a catalyzer by encouraging the employees to work in small teams of interchangeable artists and to express themselves.

2.4 THE UPA PRODUCTION SYSTEM

2.4.1 The Units

Being a unionist and a Democrat, Bosustow structured the studio in "units" and allowed his employees to freely form teams of interchangeable artists. These units were very small, "with a central head that serviced them with camera and ink and paint."[127] Every unit consisted of a director who could select people to work with: a layout artist (designer) and a background painter.[128] The novelty lies in the ability of the director to work with different artists for every single project, differing from the fixed production system at Warner Bros. and MGM or the assembly line setup of Walt Disney Productions. At UPA, "each director, in a sense, had his own unit there. He may not have had the same group of animators—the animators all worked in one pool."[129]

The lack of an assembly-line approach did not go unnoticed by journalists and film critics: UPA "was set up in conscious reaction against both the Disney style and the Disney method, the method of a large-scale movie factory."[130] The difference with the Disney production system is that "UPA pictures are handled start to finish by small units, each film being the responsibility of one close group that works together on it from its original planning to the final print."[131]

The same structure was adopted in the New York studio:

> In order to keep our people individually creative, we are divided into eight independent groups working on different projects. Most of them are in California, but one is here in New York. They watch each other, but they don't give orders to each other.[132]

Presumably it was also set up in the London branch.

The unit system at UPA was something unique, never tried before in the U.S. cartoon industry. It made possible and even caused "a degree of experimentation and creative variety that hasn't really existed since."[133] UPA production manager Herb Klynn explained why:

> The lack of central leadership meant that the talent was all in friendly competition with each other, and all vying to do something distinctive and different. The units that were assembled for each project mixed the talent in different combinations where they exchanged ideas and challenged each other.[134]

Successful examples of these small units working on a single animated film from beginning to end are *Gerald McBoing Boing*, directed by animator Bobe Cannon, designed by Bill Hurtz, and colored by Herb Klynn and Jules Engel; *Rooty Toot Toot*, directed by designer John Hubley, designed and colored by Paul Julian, and animated by Grim Natwick and Art Babbitt, among others; and *The Tell-Tale Heart*, directed by Ted Parmelee, designed and colored by Paul Julian, and animated by Pat Matthews.

A unit system based on such small groups of people granted freedom and creativity, and Bosustow was able to capture this. He understood that to give complete freedom to his employees might lead to outstanding creative results: "Bosustow, for the first time within the history of American animated cinema, allowed groups of artists to freely work in studios that belonged to them."[135] The question here might be, therefore, who really ran the studio: Bosustow or the artists?

2.4.2 Freedom Is Granted

The UPA studio was a team and a family, "a group of people working together as a whole: the artists gave their input, the animators gave their input, and other artists from other units (or projects) gave their input as well."[136] No hierarchy was present: "Stephen Bosustow owned UPA, but each person had a voice!"[137]

Whereas at Disney animators were venerated like actors in the studio system, at UPA, in the early days, "everyone was relaxed, and free to contribute, and there was a great warmth and compatibility, which generated the enthusiasm, which ended up on the screen."[138] Everyone respected the other:

> [T]he animator had respect for the layout man, the layout man had respect for the animator, the layout man had respect for the color man, and the color man had respect for the story man. ... They knew they were good, therefore they respect[ed] each other. At Disney, if you were not an animator, you were probably a third- or fourth-class citizen.[139]

At the very beginning of UPA, all artists were doing multiple jobs within the studio:

> If Bill [Hurtz] was directing, he [Zack Schwartz] did layout... Jules [Engel] would do certain things and overlaps. Ade [Woolery] was doing stuff in camera. It wasn't a matter of what our job qualification, so to speak, was; it was the fact that we were part of this cohesive creative team.[140]

UPA was the place where everybody wanted to be to experiment. Director Leo Salkin joined UPA London after working for 15 years at another studio. Asked how he felt about this new adventure, he enthusiastically affirmed: "If you want to do a film a certain way, you do it that way. No one stops you."[141]

Another example of how the UPA unit system granted creativity and freedom to the artists was the fact that there were no fixed musicians. Composers were hired from project to project, according to how their music would fit the story of the animated films. Ed Penney explained:

> They do not have "staff composers," that is, salaried men who grind out so many bars of "chase," "laugh" or "suspense" music by the bar, as if they were grinding out sausage. Instead they have done what some forward looking producer-directors in France, England and even the United States have done, and that is, commission a leading composer to write a special score.[142]

This led to a great variety of scores belonging to different styles and composed by many musicians: Gail Kubik, Ernest Gold, Benjamin Lees, David Raksin, George Bruns, Shorty Rogers, Boris Kremenliev, Chico Hamilton, Phil Moore, and many others. The same approach can be seen in the visual product: many UPA artists were accomplished painters and sculptors who had already exhibited in galleries, such as Jules Engel, John Hubley, Robert Dranko, Paul Julian, Robert McIntosh and Abe Liss.[143]

The great variety of artists and composers allowed a great variety of audiovisual styles. As Bosustow noted, "One day … we work with contemporary art—the next we create spots based on the work of the old masters. We constantly change."[144] Cannon added: "We use creative people in *all* departments, even for technical processes."[145]

2.4.3 A Matter of Style

One day, Robert Cannon was in a Los Angeles cinema for the showing of a UPA cartoon. The couple sitting in front of him was overcome with surprise and bewilderment. After some minutes of heated discussion, one said triumphantly to the other: "I know what it is—it's a *cartoon!*"[146]

Since their first appearance, UPA films were welcomed as a departure from Disney photo-realism and a return to "the first and fundamental principles of cartooning."[147] UPA artists "have shied away from 'multi-plane' camera and live-action technique."[148] They work "with lines on a flat surface and they don't try to hide the fact. Instead they take advantage of it, making their lines as expressive as possible."[149]

The anti-realistic features that distinguish UPA animated cartoons are the color palette, the characters and the backgrounds designs and the movements. The design is highly stylized both in the layouts of the backgrounds and the characters, and the animation is stylized as well. One example of a highly stylized cartoon is *Fudget's Budget*, where few lines define Mr. Fudget and his wife and the environment in which they live. The animation is limited instead of full, in other words, made with fewer drawings and with poses held for longer periods of time. Not only are the lines more expressive, but also, the colors: rather than having skin-colored characters, there are silhouettes of characters that can turn upon themselves to express a certain type of mood. These kinds of innovations were already present in *Gerald McBoing Boing*, where few essential lines define the interior of the house and the characters are the same color as the background.

Film critic George Seldes brilliantly and succinctly expressed the "novelty" of UPA animated cartoons when he wrote:

> The UPA product is not so much new as it is a return to the first principles of the animated cartoon, those fundamentals which Disney understood and exploited more fully than anyone before him, and which he has abandoned. They are so simple that the name of the medium, animated cartoon, comprehends all the essentials, since a cartoon is a drawing that deliberately distorts certain salient features of the subject and animation is an exaggeration of normal movement or expression.[150]

This rediscovery of the medium was made possible in part by applying the study of graphic design in relation to Modern art. With UPA films, animation was redesigned according to graphic principles and Modern artists' examples:

> The young animators, who had formed the nucleus of United Productions of America, as the company became known in 1945, were dissatisfied with the rigid conventions of storyline and visualization that dominated the film industry. Working for well-entrenched organizations they had had no chance to deviate from the animal fable in a naturalistic setting that the cartoon industry was content to exploit endlessly. These young animators, many serious, knowledgeable, and established painters, believed that the cartoon, as it then existed, failed to do justice to its visual and narrative possibilities. They were convinced that the creative innovations of twentieth century painting, not only could be adapted to

animation, but more importantly would enhance immeasurably both visual and narrative quality. They felt that the creative potential of the cartoon film had scarcely been tapped.[151]

Gene Deitch perhaps best explained to what degree the UPA approach was revolutionary in that every film was treated as a project per se, with an audiovisual style specially developed to fit the story, and that animation was considered a *graphic (cinematic) medium*:

> Here was a small group of men and women who were onto something brand new—working on the idea that *any form of graphic art could be animated.* Out with the "house styles" of Disney, Warners, MGM, or Paramount! Every film was to be approached as an entirely new adventure, its graphic style, mode of animation, music—every element—growing out of the particular story. This seems obvious enough today, but in the early and mid-forties—in a commercial studio—it was a cosmic idea.[152]

But, these ideas were in the air even before UPA came into existence. Schwartz recalled that he experimented in the black-and-white film *Willoughby's Magic Hat* (1943), produced by Screen Gems, an extremely graphic and simple approach consisting of only two shades of gray.[153] Rather, it was the cross-fertilization between graphic design and cinema that allowed a "return to a kind of visualization that was not too close to reality, but graphic and symbolic graphic and the technique was expressive of the medium itself."[154] And, it has cross-fertilized since then.

Hilberman is sure about that: UPA was "not predictive":

"I think UPA is important because it's an example of how a revolution in style and technology comes about not by a conscious decision of a few people getting together on a strike line and saying, 'By God, when this is over we're going to set up a studio that is going to do something different.' I don't believe that anybody said, 'Jesus, let's not do anything like Disney. Let's make this one different.' I think rather you had individual talents confronted with a problem or an idea who sought the best answer to it. It's a much more of a positive exploratory kind of thing, non-predictive. It happened, it evolved."[155]

"Experimentation in style and technology was happening even before UPA,[156] but UPA explored it further and brought it to full maturity."

ENDNOTES

1. Walter Gropius, "Reorientation," in *The New Landscape in Art and Science*, ed. György Kepes (Chicago, IL: Paul Theobald and Company, 1956). The author suggests this statement can be applied to an "artistic product," too.
2. Steve Bosustow's UPA collection. See Appendix, Timeline III.
3. Stephen Bosustow, interview by Tee Bosustow, December 11, 1976; Steve Bosustow's UPA collection.
4. Ibid.
5. Typewritten notes by Stephen Bosustow; Steve Bosustow's UPA collection.
6. An inbetweener is "an individual hired to create images linking the key or 'extreme' poses created by an animator." Maureen Furniss, *The Animation Bible: A Practical Guide to the Art of Animating, from Flipbooks to Flash* (London, UK: Laurence King Publishing; New York, NY: Harry N. Abrams, 2008), 326.
7. Steve Bosustow's UPA collection. In a handwritten note, Bosustow stated that, while he was at the Ub Iwerks studio, he worked as assistant to animator Grim Natwick.
8. Stephen Bosustow, interview by Tee Bosustow, March 26, 1977; Steve Bosustow's UPA collection. Lantz, the son of Italian immigrants, hired Bosustow believing that he was Italian.
9. Ibid.
10. That same year, he married Audrey Stevenson. His son Tee was born in 1937; Nick, in 1940.
11. Stephen Bosustow, interview by Tee Bosustow, December 11, 1976.
12. Handwritten notes by Stephen Bosustow; Steve Bosustow's UPA collection.
13. Stephen Bosustow, interview by Tee Bosustow, December 11, 1976.
14. Ibid.
15. Typewritten notes by Stephen Bosustow. He taught a design sketching class once a week in the Engineering/Scientific War Training Program. At Hughes Aircraft Company, he taught three times per week.
16. Typewritten notes by Stephen Bosustow. A five-minute film on "how workers should be careful in their welding practices in the plant."
17. Ibid.
18. Ibid.
19. Ibid.
20. Ibid. Bud Fuer is misspelled: "Bosustow rented an animation camera from Bud Furer, of Acme," according to Abraham, *When Magoo Flew: The Rise and Fall of Animation Studio UPA*, 52.
21. The breach among the three partners is recounted by Abraham, *When Magoo Flew: The Rise and Fall of Animation Studio UPA*, 66–70. David Hilberman was drafted into military service during much of 1945 and when he returned to the studio, Bosustow had become the "de facto head of the studio in Hilberman's absence" (p. 67). The two argued on who should run the studio. At the same time, Hilberman was considering an offer to create animation studios that he had received from a Soviet Union delegation before World War II.

Therefore, he was already thinking about leaving the studio and selling his stocks to Bosustow. Eventually, Bosustow was able to buy stocks equivalent to 51 percent of the company thus becoming the sole executive producer.

22. Steve Bosustow's UPA collection. See Appendix, Timelines I and III.
23. Typewritten notes by Stephen Bosustow.
24. Abraham, *When Magoo Flew: The Rise and Fall of Animation Studio UPA*.
25. *The Magic Fluke*, directed by John Hubley (1949; DVD, *UPA: The Jolly Frolics Collection*, Culver City, CA: Sony Pictures Home Entertainment, 2012).
26. Typewritten notes by Stephen Bosustow.
27. *Magoo's Puddle Jumper*, directed by Pete Burness (1956; DVD, *Mr. Magoo: The Theatrical Collection*, Culver City, CA: Sony Pictures Home Entertainment, 2014).
28. Typewritten notes by Stephen Bosustow.
29. Abraham, *When Magoo Flew: The Rise and Fall of Animation Studio UPA*.
30. Maltin, *Of Mice and Magic: A History of American Animated Cartoons*, 338.
31. Abraham, *When Magoo Flew: The Rise and Fall of Animation Studio UPA*, 188.
32. Steve Bosustow's UPA collection. The New York studio was operative from 1950 to 1958; and the London studio, from 1956 to March 31, 1957. See Appendix, Timeline I. According to Bosustow's typewritten notes, the first UPA TV commercial was made in 1947, presumably at the Otto K. Olesen Building in Hollywood, or possibly at the studio's second location, also in Hollywood, on Highland Avenue (UPA moved there in July 1947, according to Barrier, *Hollywood Cartoons: American Animation in Its Golden Age*.)
33. *1001 Arabian Nights*, directed by Jack Kinney (1959; DVD, *Mr. Magoo: The Theatrical Collection*, Culver City, CA: Sony Pictures Home Entertainment, 2014).
34. Steve Bosustow's UPA collection. See Appendix, Timeline II.
35. Ibid.
36. Ibid.
37. Abraham, *When Magoo Flew: The Rise and Fall of Animation Studio UPA*, 222.
38. Ibid.
39. Steve Bosustow's UPA collection. See Appendix, Timelines II and III.
40. Dick Wong, "Search for the Magic Pen," *frameafterframe* (2006): 44–45. According to this journal article, China Paint Manufacturing Company used to house the biggest animation department in Hong Kong, "seizing 90% of the market share."
41. No document stating the year in which the new company was founded has been found by the author among the many handwritten and typewritten notes that Bosustow left to his son Tee. It can only be dated approximately to 1968–1969.
42. *Is It Always Right to be Right?* directed by Lee Mishkin (1970; Burbank, CA: Stephen Bosustow Productions). www.youtube.com /watch?v=LbWCjQ5L0ZY, accessed September 25, 2015.
43. *The Legend of John Henry*, directed by Sam Weiss (1974; Burbank, CA: Stephen Bosustow Productions).

44. Typewritten notes by Stephen Bosustow.
45. Nichols, "A Star Is Drawn: Meet Gerald McBoing-Boing."
46. Fred Hift, "'McBoing' to 'Rooty Toot,'" *New York Times*, March 16, 1952.
47. Knight, "U.P.A. Goes Boing-Boing," 49.
48. "UPA, Magoo & McBoing-Boing," 22.
49. Crowther, "McBoing Boing, Magoo and Bosustow," 15.
50. Similarly, in Penney, "U.P.A. Animated Art."
51. Crowther, "McBoing Boing, Magoo and Bosustow."
52. Bongard, "Animated Cartoons Find Higher Purpose: Film Cartoonists Try to Be More Than Just Quaint," 20.
53. Knight, "U.P.A. Goes Boing-Boing."
54. Crowther, "McBoing Boing, Magoo and Bosustow;" Knight, "U.P.A. Goes Boing-Boing."
55. *Toot, Whistle, Plunk and Boom*, directed by Charles A. Nichols and Ward Kimball (1953; DVD, *Walt Disney Treasures—Disney Rarities: Celebrated Shorts: 1920s–1960s*, Burbank, CA: Walt Disney Home Video, 2005). Otis L. Guernsey Jr., "The Movie Cartoon Is Coming of Age," *New York Herald Tribune*, November 29, 1953.
56. "How Does UPA Do It?"*Television Magazine*, December 1955; Steve Bosustow's UPA collection; Barbara Moon, "The Silly, Splendid World of Stephen Bosustow,"*Maclean's*, December 7, 1957.
57. Knight, "U.P.A. Goes Boing-Boing," 49.
58. Moon, "The Silly, Splendid World of Stephen Bosustow."
59. Ibid.
60. Knight, "U.P.A. Goes Boing-Boing," 49.
61. Ibid.
62. Winsten, "The Problem of Quality," 38.
63. Moon, "The Silly, Splendid World of Stephen Bosustow."
64. Ibid.
65. Phillips McCandlish, "Without Lisping Pigs: UPA Cartoons Penetrate TV's Culture Barrier with Esthetic Appeal," *New York Times*, March 17, 1957.
66. Abraham, *When Magoo Flew: The Rise and Fall of Animation Studio UPA*.
67. Information included in *UPA: The Jolly Frolics Collection*, DVD.
68. UPA Publicity Document; Steve Bosustow's UPA collection; Knight, "UPA, Magoo & McBoing-Boing."
69. UPA Press Release for *The Boing-Boing Show*, August 3, 1955; Steve Bosustow's UPA collection.
70. Chalais, "Le fil à couper Disney," 50. "M. Bosustow ... a rèussi là où M. Disney avait échoué: l'animation d'hommes ou de femmes dessinés ne pouvait en aucun cas avoir la perfection d'une photographie" (translated by author).
71. Georgine Oeri, "UPA: A New Dimension for the Comic Strip," *Graphis: International Journal of Graphic Art and Applied Art* 9, no. 50 (1953): 470. Although *Graphis* reported 1950 as the year of production for *Gerald McBoing Boing*, the animated short was officially released in 1951.

72. Clarens, *André Martin 1925–1994. Écrits Sur L'animation*, vol. I, 45. "L'apport majeur de Stephen Bosustow est d'avoir, pour la première fois, cessé d'animer du Disney ou assimilé. … Cette équipe a ouvert la porte à tous les styles, toutes les écritures, ce qui leur donne une place historique dans l'évolution du dessin animé en Amérique" (translated by author).

73. Clarens, *André Martin 1925–1994. Écrits Sur L'animation*, vol. I, 89. "La conception du dessin, du rythme et du sujet dans le cartoon" (translated by author).

74. Ibid., 98. "Il semble que le dessin animé retrouve tous les éléments qui, chez les primitifs, constituaient son charme spécifique: prédominance du trait plus symbolique que descriptive, du gag plus poétique et fulgurant que comique ou moralisateur" (translated by author).

75. Walter Alberti, *Il Cinema di Animazione 1832–1956* (Torino, IT: Edizioni Radio Italiana, 1957), 198. "Sembra che la 'troupe' di Bosustow abbia saltato l'esperienza di Walt Disney a pié pari e si sia direttamente ricollegata ai maestri della caricatura e dell'umorismo americani" (translated by author).

76. Robert Benayoun, *Le Dessin Animé après Walt Disney* (Paris, FR: Jean-Jacques Pauvert, 1961). For an explanation of the differences between the *I style* and the *O style*, see Chapter 3, Section 3.2.

77. Denys Chevalier, *J'aime le Dessin Animé* (Lausanne, CH: Editions Rencontre, 1962), 131. "Au contraire une infinité d'expressions graphiques, chacune correspondant à une double adéquation au modèle d'écriture inspiratrice choisi et à la personnalité de l'animateur lui-même" (translated by author).

78. Piero Zanotto, "Petite histoire du cinéma d'animation: Stephen Bosustow et l'U.P.A., " *Séquences: la revue du cinéma*, no. 44 (1966): 44. "Animateur principal" (translated by author).

79. Ralph Stephenson, *Animation in the Cinema* (London, UK: A. Zwemmer Limited, 1967), 50; *Swab Your Choppers*, director unknown (1947; Burbank, CA: United Productions of America).

80. Gene Deitch, "10. Steve Bosustow", *genedeitchcredits: The 65 Greats behind the Scenes!* (blog), April 9, 2012, http://genedeitchcredits.com/roll-the -credits/10-steve-bosustow/, accessed January 20, 2015.

81. Ibid.

82. Ibid.

83. David Hilberman, interview by John Canemaker, June 16, 1979.

84. Zachary Schwartz, interview by John Canemaker, September 18, 1979; John Canemaker Animation Collection; MSS 040; box 2; folder 40.0067; Fales Library and Special Collections, NYU.

85. Ibid.

86. Maltin, *Of Mice and Magic: A History of American Animated Cartoons*.

87. Bill Hurtz, quoted in Zachary Schwartz, "Notes from Zack Schwartz Appearance at UCLA" (Zach Schwartz animation conference, UCLA, Los Angeles, California, 7 July 1977), 7; John Canemaker Animation Collection; MSS 040; box 2; folder 5; Fales Library and Special Collections, NYU.

88. Bill Scott, in Moritz, "UPA, Reminiscing 30 Years Later," 21; The John Canemaker Animation Collection; MSS 040; box 2; folder 5; Fales Library and Special Collections, NYU.
89. Bill Scott, in Moritz, "UPA, Reminiscing 30 Years Later," 21.
90. Typewritten notes by Stephen Bosustow.
91. Ibid.
92. Ibid.
93. Handwritten notes by Stephen Bosustow.
94. Typewritten notes by Stephen Bosustow.
95. Here are Bosustow's memories, the only ones reported to have been found among his typewritten notes:

In 1951, we had to undergo our own version of the Red scare at UPA. With Senator McCarthy just beginning his investigations, the House of Un-American Activities Committee had been sniffing around Hollywood for some time. It had come up with the famed "Hollywood 10" writers, but it was attempting to ferret out others as well.

1. A remark Mrs. Bosustow had made in the 1930s about them being registered as communist party members comes back to haunt them.

2. They are cleared but he winds up having to fire one employee.

3. The committee staffers search his books for "Moscow gold." "I wish we had somebody's gold," replies Bosustow.

4. The committee gives up but the studio is psychologically shaken. Ibid.

His recollections do not specify how or why Bosustow came to force Hubley and seven other employees to leave the studio. For more information, see: Cohen, *Forbidden Animation: Censored Cartoons and Blacklisted Animators in America*; Abraham, *When Magoo Flew: The Rise and Fall of Animation Studio UPA*.
96. Typewritten notes by Stephen Bosustow.
97. Ibid.
98. Ibid.
99. Typewritten notes by Stephen Bosustow. Similarly, it was Bosustow who called Millard Kaufman to write the first Magoo episode after a meeting with Columbia president Leo Jaffe. It is also well known that the character Magoo was born from the collaboration of many artists. For more information, see: Abraham, *When Magoo Flew: The Rise and Fall of Animation Studio UPA*.
100. Typewritten notes by Stephen Bosustow.
101. Ibid.
102. Ibid.
103. Ibid.
104. Ibid.
105. Ibid.
106. Ibid.

107. Gene Deitch, "Chapter 12: The UPA Experience," *How to Succeed in Animation: Don't Let a Little Thing Like Failure Stop You!* (Van Nuys, CA: Animation World Network, 2013). www.awn.com/genedeitch/chapter -twelve-the-UPA-experience, accessed January 20, 2015,

108. Abraham, *When Magoo Flew: The Rise and Fall of Animation Studio UPA.*

109. Zachary Schwartz, "Notes from Zack Schwartz Appearance at UCLA," 5.

110. Deitch, "Chapter 12: The UPA Experience."

111. Abraham, *When Magoo Flew: The Rise and Fall of Animation Studio UPA.*

112. Deitch, "Chapter 12: The UPA Experience."

113. Cohen, *Forbidden Animation: Censored Cartoons and Blacklisted Animators in America.*

114. Ibid.

115. In 1953, Schwartz went before the HUAC and named names. Although he didn't name anyone who had not yet been named, he was no longer welcome among some of his old friends, like Hilberman. Sito, *Drawing the Line: The Untold Story of the Animation Unions from Bosko to Bart Simpson.*

116. Cohen, *Forbidden Animation: Censored Cartoons and Blacklisted Animators in America.*

117. In 1947, Walt Disney testified before the HUAC affirming that Hilberman was the brain behind the Disney strike and a Communist. An FBI report dated July 21, 1941, documents an account given by Disney three weeks after the strike began. On that occasion, Disney had said something completely different: the strike was caused by a "whispering campaign" rumoring that possibly 200 employees were going to be fired, since 19 men had just been laid off shortly before. Ibid.; Sito, *Drawing the Line: The Untold Story of the Animation Unions from Bosko to Bart Simpson.*

118. The Fleury couple is considered "HUAC's star witnesses regarding communist infiltration into the animation world." Cohen, *Forbidden Animation: Censored Cartoons and Blacklisted Animators in America*, 170. Both had painted backgrounds for *Hell-Bent for Election.* On September 24, 1951, Bernyce Fleury publicly affirmed that Hilberman could have been connected to the Communist Party. Mrs. Fleury's testimony was used in the examination of Eastman, Hubley, Schwartz and Mortimer William Pomerance. The latter had worked as an animator at Walt Disney studio. After taking part in the strike, he left the company and became business agent for the Screen Cartoonists' Guild from 1941 to 1944. Later, he moved to NYC and became a partner at TEMPO, a commercial animation studio founded by Hilberman and joined by Eastman and Schwartz. TEMPO soon attracted HUAC attention, clients broke off contracts and the studio closed. Ibid.

119. Abraham, *When Magoo Flew: The Rise and Fall of Animation Studio UPA.*

120. Sito, *Drawing the Line: The Untold Story of the Animation Unions from Bosko to Bart Simpson.*

121. Ibid.

122. Cohen, *Forbidden Animation: Censored Cartoons and Blacklisted Animators in America*.

123. Stephen Bosustow, interview by Tee Bosustow, June 1977; Steve Bosustow's UPA collection.

124. Adrian Woolery quoted in Maltin, *Of Mice and Magic: A History of American Animated Cartoons*, 340.

125. Gene Deitch, "10. Steve Bosustow", *genedeitchcredits: The 65 Greats behind the Scenes!* (blog), April 9, 2012, http://genedeitchcredits.com/roll-the -credits/10-steve-bosustow/, accessed January 23, 2015.

126. One film director whose compliant behavior with the HUAC caused controversy in Hollywood was Elia Kazan. Unlike Bosustow, Kazan had been a member of the American Communist Party during the depression, specifically from 1934 to 1936. In 1952 he testified before the HUAC, becoming a friendly witness: he mentioned names of people who had belonged to the Group Theater, such as screenwriter and personal friend Clifford Odets (for deeper insight, see: Kazan, *A Life*). His later disillusionment and disappointment with Communist and Socialist ideals can be found in his film *On the Waterfront* (1954), which offers a harsh critique of unions and their corruption. See also Chapter 1, Section 4.3.

127. Bill Hurtz, quoted in Zachary Schwartz, "Notes from Zack Schwartz Appearance at UCLA," 7.

128. Abraham, *When Magoo Flew: The Rise and Fall of Animation Studio UPA*.

129. Bill Hurtz, quoted in Zachary Schwartz, "Notes from Zack Schwartz Appearance at UCLA," 7.

130. Knight, "UPA, Magoo & McBoing-Boing," 22.

131. Hift, "'McBoing' to 'Rooty Toot.'"

132. Stephen Bosustow, quoted in Winsten, "The Problem of Quality," 38.

133. Herb Klynn, in Moritz, "UPA, Reminiscing 30 Years Later," 22.

134. Ibid.

135. André Martin, in Clarens, *André Martin 1925–1994. Écrits Sur L'animation*, vol. I, 116. "Bosustow a pour la première fois dans l'histoire du dessin animé américain permis à des créateurs, de travailler librement dans des studios leur appartenant" (translated by author).

136. Herb Klynn, quoted in Becki Lee Parker, "UPA Animation: No Animals, No Violence, Just Good Stories" (unpublished paper, University of Oregon, Eugene, OR, 1993); Giannalberto Bendazzi's collection.

137. Jules Engel, in Moritz, "UPA, Reminiscing 30 Years Later," 16.

138. Herb Klynn, quoted in Zachary Schwartz, "Notes from Zack Schwartz Appearance at UCLA," 4.

139. Jules Engel, quoted in Zachary Schwartz, "Notes from Zack Schwartz Appearance at UCLA," 4.

140. Herb Klynn, quoted in Zachary Schwartz, "Notes from Zack Schwartz Appearance at UCLA," 6.

141. David Fisher, "U.P.A. in England," *Sight and Sound*, 45; Abe and Charlotte Levitow Papers, Margaret Herrick Library, Academy of Motion Picture Arts and Sciences.

142. Penney, "U.P.A. Animated Art," 13.

143. Ibid.; Knight, "UPA, Magoo & McBoing-Boing."

144. Stephen Bosustow, quoted in "How Does UPA Do It?," 76.

145. Bobe Cannon, quoted in "How Does UPA Do It?," 76.

146. Fisher, "U.P.A. in England."

147. Knight, "U.P.A. Goes Boing-Boing," 112.

148. Knight, "The New Look in Cartooning," 30.

149. Knight, "U.P.A. Goes Boing-Boing," 112.

150. Seldes, "Delight in Seven Minutes," 27.

151. Jules Langsner, "UPA," *Arts and Architecture*, December 1954, 13.

152. Deitch, "Chapter 12: The UPA Experience."

153. Zachary Schwartz, interview by John Canemaker, September 12, 1979.

154. Zachary Schwartz, interview by John Canemaker, September 12, 1979.

155. David Hilberman, interview by John Canemaker, June 16, 1979. Hilberman recalled that the change from the Disney style happened over a period of two or three years:

"Early on Chuck Jones at Warner experimented. He had a fella named McGrath who was quite a design man and had experimented with some design in *The Dover Boys* (1942). Bobe Cannon was involved [as animator] and beginning to reach out for animation style. Screen Gems under Frank Tashlin after the strike brought as many top strike people as possible. So, you had those early design ideas happening before UPA came into being. It was simply that you had designers who had art training who were beginning to push out and feel their oats. People who knew who Picasso was and could recognize a Matisse across the room. And here they were at Disney, Warners, working with this really corny cute staff. They were ready. UPA was the first studio that was run by design people and we were talking to an adult audience, to our peers. Not the family audience, not the kiddies. So given that, the design just came out. The limited animation grew out of our need to economize on budget." Ibid.

156. Ibid.

CHAPTER 3

The Birth of a Style
Modern Art, Graphic Design, Advertising and Animation in the 1940s and 1950s

The suprematists and the constructivists can be understood as investigating the elements of motion which achieves its greatest visual importance in the animated cartoons of the motion picture.

LÁSZLÓ MOHOLY-NAGY[1]

Reductionism and minimalism are leitmotifs in 20th-century visual arts, expressions of a revolution that had started with such Modern movements as cubism, futurism, expressionism and constructivism, among others. Graphic design's relationship with Modern art, from which it took inspiration, began in the 1920s, and these new trends spilled over into UPA animation: UPA animators, layout men and story men learned from the Modern masters and incorporated Modern art and Modern graphic design into their films, thus developing a simplified audiovisual language in animated cartoons.

This chapter focuses on those features that define Modern art, graphic design and advertising illustration and their influence on UPA animated films.[2] This chapter's very end considers animation as a *graphic cinematic medium* that, in the case of UPA animations, was born from the cross-fertilization between all these art forms: painting, graphic art, graphic design and advertising illustration.

3.1 MODERN ART

In painting, it started with cubism, or even before that, with Paul Cézanne and his rendition of nothing else but those elements that can depict the object through "pure spatial properties of color."[3] Cézanne was the first painter to intentionally abandon the vanishing point perspective and use colors for their direct sensory impact. The cubists and post-cubists then followed, continuing this investigation by rendering only the essential of an object, its true *nature*. They aimed at representing an object in its totality through simultaneous views of it: from above, from profile, from three-quarter profile, in frontal elevation and so on. This attempt at rendering simultaneous perspectives had the effect of flattening the objects so that the spectator could see more of them from a normal fixed viewpoint. Moreover, a multitude of details were added since the object was depicted from every possible point of observation.

This attempt departed from the Renaissance linear perspective that allowed the faithful representation of an object as it was seen from a fixed point, which was the "unalterable position of the first spectator, the painter."[4] If Renaissance painters were interested in the complete illusion of naturalism and therefore used the vanishing point perspective to render a representation as faithfully as possible to reality, Modern painters "had discovered that one observation point, in spite of emphasis by distortion, was not sufficient to give the spatial essence of an object."[5] Therefore, they "shifted the point of vision into a kind of cinematographic sequence, and represented the projection of several points of view in one picture."[6]

Designer, painter and art theorist György Kepes explained the limitation of the vanishing point perspective and how Modern artists freed themselves from the imitation of nature:

> Linear perspective gave a unified formulation of space, but it restricted the spatial relationships to one angle of vision, one fixed point of view, that of the spectator, by creating an illusory depth between the objects and an illusory distortion of their actual shape.[7]

To escape the illusion of naturalism, Modern artists looked for simultaneous vistas via superimposition, and from their experimentation emerged the collages of the cubists. Others used amplified perspective or introduced into one picture a number of vanishing points and several horizons. In photography, the camera could avoid the frontal and profile views by rendering views from above, from below, with a bird's-eye view and so on.[8]

This aesthetic revolution led to a new representation of space. To depict simultaneous perspectives meant to provide a new space-time relationship: a new spatial illusion on the picture plane. Far from the Renaissance fixed perspective, this new articulated space suggested movement in space. The new visual arrangement did not emerge from the desire to copy nature; instead, "[Pablo] Picasso's analyses of the pictorial space," for example, "were the outgrowth of his efforts to attain a precise rendering of his experience of objects."[9]

Next, it was the turn of the neoplasticists, the suprematists and the constructivists, who shifted attention toward "the constructive potential of the visual fundamentals."[10] They went further in the investigation started by the cubists by expressing a new conception of pictorial space. They returned to those basic geometric elements, mainly the rectangular shape, and placed emphasis on their relationships within the pictorial space. Colors were used as well to provide new spatial relationships. The effect was "a new kinetic space-time rendering."[11] They completely departed from nature and the object representation to express the relationships between basic visual elements. They constructed a new pictorial space suggested by the juxtaposition of the/those "forces" expressed by different colors. By introducing the diagonal axis instead of the accepted horizontal-vertical axis, they expressed a more dynamic space,[12] and by considering only those essential elements that form the basic visual language, they reduced the image to its elementary structure.

According to Kepes and László Moholy-Nagy, pre-Renaissance painters were not as illustrative as the Renaissance painters and were able to master the relationships of the colors, the space and their positions within certain areas. Discussing the use of color in Renaissance paintings, Kepes was against the fixed illumination unit that led to model by shading. Similar to the fixed perspective, he argued that it rendered an illustrative representation of reality. Instead, children's paintings, art works of primitive tribes, early European paintings and East Asian paintings avoided it. An expression of the Modern tendencies was pointillism, in which color was not used to portray the object by the effects of illumination but became the object itself.[13] Much as in the neoplasticist, suprematist or constructivist paintings, colors were used as the basic visual elements in combination with geometrical shapes. Yet another step in abolishing this sculptural illusion was then made by the abstract expressionists, who considered the canvas as what it is: "the site of pigment laid on a flat surface."[14]

Modern artists defined a new language of vision in which the essence of the subjects portrayed was expressed via a pictorial synthesis. UPA artists were highly influenced by Kepes' book and by the study of the Modern masters of painting such as Picasso, Joan Miró, Paul Klee, Wassily Kandinsky, Raoul Dufy, Salvador Dalí, Henri Matisse, Amedeo Modigliani, Henri Rousseau, the expressionists and the fauves, among others. And, visual references are evident in UPA animated films. Similar to the Modern masters, who, according to Kepes, rejected the vanishing point perspective and its illusion of naturalism, UPA artists rejected the naturalistic illusion of life proposed by Walt Disney in such animated feature films as *Snow White and the Seven Dwarfs* and went back to an animation that had a more expressive line and color, a type of animation in which drawings are overtly drawings and do not aim to reproduce reality as faithfully as possible: "thin outlines stylized reality rather than imitating it."[15] UPA artists were pursuing the childlike and flat simplified design exemplified by some Modern masters and Chinese and Japanese drawings.[16] Therefore, UPA cartoons are as stylized as the animated cartoons of Felix the Cat, created by Otto Messmer and Pat Sullivan, or *Fantasmagorie* by Émile Cohl are.

In her book *Hollywood Flatlands*, Esther Leslie stated:

> The [Disney] feature-lengths, from *Snow White and the Seven Dwarfs* onwards, reinstitute the laws of perspective and gravity, and lead a fight against flatness, while producing traditional dramaturgical characters. They no longer appear to explode the world with the surrealistic and analytical cinematic dynamite of the optical unconscious.[17]

A photo-realistic layout design can have negative repercussions on the movement of the character (its animation), as animator Ülo Pikkov pointed out:

> The poise and movements of the dwarfs in Walt Disney's *Snow White and the Seven Dwarfs* (1937) make them seem much more alive than Snow White, whose appearance was designed to be as lifelike as possible, yet whose behavior and movements still feel rigid.[18]

By detaching themselves from the Disney realism, UPA animated cartoons got closer to the art of the avant-garde films and that elastic world and expressionistic line of the early animated films, since "avant-garde film surfaced out of the extension of problems posed in fine arts: how to represent rhythmic process not just in space and on a flat surface but also in time."[19] Indeed, as will be discussed below, animated cinema has a proper specificity that differentiates it from live-action cinema and connects it with the Modern fine arts:

> It became possible in animation to associate the figures of fine art with the aesthetic of the moving image, which, contrary to live action fiction films and documentaries, escaped the laws of gravity and overcame the anatomical limits of characters.[20]

Much as Modern artists finally considered the canvas a graphic space made by purely graphic forms, UPA artists considered the frame to be a graphic space in which forms and shape could be animated in nonlinear, convoluted time.[21] In *Christopher Crumpet*, for example, a door is animated as it is drawn frame after frame; the time of the narration is not linear but rather the convoluted time of animated cartooning, and the space is made by the few essential lines that define the characters, the door and, when necessary, a few other elements to suggest the passing from the exterior to the interior of the house.

Norman Klein emphasized how much more expressively anarchic the line is in UPA cartoons than in Disney feature films, more similar to the animation of Felix the Cat, in which the cat's tail even becomes a question mark when necessary.[22] Rather than serving a mere slavish imitational purpose, the UPA line is liberated from tracing naturalistic contours and becomes expressive of a new, invented, often humorous reality, much as in a Saul Steinberg cartoon. Leslie went a step further by affirming that:

> When Rodchenko decided in 1919 that the line stands firm against pictorial expressivity, that it has revealed a new conception of the world—truly to construct and not to represent—he could have been describing cartoons' flexible and cavalier attitude to representation.[23]

UPA artists also used color as means of expression differently than Disney artists, who used colors realistically to increase the illusion of depth or to depict as much detail as possible. In *Gerald McBoing Boing*, for example, colors are used as in an expressionist painting to convey Gerald's emotions. After being rejected by his peers, Gerald seeks understanding from his father. Turned away by his father also, Gerald sadly goes upstairs to his room: the interior of the house is sketched in purple, the staircase appears as huge as Gerald's solitude. Then, he runs away from home immersed in a melancholic blue and desperate black. The spectators are brought into Gerald's subjective world, the one that he experiences and feels, much as it happens to someone standing in front of an abstract expressionist painting. The linear naive style also expresses Gerald's childish subjectivity.

By coming back to a more expressive use of lines and colors and by turning to flatness, UPA cartoons embraced Modernism; the essential expressive drawings were "an aesthetic reaffirmation of modernism, now located, in the main, in New York, the newly minted world cultural epicentre, crucible of the new art trends of abstract expressionism, colour field painting and gesture painting."[24] And by embracing Modernism, UPA cartoons got the attention of the highbrow film critics, such as George Seldes and writers for the *Cahiers du Cinéma* or *Graphis International*.

3.2 MODERN GRAPHIC DESIGN

3.2.1 Functional Design

Alfred H. Barr Jr., director of the MoMA in New York City, declared: "The Bauhaus is not dead; it lives and grows through the men who made it, both teachers and students, through their designs, their books, their methods, their principles, their philosophies of art and education."[25] These words were printed in 1938, in the introduction of the catalog that complemented the museum's exhibition, *Bauhaus 1919–1928*.[26]

The Bauhaus had reached America. He added: "It is no wonder then that young Americans began to turn their eyes toward the Bauhaus as the one school in the world where modern problems of design were approached realistically in a modern atmosphere."[27]

The Bauhaus school developed a theory for a new Modern visual expression: it formulated theoretical principles for a universal design style, in which craft is combined with art, form follows function and clarity is given preference over beauty. Together with the De Stijl movement, the Bauhaus "deliberately sought principles which could be applied to all design, marrying art, architecture and industry in a way never before attempted."[28] Its influence on Modern graphic design, especially advertising, is still evident today, as is its impact on Modern and contemporary art. This new visual language also affected typography, posters, book design and photography.

In his catalog introduction Barr wondered, "What have we in America today to learn from the Bauhaus?"[29] He then proceeded to enumerate the Bauhaus principles. The Bauhaus fundaments that follow are relevant to the purposes of this study.

The Bauhaus was a school that combined crafts and fine arts. Its principles went against academic education and were based on the idea that "art is not a 'profession'. There is no essential difference between the artist and the craftsman. The artist is an exalted craftsman."[30] Therefore, manual experience was essential to the student, who had to attend practical workshops as well as listen to "theoretical instruction in the laws of design."[31] This principle was further grounded in the belief that the conventional distinctions between the "fine" and "applied" arts had no meaning. Instead, the Bauhaus school promoted a synthesis that brought together the many arts of painting, sculpture, architecture, graphic art, theater, photography, weaving, typography and so on. The idea was to combine the theoretical curriculum of an arts academy with the practical curriculum of an arts and crafts school, since "no barriers exist between the structural and the decorative arts."[32] Students, therefore, were instructed by two masters, one a craftsman and the other an artist, who worked in close cooperation.

Another principle was rooted in the question: how to reconcile art with an industrialized society. The school also suggested a synthesis between technology and art by including engineering into art, since "the Bauhaus believes the machine to be our modern medium of design and seeks to come to terms with it."[33] Industrial design was one of the outcomes.

A practical knowledge of craftsmanship, together with a theoretical education and a familiarity with science and economics, led to a new type of designer/layout man who adopted the principle of *functional design*, according to which "form should follow function," or in other words, "the shape of an object is defined by the work it has to do."[34] The spirit of functional design was carried over into the fine arts. Graphic art and the fine arts cross-fertilized each other. In fact, graphic design was influenced by Modern movements such as cubism and futurism, dadaism and surrealism, De Stijl, suprematism and constructivism and expressionism to the point that "the evolution of twentieth-century graphic design closely relates to modern painting, poetry, and architecture."[35] Examples can be found in the theory about color and form as formulated by Kandinsky and Klee, who were masters at the Bauhaus, and the new approach to visual composition and geometric abstraction expressed by Piet Mondrian, Theo van Doesburg, Kazimir Malevich, El Lissitzky and Fernand Léger, as well as others.

In the case of the Bauhaus, the contact with van Doesburg, who gave lectures and offered De Stijl courses at the school, marked a shift from an expressionist approach to a neoplasticist one. Van Doesburg organized a conference for dadaists and constructivists in Weimar, Germany, in September 1922. Among the participants were Moholy-Nagy, Lissitzky and Hans Richter.[36] Van Doesburg's De Stijl theory influenced masters such as Kandinsky, Klee and Johannes Itten and affected a group of Hungarian Bauhaus students who wrote the *Kuri Manifesto* (December 1921) in which they advocated for a more "constructive, utilitarian, rational, international"[37] design. As noted by Magdalena Droste, "Many of the projects at the Gropius Bauhaus echoed the practices of avant-garde groups."[38] In fact, starting in 1926, and like other avant-garde movements, the school also founded a Bauhaus magazine.

Bauhaus Modernism was embraced by American Modern design, yet the American approach was more pragmatic and intuitive and less theoretical, despite its European roots. Instead, the U.S. being "an egalitarian society with capitalistic values, limited artistic traditions before World War II, and a diverse ethnic heritage, ... emphasis was placed on the expression of ideas and an open, direct presentation of information."[39] The U.S. soon developed its own modern visual aesthetic and taste.

Paul Rand was "the leading American proponent of functional design."[40] He used signs and symbols and visually engaged the audience by altering and juxtaposing them. He wanted to combine art with a message by playfully using visual contrasts of shape, colors or texture, such as red against green, or organic shapes against geometric shapes, or photographs against flat colors.[41] In a famous 1940 *Direction* magazine cover, he visually expressed the spirit of Christmas by associating it with current events, specifically war. On a white background, he used barbed wire as a gift wrap, while the holiday decorations of red dots suggested drops of blood.

Inspired by the German advertising arts magazine *Gebrauchsgrafik* at an early age, Rand claimed an influence by the Bauhaus in his designing of the *Direction* covers and that he was working "in the spirit of Van Doesburg, Léger, and Picasso."[42] He went even further, saying, "I never claimed that this was great original stuff. ... Other guys in Europe were doing this kind of thing."[43] Still, it was highly innovative for the American art scene, and Rand ultimately defined design as "the integration of form and function for effective communication."[44]

If Rand used complex contrasts that were frequently asymmetrically balanced, Saul Bass often reduced his message to one effective image. His modern simplicity revealed a reductionist approach. In the animated opening of the film, *The Man with a Golden Arm*, designed by Bass, the drug addiction of the protagonist is suggested by a white arm on a completely black frame. The entire film's story is reduced to its essence from the very beginning. The opening titles anticipate the plot and express the idea behind the film. As Bass affirmed:

> In every title I've done, I've been very conscious of the fact that the title has a responsibility to the film, that it is there to enhance the film, to set it up, to give it a beginning—and not to overpower it and preempt it.[45]

According to Bauhaus School founder Walter Gropius, the intention of the Bauhaus was "not to propagate any style, system, dogma, formula, or vogue, but simply to exert a revitalizing influence on design."[46] Therefore, a permanent Bauhaus style did not exist—at least not intentionally. The Bauhaus masters refused to refer to a fixed style as if it could become something dogmatic, much in the way that it would be technically incorrect to talk about a UPA style. Rand and Bass did not have a fixed style, and Bauhaus and UPA should more correctly be considered as having an *attitude*, the former toward design, and the latter toward animation. Design itself is an attitude, according to Moholy-Nagy, who associated the revolutionary spirit of democracy with functional design:

> The attempts of the "Jugendstil" (art nouveau), the rise of socialist doctrines and anti-authoritarian, republican tendencies supported a movement toward true, functional design. This had its climax in the years from 1920 to 1930. Then "functional" design

began to be taken up in this country [America] too, but as an advertising stunt, a kind of novelty rather than a sincere effort to create lasting social values. The moral force behind the original efforts quickly dissipated (perhaps it was never understood), and the designers feel themselves free today to mix the "new" with the old. The present policy of decoration and embellishment and other compromises of design signify most probably a re-emerging reactionary outlook since designing is not a profession but an attitude.[47]

Moholy-Nagy's considerations were published in a book by an American publisher. It was 1956.[48]

Bauhaus masters believed that the design had to be functional to society's needs. Similarly, UPA artists believed that art, particularly the popular art of animation, could address society's needs—as the WPA artists had shown them.

3.2.2 Functional Design in UPA Animated Cartoons

It was UPA animator Herb Klynn who, among others, specified that it was not correct to talk about a "UPA style":

> In everything we do, no matter whether it's a television spot or a feature picture, we follow the creative philosophy that the story is essential. A solid story gives a solid foundation. From there, we develop creatively as each individual situation demands. In recent years there has been more and more talk about a "UPA style." But there is really no such thing as a UPA style, because we are experimenting continually, and we tailor the animation to fit the particular need of whatever we're turning out.[49]

In UPA animated cartoons, the audiovisual style fits the story. This idea sounds like an applied version of the Bauhaus principle that "forms follows function," as Bill Hurtz, designer of *Gerald McBoing Boing*, explained:

> One of the things that evolved at UPA a bit later, when the Columbia shorts got going, one of the things that kept a degree of freshness, was that a group of us who were designing felt that the design came out of the story, came out of the material. That sort

of followed the precepts of modern architecture at the time, "form follows function." It was a marvelous liberating notion that you were not tied to your particular desire for flat shapes or silhouettes or this kind of color or that kind of line divorcement or off-register line and shape, or anything like that. Those only became means, and the style came out of the content of the film.[50]

That every UPA animated short had a unique audiovisual style developed according to the story is validated by the fact that most UPA cartoons are adaptations of published stories. Some of these published stories were also illustrated, as was the case of *Madeline*, by Ludwig Bemelmans, and *The Unicorn in the Garden*, by James Thurber. Other adaptations are *Gerald McBoing Boing*, from a character and story created by Dr. Seuss; *Rooty Toot Toot*, from a popular ballad; *The Emperor's New Clothes*,[51] from a short tale by Hans Christian Andersen; and *The Tell-Tale Heart*, from a story by Edgar Allan Poe.[52]

The illustrated children's book *Madeline* provided strong visual and aural sources of inspiration for UPA artists. Regarding sound, the music was composed by David Raksin, and female voice actor Gladys Holland narrated the story. The narration is extremely faithful to the original text. Only a few, very short comments were added to the film, for example, by Miss Clavel who is a speaking character. As in the original story, she affirms with a very strong French accent, "Something is not right," but a few sequences later in the film, she adds: *"Madeline est malade. Elle est malade!"* Very few urban sound effects complete the animated short.

Similarly, since *Madeline* is an illustrated book, visual references are evident as well. In the opening titles, for example, there is a rectangular shape that reminds the viewer of a book with the title MADELINE and the byline "a story by LUDWIG BEMELMANS."

Another strong reference in the film adaptation is to the paintings of the French artist Raoul Dufy, which helped set the story in a fauvist Paris. As in a Dufy painting, there is an apparently childish linear technique: the objects are addressed by only a few lines, and the colors are used expressively, not realistically, to suggest the idea of the object as, for example, the Eiffel Tower.

Another example is *The Unicorn in the Garden*, adapted from the short story of the same name written by humorist James Thurber and first published in the *New Yorker* on October 31, 1939. The story later appeared as part of the collection *Fables for Our Time & Famous Poems Illustrated*, in 1940. In the UPA animated cartoon, Thurber's drawing style is maintained almost literally, while a dualist palette of colors[53] and limited movements are freely added by UPA artists. Also, here, the viewer can see the allusion to Thurber's book from the opening title, which refers to "A Fable of Our Time…"

Using the simplicity of Modern design to functionally express stories with adult themes became a trademark of UPA animated cartoons. Inspired by a popular ballad, *Rooty Toot Toot* is told in rhythmic jazz; in *The Tell-Tale Heart*, the visual setting is surrealistic in order to express the idea of being in the mind of a crazy murderer; in *Gerald McBoing Boing*, the subjective world of Gerald and his (dis)ability are expressed through sounds, colors and subjective space. Hurtz explained the concept behind the latter by comparing *Gerald McBoing Boing* with the Mr. Magoo cartoons:

> GERALD McBOING BOING became completely different from the Magoos. The Magoos, of course, had a more traditional base, a little more roughhouse realistic drama to them. They took one form, and it was a correct form—for them, because Magoo had certain physical demands, to go in a certain kind of space. Gerald McBoing Boing created his own space, through his own motion. The shapes took form around him, based on what the needs of the story were.[54]

A design functional to the story, was not the only lesson UPA artists took from the Bauhaus masters. According to the Bauhaus principles, the distinction between fine and commercial art had no meaning, since the artist was considered an integral and necessary part of society whose creativity had to serve the purposes of a larger public. The UPA studio was "a unique combination of industry and independent artists."[55] It represented one of the few attempts to combine Hollywood production with something that could be looked at as art. Disney, of course, did the same, although differently. At UPA, the artists were in charge of the creative process, and every voice had the same weight.[56] The animated cartoons were, of course, produced for the market, in this sense being far away from the avant-gardist concept of "art for art's sake," a concept of Romantic and individualist origins. But, at the same time, they were made by artists and "they were meant to be artworks in the first place."[57]

Another essential element of the Bauhaus teaching was economy: "Economy is the sense of thriftiness in labor and material and in the best possible use of them to achieve the effect that is desired. Economy of labor is as important as economy of material."[58] At UPA, something similar was the use of limited animation. Not only did it allow for fewer drawings on a film, as compared to using full animation, but it also led to "constructive thinking,"[59] which ultimately gave birth to new and interesting stylistic solutions, such as the little hops that characterize Gerald's walking in *Gerald McBoing Boing*. In that sequence, the frame consists of an aerial view of the school and the schoolyard: we see a very little Gerald entering the frame from the left and walking fast horizontally toward the school, which is located on the right. The limited animation is used to make Gerald look as if he is walking very quickly and hopping intermittently, thus suggesting his eagerness to go to school.[60]

3.3 GRAPHIC (ANIMATED) MODERNISM

3.3.1 Line Drawing

In 1946, an article penned by John Hubley and Zachary Schwartz, appeared in the *Hollywood Quarterly*. In it, animation is defined as a new language:

> We have found that the medium of animation has become a new language. It is no longer the vaudeville world of pigs and bunnies. Nor it is the mechanical diagram, the photographed charts of the old "training film." It has encompassed the whole field of visual images, including the photograph. We have found that line, shape, color, and symbols in movement can represent the essence of an idea, can express it humorously, with force, with clarity. The method is only dependent upon the idea to be expressed. And a suitable form can be found for any idea.[61]

What Hubley and Schwartz wanted for animation was independence from those animated cartoons that depicted animals chasing each other and from the informational and educational training films that were produced during the war.

This idea of animation is actually closer to *graphic art* than photography because of the emphasis on the graphic essence of the medium: by means of "dynamic *graphic* symbols,"[62] that is, drawings animated frame by frame, "animation represents the *general* idea directly."[63] It creates a "synthesis of reality"[64] as much as the drawings of Modern masters such as Matisse or Picasso are each an "independent and complete statement of an artistic idea."[65]

British art critic and painter Roger Fry explained that:

> The revolution in art which our century has witnessed would, precisely because it has released the artist from this particular bond of representational accuracy, enable the artist to find fuller expression in line drawing than has been the case since the 14th century.[66]

He specifically praised a Matisse drawing that depicts a glass of flowers, in which "certain aspects of a rather complex vision are recorded in a few lines which have the appearance of being, as it were, scribbled with great rapidity and extreme freedom."[67] In another drawing by Matisse, a portrait, Fry noted that "the lines are forced into a scheme of extreme simplicity."[68]

UPA cartoons marked the return to the animated line.[69] A few "scribbled" lines, for example, defined the audience in the theater of *The Magic Fluke*, designed by John Hubley in 1949. A great simplicity in the drawings and the decision to include only those elements that are *essential* to the narration of the stories make UPA cartoons a mixture of Modern art and Modern design. In short, UPA cartoons defined Modern animation.

The praise of the line as a mean of expression in Modern art—and, one might add, in modern animation—is linked to its endless possibilities. Hubley and Schwartz stated: "The significance of the animated film as a means of communication is best realized in terms of its flexibility and scope of expression. It places no limitations upon ideas; the graphic representation grows out of the idea."[70] Fry defined the Modern attempt at linear design similarly:

> It is typical of the kind of synthesis which has become possible to the modern artist who regards no particular facts of nature as sacred, and who is free therefore to aim at the elimination of all but the essential forms, not of description but of plastic construction.[71]

Moreover, he added: "The line is capable of infinite variation, of adapting itself to form at every point of its course."[72] For example, his focus on a Picasso drawing turns to the fact that the lines are not anatomically functional, but they work plastically; they have a plastic validity, thus suggesting a freer rhythm, " subtler, more elastic and more adaptable than any of the rhythms … obtained for some centuries."[73]

A free, plastic line is present also in UPA animated cartoons. In juxtaposition to Disney's animated features, UPA lines are not anatomically functional but do work as caricatures. This is evident in the portraits of *Rooty Toot Toot*'s characters: Frankie, Johnny, Nelly Bly and Frankie's lawyer. We admire, for example, the way Frankie's lawyer walks as a caricature of his ability to deceive people by distracting them, or the way Frankie's anger and surprise in knowing that Johnny is with Nelly Bly is expressed by a dancing jump,[74] or the way Nelly Bly's sensuality is suggested by the affected movement of her arms and legs. The defense attorney, Frankie, Johnny and Nelly Bly and their backgrounds are designed to reflect their motives, their take on events and on the intentions of other characters, their feelings and moods.[75] The characters thus become caricatures of themselves.

Not to be overlooked are the strong connections that animated cinema has with illustration, cartooning and, especially in the U.S., the comic strip. Chronologically speaking, the idea of an essential, not overdetailed but almost sketched design in animation derived from cartooning, not from Modern art. Winsor McCay, perhaps best known as the director of *Gertie the Dinosaur*,[76] one of the earliest American animated films, was primarily a cartoonist whose drawing skills were later applied to animation. In fact, his first animated film, *Little Nemo*,[77] set in motion the adventures of Little Nemo, a character he had illustrated in comic strip form for some time. The film, therefore, is an animated version of the namesake comic strip.

It is more than plausible that UPA artists were influenced not only by Modern artists but also by cartoonists and illustrators active during the 1940s and 1950s whose drawings expressed a graphic Modernism. These included Virgil Partch, Robert Chesley Osborn and Saul Steinberg.

3.3.2 Animation as a Graphic Cinematic Medium

Zachary Schwartz stated very clearly that animation is closer to the graphic arts than it is to live-action cinema:

> The thing we were striving for at UPA; this melding of all of the arts, came about more from our very strong appreciation that it was a graphic art, and not another arm of motion pictures. ... Young people today are thinking more of animated films as personal expressions, the way a graphic artist or a painter thinks of it... Our efforts at UPA really grew out of the fact that our work was closer to the work of the graphic artist than it was to [the work of] the motion picture director.[78]

Early historians of animation struggled to define animated cinema as a medium in its own right, separate from live-action cinema, to which it had often been associated as a genre. The search for a definition of what animation could be went hand in hand with the examination of style. From a European perspective, the conflict came to be played out by two different graphic styles, the *O* and the *I styles*: the first refers to a manner of designing characters that confers roundness (and three-dimensionality) to them and their movements; the second is associated with the idea of angular (and two-dimensional) characters whose movements are stylized.[79] The *O style* is mainly achieved via full animation; and the *I style*, via limited animation. Under these premises, discussions of Disney and UPA would inevitably place them in opposite corners as antagonists.

There is a historical distinction between American and European animated film that is useful in explaining European appreciation for UPA: while animation in the United States derived from editorial cartoons and subsequently from slapstick comedy, in Europe it resulted from experimentation of avant-garde painters and filmmakers.[80] Although the slapstick influence was evident in all American animated cartoons (in the use of devices such as the chase, the gag, the pratfall, and so on), by the time UPA films reached Europe, critic André Martin focused more on the "graphic renovation of UPA,"[81] adding that the animated film no longer could be reduced "to the unique and burlesque blossoming of the satirical American animated cartoon."[82]

Animation needed a technical and aesthetic definition that could help interpret the various and different audiovisual styles; from hand-drawn animation to puppet animation, from Disney cartoons to the abstract films. The heterogeneous examples of animators Jiří Trnka and Norman McLaren and of UPA studio were used in this search for a definition.

The first to attempt a partial definition was Giuseppe Maria Lo Duca, who in 1948 saw in the introduction of cels a relevant progress for the art of animation:

> After Hurd, up to sound and color, the technique of the animated cartoon doesn't have anything new. The cartoon will evolve and transform from a vague process to a fine and lively graphic, the ideal support for irrational movements imposed to the two dimensional characters.[83]

Robert Benayoun offered another turning point in animated cinema studies when he stated that the animated film is an art form independent of live-action cinema. Moreover, he affirmed that after World War II, it was possible to look at animation not only as a cinema made up of gags and caricatures but also as an art form of personal expression owing to the many techniques and styles independently developed, especially in Europe.[84]

According to Denys Chevalier, animation needed to detach itself from the gag as the only film structure to follow. In the attempt to describe what is peculiar of animated films, Chevalier instead focused on the "plastic composition,"[85] considered as the connection between animated cartoon and modern painting. This assumption led him to state: "the animated cartoon … is a plastic expression completely distinct from the live-action cinema."[86] Similarly, Ralph Stephenson pointed out that animators do not work with "bits of reality"[87] as filmmakers do and do not rely on the camera as much as filmmakers do. Instead, "cartoons in telling a story will have to go from one place or one time to another, but these switches are most effectively achieved by conventions of graphic art, not of camera photography."[88] From here, a technical definition was but a small step away: "an animated film is one that is created frame-by-frame."[89]

Moving further in this direction, Gianni Rondolino observed the reasons why the visual look of the images and the rhythmic movements in animation are emphasized. He pointed out that while live-action cinema refers to a tradition that has literature and theater as sources, the animated cinema has among its references cartoons and children's literature as well as paintings, graphic design and visual arts.[90] By the mid-1970s, animated films came to be defined technically.

Regarding the aesthetics of animated films, far from finding a definition of what animation could be aesthetically, given its vast and various techniques (resulting in a vast variety of audiovisual styles), early historians offered interesting interpretations of the different styles, and especially of the "UPA style." Walter Alberti interpreted UPA animated shorts as a reminiscence of Émile Cohl animations: their refined and sophisticated graphic design and almost childish drawings resulted from a "graphic modernism."[91] This "plastic revolution"[92] could only be achieved by departing from the Disney *O style* and by embracing European art.

Being a surrealist, Maurice Benayoun considered Disney films "vulgar" in their attempt at reproducing reality, while he found UPA's, Trnka's and McLaren's animated shorts to be the *quintessence* of animated cinema, once they had finally "discovered the form."[93] Interestingly, Benayoun believed that the UPA rebellion against the Disney style led to a "revolution" in animation, but not one inspired by the stylized and primitive art of the Quakers, the Navajo paintings on sand or the stylization of Grant Wood. Instead, the UPA *I style* was accomplished, he argued, only after European art had been interiorized in the American visual culture. As an art form, animation integrated contemporary art:

> It is impossible to mention the animated films produced after World War II without blatantly asserting the influence exercised on them by people like Klee, De Chirico, Kandinsky, Picabia, Kubin, Mondrian, Ernst, Tanguy, Miró, Fischinger, Calder, Saul Steinberg, Sutherland, Morris Graves, Ben Shahn, Jackson Pollock, Stuart Davis, etc.[94]

This assertion clearly resonates with the idea that an animator is basically a graphic artist or a sculptor and that animated films are closer to graphic arts than to live-action filmmaking, although they are both screened in cinemas and shot on celluloid.[95] Considering the *plasticity* of animated films as its *essence*, the slapstick tradition could only be abandoned: as UPA films refused to tell stories based on violence and gags and used a unique audiovisual style for every film, animations had to follow a different path from that moment on and eventually would be defined differently from an aesthetic perspective: "If the plastic revolution reaches out into all branches of animation, it will be evident in the development of a different narrative, which I will gladly associate with the disappearance of the 'pratfall.'"[96]

Similarly, Chevalier affirmed that UPA did not develop a unique style but as many styles as ideas that were turned into animated films.[97] Martin believed that in UPA's, Trnka's and McLaren's animations lay the aesthetic principles of an adult cinematographic genre that had nothing to do with live-action cinema and that had freed itself from the Disney style that had dominated the industry up to that moment.[98] Stephenson reinforced this opinion, adding that UPA had inaugurated a new global trend:

> Not only did UPA encourage individual and different work. It marked a general change in style which pointed the way to what has become almost a new approach to the cartoon, not only in America but all over the world. The trend can be described as moving away from realism, but towards greater economy and towards a more appropriate use of the cartoon medium.[99]

"A more appropriate use of the cartoon medium" meant simplicity of design [stylized characters and backgrounds], economy [stylized animation] and graphic visual solutions rather than photo-realistic ones. Schwartz summarized:

> We were working with a medium that was not hooked to reality. It was really a graphic medium. It had all of the possibilities of graphic art that could take off and go in any direction at all. It did not have to be tied to what a motion picture camera could shoot.[100]

He clarified by using the way Bobe Cannon animated *A Few Quick Facts about Fear* as an example:

> He [Cannon] had a wonderful natural feeling for shapes, the animation of shapes, and this impressed me very much. Having been schooled at Disney's, where so much of the effort was put into achieving this roundness of form—even though everything was drawn in line, the effort to give things this kind of volume … was something that everybody really struggled for, and it was a thing that Don [Graham] taught, in drawing. I began to get a glimpse of something, here and there, of a kind of acting, which was possible in a graphic way that was not a kind of exaggeration

or a caricature of reality, but took its life from pure design elements and became characterization and personality and acting—expression of ideas in acting—greatly from the design elements, the graphic elements. Bobe had a real feeling for this.[101]

A brilliant example is from *Christopher Crumpet*, directed by Cannon. It is a sequence in which Billswater, a colleague of Christopher Crumpet's father, is leaving Christopher's house: here, the spectator sees the action of leave-taking as "traced" on frames from the beginning until the end. So, instead of just seeing Billswater walking away, as in classical animation, the poses that compose Billswater's leaving are kept frame after frame, thus leaving a *trace* of them on the frames as the animation unfolds. The innovation lies in the final visual effect of the movements being "traced" on the sequence's frames. This highly graphic solution may have inspired Norman McLaren's *Pas de Deux*.[102] Before this sequence, there is another one in which the frame is split in two parts suggesting the passing of time/space: from the exterior to the interior, from an external reality to Christopher's world. This is another reminder of the graphic nature of the animated cartoon medium.

In *Little Boy with a Big Horn*, also directed by Cannon, there is another animated graphic solution that traces the movements of the father after the son has played his big, noisy horn. The father is animated while jumping up in the air and bouncing off the ground; his figure is horizontally multiplied as to suggest his multiple movements and the reverberation of the sounds emitted by the horn.

3.4 CROSS-FERTILIZATION BETWEEN ANIMATION, MODERN ART AND GRAPHIC DESIGN

3.4.1 Advertising Art

Even before the Bauhaus exhibit of 1938, the Museum of Modern Art in New York City was promoting the idea that advertising posters might be appreciated as art. Alfred Barr, director of the new museum, tried to "incorporate the poster into a new canon of modern art"[103] and, therefore, wanted to improve poster design. Within this context, the museum organized a competition for high school students in 1933 and held exhibitions of advertising posters by the Ukrainian-French artist and designer Cassandre, the pseudonym of Adolphe Jean-Marie Mouron, in 1936 and the American artist and designer Edward McKnight Kauffer in 1937.[104]

Since the 1920s attempts were made by art directors to link advertising with Modern art, experimenting with new styles and techniques derived from European avant-garde movements like cubism and futurism. Those advertisers who embraced Modern art favored:

> [T]he sweeping diagonal line and asymmetrical "off-center layout," ... a sense of unresolved tension ... and "expressive distortion," rejection of more traditional mimetic or academic conventions of representation in favor of images that connoted subjective experience and a "feeling" for the product.[105]

But, it was thanks to two figures, in particular, that Modern art definitively entered the advertising world. The first is Charles Coiner, art director at N. W. Ayer and Sons from 1929 to 1964, who, during the 1930s and 1940s, commissioned paintings and drawings from such artists as Picasso, Man Ray, Moholy-Nagy, Dalí, Dufy, Georges Rouault, Herbert Bayer and Cassandre, among others. Famous is the Hawaiian Dole Pineapple campaign for which caricaturist Miguel Covarrubias, poster designer Cassandre and painter Georgia O'Keeffe were hired. The second is Walter Paepcke of the Container Corporation of America (CCA), who hired Coiner for some campaigns, appointed Egbert Jacobson as art director of the CCA and became a close friend of Moholy-Nagy. With Jacobson at the artistic helm, the Bauhaus and constructivist aesthetics took root in American advertising: "art literally absorbed advertising; the two became one."[106]

The CCA produced paperboard packaging for clients like Campbell's Soup and Hunt's Foods. Elizabeth Nitze Paepcke, an influential figure on her husband Walter, persuaded him to associate CCA's image with design excellence. This meant: "modernism, especially the montage, the bold type, the bright color, and the simplified asymmetrical composition pioneered by French, Swiss and German designers (especially by members of the German Bauhaus) and seen in such European journals as *Graphis* and *Gebrauchsgraphik*."[107] The first CCA campaign was meant to reinvigorate CCA's image. It started in 1937 and included 12 posters designed by Cassandre, and other ads created by Jean Carlu, Bayer and Kepes, among others. These posters were highly innovative for the American advertising industry and laid bare the gap between Americans and avant-garde Europeans:

The CCA images were nonanecdotal; they did not, strictly speaking, illustrate. Meanings were intended to be suggestive, not definitive. Symbolic association between images and text, between design, paperboard, and the Container Corporation, were metaphorical, poetic, and comparatively subtle. Several of these artists favored montage, a device that did not employ clear, sequential narratives. Each advertisement, as a whole, privileged art, complexity, autheticity, and class, contrasting sharply with the hysterical, hard-sell, direct approach seen in the comic book and photographic advertisements pitched to the less affluent and educated.[108]

Other series of CCA advertisements followed in which less priority was given to the aesthetics of German and Russian Modern design and more to Modern paintings, depending on the artists selected for each campaign. The CCA Modernist aesthetic endeavor was publicly validated in 1945 with the exhibition entitled *Modern Art in Advertising, An Exhibition of Designs for Container Corporation of America*, held at the Art Institute of Chicago.[109]

According to Kepes, advertising art, once liberated from the burdens of tradition, could freely experiment with photomontage: "The idea of dissecting and rearranging photographic elements and combining them with drawings was carried further in the experimental forms of photomontage."[110] Also for Moholy-Nagy, applied photography was an essential tool for advertising: "The two new resources for poster art are: (1) photography, which offers us a broad and powerful means of communication; (2) emphatic contrasts and variations in typographical layout, including the bolder use of color."[111] The advertising poster thus became a dynamic space in which the spectator played a role in reading the meaning and interpreting the suggestions evoked:

> To put an advertising message through effectively, the most heterogeneous elements—verbal message, drawing, photography and abstract shapes—were employed. This variety of meaningful signs and symbols could only be integrated by a dynamic meaning organization. Visual advertising, however, has the eye as its customer. To satisfy this customer, it must be vital as a visual experience and it must offer comfort to the eye.[112]

Art joined advertising. But advertising being a commercial art, its interest in (Modern) art must be explained especially by economic considerations:

> [F]irst, a self-conscious concern with developing art in the interests of selling, thereby exploiting the possibilities of commercial design; second, a sense that modernism, still new to Americans in the 1920s, formed a visual vocabulary offering special opportunities to the business corporation; and third, a belief that the corporation could become a major patron, stimulating creativity even while it used art to enhance salesmanship, public relations, and employee efficiency.[113]

Similarly, in the 1940s and 1950s, American animation industry, animation was used as a commercial art (animated TV commercials), in addition to its use as an entertainment product (theatrical releases). At UPA, the same approach was applied whether the artists were dealing with a theatrical short or a commercial spot: the style was functional to the story.[114] As Bobe Cannon declared, "the story is just as important in the TV spot as it is in any other form of expression."[115] Furthermore, in television commercials, as in any type of advertising, one could add that the style was functional to the product.

As already established, UPA artists felt the necessity to distance themselves from the Disney tradition and incorporate into their animations Modern graphic design and Modern art. It is neither possible to comprehensively analyze UPA TV commercials due to a lack of availability of the films, nor is it the intention of this book to consider TV commercials in the analysis of UPA films. By watching a popular UPA commercial such as the one made for Piels Beer, the viewer could suppose that there was also cross-fertilization between UPA TV commercial design and Modernism by identifying those features that characterize the studio's approach to animation: reductionism and minimalism within the "less is more" tradition. This particular ad also suggests that the success of UPA TV spots was probably owing to their ability to make people laugh while they advertised. As Cannon put it, "our TV commercials combine entertainment with information."[116]

UPA TV commercials were mostly produced in the New York studio.[117] Several of them received awards from the Art Directors Clubs of New York, Los Angeles and Chicago. Some of the products advertised for different clients were Lucky Strike and Camel cigarettes, Coca-Cola, Motorola, Jell-O Instant Pudding and Piel Brothers Beer.[118] As of 1955, UPA had made TV commercials for 77 different products.[119] Information on the workflow of UPA animated TV commercials were summarized by UPA artists in a drawing (see Figure 3.1).

3.4.2 Primitivism and Children's Art

Kepes suggested the superiority of Modern art to Renaissance art lay in the possibility with the former of reproducing reality according to multiple perspectives. European Modern artists, indeed, sought to express the spatial essence of an object by adopting multiple perspectives and by showing the essential part of it in combination, similar to what had been attempted in primitive art.[120] It was similar not only to primitive art in these goals, however, but also to Chinese and Japanese paintings and drawings made by children, in which lines "open up the space instead of closing it" and "the picture space … [is] a medium of experience,"[121] Kepes noted. Rand also addressed the subject, in 1947:

> Contemporary as it may seem, the concept of simultaneity takes us back to ancient China. The Chinese, aware of the need for a means of expressing in one picture simultaneous actions or multiple events, devised a form of oblique projection. They also devised a means of showing one object behind, above, or below another, by free disposition of elements in a composition, completely disregarding the illusions of visual perspective. This was essentially a method of formalizing or "neutralizing" the object. It was a transformation resulting in formal arrangements rather than conventional illustration.[122]

Asian paintings, especially those coming from Japan, had already played an important role in the initial phase of the Modern movement. In the last decade of the 19th century, European artists were influenced especially by Kitagawa Utamaro and Katsushika Hokusai. In Japanese paintings, "subjects often became emblematic symbols, reduced to graphic interpretations conveying their essence"[123] by means of calligraphic line drawings,

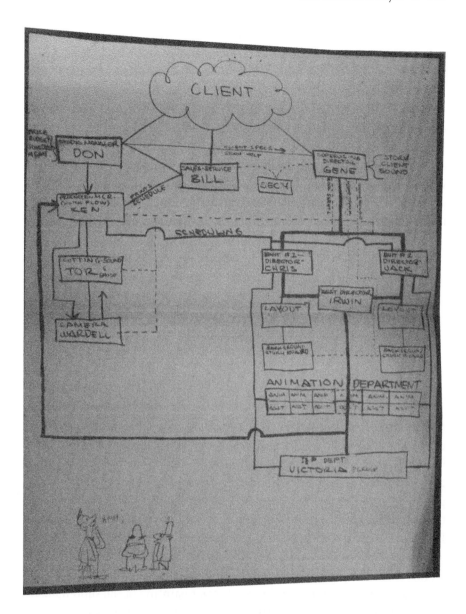

FIGURE 3.1 Flow Chart of the UPA Creative Process for Animated TV Commercials, author unknown. Reprinted with permission from Tee Bosustow (*Steve Bosustow's UPA collection, in the care of his son, Tee Bosustow*).

abstraction and simplification of natural appearances, unconventional use of flat colors, silhouettes, bold black shapes and decorative patterns.

In the U.S., primitive art was highly regarded during the 1930s and 1940s.[124] The first study that established a connection between primitive art and Modern art was written by Robert J. Goldwater in 1938 under the title *Primitivism in Modern Painting*. In it, Goldwater outlined the aesthetic features of 20th-century primitivism in relation to Modern paintings. He especially focused on the influence on and assimilation of "primitive" works of art by different Modern artists and artistic movements. He also pointed out the great variety of interests in primitive works of art and differing interpretations by Modern artists of what was "primitive":

> For Gauguin they were the Egyptian, the Indian, and the Polynesian alike; for the *fauves* the "curious" phases of African sculpture and the *images d'Epinal*; for the *Brücke* and the *Blaue Reiter* the sculpture of the exotic peoples generally, the drawings of children and their own provincial folk art; while for Picasso primitive meant Ivory Coast sculpture and the painting of Henri Rousseau.[125]

There was a common denominator, however: the primitiveness lay in the quality of simplicity that was attributed to these different works of art by those Modern artists that Goldwater had considered. After specifying that primitivism was not an artistic movement per se but rather grew from the general social and cultural setting of Modern art to the point of pervading many Modern paintings, he then identified different types of primitivism, thus outlining a history of primitivist evolution: a Romantic primitivism (Gauguin and the Pont-Aven school, the fauves), an emotional primitivism (Die Brücke and Der Blaue Reiter), an intellectual primitivism (Picasso with the direct influence of primitive sculpture and primitive tendencies in the abstract painting of the suprematists, the purists and the neoplasticists), and a primitivism of the subconscious (the Modern primitives such as Henri Rousseau, Louis Vivin and Camille Bombois; those artists who expressed a "child cult," such as Paul Klee; and dadaists and surrealists).

Modern artists achieved their own rendering of the primitive by "primitivizing" their pictorial formal elements according to their theoretical principles and intentions. In spite of the evident differences in styles, there are common traits among Modern paintings that can be ascribed to the assimilation of stylistic features expressed by primitive works of art: a tendency to abstraction, a pictorial simplification, a longing return to simplicity and immediacy and a reductionist effect. So, for example, the fauves used broad, unfinished lines, large areas of undifferentiated color, pure colors and a lack of perspective to render "a symbolic scene which is to work upon the beholder by its symbolic qualities, by the suggestion of things outside itself, rather than a scene complete in itself and external to the spectator."[126] Picasso, on the other hand, after being exposed to sculptures from the Ivory Coast, offered a personal interpretation of them by geometrizing and stylizing the original contours of the sculpted figures. Amedeo Modigliani was also influenced by African sculpture, but he was able to synthesize formal elements derived from African art (the long oval of the heads and the long nose, for example) and expand them into a personal visual style (the long oval of the heads, long necks, flat long noses and small mouths).[127]

Modern artists also looked to the art of the child for inspiration. Among them were, for example, Klee, Dufy, and Marc Chagall. In Klee's compositions, there is often a naive look that takes inspiration from children's and primitive art and at the same time synthesizes all Modern movements. In his *Pedagogical Sketchbook*, published in 1925 as a Bauhaus student manual, he invited students to approach art intuitively and to use external features such as eyes, legs, roofs, sails and stars as means for reaching a spiritual reality. Sibyl Moholy-Nagy wrote in the introduction to Klee's book: "Just as a magician performs the miraculous with objects of utter familiarity, such as cards, handkerchiefs, coins, rabbits, so Paul Klee uses the familiar object in unfamiliar relationships to materialize the unknown."[128] Klee often rendered distortions of the human forms as if they were child-drawn figures. He associated personal meanings to them, leaving the spectator with the task of grasping them by means of their being common symbols.

UPA artists, especially Bobe Cannon, often favored a naive look for the pictures that would reflect children's sensibility, although achieving the final "childish" visual effects required a conscious effort. *Gerald McBoing Boing, Madeline* and *Christopher Crumpet* are stories about children. The visual styles of these animated cartoons are intentionally rendered as if the drawings were made by children: it is like experiencing the world through the eyes of Gerald, Madeline or Christopher. Moreover, UPA animated cartoons express some of primitivism's aesthetic features expressed in Modern art, such as the use of broad areas of color applied flatly and in strong contrast with each other, especially in the backgrounds, and the lack of perspective (which, in turn, became the adoption of multiple perspectives, as will be discussed in Chapter 4).

Willie the Kid, written by T. (Thornton) Hee and Cannon, is the story of a group of children playing cowboys in suburban America. The film was designed by Hee and directed by Cannon. As we witness the adventures of Willie and his little friend Roger, we enter their fantasy world by means of visual transformation: the green backyard where his father is talking with the neighbor becomes an ocher desert with canyons and cacti. According to the children's imagination, even the legs of Willie's father metamorphose into a cactus, dogs become horses and the garage becomes the bank. We are carried into Willie's world. For example, when he needs help from his mother to read a map, she appears among the rocks, which are then revealed to be the house window from which she is leaning out. The two worlds—the real one and the fantasy one—metamorphose one into the other as proof that we are experiencing Willie's imaginary play.

The Family Circus[129] is an ordinary story about a jealous daughter who feels neglected by her father who showers attention on her baby brother. Since Patsy's father is often busy caring for the child, Patsy plays pranks on him. Annoyed by the situation, he scolds her until a daydreaming sequence reveals to him the reasons for her behavior. In this sequence, the father and Patsy take part in a circus. They are drawn and animated in a very naive visual style, as if the characters and the backgrounds were drawn by children, not skillful artists. The animation is very simple as well.

Baby Boogie is drawn and animated entirely in a childish, naive style. The film revolves around a little girl who wants to find out "where babies come from." Backgrounds are made of areas of colors, and the characters are stylized as if they were sketched by a child. Despite this being an attempt to render visually the manner in which the little girl perceives and interprets the world, the visual designs are so childish as to look simplistic.

A child's sensibility became a means of expression also in John and Faith Elliott Hubley's films. In them, however, the metamorphosis is taken a step further, as the married couple used the actual recorded voice of their son and daughters as soundtracks for their films.

In UPA films, an opening up of the space meant a release from the Disneyesque mimetic approach and the adoption of multiple perspectives.

As in *Willie the Kid*, the spectator is thereby able to experience two different realities. *Gerald McBoing Boing* and the way the characters are animated in relation to the space is another example. Gerald and his parents appear to be floating in a flat, two-dimensional background, and poses are kept for seconds—approximately two seconds, for example, when Gerald's father jumps in the air at the beginning of the film as a way to emphasize psychological reactions or subtleties. In another example, when the doctor hangs his hat on Gerald's father's leg, the pose of the leg is kept for a few seconds. This animation gains meaning through its relationship with other elements, such as the way the doctor keeps on walking while the father is still. Similarly, when Gerald's mother, father and the doctor jump in the air from the chair, after Gerald emits loud noises, their position is held; the trio is up in the air for some seconds, while Gerald is still.

3.4.3 Some Examples of Cross-Fertilization

Modern animation, graphic design, advertising posters and painting mutually influenced one another. Examples of cross-fertilization between these arts not only illustrate their impacts on each other; often they also help illustrate the renown of the UPA studio and the high regard in which artists of other fields held UPA during the 1950s.

One of the earliest examples was Paul Rand's cover for the fall 1945 issue of *Direction*, which he dedicated to *Brotherhood of Man* (Figure 3.2). Inside the issue, an article about the artists creators stated:

> Watch for their "neon-outline" technique which is far more original than anything Disney has been doing lately, and a far cry from the new mixture of animated cartoon and Technicolor photography with which Disney ran amok in *Three Caballeros*, and which these producers—and DIRECTION—consider highly unfunctional.[130]

Other examples of cross-fertilization between graphic design and animation are a *Harper's Bazaar* publicity article that discusses *Rooty Toot Toot* before its theatrical release and an article on *Gerald McBoing Boing* in *Life* magazine.

Continuing with Rand, the 1946 cover of *Jazzways* is yet another example of cross-genre exchanges with UPA. Rand's dynamic composition for the jazz magazine is made of contrast of bright colors through the collage

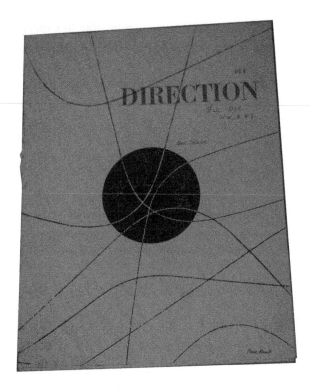

FIGURE 3.2 Paul Rand, Magazine Cover of *Direction*, Fall 1945. Reprinted with permission from Tee Bosustow (*Steve Bosustow's UPA collection, in the care of his son, Tee Bosustow*).

technique. A similar technique based on the use of animated cutouts and a similar use of contrasting bright color are at the base of *The Oompahs*,[131] a UPA animated short released in 1952 about a generational conflict. Orwell, a little horn, belongs to a family of musical instruments, the Oompahs; the father is a tuba and the mother is a mellophone. His father would like him to learn classical music, while Orwell enjoys improvising jazz music with his friends of South Tempo Street.

In the 1954 short *Fudget's Budget*, Mr. and Mrs. Budget are animated first as lines moving on a sheet of graph paper; then they metamorphose into the caricature figures of the family members. White lines on a black background are also animated in the opening titles of *The Man with the Golden Arm* (1955). It is possible that the latter may have found inspiration in the UPA animated short.

Saul Steinberg, whose drawings were certainly a source of inspiration for *Brotherhood of Man*, directly collaborated with UPA on a one-minute commercial for Jell-O Instant Pudding in 1954. The TV spot, commissioned by Young & Rubicam ad agency, was made at the UPA New York studio. It was designed by Saul Steinberg and directed by Gene Deitch.[132]

In a *Gerald McBoing Boing* sequence, the boy is running toward an approaching train in an attempt to jump on it. The train is huge compared to Gerald, and for a few seconds the spectator only sees its massive wheels on the right side of the frame. A similar graphic composition is present in the 1952 advertising poster *The Most Important Wheels*, designed by Joseph Binder. The poster conveys the idea of movement by means of converging lines toward a point placed outside of the image, on the right side of it. As *Gerald McBoing Boing* was released on January 25, 1951, a year before the poster was designed, it is possible to assume a visual influence of the film on the poster design, or, at least, a common vision of intents.

UPA artists redesigned animation according to the same principle of simplicity that was at the base of Modern art and Modern graphic design. Through cross-fertilization and in-house inspiration and experimentation, they molded a simplified audiovisual language that could be applied to animated film. Their preference for flat, simplified layouts and stylized animation made of expressive colors and "anarchic" lines were the result of a reappraisal of early animation and the borrowing of Modern aesthetic features already expressed in other art forms. In the process, UPA artists raised the animated cartoon medium to the level of art within a market-oriented context, and in doing so, competed with Walt Disney productions.

How UPA production incorporated Modern art and graphic design into the animations and how this resulted in highly original audiovisual styles will be the focus of Chapter 4. This analysis will help in understanding how UPA laid the foundations for a Modern animation.

ENDNOTES

1. László Moholy-Nagy, *Vision in Motion* (Chicago, IL: Paul Theobald and Company, 1956), 269.
2. Emphasis is put on the analysis of a modern visual language provided by György Kepes in his book *Language of Vision*, since it was a source of inspiration for UPA artists.
3. László Moholy-Nagy, *The New Vision and Abstract of an Artist*, 4th ed. (New York, NY: Wittenborn Schultz, 1949), 156.

4. Ibid., 35.
5. Kepes, *Language of Vision*, 95.
6. Ibid.
7. Ibid., 87.
8. Ibid.
9. Moholy-Nagy, *The New Vision and Abstract of an Artist*, 36.
10. Moholy-Nagy, *Vision in Motion*, 114.
11. Ibid., 38.
12. Kepes, *Language of Vision*.
13. Colors were used as means of expressions also by Cézanne, the fauves, the postimpressionists like the pointillists, and the expressionists. Ibid.
14. Leslie, *Hollywood Flatlands*, 297.
15. Ibid., 291.
16. The stylized look of UPA animated cartoons with thin expressive lines, almost empty backgrounds and flat characters resonates with the idea of simplicity (and therefore beauty, according to Japanese aesthetic canons) evoked by Noh theater. This idea is masterfully expressed by director Akira Kurosawa in *Throne of Blood* (1957; DVD, New York, NY: The Criterion Collection, 2003), a contemporary film adaptation of William Shakespeare's *Macbeth*. The story is set in medieval Japan during a historical period of intense wars between different clans, and revolves around the ambition of samurai Washizu, incited by his evil wife, Asaji.

To express the complex psychology of the characters and their intimate desires, Kurosawa favors a visual language with features intentionally borrowed from Noh theater: the stylized performances of the actors; references to the mask, especially Asaji's facial expressions and even the makeup; the bare sets and dramatic use of the cinematic space/theatrical stage. But one example is the confrontational sequence in which Asaji instigates Washizu to kill His Lordship, a scene that is visually rendered via stylized movements of the couple: first, Washizu walks diagonally toward his wife who is sitting on the ground; then he makes a circular walk around his throne, while his wife explains that she firmly believes in the ghost woman's prophecy, and finally, while the murder is being executed, Asaji makes a circular stylized dance around herself, in front of the wall where the traitor's blood has collected. The visuals of the film can be likened to a Japanese painting or an animated film's background upon which abstract elements are moved in relationship to one another: the circle, the line and the diagonal are visually expressed by the stylized movements of the actors and substitute the verbal language.

The idea of simplicity is also visually evoked by the interplay between emptiness and full spaces, which clearly makes reference to Japanese ink drawings and folding screen paintings: the settings consist of few natural elements, such as the trees and the wind, the forest and the fog. They are cinematographically composed so that often a large part of the picture is unfilled, and thus the emptiness plays an active compositional role. Simplicity is also aurally evoked by the interplay of silence and music, which stresses topical moments of the drama.

Kurosawa dialogues with Western theater by keeping the basic plot but eliminating the verbal mannerism, turning back instead to the essential minimalism of Noh theater. In this regard, he may have also been influenced by UPA simplicity, much as Sergei Eisenstein acknowledged he was inspired by Walt Disney animated cartoons, especially by the "poetry's principle of transformation [that] works comically in Disney, given as a literal metamorphosis" (Sergei Eisenstein, *Eisenstein on Disney*, 40).

On the influence of Noh theater on Kurosawa's film: Minae Yamamoto Savas, "The Art of Japanese Noh Theatre in Akira Kurosawa's *Throne of Blood*," *Bridgewater Review* 30, no. 2 (2011): 19–23. http://vc.bridgew.edu/cgi/viewcontent.cgi?article=1279&context=br_rev, accessed June 16, 2016. On the interplay of silence and sound: Lei Jin, "Silence and Sound in Kurosawa's *Throne of Blood*," *CLCWeb: Comparative Literature and Culture* 6, no. 1 (2004). http://docs.lib.purdue.edu/cgi/viewcontent.cgi?article=1206&context=clcweb, accessed June 16, 2016.

17. Leslie, *Hollywood Flatlands*, 121.

18. Ülo Pikkov, *Animasophy: Theoretical Writings on the Animated Film* (Tallinn, EE: Estonian Academy of Arts, 2010), 82.

19 Leslie, *Hollywood Flatlands*, 37.

20. Pikkov, *Animasophy: Theoretical Writings on the Animated Film*, 94.

21. Animator Ülo Pikkov provides a metaphor for describing time in animation. It stresses the idea of non-linearity and multiple (sound) perspectives: "Time in the animated film resembles a cubist painting, the image of which has been first divided into odd, manipulated pieces and then reassembled as a new totality." Ibid., 49.

22. Klein, *Seven Minutes: The Life and Death of the American Animated Cartoon*.

23. Leslie, *Hollywood Flatlands*, 19.

24. Ibid., 294.

25. The Museum of Modern Art, New York, "Bauhaus 1919–1928," ed. Walter Gropius, Herbert Bayer and Ise Gropius (New York, NY: 1938), 5.

26. Before 1938 small exhibitions on the Bauhaus were held in the U.S., as asserted in the same catalog:
"the bauhaus painters, especially feininger, klee and kandinsky, participated in many american exhibitions during the 1920's, notably those organized by the *société anonyme* of new york, under the direction of miss katherine dreier, and the *blue four* exhibitions arranged in new york and on the west coast by mrs. galka scheyer. schlemmer and others of the bauhaus theater exhibited at the international theater exhibition, new york, 1926. the bauhaus was represented in the machine age exhibition, new york, 1927, and in an exhibition of modern printers and typography, wellesley college, 1928. small exhibitions entirely devoted to the bauhaus were given by the harvard society for contemporary art, under the direction of lincoln kirstein, cambridge, december, 1930 – january 1931; at the john becker gallery,

new york, january–february 1931; and at the arts club of chicago, march, 1931" (printed without capital letters in the original text, according to the Bauhaus typographical practice introduced in 1925). Ibid., 205.

27. Ibid.
28. Bartram, *Bauhaus Modernism and the Illustrated Book*, 12.
29. The Museum of Modern Art, "Bauhaus 1919–1928," 6.
30. Ibid., 16.
31. Ibid., 22.
32. Ibid., 23.
33. Ibid., 25.
34. Moholy-Nagy, *Vision in Motion*, 33.
35. Meggs, *Meggs' History of Graphic Design*, 248.
36. Magdalena Droste, *Bauhaus* (Cologne, DE: Taschen, 2014).
37. Ibid, 33.
38. Ibid., 60.
39. Meggs, *Meggs' History of Graphic Design*, 374.
40. Heller, *Design Literacy: Understanding Graphic Design*, 53.
41. Meggs, *Meggs' History of Graphic Design*.
42. Paul Rand, quoted in Heller, *Design Literacy: Understanding Graphic Design*, 54. See also Chapter 1.
43. Ibid.
44. Meggs, *Meggs' History of Graphic Design*, 374.
45. Saul Bass, quoted in Heller, *Design Literacy: Understanding Graphic Design*, 159.
46. Walter Gropius, quoted in Heller, *Design Literacy: Understanding Graphic Design*, 110.
47. Moholy-Nagy, *Vision in Motion*, 49.
48. His thoughts were written much earlier and published posthumously; Moholy-Nagy died of leukemia in 1946.
49. "Creativity Basic," 47.
50. Bill Hurtz, quoted in Schwartz, "Notes from Zack Schwartz Appearance at UCLA," 5.
51. *The Emperor's New Clothes*, directed by Ted Parmelee (1953; DVD, *UPA: The Jolly Frolics Collection*, Culver City, CA: Sony Pictures Home Entertainment, 2012).
52. For a detailed analysis of some of these animated films, see Chapter 4, Section 2.2.
53. For more information and a detailed analysis of the film, see Chapter 4, Section 2.2.3.
54. Bill Hurtz, quoted in Schwartz, "Notes from Zack Schwartz Appearance at UCLA," 5.
55. Jules Engel, in Moritz, "UPA, Reminiscing 30 Years Later," 15.
56. For more information, see Chapter 2, Section 4.2.
57. Jules Engel, in Moritz, "UPA, Reminiscing 30 Years Later," 15.
58. The Museum of Modern Art, "Bauhaus 1919–1928," 116.
59. Ibid.

60. On this aesthetic visual solution, see also Chapter 4, Section 2.2.1.
61. John Hubley and Zachary Schwartz, "Animation Learns a New Language," *Hollywood Quarterly* 1, no. 4 (1946): 363. www.jstor.org /stable/1209495?seq=1#page_scan_tab_contents, accessed November 4, 2012.
62. Ibid., 362.
63. Ibid.
64. Ibid.
65. Roger Edward Fry, "Line as a Means of Expression in Modern Art," *Burlington Magazine for Connoisseurs* 33, no. 189 (1918): 202. www.jstor .org/stable/860829?Search=yes&resultItemClick=true&searchText=Line &searchText=as&searchText=a&searchText=Means&searchText=of&sea rchText=Expression&searchUri=%2Faction%2FdoBasicSearch%3FQuer y%3DLine%2Bas%2Ba%2BMeans%2Bof%2BExpression%26amp%3Bacc %3Doff%26amp%3Bwc%3Don%26amp%3Bfc%3Doff%26amp%3Bgroup %3Dnone&seq=1#page_scan_tab_contents, accessed February 17, 2015.
66. Ibid.
67. Ibid.
68. Ibid.
69. Klein, *Seven Minutes: The Life and Death of the American Animated Cartoon.*
70. Hubley and Schwartz, "Animation Learns a New Language," 362.
71. Fry, "Line as a Means of Expression in Modern Art," 206.
72. Ibid.
73. Ibid.
74. To choreograph the entire film, UPA hired dancer Olga Lunick to provide examples of movements to be studied by John Hubley and the artists working on the film. In this example, it is evident the influence of Lunick's ballet movements as a reference source. For more information, see: Abraham, *When Magoo Flew: The Rise and Fall of Animation Studio UPA.*
75. For more information and a detailed analysis of the film, see Chapter 4, Section 2.2.2.
76. *Gertie the Dinosaur*, directed by Winsor McCay (1914; New York, NY: Vitagraph Studios). www.youtube.com/watch?v=lmVra1mW7LU, accessed September 25, 2015.
77. *Little Nemo*, directed by Winsor McCay (1911; New York, NY: Vitagraph Studios). www.youtube.com/watch?v=kcSp2ej2S00, accessed September 25, 2015.
78. Schwartz, "Notes from Zack Schwartz Appearance at UCLA," 5.
79. For more information, see Chevalier, *J'aime le Dessin Animé.*
80. Alberti, *Il Cinema di Animazione 1832–1956.*
81. Clarens, *André Martin 1925–1994. Écrits Sur L'animation*, vol. I, 103. "Renouvellement graphique de l'UPA" (translated by author).
82. André Martin, quoted in Benayoun, *Le Dessin Animé après Walt Disney*, 171. "À la seule et burlesque floraison du dessin animé caricatural américain" (translated by author).

83. Giuseppe Maria Lo Duca, *Le Dessin Animé: Histoire, Esthétique, Technique* (Paris, FR: Prisma, 1948), 25–26.
"Après Hurd, jusqu'au son et jusqu'à la couleur, la technique du dessin animé n'est plus rien de nouveau. Le dessin évolua et, d'un vague schéma, il passa à une graphie déliée, agile, support idéal des mouvements irrationnels imposes aux personnages à deux dimensions" (translated by author).

84. Benayoun, *Le Dessin Animé après Walt Disney.*

85. Chevalier, *J'aime le Dessin Animé,* 12. "Formulation plastique" (translated by author).

86. Ibid., 26. "Le dessin animé … est un expression plastique absolument distincte du cinéma" (translated by author).

87. Stephenson, *Animation in the Cinema,* 10.

88. Ibid.

89. Ibid., 13.

90. Gianni Rondolino, *Storia del Cinema D'animazione,* 2nd ed. (Turin, IT: UTET, 2003).

91. Alberti, *Il Cinema di Animazione 1832–1956,* 200. "Modernismo grafico" (translated by author).

92. Benayoun, *Le Dessin Animé après Walt Disney,* 17. "Révolution plastique" (translated by author).

93. Ibid. "Le cartoon découvrait le forme" (translated by author).

94. Ibid., 7.
"Il est impossible de mentionner les dessins animés de cet après-guerre sans constater de criante manière l'influence exercée sur eux par des gens comme Klee, De Chirico, Kandinsky, Picabia, Kubin, Mondrian, Ernst, Tanguy, Miró, Fischinger, Calder, Saul Steinberg, Sutherland, Morris Graves, Ben Shahn, Jackson Pollock, Stuart Davis, etc" (translated by author).

95. Stephenson, *Animation in the Cinema.*

96. Benayoun, Le Dessin Animé après Walt Disney, 38. "Si la révolution plastique s'étend à toutes branches de l'animation, il faudra de toute évidence que se développe une forme différente de récit, que je situerais volontiers vers l'absence de 'chute'" (translated by author). In this context, chute (fall) refers to the slapstick comedic device.

97. Chevalier, *J'aime le Dessin Animé.*

98. Clarens, *André Martin 1925–1994. Écrits Sur L'animation,* vol I.

99. Stephenson, *Animation in the Cinema,* 48.

100. Schwartz, "Notes from Zack Schwartz Appearance at UCLA," 9.

101. Ibid., 4.

102. *Pas de Deux,* directed by Norman McLaren (1968; DVD, Norman McLaren: The Master's Edition, Ottawa, ON: National Film Board of Canada, 2006).

103. Michele Helene Bogart, *Artists, Advertising, and the Borders of Art* (Chicago, IL: University of Chicago Press, 1995), 122.

104. Ibid.

105. Ibid., 139.

106. Ibid., 167.
107. Ibid., 260.
108. Ibid., 263.
109. Neil Harris and Martina R. Norelli, "Art, Design, and the Modern Corporation," ed. National Museum of American Art (Washington, DC: Smithsonian Institution Press, 1985).
110. Kepes, *Language of Vision*, 219.
111. The Museum of Modern Art, "Bauhaus 1919–1928," 152.
112. Kepes, *Language of Vision*, 221.
113. Harris and Norelli, "Art, Design, and the Modern Corporation," 8–9.
114. "Creativity Basic."
115. "How Does UPA Do It?," 76.
116. Ibid.
117. Steve Bosustow's UPA collection.
118. Steve Bosustow's UPA collection.
119. "How Does UPA Do It?"
120. Kepes, *Language of Vision*.
121. Ibid., 86.
122. Paul Rand, *Thoughts on Design*, 4th ed. (San Francisco, CA: Chronicle Books, 2014. Originally published: New York, NY: Wittenborn Schultz, 1947), 48.
123. Meggs, *Meggs' History of Graphic Design*, 194.
124. Genter, *Late Modernism: Art, Culture, and Politics in Cold War America*.
125. Robert J. Goldwater, *Primitivism in Modern Painting* (New York, NY: Harper and Brothers Publishers, 1938), 172–173.
126. Ibid., 78.
127. Ibid.
128. Paul Klee, *Pedagogical Sketchbook*, 7th ed. (New York, NY, and Washington, DC: Praeger Publishers, 1972), 7.
129. *The Family Circus*, directed by Art Babbitt (1951; DVD, *UPA: The Jolly Frolics Collection*, Culver City, CA: Sony Pictures Home Entertainment, 2012).
130. "United Films," Direction 1945, 3; Steve Bosustow's UPA collection. At the time the article was written, the studio was called United Film Productions, or simply United Film. Its name had been changed from Industrial Film and Poster Service in May 1944, and by December 1945, the studio would be renamed United Productions of America, soon better known as UPA. Abraham, *When Magoo Flew: The Rise and Fall of Animation Studio UPA*.
131. *The Oompahs*, directed by Robert Cannon (1952; DVD, *UPA: The Jolly Frolics Collection*, Culver City, CA: Sony Pictures Home Entertainment, 2012).
132. Gene Deitch, "19. Saul Steinberg meets Margaret Hamilton!" Genedeitchcredits: The 65 Greats behind The Scenes! (blog). http://genedeitchcredits.com /roll-the-credits/10-steve-bosustow/, accessed September 24, 2015.5

UPA Films as Case Studies for a Simplified Visual Language in Animation in the 1940s and 1950s

> UPA was the first to break out of traditional forms. We don't hide the fact that our characters are drawn. If we want a door or chair, we pop it in when we need it, and take it off when we don't. We've developed a simplified form—simple in attitude, poses and minimum movement.
>
> ROBERT CANNON[1]

As a graphic cinematic medium, animation is a relatively young art form. It arrived at that synthesis of minimalism and reductionism typical of the 20th century later than all the other visual arts but was firmly situated in that trend, nonetheless, finding special affinity with and inspiration from graphic design. UPA animated shorts were ahead of the game, anticipating this synthesis in animated cinema that occurred internationally in the industry during the 1950s and 1960s. This chapter presents selected UPA films that are examples of a simplified audiovisual language in animation: these films are analyzed as case studies in order to see if and in which terms UPA was a groundbreaking studio for modern animation.

4.1 PRE-COLUMBIA FILMS

As of June 1, 1946, UPA had made 50 animated motion pictures and sound slide films, three silent strip films, and three 2" × 2" slides.[2] More films were to be produced before the Columbia agreement was signed in 1948. Very few films have survived the passage of time and are available today. Among them, *Hell-Bent for Election* and *Brotherhood of Man*, made both for the UAW, and the U.S. Navy training film *Flat Hatting* merit attention.

The first animated cartoon made by Industrial Films and Poster Service was *Hell-Bent for Election*, a promotional animated short that supported Franklin Delano Roosevelt in his candidacy for reelection in the upcoming 1944 presidential election. Directed by Chuck Jones, the allegorical film is about two trains: the Win the War Special races against the Defeatist Limited. The first train is modern and streamlined; the second is old and decaying. "A giant step away from Disney styling,"[3] in Maltin's opinion, the film is interesting for the sequence in which Joe, the railway worker who is in charge of derailing the Defeatist Limited, is lulled asleep by a sinister "Wrecker" that might be "a caricature of a Southern politician"[4] and dreams about the two trains coming to the station. This dream sequence, animated by Bobe Cannon,[5] depicts worker Joe struggling to stop the right train. Here, figures and objects are defined mostly by white lines on a dark blue background. For example, only lines define the contours of the two trains arriving at the station, almost if they belong to a sketched drawing. After this sequence, worker Joe wakes up in time to throw the switch and help the Win the War Special win the race.

As David Hilberman affirmed, there is a contrast between the backgrounds, Modern in design, as in this sequence, and the characters that were animated mostly by Warner Bros. animators.[6] And, as Estonian animator Ülo Pikkov pointed out, "the harmonic relationship between the characters and space require[d] that both the characters and space be conceived according to the same concept and related to each other by coherent stylistic means; otherwise, the characters and space [would have] collide[d]."[7]

As for the short's aural features, the film does not indicate a Modern approach but instead quite a traditional one for animated cartoons. A good balance is achieved among a sung musical score, which is present at the beginning, in the middle, and at the end of the film; the sound effects, such as the noise of the approaching trains; and the dialogue. Further, the melody turns sinister and intimidating during the sequence in which Joe is dreaming.

The film was successful and convinced the UAW to finance a second animated short, *Brotherhood of Man*, which was designed by John Hubley and animated by Bobe Cannon. This second UAW commission anticipates such future UPA visual solutions as angular, two-dimensional, flat characters, almost sketched backgrounds and stylized movements. The film is based on the pamphlet *The Races of Mankind*,[8] written by anthropologists Ruth Benedict and Gene Weltfish. It is about a white man who is confronted with other races and discovers that there are no differences among people of different skin colors in physical strength, individual brain capacity or a group's contribution to human civilization.

The film opens with the white man awakened by his barking dog. Surprisingly, he discovers that the Earth has shrunk and "people and places we used to just read about are practically in our own backyard," the narrator says. A green demon version of the man goads his prejudices and prompts the man to question the differences between the human races. "We'll get along," affirms the white man. "We've got to. The future of civilization depends on brotherhood!" But, these same suspicions exist among all people of different races. A voice thus starts explaining scientific facts beginning from Adam and Eve up to current times: as prehistoric people drifted apart, little differences began to appear. Three groups developed among the population defined by differences in skin color and gave rise to the idea of three separate races, as the narration says: "the Caucasian, the Negroid, and the Mongoloid." But in spite of the differences, all human races are equal: "If you take their skins off, there's no way to tell them apart," the narrator affirms.

Interestingly, there are few frames that suggest the skin color of the three races; shapes, rather are defined over colored areas without precisely filling in the outline, an effect that was later used extensively in *Gerald McBoing Boing*. When the narrator is explaining how "all people contributed to civilization," the wheel and its application for transportation becomes the common thread in an entire sequence that travels from pre-historic times to modern times and the airplane.

For the entire duration of the film, the narrator and the white man carry on a dialogue: the former plainly and firmly explains all the scientific facts necessary to prove that all people are equal, while the latter expresses doubt. A musical score adds emphasis to the actions, the narrator's points and the characters' emotional reactions.

Brotherhood of Man stands out most perhaps for how "the animation and the design complemented each other."[9] Hubley later described the intentions behind the film:

> We went for very flat, stylized characters, instead of the global three-dimensional Disney characters. It was very influenced by Saul Steinberg and that sharp-nosed character he was doing at the time. Bob Cannon did most of the animation; in fact, he was the director. ... Paul Julian did all the backgrounds very flat; he used areas of color that would be elided from the line. Very advanced graphics for that period."[10]

Cannon was responsible for having developed the style that could move flat, angular characters inspired by Steinberg's cartoons, as Hilberman recalled: "Bobe was the first animator who developed a style that organically grew out of the kind of characters we were designing."[11]

Flat Hatting, too, anticipates future UPA visual and aural expressions. The film is about Murphy, a U.S. Navy pilot who used to flat-hat[12] in urban areas, especially in San Francisco. The reason for his reckless behavior was immaturity. The film, therefore, compares how Murphy used to behave when he was younger and what he does now. Similar to *Brotherhood of Man*, the passage of time is shown through metamorphosis—the airplane become a car, then a bicycle, later a toy and finally a small hatchet—to symbolize a regression to Murphy's childhood. In *Flat Hatting*, the characters and the movements are stylized, as are the backgrounds. Sources of inspiration were Picasso, particularly in the drawing of women lying on the beach, illustrator Robert Osborn and artist John McLeish.[13] The distance from the Disney style is evident. As Hubley later reminisced, "in the early days it was Picasso, Dufy, Matisse that influenced the drive to a direct, childlike, flat simplified design rather than a Disney 18th Century watercolor."[14]

Peculiar to this film's visual style is the emphasis on line drawings that look as if the characters are just scribbles. This is clear, for example, when Murphy is at school: his classmates appear as flat as a Picasso drawing. There is no attempt to portray them in perspective or realistic terms. Similarly, when Murphy is at a social event, surrounded by men and women, everything is rendered flatly.

The film is music driven. A musical score accompanies Murphy's misbehaviors and stresses decisive moments, such as a very dangerous flat-hatting operation over a populated beach, which is aurally expressed with a climax in the melody. Most of the time, both the musical score and the narrating voice illustrate the images by explaining or emphasizing Murphy's actions, but there are also interesting examples of interactions between sounds and images without them overlapping. There is a sequence, for example, in which the spectator learns that now that Murphy is an officer and a gentleman, he has accepted the codes of civilization. The narrating voice informs: "He wouldn't think of doing this …, or this …, or this." After each "this," the spectators sees first, Murphy showing a rat at a social gathering while he is surrounded by other gentlemen and ladies; second, Murphy hanging from a chandelier in the same room; and finally, Murphy beating a trophy over the head of an old lady seated on a couch. Other similar examples exist throughout the animated short.

The film ends with Murphy before a court-martial. Members of the jury appear as silhouettes while the verdict is read; only Murphy is recognizable by his face. In the last frames, we see him in civilian clothes outside a military airport.

4.2 THE *JOLLY FROLICS* SERIES

4.2.1 An Overview

The first *Jolly Frolics* animated cartoon was theatrically released in 1948. As part of the Columbia agreement, *Robin Hoodlum* features the Fox and the Crow, as do *The Magic Fluke* and *Punchy de Leon*.[15] It was only after the success, both in terms of box-office earnings and Academy Award nominations for the first two Fox and Crow cartoons, that Columbia allowed UPA to come up with its own character—Mr. Magoo, who made his first appearance in *The Ragtime Bear* in 1949.

The *Jolly Frolics* series consists of 38 cartoons produced by UPA and theatrically released by Columbia from 1948 to 1959.[16] The majority of them are one-shot cartoons, something UPA artists favored. It is known, for example, that both Hubley and Cannon did not like to repeat themselves creatively.[17] Nevertheless, Hubley did direct three Mr. Magoo animated shorts,[18] while Cannon directed three more cartoons featuring little Gerald after the success of the original *Gerald McBoing Boing*, as well as two Mr. Magoo animated films.[19]

Among all these animated cartoons, the stories are heterogeneous, as are the audiovisual styles developed for each animated short. Still, it is possible to recognize those aesthetic features that made UPA internationally a trademark: stylized characters, flat backgrounds and simplified animation, which came to be known as limited animation. The music and sound effects were developed in each short according to the story, and different musicians were hired from time to time. Jules Engel was in charge of the color department, thus providing inventive aesthetic visual solutions such as the use of colors for the backgrounds that suggest the psychology of the characters, or the use of the same color for both the background and the characters, as in, for example, *Gerald McBoing Boing*.

Regarding the stories selected, it is noteworthy that the protagonists are often outsiders. In line with the zeitgeist of the 1950s, we find children who are not understood by their parents and peers, as in Gerald, Patsy of *The Family Circus*, Ollie of *Little Boy with a Big Horn* or Johnny of *Bringing up Mother*[20]; an old man who lives in a quite unrealistic Ionesco world, namely Mr. Magoo; or people who have imaginary friends, as in Christopher Crumpet and his father's boss of *Christopher Crumpet's Playmate*. If the world outside is itself in a precarious state, owing to the international and domestic political situation, these UPA characters give evidence of the ability to survive thanks to their imagination and, especially, their being different from ordinary people. As Georgine Oeri affirmed in *Graphis*:

> The story of GERALD McBOING BOING criticizes, without saying as much, the belief in the adjustment of young people to their existing environment—the idea that they should fall into line with the others and be a "success" in life.[21]

After the very early period in which experimentation took place at the Otto K. Olesen building or at the studio's second location on Highland Avenue in Hollywood for the pre-Columbia films, the more creative years came in conjunction with *Gerald McBoing Boing* and *Rooty Toot Toot*. But before that, even as early as *The Magic Fluke*, we can recognize the tendency to flatten the characters and to avoid a realistic, detailed representation: in the latter film, especially, only the essential elements are portrayed when depicting a crowd of people. In this animated short, whose title makes parodistic reference to Wolfgang Amadeus Mozart's *The Magic Flute*, the Fox and the Crow are a musical duo until the Fox abandons the Crow, who, nevertheless, remains loyal to his old friend and provides him a magic wand. As Steve Bosustow told Howard Rieder,

> It was the old animal stuff. But even in the first "Fox and Crow" we caricatured human beings. We didn't use animals for the other characters. The first picture we made was *Robin Hoodlum*, a satire on Robin Hood. We moved up a notch from straight hit-them-over-the-head cartoons. We moved up into satire and we initiated a more modern graphic approach. Most of us were from the era where contemporary graphics were popular. We had gone to art school, and developed during this period, where Disney hadn't. This was a new era.[22]

After the Fox and Crow cartoons, the desire among UPA staff to distinguish themselves from traditional animation by dealing with stories for adults and animating human beings came into effect. Herb Klynn later recalled: "Animals were boring; all of the other studios were using them. It was done, done, done! How do you use animals in the story of *The Tell-Tale Heart* or *Rooty Toot Toot*? You don't. You need to use people."[23] Therefore, people are the protagonists of *The Popcorn Story*,[24] *The Family Circus*, *Georgie and the Dragon*[25] and *The Wonder Gloves*,[26] among other shorts.

The years from 1951 to 1954 marked a more creative period. *Gerald McBoing Boing*, *The Oompahs*, *Rooty Toot Toot*, *Willie the Kid*, *Madeline*, *The Emperor's New Clothes*, *Christopher Crumpet*, *The Unicorn in the Garden*, *The Tell-Tale Heart*, Ballet-Oop[27] and *Fudget's Budget* were all produced in this lapse of time. Noteworthy are the highly stylized backgrounds of *Pete Hothead*,[28] designed by Ted Parmelee, and *The Emperor's New Clothes*, an adaptation of the Hans Christian Andersen fable, designed by Paul Julian, for the architectural space of their backgrounds.

In *Ballet-Oop*, directed by Bobe Cannon, Mr. Hot-Foot, the proprietor of a dance school, asks Miss Placement to prepare her group of four students for the competition of the Glendale Ballet Festival in three weeks' time. Certain visual solutions particularly highlight the nature of animation as a *graphic cinematic medium*. To indicate the passing of time, for example, the days of the week appear in writing along with two legs in a ballet position, pass one after the other. In another sequence, just silhouettes of girls perform ballet movements, added frantically on the screen, to suggest all the positions that they should remember to properly perform a ballet.

In the film there are two different musical scores. The film's principal score, reminiscent of classical compositions, is heard while the girls rehearse their ballet. The secondary score is used when the little girls perform the ballet on stage at the event. The scores have accelerating and decelerating rhythms, according to the animated dance steps. Sound effects emphasize some visual elements or actions, such as in the opening credits, when the word *Oops* is accentuated by a thud.

Ballet-Oop ends with the female group winning the competition and Mr. Hot-Foot asking for another ballet performance to be prepared, this one for a festival in two weeks' time.

Cannon's next film, *Fudget's Budget*, goes a step further in using visual abstractions. As the viewer sees and hears at the very beginning of the short, the film is "dedicated to all those courageous people who manage to live within a family budget." The sentence appears on the frame, while a narrator reads it. The film is about Mr. and Mrs. Fudget and their family budget, as we can guess from the opening titles. What is interesting here, however, is that Mr. and Mrs. Fudget are introduced as orange lines moving on a flat sheet of graph paper that then metamorphose into the characters. The space within the frame is defined by the lines of the sheet of paper: we see, for example, Mrs. Fudget disappearing behind a vertical line, as she walks horizontally on the screen from left to right. To stay within their budget, Mr. and Mrs. Fudget must cut some purchases and activities, so they go down the list to see what can be eliminated. Here, a list scrolls down as if written on a notepad. Visual solutions go hand in hand with the narration: when we hear that George (Mr. Fudget) has gotten a raise, we see the $ sign repeated on the screen under the Fudgets' house. When the family is close to bankruptcy, there is a visual metaphor: a storm tears down the house, which then transforms into a boat floating on a stormy sea. A loan from the bank is now necessary: buckets with $ signs help eliminate the water from the boat. Eventually the storm is over, and the Fudgets pay all their bills.

Fudget's Budget is also rich in acoustic solutions and a fine example of the complementarity between images and sounds that characterizes UPA films. First, there is a musical score whose pace changes according to the narration, although it has a quite fast rhythm for most of the film. A slightly different tune is played when George and Irene Fudget are enjoying an evening out, in a different environment than the usual house. Second, there is a narrating voice that helps explain the story (Who are the characters? What do they do? What happens to them? How do they solve problems?) and dialogues with the characters. At the very beginning, for example, the narrator asks Mr. Fudget, "George, where is Irene?" Third, there are sound effects that accompany visual metaphors: the noise of a vacuum cleaner while we see Mrs. Budget using it and after the narrator has explained that Irene takes care of the house; the noise of water spurting out of lead pipes while we see them broken; the noise of water pouring down from the roof into pots; or the noise of a car passing by as we see Mr. and Ms. Fudget in their car. Additionally, there is a second narrating voice that sometimes appears on the frame as a huge red line representing the profile of a face. We hear it asking, "How much did they pay?" or "How did they do it?" until at the very end, it dialogues with the principal narrating voice, which is finally portrayed as a similar huge blue face line.

A budget is an abstract thing. To suggest its complex essence, there are several visual and aural metaphors. *Fudget's Budget* effectively conveys its message thanks to a highly stylized design, both of the characters and the backgrounds, and the use of limited movements. The house, for example, is itself a visual metaphor for the budget: it shrinks or enlarges according to the family's financial situation. Thus, we can relate the idea of a budget with that of a family composed of four people who live together under the same roof. And, as in every family, there are the little expensive passions, as Irene's for new hats, a comic situation that helps the spectator sympathize with the characters.

As these two films illustrate, by 1954, UPA's simplified audiovisual language had come to full maturity and was about to inspire international productions. But, there is another Cannon's film that deserves mention: *The Jaywalker.* It is about Milton Muffet, a man who can't stop jaywalking.[29] Here, of note is that the idea of heavy car traffic is suggested by abstract sounds and images and a jazz rhythm. The film is told through a first-person narration: Milton Muffet talks about his awful addiction. In fact, Milton introduces himself at the very beginning in this way:

"Just to look at me in a crowd, you'd think I was perfectly normal. ... I have a confession to make: I am a jaywalker." His introduction is prefaced by a musical score and foreground sound effects, such as traffic signal sounds. Often there are also background sounds to convey the idea of traffic noises: cars passing by, cars slowing down, multitudes of people walking by and so on.

4.2.2 Four Case Studies

4.2.2.1 Gerald McBoing Boing

Gerald is a little boy who does not speak words but goes "boing-boing" instead. From the very beginning, we are introduced to the subject of the story, a boy with a disability that causes him the rejection of his peers and even of his father. In *Gerald McBoing Boing*, everything is *essential*: from the characters' design to the backgrounds, from the animation to the music and up to the color, nothing but necessary elements are used to tell the story. Minimalism and reductionism are the leitmotifs of the audio-visual style. Moreover, as the Production Notes written by Charles Daggett, the publicity man at UPA, state, *Gerald McBoing Boing* is:

> [T]he first attempt to put on the screen a picture that would look like a drawing. It is marked by an utter simplicity of background, character delineation and movement—a simplicity most neces-sary in telling the simple, touching story of a little boy who is a strange one in a strange world.[30]

The opening titles, in fact, are designed as if they were written by an elementary school child. They thus bring us immediately into the world of a little boy. In the first frames, Gerald is animated as if he is being drawn then and there: we see the drawing lines composing his figure. All the characters are designed as if they were drawn by children as well, and they literally seem to float in the space. The backgrounds consist of few elements: a carpet, a window, a chandelier, a coat rack and an armchair. There is no conventional use of the space: the backgrounds do not provide a unique perspective with a singular point of observation; the frame is broken into multiple perspectives, since the space is only addressed by a few visual elements.

Gerald McBoing Boing is another example of a UPA film extremely rich in sounds. As in many UPA cartoons, it is narrated by a male voice. There is also a musical score, composed by Gail Kubik, that together with abstract sounds emphasize Gerald's actions. Generally cheerful, like Gerald's personality, the score takes a heartbreaking turn when Gerald is facing the rejection of his father. As the characters do speak and verbally interact with each other, there are several "voices" conveying aural information that are never overlapping. It is as if the whole narration of the film comprises several alternating aural sources of information. When the doctor arrives, for example, we hear him say, "I see," immediately followed by the narrator saying, "said the doctor," creating the effect of the two voices being linked together. In fact, they are part of the same story, a story that is not simply read by a narrator and visually illustrated but that is brought to life by the animation of the characters. In addition, there is a major novelty: sound effects are the language that Gerald uses to communicate, and for this reason, they express his emotive language. So, for example, when he tries to get his father's attention, we hear a claxon-like sound, as if a truck were passing by and announcing itself. Or, when he tries to play with other kids, Gerald emits loud noises that are inevitably identified as too loud and "different" by his peers. Since Gerald's sounds successfully express his intentions and feelings, they are followed by the reactions of those who interact with him: his father jumping in the air after a very loud "boing boing," other kids falling to the ground after he emits a loud "beep beep." Finally, when Gerald is the featured star of a radio show, the viewer hears an entire performance of sounds, and it is the task of the public to imagine it visually.

For their "emotional" quality, Gerald's sounds function as poetic devices: they address a world that we cannot see but only imagine. In fact, Gerald's sounds do not convey specific connotative meanings as might be the case of sentences made of words. Instead, they evoke Gerald's feelings, moods and emotive reactions as responses to what happens around him, and as spectators, we are prompted to guess what exactly he is trying to convey via our imagination. For example, when Gerald goes to his father after being rejected by his peers, he cries and emits a claxon-like sound to get his father's attention. At the same time, he is pointing at the door, suggesting that he is somehow referring to what has just happened outdoors at the park with the other kids. Here, sounds and images do complement each other, providing valuable hints to understand Gerald's feelings and, more generally, the entire story that is being told. At the same time, it is our task to put all the visual and aural information together.

The animation is stylized. Interestingly, it is used to stress some poses rather than others, according to what Gerald is doing or how people react to him. So, for example, to show Gerald's father's astonishment when he hears Gerald's first "boing-boing," we see him jumping in the armchair and the position is sustained in the air for few frames as to stress this unrealistically rather than reproducing a natural flow of action. Or, when the doctor enters the door, Gerald's father is designed in a funny position, as if he is waiting for something extraordinary to happen: his legs do not touch the ground, and the position is held for a few frames. Funnily, the doctor mistakes the father's foot for the coat rack and hangs his hat on it. These little elements are used to define the personality of the characters and help the viewer enjoy ironic subtleties. To suggest the carefreeness with which Gerald goes to school, for example, he does not walk normally but hops. About the animation, director Bobe Cannon said that he wanted the film to express "an understatement in movement as opposed to dynamic movement."[31] He added:

> This, we felt, would be more effective because there has been a traditional excess of movement in cartoons produced at other studios. The story-book treatment we have achieved, as opposed to live action technique too often borrowed for cartoons, was dictated by the story idea.[32]

Another interesting sequence is when Gerald returns from school. The passage of time is shown with a synthesis. From the footstool where he is standing up, we see him riding a small tricycle by means of transformations: the footstool gets smaller, Gerald's clothes change and finally he is on his tricycle performing a new action. A compression of time is thus suggested. As Ülo Pikkov observed:

> Time in animation film is generally compressed and elliptical—events occurring over an extended period of time are compressed and the less important details and story lines are omitted, as filmic events are reduced to the essence of the represented events (and their duration), instead of merely imitating them. Spectators comprehend subconsciously that they are being presented with elliptical cinematic narrative, purified of secondary minutia, and they are able to mentally "unwind" the narrative.[33]

The colors as well are used in an unconventional way. The characters' skin color is the same as the backgrounds. Areas of color are used to suggest the essence of the objects without filling in completely the shapes defined by the outlines. Sometimes, different colors define different shapes according to the principle that "if a shape can be identified by a color separation, there is usually no need for a line around the shape."[34] Interestingly, colors also express the psychology of Gerald: when he is running away from home, it is night and everything is dark as to underline his desperation, while when he is happily working as a "sound-effect boy," a bright yellow defines the interior of the location.

As much as the sound expresses an emotive language and the colors stress Gerald's psychological reactions, the frame illustrates an emotive space: it is *subjective* because it shows what Gerald perceives. So, for example, we see a very little Gerald climbing the stairs of a big purple house, the house as large as his feeling of loneliness; or, we see little Gerald trying to jump on a big train in motion. The man who is going to hire Gerald is tall and majestic, while scared Gerald is little compared to him. What we see is what Gerald sees; we adopt his same point of observation, which is his *subjective* space. A last example is at the end of the animated cartoon when the narrator explains that Gerald is now rich and famous, known "from coast to coast." Visually, we see a limousine that is so unrealistically long that it stretches the length of two different groups of people gathered to revere Gerald, as if Gerald's huge popularity is symbolically illustrated by the car that goes from coast to coast of the U.S.

4.2.2.2 Rooty Toot Toot

In *Rooty Toot Toot*, John Hubley's UPA masterpiece and his personal response to Cannon's *Gerald McBoing Boing*, the use of the subjective space is pushed even further. The film is an adaptation of the popular ballad "Frankie and Johnny." The story is of a murder: Frankie shoots Johnny to death after discovering that he betrayed her with Nelly Bly.

The layout designs and the colors, both made by Paul Julian, function to illustrate the personality of the characters. Moreover, different backgrounds with different colors are used to express three versions of the events provided by three different people in the courtroom. The same can be said about the animation, which enriches with little touches the personalities of Frankie, Johnny, Nelly Bly and Frankie's lawyer.

The opening credits introduce the theme. The lyrics of the ballad are sung by a female voice to a jazz melody. The spectator sees a pianola as the credits appear on the piano roll and later sees and hears the title of the short, which is onomatopoeic for the three shots with which Johnny "wound up dead." From the exterior of the courthouse, which is designed by simple black lines on a neutral white background, the viewer enters the court, and Frankie appears. Her attitude—the way she moves, her expressions and the color of her dress—reveals her true nature and suggests that she really might have killed Johnny. Frankie's lawyer is a character in his own right: he is portrayed as someone who knows how to deceive people by distracting them with alternative stories. Some details reveal his personality as well: his physicality, his pretentious attitude and the way he walks, especially some little movements of his legs and feet. The backgrounds are rich in decoration: scribbled lines define the interior of the room and the people are designed by few lines, as if they were sketched.

The first reconstruction, given by the bartender, follows: he starts to wipe a glass, and with a fade-in, we are brought into the Sordid Bar. The backgrounds are of gray, black and white but especially of white and black lines on a gray background. Johnny arrives at the bar and enters a secondary room; Frankie arrives a few seconds later and receives the information from the bartender that Johnny is with Nelly Bly. Here, Frankie is animated with a jump up in the air, as to stress her astonishment. She runs to the other room, and we hear, without seeing it, the three shots. A small detail is shared: she enters the bar with the gun in her hands, thus suggesting that she already has negative intentions. With another fade-out, we go back to the courtroom, where it is now Nelly Bly's turn.

While we listen to the testimony of Nelly Bly, the background colors change from the beginning of the short. Here, darker tonalities, similar to the ones used for the deposition of the bartender, are used. In fact, the two testimonies are similar. Nelly Bly introduces herself as a "singer, a singer of sweet melodies." Here, the design and the animation brilliantly suggest that she is a seducer, such as, when she is animated crossing her legs, or overdramatically touching her hair, or twisting her arms. She brings us into the secondary room of the Sordid Bar, where she is rehearsing with Johnny; Frankie arrives and shoots him.

Back in the courtroom, we now hear Frankie's lawyer. He pompously begins by saying, "*Facto factotum.* Picture, if you will, the true events," and then tells a story in which Frankie appears as "pure and demure." A sweeter melody leads us to where Frankie is, "in her garden, in her inno-cence": the backgrounds are white—the color of purity—filled by purple flowers, birds and a blue butterfly. Johnny tries to kill her, but in a series of (mis)fortunes, he has to run away from the bullets. Once he reaches the secondary room of the Sordid Bar, we see the same scene as before, but the colors of the backgrounds are now different, as if they are fading away. We are dealing, in fact, with a different version of the events.

Back in the courtroom, we easily understand that the story told by Frankie's lawyer is of pure invention, in part because he says, "I have performed this..." and uses the word *fiction* in place of *function*. With a mischievous coup de théâtre, he proposes to Frankie, the people of the jury applaud enthusiastically and Frankie is declared not guilty. But, as soon as she sees the lawyer dancing with Nelly Bly, she shoots him. Here the colors of the backgrounds are again different from before. We are in the present, new events are occurring and the situation turns dark: first an intense red completely fills in the courtroom, then, after Frankie kills the lawyer, everything turns cold blue. The film ends the same way that it started, but instead of the opening credits on the piano roll, Frankie enters the jail.

As in *Gerald McBoing Boing*, *Rooty Toot Toot* is a Modern film also for the sound achievements. There are multiple narrating voices, which have in common the fact that they do not simply speak but sing. An unidenti-fied female voice introduces the ballad at the beginning of the film, while we see the opening credits, and closes the film at the very end. In addition, some of the characters, specifically the lawyers, the bartender, and Nelly Bly, express themselves singing or in tune with the background jazz mel-ody. Also, when Frankie exclaims, referring to Nelly Bly, "That's a lie, that's a lie. She's no singer," her sentence perfectly fits the background musical score. Of course, the score changes its pace according to the rhythm of the events narrated and the different reconstructions. In addition, there are several onomatopoeic sounds and background sound effects, such as the buzz in the courtroom. All the sound effects contribute to highlighting the personality of the characters as much as how they are designed and animated.

In *Rooty Toot Toot*, everything is functional to the storytelling, from the character design to the stylized animation, from the music to the layouts. The spectator is brought into the story by means of audiovisual changes: small details in the music, the way the characters perform an action, or the colors of the backgrounds help us to follow the story and reveal hidden meanings. The psychology of the murder is well reconstructed, and we are able to grasp the personality of the characters by means of stylized movements and the designs of the characters and backgrounds.

Among Hubley's sources of visual inspiration were the illustrations of David Stone Martin, an artist who designed many jazz album covers during the 1950s and 1960s. His works were characterized by thinly outlined figures of musicians with their musical instruments and often broad areas of flat colors. Sometimes one color filled the entire surface of the cover; sometimes areas of strikingly different colors were used to create a visual chromatic contrast. Almost never did colors realistically illustrate a scene or a subject, and rarely did they completely fill in the contours of the figures and the objects outlined. Paul Julian recalled what Hubley admired of Martin's work: it "almost always had an asymmetric inventiveness about it that John found related to his own sense of exploration at the expense of order and/or inertia."[35]

Another person who inspired primarily John Hubley and secondarily those UPA artists who worked closely with him was Lithuanian-born Ben Shahn, a leading influence in the social realism art movement. His empathic depictions of the harsh conditions of the urban working class and proletariat could not but be considered of great interest by the leftist-oriented UPA artists.

4.2.2.3 *The Unicorn in the Garden*

From the opening credits of *The Unicorn in the Garden*, the spectator is aware that the film, directed by William T. Hurtz, is an adaptation of humorist and cartoonist James Thurber's work. The visual style is quite faithful to Thurber's drawings. The film is about a domestic conflict between a husband and wife; a cheerful and playful man versus a dark and mischievous woman. The layouts underline these different personalities: the outside garden where the man finds the unicorn is bright and sunny, while the inside of the house where the couple lives, and especially the bedroom where the woman is lying on the bed, is black and dark. About the style, the Production Notes remark:

> The designing of the characters to achieve a Thurber feeling took extensive research through all the books of Thurber cartoons. The poses of the Thurber man and woman were studied carefully and

this search provided the artists with a clue to how the character should act. For example, very often the man or woman would be shown looking back over the shoulder. This attitude, which suggests an air of great deliberativeness, can be seen quite often through the "Unicorn in the Garden."[36]

Yet, the greater challenge for the UPA artists in turning into motion a cartoon story was the use of colors, which were applied "freely and roughly."[37]

After the opening credits, viewers are brought into the fable by means of the classical line "Once upon a sunny morning. ...," which appears together with a tweeting bird. Next, we have an aerial-like view of the sunny garden in which some of the scenes are going to take place. A fade-in shows the interior of the house: a man is trying to cook some eggs, one falls to the floor and we hear the sinister voice of the wife asking, "What's going on down there?" We thus surmise that she is upstairs and does not get along very well with her husband, and especially, we can grasp a little bit of her personality. The color of the interior is a neutral azure. From the kitchen's window, the man sees the unicorn in the garden and decides to go out to greet it while it is eating roses. He touches its horn and runs into the house to communicate the news to his wife. Here, the backgrounds are completely black except for a few decorations on the wall, necessary to suggest the idea of being in a house. He runs upstairs, opens the window and says, "There's a unicorn in the garden." But, the wife laconically replies: "The unicorn is a mythical beast." He exits the room, remembering to close the venetian blinds before going downstairs. The woman rests in her darkness.

The scene repeats itself: the man is in the garden with the unicorn eating flowers. He runs upstairs and says to the wife: "The unicorn ate a lily." She answers: "You are a booby and I am going to put you in the booby-hatch." After he exits the room, the woman runs to the telephone and calls the police and a psychiatrist, Dr. I. Ego. In the meantime, the unicorn has disappeared from the garden.

By means of a fade-in, we pass from the studio of Dr. Ego to the house of the couple, where the woman is telling the story of what she heard from her husband to the doctor and to two astonished policemen. Here the backgrounds are first pink and violet, then later purple-blue and orange. The scene ends with the doctor ordering the policemen to capture the woman.

From a dark interior, we come back to a neutral green background where we see the wife tied in a straitjacket and the husband calmly entering the frame from left to right. A few frames later, she is taken away by the policemen, while we hear the wedding march in an accelerated rhythm as a closing tune. The film ends how it started: on a yellow background we read the moral of the fable "Don't count your boobies until they are hatched," with the blue bird happily chirping.

The domestic conflict is also expressed by shifts in the score, which was composed by David Raksin, who also worked on *Madeline*. The music is peaceful and relaxing when we see the man and the unicorn, whereas it accelerates and becomes anxious when the wife appears. The atmosphere of the fable is suggested by a harpsichord; the unicorn, by an "ancient woodwind;" and the wife, by a "complaining saxophone."[38] In his essay "'A Sound Idea': Music for Animated Films," Jon Newsom analyzes *The Unicorn in the Garden* by breaking down the actions according to the composer's score, not the animators' worksheets. Newsom remarks that the unicorn motif, which is the principal theme, is lyrical and diatonic and is played by the alto recorder. The high soprano saxophone, whose melody is made of whining sounds, is used for the wife and "corresponds more to the pathetic than the sinister side of the wife's nature. She is drab, unimaginative, and the victim of her own cunning."[39] Newsom considers *The Unicorn in the Garden* necessarily both funny and beautiful in order to make bearable to the spectator a story that is both horrible and realistic: "Only the fantasy, which is the beauty and the humor, makes that marital cold war tolerable. Thurber's suave, gentle, Freudian mythical beast and Raksin's acoustically informed and sinuous unicorn melody for the ancient recorder give hope through their art."[40]

The film space is *subjective* since it shows the conflict's dichotomy by expressing the different personalities of the woman and the man by means of characters' design, colors, backgrounds and movements. The characters are brilliantly animated: the way the woman moves suggests suspicion and a menacing attitude, while the man walks peacefully when he is in the garden or runs crazily as soon as he enters the house.

4.2.2.4 The Tell-Tale Heart

The Tell-Tale Heart is an adaptation of the story of the same name written by Edgar Allan Poe in 1843. It is about a madman who strangles an older man with whom he has lived, hides the body under the floor and reveals the murder to the police after being betrayed by his own egotism. The film was originally intended to be released in 3D.

The short opens with a few sentences written on the frames explaining, "The film that you are about to see is based on a story told a hundred years ago by America's greatest master of drama and suspense. ..." What follows is key to understanding the stylistic choices of the entire animated short: "This story is told through the eyes of a madman ... who, like all of us, believed that he was sane." In other words, what we are going to see is a psychological drama as the killer experienced it. The space is therefore highly *subjective*: we do not see a realistic house but an imaginary house, specifically the house as it appears in the mind of the madman. The same goes for the sounds, especially the beating of the old man's heart, which constitutes two different climaxes, as director Ted Parmelee explained in the Production Notes:

> The story has two climaxes which occur too rapidly in seven minutes of story-telling. The first climax has to be high enough in emotion to carry the audience with it, but cannot rob the second climax. This compression of climaxes seems similar to the series of climaxes Beethoven carries through in his Eighth Symphony. He reaches a climax and follows with such a calm that you are unaware that the second climax is really no higher than the first. He attains the second climax by repetition with slight modification of the music. We arrive at the climax in the same way, editorially and graphically.[41]

The opening credits are reminiscent of Salvador Dalí's surrealism: we see a perforated canvas inside another perforated canvas, with an old house on the background, a disturbing Victorian house. Here it is also possible to see some resemblances to Grant Woods' depictions of the rural American Midwest, with its houses and landscapes, as well as Edward Hopper's portrayals of American architectural and rural scenes.

After the opening credits, we see the shadow of the madman and hear his voice. We will never see the face of the man, only his shadow the way he sees it. We then go into the house by means of a first-person camera technique. The backgrounds are mostly made up of stairs and stylized furniture; we often have an observation point from the stairs as if the madman lives on the second floor and is constantly looking from above. What obsesses him is the eye of the old man; it is what he must get rid of.

We see the face of the old man in the foreground and an animated white shape that looks like lightning. A similar lightning shape appeared in the opening credits, following the title of the film. The madman's obsession refers to everything that can remind him of the eye, such as the moon and a white water jug. About these objects, Parmelee stated:

> We chose very definite, unmistakable shapes for each object relating to the old man—the table, the stairs, the door, the bed, and quilt—so that the objects would never be confused no matter how much they might be distorted in any future appearance in the picture. The quilt was sharply patterned because its use and appearance are so brief that the audience must identify it later in a matter of a second as a thing closely related to the old man.[42]

Next follows a sequence in which the madman explains how he waited for the right moment to kill the old man and how he watched over him. He waits seven days. Then, during the eighth night, the murder is executed. Here, there is a startling scene in which it is suggested how the madman is waiting for the proper moment and how time passes: there is a fade-in to the interior of the house, with skeletal stairs that remind of the clock's gears, a pendulum, and the shadow of the old man at the center of it. Then, the superimposition of two layers is carried on for some seconds until the gears of the clock are truly shown, and time, as the madman says, stops. Parmelee explained: "In less than a minute, we express seven days of waiting. The pendulums, because of their mechanical action, indicated a feeling of unalterable and premeditated behavior. We played the clocks and pendulums heavily to convey the suspension of time."[43]

In the following scene, the old man is awakened and is frightened by something in the air, which is the madman getting closer and closer with an oil lamp. The old man hits the oil lamp with his hand, and we, like the two characters, are immersed in full darkness. Here, the mastery of UPA artists in combining innovative and striking aural and visual solutions is evident: while the frame is totally black, we hear the madman say: "For an hour I did not move a muscle." While he continues to narrate, the frame stays black for some seconds until the beating of the old man's heart pushes him to strangle him. Here, too, an original visual solution is employed: as the madman's eyes gets used to the darkness, he starts to visualize what surrounds him; the beating of the old man's heart gets louder and louder, and the black frame is intermittently illuminated. Still, what we see, through the madman's eyes, during these intermittences that aurally correspond to the sounds of the old man's heartbeat is a dark violet-blue surface crossed by cracks. These abstract animations, accompanied by the accelerating sounds of the heartbeat and a pressing score, reach a climax: the frame returns to black and, immediately after, we hear a scream. Then, the quilt is animated to be move very quickly, and in a disorderly way. We grasp that the old man has been killed, although we do not see any blood, only his hand lying on the floor, sticking out from the quilt.

The madman feels liberated from the eye now, and he looks up to the moon from his point of observation; the house has no walls but is open to the nocturnal sky "to achieve a madman's release."[44] With a fade-in, we come back to the interior, where the madman hides the dead body under the floor. A few seconds later, policemen knock on the door. They are drawn in a style reminiscent of German expressionist paintings. They start asking questions and looking for the old man. Camera movements, which are quite frequent in all the film, illustrate again the skeletal interiors with no walls at all. The policemen are everywhere, up on the stairs, down on the first floor looking for the old man. A mistake, the spilling of water, preludes the madman's confession. He hears anew the beating of the old man's heart. This scene depicts water dripping down, drop after drop, while on the background we see a policeman with a tea cup in his hands that the madman had offered him earlier. The dripping of the water continues without intermission; it gets louder and louder until the madman confesses. The film ends with the madman in prison: we see from behind bars and hear his voice repeating the same sentence he had uttered at the beginning of the film: "True, I am nervous, very very dreadfully nervous, but why would you say that I am mad?"

The film is rich in detail and cross-reference. For example, the passing of time is shown with the changing of the madman's shadow on the floor. The reference to the lightning is repeated in the mirror after the water jug breaks. The design and colors were made by Paul Julian, who probably made his most startling and effective contribution at UPA with this film.

The first-person narration is by actor James Mason, who brought life to the character's presence through his deep voice, which also majestically enhances the feeling of claustrophobia and mental disease. The music was composed by Boris Kremenliev. The musical score and the narrating voice match each other, anticipating in tonality and intensity the events that are visually expressed in the frames. As mentioned by the director, the film is built around two climaxes, whose suspense is visually and aurally very well calculated. Sound effects do not appear casually but at specific frames. Apart from the aforementioned two sequences in which the beating of the old man's heart is heard and metaphorically seen, there is a general surreal silence during the film. Sporadic sound effects are used to suggest the monotonous passing of time and its accelerations (in correspondence to climactic events), as perceived by the madman awaiting his moment to kill the old man. Time is rendered by both superimposed visual clocks and the sound of the clock's ticking. In addition, there are noises of creaking doors, of a fluttering butterfly, of the breaking of a water jug and others. In the second climax, the confession of the madman, we hear his voice screaming, the background music and the noise of water dripping. All these acoustic elements are carefully balanced in order to enhance the intensity of the truth.

The film marked a high point in UPA artistic production for its outstanding originality, both in terms of story subject and of audiovisual style. Many elements contributed to its high quality, visually and aurally. *The Tell-Tale Heart* can be considered the most "cinematic" of UPA animated cartoons for the use of camera movements and for the way the space in which the characters are animated is rendered in the frames. It might be a daring comparison, but UPA artists could have been influenced by Edward Hopper in the dramatic use of light and dark to suggest a psychological mood (liberating lunar source of light versus dark oppressive interiors of the house), in the study of the interaction of human beings with their environment (the positions of the old man, the policemen and the murderer in relation to the interiors of the house and its objects), in the juxtaposition of the interior and exterior of the house and its many psychological implications (in many sequences there are doors and windows sometimes opened, sometimes closed) and in the cinematic composition of the frames. Moreover, the very last frames of the film visually express what the madman is observing from the jail where he is now imprisoned: he sees a building whose perspective reminds the spectator, again, of some of Hopper's architectural representations of contemporary America.

4.2.3 Series Attempts

UPA made several attempts at series. The most relevant consists of four animated shorts dedicated to Gerald McBoing Boing. After the success of the first film, released in 1951, another three animated cartoons were directed by Cannon: *Gerald McBoing Boing's Symphony*,[45] *How Now Boing Boing*[46] and *Gerald McBoing! Boing! On Planet Moo*.[47]

In *Gerald McBoing Boing's Symphony*, Gerald is asked to reproduce a symphony for the Bong Bong Bong radio station. Gerald's popularity is still high, and he now has his own radio show. One day, the radio station owner is in a fix: the orchestra hasn't shown up for the performance, and "silence on the air is strictly taboo." He therefore asks Gerald to do the show. But just when everything seems to be all right, we realize that Gerald has gotten the scores of two different radio shows mixed up, and the classical piece is interspersed with sounds like, for example, a train roaring by. The station owner dismisses Gerald until he discovers that the show was a successful, and then Gerald gets a raise.

In the film, we can recognize all the aesthetic features present in *Gerald McBoing Boing*: colors do not fill the outlines, the same color is used for the backgrounds and the characters' skin, multiple "voices" interact with each other and colors are used dramatically to highlight topic moments in the narration, as when Gerald has difficulty in performing the piece without the orchestra and the background turns alarmingly red. Interestingly, at the very beginning, the shapes of different people appear on the screen the same way as they are drawn: we see only the outlines of caricatures suggesting a crowd of people.

In *How Now Boing Boing*, Gerald is brought to Professor Joyce, "teacher of voice," to finally learn to speak words and not sounds. Gerald takes private lessons, but he does not progress. The reputation of Professor Joyce is ruined, and Gerald phones him one last time. Thus, Professor Joyce discovers that when Gerald talks by phone, his emissions are perceived as words and not sounds.

There are some details in this film that are noteworthy. First is the use of colors in the backgrounds as a device to pass from the exterior to the interior: here, going from pink to green suggests the evolution of a situation. Second, the three doctors are animated as having wheels instead of feet, a detail that suggests a fast walking in unison. Third, Gerald's father and Professor Joyce talk in rhythmical rhymes. Moreover, the words "How now brown cow" are the leitmotif of the film: they are first uttered loudly in an elementary classroom by a group of students; they are later silently mimed by Gerald as Professor Joyce tries to teach Gerald how to speak; and they are finally pronounced by Gerald at the end of the film. Funnily, the professor is named after novelist James Joyce, whose literary legacy rests in his stream-of-consciousness technique and related use of words.

In *Gerald McBoing! Boing! On Planet Moo*, Gerald is kidnapped by aliens from the planet Moo. The Moo people speak perfect English, but the Moo king believes that people on Earth speak like Gerald. He tries to interpret what Gerald says. Once on Earth, the Moo king will communicate with the Earth people by boing boing sounds. The story is weaker than the previous Gerald sequels. All three *Gerald McBoing Boing* sequels, nonetheless, show a remarkable use of abstract sounds.

Other efforts at series were *Bringing up Mother*, which followed *Family Circus*, and *Four Wheels No Brakes*,[48] in which the main character is Pete Hothead, who originally appeared in the 1952 film of the same name. Another is *Christopher Crumpet's Playmate*. In the original, *Christopher Crumpet*, there is a sequence—when Christopher exits his house to see the real rocket ship that his father has brought him—in which the visual style is reminiscent of children's art and harks back to Cohl's animation. In the sequel, the imaginary elephant is drawn only by contour, as if it is transparent, or, better, invisible to some people and visible to others. These devices allow the audience to empathize with the films, since it is easier to follow a story in which the content (a story about a child who wants something almost impossible to get or has an imaginary friend) matches the style (achieved by almost "naive" drawings).

Another UPA series was *Ham and Hattie*, developed and released from 1957 to 1959. Four animated cartoons were produced: *Trees and Jamaica Daddy*,[49] *Sailing and Village Band*,[50] *Spring and Saganaki*[51] and *Picnics are Fun and Dino's Serenade*.[52] Although *Trees and Jamaica Daddy* brought UPA an Academy Award nomination—its last—the series was not successful. Every short is divided into two parts: the first is about Hattie, a little blond girl; the second is about Ham, a brown middle-aged man. Hattie is portrayed enjoying her fantasies, such as having a picnic in a city that resembles Manhattan or sailing a small boat in a fountain; while Ham performs a different character in every short, such as a British dog or a Japanese warrior. In the animated films, the narration is predominant over the visual counterpart: the stories are sung, and the visual style is pretty much the same for every cartoon. It seems that with this last series, UPA artists had forgotten the principle of "form follows function," since there is a lack of balance between the content and the style. Limited animation is not used to illustrate the psychological subtleties of the characters as it was done, for example, in Cannon's animations. Overall, the films are neither funny enough for children nor serious enough for adults. There was, however, one other UPA series that had enormous success during the 1950s.

4.3 MR. MAGOO THEATRICAL RELEASES

4.3.1 Who Is Mr. Magoo?

Mr. Quincy Magoo is a grouchy, cantankerous and stubborn man, probably in his mid-60s. When he was young, he attended Rutgers University and got his driver's license in 1922. He smokes cigars, drives a car and has a scatterbrain nephew, Waldo. When he first appeared in *Ragtime Bear*, Magoo mistakes Waldo for a bear, goes into a cottage with him/it and almost kills him instead of killing the animal. Mr. Magoo, in fact, is nearsighted: he can't read the signs, but he is so self-confident as to believe the opposite.

The gags in the Mr. Magoo series are based on his nearsightedness: in *Magoo Goes Skiing*, he mistakes Waldo for a dog; in *Kangaroo Courting*,[53] he courts a kangaroo, instead of a lady, for Waldo; and in *Destination Magoo*,[54] he believes himself to be on the moon while he is actually at Luna Park in Coney Island. The gags are endless: in *Spellbound Hound*, he talks with a dog instead of his friend Ralph; in *Calling Doctor Magoo*,[55] he ends up on a boat believing he is at the hospital; in *Pink and Blue Blues*,[56] he babysits the neighbors' dog instead of their son. John Hubley recalled that as Magoo evolved as a character in the first film, "the myopia was a story necessity; one of the many ingredients that make the narrative workable."[57] It also became the most recognizable trait of Mr. Magoo.

Due to his nearsightedness, Magoo often ends up in trouble: he touches what he shouldn't touch and pushes those buttons that put him in extreme danger. But, as he cannot see the danger, Magoo thinks everything is fine. He is so convinced that what he sees is what truly exists, that he has an explanation for every apparently inexplicable situation. UPA director Pete Burness recalled that "the important thing is the big mistake in Magoo's mind of thinking that he sees something that he does not."[58] In fact, Mr. Magoo says in the opening theme song of the animated shorts: "I tell you boy, that's a corker!" So, when he doesn't have an explanation for what he truly sees, he simply admits the strangest events into his personal world of paradoxical explanations. Burness added: "The important thing was Magoo's absolute self-confidence, the absolute certainty that he is right at all times."[59] An article that appeared in *Graphis* described Magoo as follows:

> [He is] a character who sows confusion along the borders of the real and the unreal. He has, in his nearsightedness, a touching and unshaken confidence in the reasonableness of the world, which therefore functions in accordance with his own conceptions, no matter how wild the chaos which surrounds him.[60]

Amazingly, not only does everything turn out right for Magoo, but he often comes out winning. In *Magoo's Masterpiece*, he ends up getting the police to capture a diamond thief. The same gag is repeated over and over as a comic device: there are villains in *Spellbound Hound*, *Magoo Express* and *Magoo's Canine Mutiny*.[61] In *Trouble Indemnity* (1950), an insurance agent tries to convince Magoo to buy an unfair insurance policy, or in *Bungled Bungalow*, a thief tries to steal Magoo's entire house. It all always works out.

Mr. Magoo is conservative: he stands for traditional values and has difficulty understanding the younger generations. In *Hotsy Footsy*, he says, "The younger generation doesn't understand…," while in *Magoo Makes News*,[62] he complains about a newspaper editorial saying: "This is the age on nothing." In *Magoo's Three Point Landing*, he exclaims: "What's the matter with people these days, never time to lend a helping hand, rush rush rush, rush!" In *Magoo Saves the Bank*,[63] he encourages to save money in a bank account for a bright future: "It's my patriotic duty," he declares.

From the point of view of his creators, Magoo is a human being character, neither animal nor caricature. Therefore, he is almost "live action in his nature. He doesn't move, talk, or act like a cartoon. He behaves almost like a live character actor."[64] And for a human character, he is quite a talkative one. Magoo's thoughts, in fact, are constantly revealed to the public by himself: he is used to thinking out loud. Thus, the Magoo films are more photo-realistic than any other UPA cartoon. If Gerald is a "drawing on the screen,"[65] Magoo is three-dimensional, leading Burness to describe the Mr. Magoo cartoons as "a halfway point between the extreme literalism of Disney and the ultrastylistic animation of the more offbeat UPA films."[66]

Mr. Magoo was created in 1949, after the success of the first two Fox and Crow cartoons (*Robin Hoodlum* and *The Magic Fluke*), made by UPA under the conditions imposed by the Columbia contract. With the success came a certain freedom: Columbia agreed to let UPA create a completely new character. In very few years, Mr. Magoo became so popular that Columbia then pressured Bosustow to favor the production of shorts based on him over the one-shot cartoons so loved by UPA artists. As Steve Bosustow recalled:

> Columbia was becoming more and more unhappy over our offbeat pictures. They told me frankly that unless we came up with a series character that could be accepted and successful under their selling methods, that our contract would not be renewed.[67]

The success of the series provided financial continuity to the studio, but, with the passing of time, the gags and situations became repetitive and Magoo lost his original verve. For example, by 1957 *Magoo's Private War*[68] was simply a weaker version of 1954's *When Magoo Flew*, both having the cinema as the main place of reference, although the situations are reversed. In the former, Magoo is at the cinema and believes himself to be at war with aliens, while in *When Magoo Flew*, he is in an airplane but thinks he's at the cinema.

Over the years, his character underwent a series of changes and became sweeter: instead of a grouchy uncle, he became a sentimental grandfather. After featuring in 53 cartoons in the span of a decade, the original Magoo had been lost. Pete Burness, who directed the majority of the Mr. Magoo films, expressed doubts about it:

> I have later wondered if I was right. I have wondered because he got progressively warmer until he was weakened. ... I think that giving him a warm side was good, but towards the last of the theatrical series he became entirely warm and sweet. He was now basically sweet with occasional breakouts of temper ... For a long time we kept a good balance.[69]

John Hubley, the first to direct a Mr. Magoo film, was similarly perplexed about what happened to the character:

> A great deal in the original character, the strength of him, was the fact that he was so damn bull-headed. It wasn't just that he couldn't

see very well; even if he had been able to see, he still would have made dumb mistakes, 'cause he was such a bull-headed, opinionated old guy. When they started cutting the budget, they used very simplistic animation and gags became obvious. We used to dream up a lot of subtleties and we ad-libbed a lot of the dialogue.[70]

4.3.2 Case Studies

4.3.2.1 Trouble Indemnity

A parody of the film *Double Indemnity*,[71] *Trouble Indemnity* was the first Mr. Magoo cartoon directed by Pete Burness. It tells the story of Magoo who risks death in an attempt to file a claim at the insurance building. The film opens in Mr. Magoo's house. In a living room full of decorations and details, Magoo goes to see who has just rung the bell. It is Aloysius Q. Tirefighter, who tries to sell him an insurance policy. Magoo refuses and escorts him to the door. Accidentally, Magoo has led the salesman to the closet instead of the front door. In the closet, Tirefighter finds all sorts of Rutgers paraphernalia. He dresses himself as a Rutgers alumnus, emerges from the closet and re-introduces himself as "Ron Rutgers of Rutgers College Alumni Association." Magoo is captivated: "Did you say Rutgers?" And, he immediately buys an insurance policy.

Tirefighter, happily astonished, leaves the house, and Magoo stumbles on his tiger carpet. Believing he was bitten by a dog, Magoo decides to go to the insurance company to file a claim. In the vicinity of the insurance building, he ends up perilously perched on beams in mid-air at a construction site. Unaware of what is happening, Magoo believes he is on an elevator and in the corridors of the insurance building. He even mistakes a bag of cement for a man, telling it, "… Don't stand there like a bag of cement, boy!"

Back in the office, Tirefighter informs his boss that he has just sold Magoo a $400,000 policy. "This Magoo, is he a good risk?" asks the boss. "… Don't worry, chief, he's the quiet refined type," says Tirefighter. He then looks out the window and sees Magoo walking on the beams. "Get him! If he falls, the company falls!" screams the chief. The two will uselessly try to capture Magoo.

The animated film is funny and stylized at the same time. As Burness noted, "*Trouble Indemnity* was a good balance of humor and situation with a high level of production design."[72] Due to the nature of the Mr. Magoo animated cartoons, the films had to be entertaining to ensure sales to theatrical exhibitors. Comic devices such as the chase or the introduction of the villain, as well as comic sound effects typical of the animated cartoon tradition, were therefore necessary to make the story workable and sellable. At the same time, however, being a film done by UPA artists, and considering the three-dimensional nature of Mr. Magoo as a character, *Trouble Indemnity* shows a stylization of only the backgrounds. We see, for example, very stylized skyscrapers in the backgrounds, especially when Magoo is in mid-air walking along the beams of the building under construction. According to Burness, the film was one of the most successful Mr. Magoo films[73] and was nominated for an Academy Award in 1950, the same year that UPA's *Gerald McBoing Boing* received the Oscar for Cartoon Short Subject.

4.3.2.2 When Magoo Flew

The first Columbia cinemascope cartoon[74] features Mr. Magoo taking a wrong direction on the way to the movie theater and ending up on a plane at the airport. Once in his seat, he reads the sign "Fasten seat belts" and exclaims: "Interesting title!"

The gags are several. When the flight takes off, Magoo remarks: "This 3-D is extraordinary!" Later a cop appears looking for a man with a briefcase. Magoo believes he is part of the plot of the film that he is watching. Close to him is the man the policeman is looking for. The man leaves the briefcase and goes to hide elsewhere. Magoo notices that the man has forgotten his briefcase and goes after him. He ends up on the wing of the airplane, still believing he is at the cinema: for example, he mistakes a stream of clouds for the smoking lounge. At the end, once on the ground, Magoo has but one complaint: "No cartoons!" About Magoo's wandering around the exterior of the plane, Burness commented:

> This was the basic ingredient of most successful Magoo pictures. In *Trouble Indemnity* we see the best use of this technique. He wandered around on a building under construction and was in danger of falling. A time or two he did fall, but was saved by some near-miraculous happening. Barbara [Hammer] sensed this and wanted to get this danger of falling.[75]

Barbara Hammer was the writer of the *When Magoo Flew* story. She sent a script to the studio with the story of Magoo ending up on a plane while believing he was at the cinema. Tedd Pierce then added the idea of the man with the briefcase as a comic device for Magoo.

The musical score is acoustically rich with diverse instruments. The sounds of a trombone are easily identifiable, for example. The score resonates with the images: a switch in rhythm and style of the music complements a scene in which an unaware Magoo lines up to board the flight behind a group of musicians.

Burness felt that *When Magoo Flew* was the high point of the Mr. Magoo series and that after it, the stories became weaker and the shorts less entertaining.[76] The cartoon premiered in December 1954 and was awarded the Academy Award for Short Subject, Cartoon for that year (Figure 4.1). In 1956, another Magoo cartoon would be an Academy Award winner: *Magoo's Puddle Jumper* (Burness, 1956). When receiving the Oscar in 1956, Burness exclaimed: "I'm sure you all know it, but I feel I must say it. It's not a one man job. Thank you (Figure 4.1)."[77]

4.3.3 Mr. Magoo's World

Although the comicality of the animated series relies on a specific comic device (Mr. Magoo's nearsightedness), which leads to repetitive gags, the character itself is not repetitive. The contexts in which Mr. Magoo is placed are always different and the environment in which he is animated also varies from short to short. His absolute self-confidence and the big mistake he inevitably makes of believing what he hears and sees is rendered by means of contrasts between the character and the world in which he lives, which on screen is represented by the backgrounds.

The backgrounds play an important role in defining Magoo's personality. At the very beginning of *Ragtime Bear*, Magoo stops in front of a road sign in which is written "Straight Ahead for Hodge Podge Lodge." Of course, he hasn't even seen it. So, he asks: "Which way to Hodge Podge Lodge?" looking at the camera, toward the spectator. As if someone is watching the scene from the outside, just like the spectator, an offscreen voice says: "Can't you read the sign?" In his typical self-assured manner, Magoo asserts: "Certainly I can read the signs." He puts on his glasses, looks at the road sign but still can't see it properly. He asks: "What does it say?" and the voice replies: "Straight ahead!"

This dialogue, from the first Mr. Magoo short, exemplifies the dialogue that is continued through the entire series. It is a dialogue between Magoo and the world that surrounds him: the other characters, the environments

FIGURE 4.1 Director Pete Burness with the Oscar in His Hands. Reprinted with permission from Tee Bosustow (*Steve Bosustow's UPA collection, in the care of his son, Tee Bosustow*).

in which he performs his actions and the backgrounds of the films. These backgrounds include objects, houses, streets, cars, hotels, other characters and animals. Everything around him has an almost three-dimensional realistic look, as to reinforce the idea that the world in which he lives is real; it exists outside his mind, although it is his mind that plays tricks to him—and the spectator. It is the lack of synchronicity in the dialogue between Magoo and what surrounds him that we get to know his personality.

Compared to other UPA films, the Mr. Magoo animated cartoons are more talkative. More than dialogues between different "voices" or characters, there is a constant flow of words. Mr. Magoo thinks out loud, and his thoughts prove that his way of interpreting the reality is sincere. It is from this uninterrupted verbal flow that we understand the comicality of the absurdity in which Mr. Magoo lives. The gags are funny because they combine images and sounds: what Magoo wrongly but firmly thinks he has seen, together with what he verbally reveals to us, his explanations of the reality.

To express the complexity of the chaotic external world in which Mr. Magoo lives (while his internal world is made of simple, firm and resolute beliefs), UPA artists designed backgrounds rich in details and colors. Far from the minimalism of the layout design of the one-shot cartoons, the Mr. Magoo animated series shows an explosion of colors and an abundance of refined details in the backgrounds. So, for example, Magoo resides in a cluttered and over-decorated Victorian-style house, far from the Modern interior design recalled, for example, in the furniture of *Gerald McBoing Boing*. An Eames chair could never be found in Mr. Magoo's living room, where every object is ornamental and a reminder of time past.

In *Spellbound Hound*, there is a scene in which Magoo is leaving his cottage on a lake by boat. We see a sign up on the cottage, drawn on the background. It says: "Point Dim View." In *Ragtime Bear*, when Magoo reaches the hotel followed by a bear instead of his nephew, another sign appears: "Rough it at the Hodge Podge Lodge." In *Barefaced Flatfoot*, Magoo and Waldo end up in an empty theater. The stage, the settings and the dressing rooms are like a labyrinth in which they got lost. In *Bungled Bungalow*, Magoo does not recognize his own house, let alone his nephew Waldo, his car, his dog or anything else around him. Therefore, the backgrounds do metaphorically express the confused, hectic and new Modern world in which Magoo performs. America has turned Modern, but he can't see it. Magoo is blind to Modernism.

Traits of Magoo's personality emerge from the backgrounds of the films. He is defined by the backgrounds: they are rich in details as much as a character's personality is full of different sides. And, Magoo's house is as cluttered as the outside world is chaotic. After the HUAC hearings indirectly forced UPA story men to be less satirical, Mr. Magoo's stories began to lack originality, and from here derived the repetitiveness of gags. Nevertheless, UPA artists continued to find ways to express their creativity in the backgrounds' designs, which not only are pertinent to the story and suggest Magoo's personality but also are visually extremely varied in the entire animated series. Perhaps Mr. Magoo was such a successful character because the public got to know him little by little, short by short. As every film revealed how he behaved in a new circumstance, the public got to see another aspect of his personality. By the end, his character was well defined.

4.4 *THE BOING-BOING SHOW*

4.4.1 An Overview

The Boing-Boing Show premiered on Sunday, December 16, 1956, at 5:30 p.m. on the U.S. East Coast, 2:30 p.m. on the West Coast.[78] The animated cartoons that composed the 30-minute show vary greatly both in duration and in content. Animated segments range in length from two minutes to 14 minutes. The contents are also extremely different from one to the other: some seem designed for four- and five-year-olds; others seem intended for an adult audience. The heterogeneity can be explained by the new talents hired to produce the show and the great amount of freedom granted to the new and old directors in terms of contents and styles.

Among those who were hired for the production of the show were animators Ernest Pintoff, Fred Crippen, Teru "Jimmy" Murakami and George Dunning; illustrator Aurelius Battaglia; and musician Mel Levin. Writer Bill Scott was rehired to add humor to the animated segments.[79] People from all the arts were involved, as Jules Engel recalled:

> Musicians like Ernest Gold and Boris Kremenliev and Shorty Rogers, who might never have done music for a cartoon, were hired by UPA. Dory Previn wrote rhyming scripts for the "Twirlinger Twins." Filmmakers from the avant-garde, like John Whitney and Sidney Peterson, were also hired.[80]

Engel also remembered that the studio tried to invite Oskar Fischinger, but he refused, possibly owing to his traumatic experience at Disney.[81]

From a stylistic point of view, the animated segments are extremely varied, although the general trend seems to lean toward a more striking minimalism both in the characters' and backgrounds' designs. Furthermore, less care in the sound effects and in the dialogues seems to have been given to these segments, which are often musicals or mostly narrated by voice actors. Yet, all those UPA aesthetic features already present in the *Jolly Frolics'* animations are brought here to an extreme. In *The Fifty-First Dragon*, for example, we see only a few essential elements that define the space, the characters and their relationship in the space. So, at the very beginning, the dragon is presented only through the shapes of three rhombi, and later the interior/exterior of the castle is defined by colored areas. The film is based on a story by Heywood Broun and is narrated by a male voice actor. There is a musical score and few dialogues between the characters. There are no sound effects.

The influence of Modern art is present in *The Boing-Boing Show*. In *The King and Joe*, for example, there are strong visual references to the art of Paul Klee. Minimalism is evident, for example, in *One Wonderful Girl* and in *Pee-Wee the Kiwi Bird*, where, the characters are literally floating on green backgrounds.[82] A similar approach is present in *Two by Two*, conceived by Howard Beckerman and directed by George Dunning.[83] These last two segments are both narrated in the form of musicals.

Abstractions are present in *Lion Hunt, Blues Pattern* and *The Performing Painter*, all three designed by experimental filmmaker John Whitney Sr. in collaboration with Ernest Pintoff and Fred Crippen.[84] Whitney explained how *Lion Hunt*, a musical piece, was conceived:

> The lively music was sung by two girls who nominally were bragging about going on a lion hunt and boasting, "Who's afraid?", but each time they repeated this, new innuendos crept in. I did the visual in black-and-white. For the background jungle, I used real philodendron plants (black-lit) that I would shake at specific intervals when a particularly comic percussive beat occurred in the music. In front of the plants, I optically printed silhouettes of safari bearers, spears, underbrush, etc (all cut-outs), and stylized drawings of the lion—all of which I had "animated" by manipulating the paper in real-time under the camera.[85]

In *Blues Pattern*, Whitney made "abstract designs to express the jazz improvisation of the combo."[86] Here, the animation of a group of jazz musician alternated to the animation of blue(s) rectangles: the geometric figures "dance" according to the rhythm of the jazz music, composed by Milton "Shorty" Rogers. *Blues Patterns* is an attempt at combining character animation with visual music.[87]

The Performing Painter also strives to combine character animation with visual music. Here, we see the visualization of the "abstract expressionism" of an "action" painter[88] who improvises on the canvas. His brush strokes spark on the screen as flashes of colors.

The Performing Painter is part of a mini-series of animated cartoons called *Meet the Artist*. Originally, there were three cartoons conceived for the Museum of Modern Art's "Television Project"[89] by Sidney Peterson: *The Invisible Moustache of Raoul Dufy, The Merry-Go-Round in the Jungle*, about Henri Rousseau, and *The Day of the Fox: A Legend of Sharaku*, about the Japanese print artist Tōshūsai Sharaku. After the production of *The Invisible Moustache of Raoul Dufy*, the MoMA abandoned Peterson's project, and UPA carried on the production of the subsequent animated shorts.[90] Following are Peterson's recollections on the project:

> Each one was animated by a different team—Aurie Battaglia did DUFY, I think T. Hee or maybe Bobe Cannon did MERRY-GO-ROUND based on Lew Keller's designs, and Alan Zaslove did SHARAKU. The results are quite different. MERRY-GO-ROUND has a regular cartoon style that even renders Rousseau's paintings in a stylized version. But Alan Zaslove was crazy about Sharaku's work, and respected it so much that he kept the images of Sharaku's prints in the film very faithful to the originals. I made up the fable of Kitsuné the Fox to explain the mysteriously brief career of "Sharaky." I think it worked very well—it was really in the Japanese tradition and sensibility.[91]

A similar mini-series was *Meet the Inventor*. It consisted of three cartoons about Eli Whitney, Robert Fulton and Samuel Morse. For the *Dusty of the Circus* cycle, six cartoons were produced: *Turned around Clown*, *The Five-Cent Nickel*, *Lion on the Loose*, *The Elephant Mystery*, *The Sad Lion* and *The Bear Scare*.[92] The main character of the series is Dusty, the son of a circus owner, who has the ability to talk with animals. In *Turned around Clown*, for example, Dusty helps the troupe's clown recover his smile.

Mr. Longview Looks Back is yet another series, created by T. Hee,[93] consisting of four cartoons. It opens with Mr. Walter Longview, a journalist at his news desk, who introduces a historical event and, eventually, the reporter who will interview people on the spot. In *The Trojan Horse*[94] segment, for example, the viewer is taken back to August 14, 1190 BCE, in the middle of the Trojan War. The other three episodes cover the trial of Zelda Belle, the Great Fire of Rome and Christopher Columbus' "discovery" of the Americas. The series signaled the pervasiveness of television in the American household. *The Twirlinger Twins*, another series, focused on two little twin girls whose stories are told by them singing. It was created by Osmond Evans and Rudy Larriva.[95]

A noteworthy and funny cartoon is *Mr. Tingley's Tangle*, directed by T. Hee. Mr. Tingley commutes every day from suburbia to the city. His life, therefore, seems rather uninteresting, but when he gets home every evening, he ends up being "amused" by his family life, as happens one night when they all go to a drive-in cinema. Mr. Tingley would love to just sit back and enjoy the movie, *Passion Under the Pyramids*, with its beautiful Egyptian dancing girls, but he is frequently interrupted by his sons getting out of the car: every time they exit the vehicle, the interior light switches on, disturbing Mr. Tingley from properly watching the picture. The cartoon is another example of a UPA short that has a suburban environment as a relevant landscape for the story.

Some animated segments of *The Boing-Boing Show* are repetitive of previous UPA films. *The Little Boy Who Ran Away*,[96] for example, is about a little Gerald-like boy who leaves his suburban home to go to the city and discovers that he misses his dog and everything else too much to be far from home. *A Little Journey*[97] seems to be inspired by *Madeline*, at least in the general mood. It is about the French village of Avignon and its inhabitants, busy in their typical-day activities.

The Boing-Boing Show was not as successful as its creators had hoped. According to Bosustow, both CBS and the UPA crew were to blame: "We were 10 years ahead of our times, and CBS gave us a lousy time. … Sometimes we were so deep we didn't understand it ourselves."[98]

4.4.2 Case Study: *The Invisible Moustache of Raoul Dufy*

Written by Sidney Peterson and directed by Aurelius Battaglia,[99] *The Invisible Moustache of Raoul Dufy* premiered at the 1955 MoMA exhibition on UPA cartoons. It is the story of the French painter Raoul Dufy, who spent his entire life working during the day and painting at night, until he became old and famous.

The film opens with an introduction: "This is the story of Raoul Dufy, the painter…," and we see a little blond boy drawn on a framed canvas. Raoul, the narrator informs us, looks like an English millionaire, but he neither is English nor a rich boy. His blue eyes and blond hair come from his ancestors, particularly his "great great great great great great grandfather," who was a Scot and fought "a great battle" in Scotland. Here, we see the scene of the battle: armored knights coming from the left attack horizontally Dufy's ancestor, who is coming from the right. In the UPA tradition, the knights look like sketched figures drawn on a two-dimensional, flat violet and blue surface. Next, we learn that the ancestor moved to France, where people started to call him "Duf" and, after a while, "Dufy." We see a woman and a man and some trees on the backgrounds: the characters resemble the main characters of Georges Seurat's painting *Un dimanche après-midi à l'Île de la Grande Jatte.*[100]

"So, many years later, Raoul Dufy lives in the port of Le Havre," the narrator continues. Here, the harbor of Le Havre resembles some of Dufy's paintings that might have been used from UPA artists as source of reference, such as *Regatta at Cowes.*[101] In the UPA cartoon, there are no fauvist colors, only sketched boats in the harbor.

After being introduced to Dufy's family, we are informed that Dufy likes to draw and paint. Le Havre, we come to know from the narrator, was a cradle of painters. Raoul would like to be a painter and a millionaire, to the point that he makes up a song:

> If I can be a painter, I'll be a millionaire. I'll buy a lot of pictures and put them everywhere... if I can be a painter, a rich man I will be. My castle will be famous as a pictures' gallery.

But his father wants him to earn money and not be another painter. Mr. Dufy speaks to Raoul:

> It was a fine thing to paint, but there was a tiny set and a place for everything, especially a time to make money and a time to paint. The time to make money was from half past 6 in the morning until 6 at night. Painting could come later, after dinner.

So, Raoul went to work. He counted bags of coffee that came from ships, from half past six in the morning until six o'clock at night, as his father told him. Then, he painted.

"He worked hard, but he didn't get rich. He grew up and he even grew a moustache," explains the narrator. His mustache was so blonde that nobody could see it, not even Raoul, "although he could feel it." Therefore, it was an invisible mustache. Inspired by his mustache, Raoul thought: "I want to paint the things that people cannot see, so that they will see them." So, he kept on painting.

He grew older and continued to paint. Here, we see an abstract sequence of one canvas creating another canvas and then another and so on. Dufy's famous paintings appear on the screen one after another, until "a strange thing happened: people began to look." The narrator continues: "They began to see the world that Dufy saw: boat races, parades, beach scenes, still lifes, fountains, concerts, musical instruments." On the screen, we see all the famous Dufy paintings portraying these subjects. From one painting, an eye is animated, and we see an old man looking at us with his monocle, as if he is looking at Raoul's canvas. Then, we see a multitude of people looking at us: some men and women resemble cubist figures, and a woman in particular is drawn like a Modigliani model, as was Nelly Bly in *Rooty Toot Toot*.

We are told that Raoul's "originality was rather contagious": people start to paint in his style. "His paintings influenced women's fashion," and "eventually, his art became a part of people's daily lives": women pass behind Dufy's canvas and exit with their clothes transformed into the same patterns of the canvas. Raoul Dufy is now an affirmed painter: "[I]t was a world; the world of Dufy, of Raoul Dufy, the painter, who had blue eyes and blonde hair, and looked like a small English millionaire—and with an invisible moustache." The film closes with the same image it started with—Raoul drawn in a framed canvas—but here, Raoul is depicted with an invisible red mustache on his face, while his song is sung until the last frame. At the very end, we see only the red mustache disappearing in the center of the screen.

Different from other animated segments of *The Boing-Boing Show*, this film shows a certain complexity in the sound treatment that is equal to the UPA one-shot cartoons. A musical score, a narrating voice, talking characters, sometimes even in French, lyrics sung by the protagonist, moments of "silence" and casual environmental sound effects are all combined together effectively.

The Invisible Moustache of Raoul Dufy is a brilliant film for the way it is narrated, the audiovisual style adopted by its creators and the numerous visual references to Modern art. It is not surprising, therefore, that it was commissioned by the Museum of Modern Art, which by that time, was trying to bring Modern art closer to the people, especially by courting the female public through television.[102]

4.5 THE ANIMATED FEATURE FILM: *1001 ARABIAN NIGHTS*

1001 Arabian Nights premiered in December 1959. By that time, the UPA studio was finding it hard to make a profit by doing just short cartoons. Further complicating matters, TV had inaugurated a new era for cartoon production and distribution, and Columbia had terminated its distribution deal with UPA the year before. In reaction, UPA attempted to make an animated feature film, something only Disney and the Fleischer Studios had done before in the U.S.

Directed by ex-Disney veteran Jack Kinney, the *1001 Arabian Nights* features Mr. Magoo as Abdul Azziz Magoo, uncle of the poor but honest Aladdin, who is in love with Princess Yasminda, the sultan's daughter. Set in ancient Baghdad, the plot includes the presence of an evil, mean and avaricious character: the wicked magician Wazir. As in the famous book, *One Thousand and One Nights*, which served as a reference source for the film, there is a magic lamp with its jinni (genie) and a magic rug. The story can be reduced to its essential elements: to win Yasminda's hand in marriage, either Aladdin or the wicked Wazir must gain possession of the magic lamp, which lies in a cave that can only be opened by "a seventh son of a seventh son," who turns out to be Aladdin. Wazir needs the lamp to become the most powerful man in the land. Aladdin needs it to be the richest man in the land so that he can save the kingdom and marry the princess. Yasminda is betrothed to the wicked Wazir, but with the intervention of the jinni and with the help of a magic rug, Magoo will save the day and get Yasminda to marry his nephew (Figures 4.2 and 4.3).

FIGURE 4.2 Model Sheet of the *1001 Arabian Nights'* Accountant. Reprinted with permission from Tee Bosustow (*Steve Bosustow's UPA collection, in the care of his son, Tee Bosustow*).

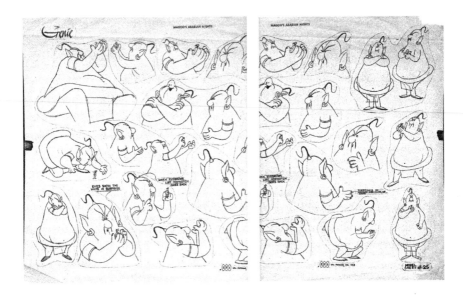

FIGURE 4.3   Model Sheet of the *1001 Arabian Nights'* Genie. Reprinted with permission from Tee Bosustow (*Steve Bosustow's UPA collection, in the care of his son, Tee Bosustow*).

From a stylistic perspective, the film seems to be closer to the Disney tradition than to the UPA heritage. It is a musical—not an effective one, but a musical nonetheless—that includes the presence of animals as a means to define the personality of the characters. Magoo, for example, has a cat, Bowzir, although he thinks it is a dog, and the wicked Wazir has several assistants in the shape of spiders, rats and bats. A review in the *Hollywood Citizen News* noted:

> It must be chronicled here that Aladdin looks just like the Prince in Sleeping Beauty and the wicked Wazir resembles the wicked witch of that other fairy screen epic. Some of the 'effects' are also not too original and remind you of the snowflakes of former cartoons.[103]

Still, the journalist praised the originality of Magoo, a character still found to be refreshing although he is now playing a role in an animated feature film intentionally aimed at children. In fact, *Newsweek* opined: "Children are likely to love it all, even though adults may feel that Magoo has turned his back on them."[104]

The film is interesting for some visuals that address the rich flavor of Persian tapestry and for the musical score that explicitly incorporates Eastern Asian melodic references. Robert Dranko was the production designer. At the beginning of the film, for example, we see a stylized Baghdad set against a blue nocturnal sky: the city with its walls is only defined by white lines on a deep blue background. When Aladdin meets Yasminda, the animation consists of flowers that start exploding on the screen in a naive children's style of drawing. Other effective visual solutions are evident, for example, in the illustrations of the exteriors and interiors of the sultan's palace, which are reminiscent of Persian architecture and rich in Persian patterns, respectively.

Although the film stands out in some scenes for this visual Persian scenery, it lacks those aesthetic innovations that made UPA famous, partly because the story is weak and partly because the characters are more three-dimensional than the other UPA flat-designed characters that were so praised by the public and the press. As Charles Stinson, journalist of the *L.A. Times* put it:

> U.P.A.'s sophisticated, semi-abstract art technique, so celebrated in art houses, has been of course, much modified for the transfer to domestic audiences. Which is to say, that it has been crossed, and not always deftly, with that kind of ordinary sentimental comic strip cartoon style represented by, say, Bugs Bunny.[105]

So, by 1959, UPA was in economic stress. In a year, Bosustow would be selling the studio to Saperstein, who later exploited the famous Mr. Magoo character for television series. Nonetheless, UPA had by now become a trademark. Numerous studios, animators and directors had been inspired by the revolution in animation design that had begun at the Otto K. Olesen building and exploded later in the Burbank studio. This UPA influence is explored in Chapter 5.

ENDNOTES

1. "How Does UPA Do It?," 44.
2. UPA Financial Statements at July 1, 1946; Steve Bosustow's UPA collection.
3. Maltin, *Of Mice and Magic: A History of American Animated Cartoons*, 326.
4. Shull and Wilt, *Doing Their Bit: Wartime American Animated Short Films, 1939–1945*, 169.
5. Abraham, *When Magoo Flew: The Rise and Fall of Animation Studio UPA*.

6. Barrier, *Hollywood Cartoons: American Animation in Its Golden Age*. This hybrid nature of the animated short (stylized design of the backgrounds and rounded characters) might be ascribed to the fact that the artists who collaborated at the film were friends who worked at different animation studios and then participated on this project after hours.

7. Pikkov, *Animasophy: Theoretical Writings on the Animated Film*, 132.

8. *The Races of Mankind*. By Ruth Benedict and Gene Weltfish. Public Affairs Committee, Inc., New York, Pamphlet no. 85, 31 pp. (10c).

9. Abraham, *When Magoo Flew: The Rise and Fall of Animation Studio UPA*, 65.

10. John Hubley and Faith Hubley, "Animation: A Creative Challenge—by John and Faith Hubley (interview)."

11. David Hilberman, quoted in Maltin, *Of Mice and Magic: A History of American Animated Cartoons*, 327.

12. According to the 10th edition of *Merriam-Webster's Collegiate Dictionary*, *flat-hat* is defined as "to fly low in an airplane in a reckless manner."

13. Abraham, *When Magoo Flew: The Rise and Fall of Animation Studio UPA*.

14. John Hubley and Faith Hubley, "Animation: A Creative Challenge—by John and Faith Hubley (interview)."

15. *Punchy de Leon*, directed by John Hubley (1950; DVD, *UPA: The Jolly Frolics Collection*, Culver City, CA: Sony Pictures Home Entertainment, 2012).

16. Each Columbia contract lasted five years: the first one from 1948 to 1953, and the second one, from 1953 to 1958. In 1958, Columbia decided not to renew it, and "cartoons in progress were completed." The last *Jolly Frolics* animated short made was *Picnics are Fun and Dino's Serenade*, directed by Lew Keller and Fred Crippen, and released in theaters on January 16, 1959. The last UPA short distributed by Columbia was *Terror Faces Magoo*, directed by Chris Ishii and Jack Goodford (1959; DVD, *Mr. Magoo: The Theatrical Collection*, Culver City, CA: Sony Pictures Home Entertainment, 2014), and theatrically released in July 1959. Abraham, *When Magoo Flew: The Rise and Fall of Animation Studio UPA*, 206.

17. Abraham, *When Magoo Flew: The Rise and Fall of Animation Studio UPA*.

18. John Hubley was also the supervising director of three Mr. Magoo animated cartoons that had Pete Burness as animation director: *Spellbound Hound* (1949), *Trouble Indemnity* (1950) and *Bungled Bungalow* (1950). He was the sole director of *The Ragtime Bear* (1949), *Barefaced Flatfoot* (1951) and *Fuddy-Duddy-Buddy* (1951). *Mr. Magoo: The Theatrical Collection*; DVD, Culver City, CA: Sony Pictures Home Entertainment, 2014.

19. These were *Magoo's Moose Hunt* (1957) and *Scoutmaster Magoo* (1958). *Mr. Magoo: The Theatrical Collection*; DVD, Culver City, CA: Sony Pictures Home Entertainment, 2014.

20. *Bringing up Mother*, directed by William T. Hurtz (1954; DVD, *UPA: The Jolly Frolics Collection*, Culver City, CA: Sony Pictures Home Entertainment, 2012).

21. Oeri, "UPA: A New Dimension for the Comic Strip," 470.

22. Stephen Bosustow, quoted in Rieder, "The Development of the Satire of Mr. Magoo," 25.

23. Herb Klynn, quoted in Becki Lee Parker, "UPA Animation: No Animals, No Violence, Just Good Stories" (unpublished paper, University of Oregon, Eugene, OR, 1993).

24. *The Popcorn Story*, directed by Art Babbitt (1950; DVD, *UPA: The Jolly Frolics Collection*, Culver City, CA: Sony Pictures Home Entertainment, 2012).

25. *Georgie and the Dragon*, directed by Robert Cannon (1951; DVD, *UPA: The Jolly Frolics Collection*, Culver City, CA: Sony Pictures Home Entertainment, 2012).

26. *The Wonder Gloves*, directed by Robert Cannon (1951; DVD, *UPA: The Jolly Frolics Collection*, Culver City, CA: Sony Pictures Home Entertainment, 2012).

27. *Ballet-Oop*, directed by Robert Cannon (1954; DVD, *UPA: The Jolly Frolics Collection*, Culver City, CA: Sony Pictures Home Entertainment, 2012).

28. *Pete Hothead*, directed by Pete Burness (1952; DVD, *UPA: The Jolly Frolics Collection*, Culver City, CA: Sony Pictures Home Entertainment, 2012).

29. According to the 10th edition of *Merriam-Webster's Collegiate Dictionary*, *jaywalk* is defined as "to cross a street carelessly or at an illegal or dangerous place."

30. Charles Daggett, Production Notes, "Gerald McBoing Boing," Early Museum History: Administrative Records, III.26.a; The Museum of Modern Art Archives, New York.

31. Daggett, Production Notes, "Gerald McBoing Boing," Early Museum History: Administrative Records, III.26.a; The Museum of Modern Art Archives, New York, 2.

32. Ibid.

33. Pikkov, *Animasophy: Theoretical Writings on the Animated Film*, 52.

34. Donald W. Graham, *Composing Pictures: Donald W. Graham* (Beverly Hills, CA: Silman-James Press, 2009. Originally published: New York, NY: Van Nostrand Reinhold Co., 1970), 83.

35. Paul Julian, quoted in Barrier, *Hollywood Cartoons: American Animation in Its Golden Age*, 529.

36. Charles Daggett, Production Notes, "The Unicorn in the Garden," Early Museum History: Administrative Records, III.26.a; The Museum of Modern Art Archives, New York, 2.

37. Ibid.

38. Daggett, Production Notes, "The Unicorn in the Garden," EMH, III.26.a., MoMA Archives, NY, 2.

39. Jon Newsom, "'A Sound Idea': Music for Animated Films," *Quarterly Journal of the Library of Congress* 37, nos. 3/4 (1980): 305. www.jstor.org /stable/29781862?seq=1#page_scan_tab_contents, accessed April 8, 2015.

40. Ibid., 306–307.

41. Ted Parmelee, in Charles Daggett, Production Notes, "The Tell-Tale Heart," Early Museum History: Administrative Records, III.26.a; The Museum of Modern Art Archives, New York, 2.

42. Ibid., 3.

43. Ibid.

44. Ted Parmelee, in Daggett, Production Notes, "The Tell-Tale Heart," Early Museum History: Administrative Records, III.26.a; The Museum of Modern Art Archives, New York, 3.

45. *Gerald McBoing Boing's Symphony*, directed by Robert Cannon (1953; DVD, *UPA: The Jolly Frolics Collection*, Culver City, CA: Sony Pictures Home Entertainment, 2012).

46. *How Now Boing Boing*, directed by Robert Cannon (1954; DVD, *UPA: The Jolly Frolics Collection*, Culver City, CA: Sony Pictures Home Entertainment, 2012).

47. *Gerald McBoing! Boing! On Planet Moo*, directed by Robert Cannon (1956; DVD, *UPA: The Jolly Frolics Collection*, Culver City, CA: Sony Pictures Home Entertainment, 2012).

48. *Four Wheels No Brakes*, directed by Ted Parmelee (1955; DVD, *UPA: The Jolly Frolics Collection*, Culver City, CA: Sony Pictures Home Entertainment, 2012).

49. *Trees and Jamaica Daddy*, directed by Lew Keller and Fred Crippen (1958; DVD, *UPA: The Jolly Frolics Collection*, Culver City, CA: Sony Pictures Home Entertainment, 2012).

50. *Sailing and Village Band*, directed by Lew Keller and Fred Crippen (1958; DVD, *UPA: The Jolly Frolics Collection*, Culver City, CA: Sony Pictures Home Entertainment, 2012).

51. *Spring and Saganaki*, directed by Lew Keller and Fred Crippen (1958; DVD, *UPA: The Jolly Frolics Collection*, Culver City, CA: Sony Pictures Home Entertainment, 2012).

52. *Picnics are Fun and Dino's Serenade*, directed by Lew Keller and Fred Crippen (1959; DVD, *UPA: The Jolly Frolics Collection*, Culver City, CA: Sony Pictures Home Entertainment, 2012).

53. *Kangaroo Courting*, directed by Pete Burness (1954; DVD, *Mr. Magoo: The Theatrical Collection*, Culver City, CA: Sony Pictures Home Entertainment, 2014).

54. *Destination Magoo*, directed by Pete Burness (1954; DVD, *Mr. Magoo: The Theatrical Collection*, Culver City, CA: Sony Pictures Home Entertainment, 2014).

55. *Calling Doctor Magoo*, directed by Pete Burness (1956; DVD, *Mr. Magoo: The Theatrical Collection*, Culver City, CA: Sony Pictures Home Entertainment, 2014).

56. *Pink and Blue Blues*, directed by Pete Burness (1952; DVD, *Mr. Magoo: The Theatrical Collection*, Culver City, CA: Sony Pictures Home Entertainment, 2014).

57. John Hubley, quoted in Rieder, "The Development of the Satire of Mr. Magoo," 61.

58. Pete Burness, quoted in Rieder, "The Development of the Satire of Mr. Magoo," 66.

59. Ibid, 74.
60. Oeri, "UPA: A New Dimension for the Comic Strip," 471.
61. *Magoo's Canine Mutiny*, directed by Pete Burness (1956; DVD, *Mr. Magoo: The Theatrical Collection*, Culver City, CA: Sony Pictures Home Entertainment, 2014).
62. *Magoo Makes News*, directed by Pete Burness (1955; DVD, *Mr. Magoo: The Theatrical Collection*, Culver City, CA: Sony Pictures Home Entertainment, 2014).
63. *Magoo Saves the Bank*, directed by Pete Burness (1957; DVD, *Mr. Magoo: The Theatrical Collection*, Culver City, CA: Sony Pictures Home Entertainment, 2014).
64. Pete Burness, quoted in Rieder, "The Development of the Satire of Mr. Magoo," 68.
65. Bobe Cannon, quoted in Rieder, "The Development of the Satire of Mr. Magoo," 86.
66. Pete Burness, quoted in Rieder, "The Development of the Satire of Mr. Magoo," 88.
67. Steve Bosustow, quoted in Rieder, "The Development of the Satire of Mr. Magoo," 57.
68. *Magoo's Private War*, directed by Rudy Larriva (1957; DVD, *Mr. Magoo: The Theatrical Collection*, Culver City, CA: Sony Pictures Home Entertainment, 2014).
69. Pete Burness, quoted in Rieder, "The Development of the Satire of Mr. Magoo," 105.
70. John Hubley and Faith Hubley, "Animation: A Creative Challenge—by John and Faith Hubley (interview)."
71. *Double Indemnity*, directed by Billy Wilder (1944; DVD, Los Angeles, CA: Universal Pictures Home Entertainment, 2006).
72. Pete Burness, quoted in Rieder, "The Development of the Satire of Mr. Magoo," 110.
73. Ibid.
74. Rieder, "The Development of the Satire of Mr. Magoo."
75. Pete Burness, quoted in Rieder, "The Development of the Satire of Mr. Magoo," 112.
76. Ibid.
77. The author thanks the archivists of the Margaret Herrick Library, Academy of Motion Picture Arts and Sciences in Beverly Hills, for providing this information.
78. Promotional book for "Television's first animated variety show," December 1956, Abe and Charlotte Levitow papers, Margaret Herrick Library, Academy of Motion Picture Arts and Sciences.
79. Abraham, *When Magoo Flew: The Rise and Fall of Animation Studio UPA*.
80. Jules Engel, in Moritz, "UPA, Reminiscing 30 Years Later," 16.
81. Ibid.
82. The directors of the three animated segments are unknown.

83. Abraham, *When Magoo Flew: The Rise and Fall of Animation Studio UPA*.

84. John Whitney, in Moritz, "UPA, Reminiscing 30 Years Later."

85. Ibid., 19.

86. Ibid.

87. *Visual music* is defined by Maureen Furniss as "equivalents to music in visual form, using color, shape, and motion to suggest musical qualities in painting, animation, or other types of art," in *The Animation Bible: A Practical Guide to the Art of Animating, from Flipbooks to Flash*, 328.

88. John Whitney, in Moritz, "UPA, Reminiscing 30 Years Later," 19.

89. In the first half of the 1950s, MoMA was interested in making art more accessible to people at home watching TV. The idea was to use television as a medium for arts education and simultaneously as an advertising tool for the museum. Therefore, MoMA tried to develop "popular television format[s] for art education." One of these formats was the animated children's series *They Became Artists*, which was supposed to be made by UPA. According to Spigel, Sidney Peterson played a relevant role in orchestrating a deal between the museum, NBC, UPA and even the artist Marc Chagall. Spigel, *TV by Design: Modern Art and the Rise of Network Television*, 159.

90. Ibid.

91. Sidney Peterson, in Moritz, "UPA, Reminiscing 30 Years Later," 20.

92. The directors of these animated segments are unknown.

93. Abraham, *When Magoo Flew: The Rise and Fall of Animation Studio UPA*.

94. The director is unknown.

95. Abraham, *When Magoo Flew: The Rise and Fall of Animation Studio UPA*.

96. The director is unknown.

97. The director is unknown.

98. "Creativity Basic," 60.

99. Aurelius Battaglia directed also *The Beanstalk Trial* for *The Boing-Boing Show*. Abraham, *When Magoo Flew: The Rise and Fall of Animation Studio UPA*.

100. Georges Seurat, *Un dimanche après-midi à l'Île de la Grande Jatte*, 1884–1886. Oil on canvas. Art Institute of Chicago.

101. Raoul Dufy, *Regatta at Cowes*, 1934. Oil painting. Washington D.C. National Gallery of Art.

102. Spigel, *TV by Design: Modern Art and the Rise of Network Television*.

103. H.F., "Oh for a Magic Lamp Like Magoo in '1001 Nights'!" *Hollywood Citizen News*, December 21, 1959; *1001 Arabian Nights* file, Core collection production files, Margaret Herrick Library, Academy of Motion Picture Arts and Sciences.

104. "Bright-Toned Fantasy," *Newsweek*, December 21, 1959; *1001 Arabian Nights* file.

105. Charles Stinson, "Mr. Magoo Triumphs over Arabian Foes," *Los Angeles Times*, December 18, 1959; *1001 Arabian Nights* file.

CHAPTER 5

The UPA Formula

From Direct Influences to Concurrent Examples of Modernism in Animation

This had always been the objective of modernism: to flatten out, to bring to the surface, in order to make the base show itself for what it is.

ESTHER LESLIE[1]

UPA's influence is extensive. During the 1950s and 1960s, both in the U.S. and internationally, animation turned toward more streamlined characters and backgrounds, limited animation, non-objective designs and an expressionistic use of colors. Some studios and some artists were directly influenced by UPA, especially in the U.S.; others, particularly those belonging to the Eastern European countries, developed a new simplified audiovisual language from their own traditions. The result was internationally similar, however: the incorporation of Modern art and Modern graphic design into animation with Modern sounds and contemporary music. This chapter focuses on the direct influence of UPA on the U.S. animation industry, its indirect international influence and what has been added to the film language by those artists and studios that referred to UPA.

The directors and animated films presented here are *illustrative examples* of a major stylistic trend in animation. They neither provide a complete overview of worldwide animated cinema of the 1950s and 1960s, nor can they be considered an exhaustive list of all the animated films in which it is possible to infer an aesthetic influence from UPA. Among worldwide production, this work presents selected films and directors that more than others exemplify, in a specific nation or geographic area, a common trend in animation. Each of these directors and films is different. Whereas they all express audiovisual features that can be ascribed to UPA films, they do so in different ways. Not only does every geographic area and nation have its cultural peculiarities, but also every director has his or her own personal audiovisual style, and even films made by the same director can be stylistically different from one to another. Therefore, UPA direct and indirect influences on international productions are analyzed as highly specific examples. The UPA example was not simply copied but assimilated by international directors. Their films thus express a certain level of "contamination" of stylistic features coming, for example, from Disney or UPA and local stylistic features belonging to their cultural heritage. Yet, in the specific case of Europe as a region, UPA-like audiovisual stylistic solutions had developed independently, even years before UPA existed. A simplified audiovisual language in animated cinema had been addressed by isolated European films as early as 1934, as was the case of *La Joie de vivre*,[2] a two-dimensional stylized animated short made in France. In sum, the breadth of the considered geographic areas and the historical transitional periods, the assorted directors and the differences in their simplified audiovisual styles need to be taken into consideration when evaluating UPA direct and indirect influences on Modern animations.

5.1 DIRECT INFLUENCES OF UPA IN THE UNITED STATES

UPA's existence was short; nevertheless, it had an impact on other studios. UPA's main rival, Disney, made some shorts that clearly incorporate graphic design and might be interpreted as UPA-inspired. Disney's *Toot, Whistle, Plunk and Boom*, awarded with an Academy Award for Cartoon Short Subject in 1953, is probably the most exemplary. It is an educational and entertaining animated short film that illustrates the principles and progress of symphonic music throughout historical achievement. The story is told by an owl that teaches the study of musical instruments to a class of bird-children. When the owl-teacher is illustrating how an orchestra performs, for example, we see a highly stylized, almost scribbled orchestra playing the instruments. The musicians are later portrayed as streamlined transparent figures made of white lines on a violet background. At times the short resembles the UPA animated short *The Oompahs*, which was distributed just one year earlier.

Similar visual solutions are present in *Melody*,[3] an animated Disney film that was part of a series of shorts called *Adventures in Music*, in which the principles of music are taught. Only two shorts were produced: the first to be released was *Melody*, followed by *Toot, Whistle, Plunk and Boom*. In *Melody*, for example, areas of colors do not precisely fill in the outlines but rather are used much as in UPA's *Gerald McBoing Boing*. The visual influence is strong and evident. In a sequence in which the students are illustrating a story by singing it, we see images drawn in a very naive style, as if they were made by children, a visual solution already proposed by UPA artists.

Furthermore, Disney productions of the 1950s seems to rely less on animal characters and more on human characters, or at least on characters that are slightly different from the traditional classic Disney formula. For example, in *A Cowboy Needs a Horse*,[4] the protagonist is a child who dreams of being a cowboy. Similarly, in *Pigs Is Pigs*,[5] the characters are human beings. This tendency was anticipated, for example, during the 1940s by *Johnnie Fedora and Alice Bluebonnet*,[6] the story of two hats that fell in love. By the 1961 animated feature film *One Hundred and One Dalmatians*[7] some stylization, especially in the background design, is evident.

A specific director influenced by UPA stylization was the highly original Tex Avery. As early as 1951, he introduced an angular flat character in *Symphony in Slang*.[8] The character resembles one of the protagonists of *The Dover Boys at Pimento University*. This trend was also present in his series *The House of Tomorrow* (1949), *The Car of Tomorrow* (1951), *TV of Tomorrow* (1953) and *The Farm of Tomorrow* (1954),[9] a funny yet harsh critique of modern innovations and technologies. In *The Farm of Tomorrow*, for example, there are segments in which the characters are designed as purely sketched colored lines on a blue background.

Sh-h-h-h-h-h[10] mocks the 1950s trends in jazz music and the experimentations with silence of artists such as John Cage. In the film, a middle-age man goes to a psychiatrist after visiting a jazz nightclub where the music was played at full volume. The psychiatrist diagnoses the man as having "a serious case of 'tremble noises.'" He suggests relaxation in some quiet and remote place, stating, "If you do not get away from these noisy horns, your entire nervous system will shatter. You will just blow up!" The man flees to a remote location in the Alps, to a lodge where no one and nothing emits sounds; all communication is through writing. We hear the sound of a tape rolling on as if no sound at all has been recorded on it; we perceive the "noisy silence," as in a John Cage's performance. Next, when the man is ready to go to sleep, his quiet is interrupted by the sound of a horn coming from the room next to him. After many vicissitudes, he will discover that his neighbors are the psychiatrist and his wife, the nurse. The film can be interpreted as a parody of the UPA "highbrow" tendency to incorporate contemporary jazz music into its animated shorts. To reinforce the parody, the opening and closing credits visually consist of three different geometric figures colored in red, yellow and blue, the colors of the UPA logo.

Avery's *Crazy Mixed Up Pup*[11] can also be interpreted as a parody, this time of *Christopher Crumpet*. In the film, a man and a dog switch their identities with a lot of crazy, mixed-up situations and gags, especially in the domestic environment, where the wife of the man goes mad in trying to understand what is happening.

The Pink Phink[12] was the first animated short produced by the DePatie-Freleng studio to feature the Pink Panther.[13] It won an Academy Award in 1964. The success of the short and of the subsequent series rests greatly on the captivating opening musical theme, composed by Henri Mancini, as well as on the main character, the Pink Panther. *The Pink Phink* is about two characters who compete over whether a house should be paint pink or blue. The Little Man paints it blue, while the Pink Panther paints it pink. As soon as the Little Man paints it blue, the Pink Panther covers it over with a coat of pink. By the end, the entire house is painted pink, and so is the Little Man. This short serves as a reminder of the nature of the animated cartoon medium, made of characters and backgrounds that do not necessarily have to be realistically represented. For this reason, *The Pink Phink* owes much to the UPA lesson. The filmic space, for example, is mostly defined by few black lines on a white background. These lines are essential to delineate the interior and the exterior of the house. Sometimes they address a door or a stair. The backgrounds are flat and stylized. Only two characters are animated on the screen, and the two colors, pink and blue, are the true protagonists of the short.

Among UPA-introduced innovations, the use of the so-called limited animation was exploited by Hanna-Barbera for *The Huckleberry Hound Show*, made for TV and broadcast in 1958.[14] Unfortunately, the stylistic innovations that went hand in hand with limited animation in UPA cartoons were disregarded by the two producers, who focused more on productivity and less on quality. During the 1960s, television became virtually the sole communication medium through which animation was broadcast in the U.S., and:

> [L]imited animation became the de facto method of production for television animation. It also became a dismissive shorthand for poor quality work, work that was batted out quickly in order to fill airtime with no consideration for the artistic uses of the technique.[15]

That's why "the graphic simplicity and flatness they [UPA artists] pioneered was the perfect foundation on which to build TV animation, given the limitations of early broadcast technology."[16]

The UPA heritage was carried on and further explored by those artists who founded their own companies or worked as independents after they left UPA. Dave Hilberman and Zachary Schwartz founded Tempo Productions; Herb Klynn and Jules Engel formed Format Films[17]; Adrian Woolery founded Playhouse Pictures, a studio where Bobe Cannon, animator Frank Smith, designer Sterling Sturtevant and ink-and-paint supervisor Mary Cain all worked after they left UPA.[18] Bill Melendez formed his own company and started to produce the *Peanuts* cartoons, which are childlike films in Cannon's tradition.

From UPA Gene Deitch joined Terrytoons.[19] Under his supervision, the studio produced *Flebus*,[20] directed by Ernest Pintoff, and *The Juggler of Our Lady*,[21] directed by Al Kouzel. *Flebus* is the story of a man who is liked by everyone, until one day, he meets Rudolph, who does not like him. Flebus can't help thinking about this all the time. In the typical spirit of the 1950s, therefore, he visits a psychiatrist who determines he is "neurotic." Rudolph, as well, cannot figure out why he dislikes Flebus, so he, too, is diagnosed as "neurotic." The two characters end up being friends. Here, the UPA lesson is brought to an extreme. Pintoff followed the trend initiated with *The Boing-Boing Show*, on which he had worked: the designs are extremely simple, the backgrounds are made of pure colored areas and the frame is filled in by one to two animated characters each. Interesting is the use of sounds, especially when considering that Pintoff was a jazz musician[22]: Flebus' every action is stressed by different sound effects or pieces of scores.

The Juggler of Our Lady is based on a book written by R. O. Blechman and is narrated by Boris Karloff. Set in medieval times, it is the story of a juggler who is ignored by all and decides to become a monk. During a festival honoring the Lady, while all the other monks are offering gifts, he decides to juggle for her until he collapses from exhaustion. The film is interesting for the layouts, which are composed of few essential lines, sometimes even white on a black background. Also, the design of the juggler is very simple and childlike.

After he left Terrytoons, Pintoff started his own company, Pintoff Productions,[23] where he produced and directed two relevant independent cartoons: *The Violinist*[24] and *The Critic*.[25] In *The Violinist*, a musician who plays the violin terribly decides to take lessons from Andreas Fillinger. The great master suggests that "to play with feeling, one must zuffer, zuffer, zuffer!" Here, very few elements are used to suggest the environment in the backgrounds, such as a stylized subway entrance. *The Critic*, awarded the 1963 Academy Award for Cartoon Short Subject, was created and narrated by Mel Brooks. It is about a man who is attending a screening and tries to find a plot in an abstract flux of images. The film features surrealistic, abstract imagery that resembles the work of Norman McLaren, while the voice of the narrator, a cranky old man, complains about the lack of meaning in the animation. At the same time, a classical tune is played: it is the score of the abstract film the man is watching.

Many of the remaining UPA artists left in 1959 to join Jay Ward Productions. The company produced the *Rocky and His Friends* TV show that was re-launched in 1961 as *The Bullwinkle Show*. Among the UPA artists who worked there were Pete Burness, Bill Hurtz, Ted Parmelee, Roy Morita and Sam Clayberger. A prominent figure was also writer Bill Scott, who worked closely with producer Jay Ward. As animation historian Darrel Van Citters explained,

> The UPA cadre consisted of two generations of artists. The first was filled with many of those who had gotten their start at Disney

where they learned their craft, and later had polished their skills during their tenure at UPA and other studios. Most of this group became directors at Ward. The second came largely from the Los Angeles art schools, schools with sterling reputations for turning out high quality artists, places like Chouinard Art Institute, Art Center School and Jepson Art School. These graduates populated the design department at Ward's. Many of these artists brought a new sensibility and excitement to animation, one unencumbered with the formulas and traditions of the past. Their new frontier was television.[26]

Van Citters added, however, that the UPA example, both in terms of limited animation and graphic simplicity, was used by Ward's artists to make funnier cartoons:

Ironically, many of the UPA artists found work at Ward's, doing almost exactly what their prior studio had philosophically rejected, namely, making cartoons with funny animals and reciting classic fairy tales. However, the difference at Ward from both UPA *and* Disney was striking—the visual styling was looser, fresher and more spontaneous. The work done by these artists at their new home was less self-conscious, less precious and more in tune with the audience. It was created solely to get a laugh and not to be admired for its own sake.[27]

If *The Boing-Boing Show* was an experiment of the mid-1950s, a period in which TV was still living its infancy, *The Bullwinkle Show* appeared when TV was already a steady presence in American homes. Production companies had become accustomed to the tastes of the audience, had improved their method of production and had developed contents more likable by the public. We can conclude that *The Boing-Boing Show* served as an early experiment from which subsequent animation studios could take examples of what worked. This could explain why *The Boing-Boing Show* was not particularly successful.

The segments of *The Bullwinkle Show* that most owe a debt to *The Boing-Boing Show* are the *Fractured Fairy Tales*. They were narrated by Edward Everett Horton, the same voice used for *The Unenchanted Princess*[28] segment of *The Boing-Boing Show*. The *Fractured Fairy Tales* employed a simplified graphic similar to UPA cartoons:

> The *Fractured Fairy Tales* produced in Los Angeles boast the sharpest graphics of any of the Ward product and are a visual delight. They were, of course, better animated than those produced in Mexico, but the talents of the UPA diaspora are clearly evident in these episodes.[29]

Among the other artists who started their own studio were John Hubley, who founded Storyboard, Inc.; Fred Crippen, who formed Pantomime Pictures; and Jimmy Murakami, who partnered in Murakami-Wolf.[30] Hubley, with his wife, Faith Elliott, was able to further explore UPA's simplified audiovisual language and to produce highly original animated shorts that were well received and appreciated worldwide.

5.2 MODERN STYLES IN WESTERN ANIMATION

5.2.1 Modern Animation in the United States: UPA Influences at Storyboard, Inc.

John Hubley founded Storyboard, Inc., in 1953. He moved the studio to New York City in 1955, the same year he married Faith Elliott and they together began a lifelong professional partnership. Aside from working on commercials, Hubley produced independent cartoons.[31] He carried on the trend inaugurated by UPA artists of the animated short being considered a work of art and a Modern production as they propose simplified animation and design both in the characters and in the backgrounds. In addition, Hubley was highly influenced by jazz music, Modern art and contemporary graphic design. In his animated shorts, American Modern animation comes to full maturity.

In *Adventure of An **,[32] for example, the asterisk is animated on colorful backgrounds that remind the viewer of the works of the masters Joan Miró, Henri Matisse, Paul Cézanne, William Turner, Pablo Picasso, Paul Klee and Fernand Léger, among others. Especially evident, for example, is the visual reference to Klee's and Cézanne's artworks in the use of colors. The animation is stylized as much as the small asterisk character. The asterisk symbolizes a man whose adventures are illustrated from his infancy to his senior years. The film revolves around the idea that the asterisk, like every man, likes to play and to learn by playing but inevitably must face the severity of his father, who has forgotten the importance of play. From the beginning, the opening credits provide a clue to how to interpret the film by displaying the written sentence:

> The Adventures of An * who lives in a [house] where he loves to play and enjoys each new thing he sees and as he grows he sees more and enjoys more unlike his father who has forgotten how to play and how to see new things.

The written words appear in synchronicity with the rhythmic jazz score. Here, the director enjoys playing with signs, images and symbols. We do not read the word *house*, for example, but we see the asterisk moving inside a very stylized house and get the idea of it from the animation. The attitude of the two characters, father and son, are underlined by the jazz music, which is joyful when the asterisk is playing and intimidating when the father gets angry at his son's activities. We hear, for example, the sound of a loud horn when the father is trying to forbid his son to perform some action. No voices are heard during the entire duration of the film, yet the music and sound effects suffice to illustrate the story. Words probably would have been redundant and reductive at the same time.

The Tender Game,[33] the story of the playful courting and seduction between a man and a woman, is based on a score interpreted vocally by Ella Fitzgerald and musically by the Oscar Peterson Trio. The song title is "Tenderly" and was composed by Jack Lawrence and Walter Gross. Among the animators who worked on the film was Bobe Cannon, who by 1958 had left UPA. Here, too, the influence from Modern art is evident and the use of a jazz score to stress the emotional reactions of the characters. No words are used. The characters as well as the backgrounds are defined by few colorful lines that change according to their moods.

Moonbird[34] was also animated by Cannon. Animation historian Michael Barrier provides a clue to the Hubley-Cannon collaboration:

> That Cannon should have worked for Hubley was really not surprising since by 1959 it was Hubley, rather than UPA, who was making cartoons most like those Cannon had once directed (the

principal characters in *Moonbird* are children, their voices those of the Hubley's two sons).[35]

Moonbird is about "Two boys [who] have an Adventure in the Middle of the Night."[36] The film is interesting not only for the simplified design of the characters and the background and the use of expressive colors but also for the sound effects. The Hubleys recorded the voices of their two male sons while they were playing at night. What we hear is exactly what they were experiencing. Sometimes the sound of crickets and birds is audible as well. The animation was developed on the base of the sound score. The spectators enter the realm of children's play; they follow the children's nocturnal adventures until the two little characters return home with a "moonbird."

Windy Day[37] is similar to *Moonbird*: it tells the adventures of Emily and Georgia Hubley, the two daughters of the artistic duo. Also, for this film, the soundtrack is made of the voices of the two little girls recorded playing on a windy day. The animated short is interesting for the way in which play and games are animated. We hear, for example, the girls fantasizing about getting married, and we see them animated while they actually perform the rite. Their fantasy and their imagination are the true protagonists of the film, which is rich in visual references to Modern art, such as, for example, the paintings of Marc Chagall.

John Hubley explained in an interview how his style had evolved over time, especially in his career as an independent filmmaker:

> My impulse then, with the help of Faith, was to develop the visual art even further than the UPA films had. The need to break-through and to play around with more plasticity led to *Adventures of An ** *. We were commissioned by the Guggenheim Museum to do a film for the public that would say there is more than one way to look at things. You can see things abstractly and you can take pleasure in visual experience without having a lot of rules to follow. We decided to do a film with music and no dialogue, and to deal with abstract characters. We wanted to get a graphic look that was totally unique to animation; that had never been seen before. So we played with the wax-resist technique; drawing with wax and splashing it with watercolor so you produce a resisted texture. We ended up waxing all the drawings and spraying them

and double exposing them in. We did the backgrounds the same way. It photographed with a very rich waxy texture, which was a fresh look. That film hit European animators like a bombshell, and pow! it set them on fire. For awhile that little * became a symbol in Europe of the breakthrough for animation. From that point on artists started exploring millions of different graphic techniques. So for our own films after that, it was always the question of finding a slightly different technique.[38]

Author Mike Barrier added that "all of their films reflect the influence of modern art—or, to be frank about it, modern art as it has been adapted and domesticated by commercial artists and designers."[39] Barrier believes that more than the graphic style itself, what is relevant in the Hubleys' work is the fact that they abolished the traditional distinction between characters and backgrounds, something that Hubley inherited from the UPA experience:

In most of the Hubleys' films, no such boundary exists; characters and settings are cut from the same bolt. Movement alone sets them apart. This integration of characters and backgrounds—not any simple enthusiasm for modern art—was at the heart of the UPA studio's rebellion against the Disney style in the middle '40s. It was a layout man's rebellion. The ultimate effect was to elevate design—the overall "look" of a film—at the expense of animation. Layout men, who had been subordinate to the animators at Disney's, were now in the driver's seat.[40]

The Hubley films *Moonbird* (1959), *The Hole* and *A Herb Alpert and the Tijuana Brass Double Feature* (1966) received Academy Awards for Cartoon Short Subject.

5.2.2 Modern Animation in Canada: UPA Influences at the National Film Board and Vice Versa

Mutual influences from UPA and the National Film Board (NFB) in Canada started as early as 1950, when Norman McLaren visited the UPA studio in Burbank. John Hubley, who admitted how much McLaren was a source of inspiration for him since his UPA days, shared his recollections of the event:

He was a great inspiration to me at a certain point in my career. It was about 1950. He came out to visit us at UPA, and he brought a new print called *Begone Dull Care* and showed it to us. It knocked us all over. It was so fantastic. It was direct on film, and it had that marvelous Oscar Peterson track. It was very stimulating to me to see that a film artist can take the path of making his own film and expressing himself. Nobody's done it better than Norman; he's been the most pure and the most devoted all his life. His mentor was Len Lye, who had the same principles as Norman; he imbued Norman with them. That is to say: that a film artist can make a film all on his own and do every bit of it if he wants to.[41]

From this historical event, it is possible that UPA artists were influenced by *Begone Dull Care*[42] and the aesthetic of McLaren's films to some extent. *Begone Dull Care* is a visual music film in which abstract animations are tied to a jazz score. Although UPA films were character based, UPA artists were able to combine the so-called character animation with "experimental animation," two categories that came to be defined as such much later at art schools and that, according to artist Vibeke Sorensen, represent "an artificial dichotomy."[43] Of course, UPA's major achievement was to bring audiovisual Modern aesthetics to the masses, as Luther Nichols, journalist at the *San Francisco Chronicle*, said:

Of course many of the modern art techniques employed in "Gerald" have been explored before, notably by Disney in such films as "The Reluctant Dragon." And part of UPA's inspiration may have come from avant-garde creations like the Canadian musical interpretations of Norman McLaren. But no one had integrated those techniques so well before with a character that had popular appeal. That was UPA's major achievement.[44]

As discussed earlier, UPA artists used abstract imagery in their animated cartoons as part of the filmic narration, especially on production of *The Boing-Boing Show*. Jazz scores were regularly used by the directors as the preferred type of music. Furthermore, the idea that a director can make small, independent, personal films is something that occurred at UPA, a studio where artists were encouraged to express themselves and produced such personal films as *Gerald McBoing Boing, Rooty Toot Toot, The Tell-Tale Heart* or *The Unicorn in the Garden*.

The influence between UPA and the NFB was reciprocal. Two examples are useful to highlight the assimilation of the UPA lesson at the NFB: *My Financial Career*[45] and *The House that Jack Built*.[46] *My Financial Career* is based on the namesake story written by Stephen Leacock and narrated by a male voice. It is about a man who goes to a bank to open an account; he is so intimidated by the institution that nothing comes out right from his mouth. The cartoon is similar to UPA animated shorts for its use of highly stylized backgrounds and characters. Sometimes the characters are animated on background of pure color as if they are floating in the space, or the furniture that define the interior of a building are addressed by few essential blue lines on a purple background. Different from the majority of UPA films, in which the characters are of the same nature as the backgrounds, since they are both drawn, here the characters stand out from the background since they are cutouts.

The House that Jack Built owes a specific debt to *Mr. Tingley's Tangle* of *The Boing-Boing Show* for the content: it is about a man who builds a house in a suburb and shares a life similar to all those who live in suburban areas, although he would like to be unique. Working hard at it, he later tires of being unique and would simply settle for being different. The character design is vaguely reminiscent of *Christopher Crumpet*. Minimalist background design characterizes the cartoon.

In addition, there is a sequence that is visually similar to one in *The Freeze Yum Story*,[47] another animated short of *The Boing-Boing Show*. In these sequences, the frame is filled with houses that look all the same in *The House that Jack Built*, while in *The Freeze Yum Story*, the frame is filled with half-open windows. It is difficult to state if the influence is direct or if it is a case of a shared sensibility for the aesthetic of the films. The second seems more probable.

One artist who worked at the NFB before joining UPA for *The Boing-Boing Show*[48] was George Dunning, later largely known for directing *Yellow Submarine*[49] in 1968. Far from the psychedelic aesthetic of *Yellow Submarine*, which was animated by Gerald Potterton, Dunning's personal stylistic evolution was influenced by UPA and was notably individually expressed during the period he spent working at TVC London, a studio he set up in 1957,[50] just after the UPA London studio was shut down.

At the NFB, Dunning showed a personal approach to animation when directing *Three Blind Mice*[51] and *Cadet Rousselle*,[52] among others. *Three Blind Mice* consists of the animation of three white mice on a completely black background. The mice move and dance according to the musical score, which is sung by Lionel Reid. Dating to 1945, the animated cartoon anticipates the anti-Disney minimalism and two-dimensional flatness that characterized UPA productions. *Cadet Rousselle* was based on a popular song and employed animated cutouts. The character has an angular look, and the backgrounds are composed of geometric cutouts. The two shorts are quite different from each other in their visual style, thus suggesting a certain eclecticism of the director, who reached a more consistent personal style during his London years.

5.2.3 Modern Animation in England: UPA Influences at Halas & Batchelor Cartoon Films, W. M. Larkins Studio and TVC London

Hungarian-born John Halas founded Halas & Batchelor Cartoon Films in 1940, together with Joy Batchelor, and they later married. The couple worked on commissioned animated shorts for Britain's War Office, Ministries of Information and Defence, Central Office of Information and the Admiralty.[53] Famous for directing the first British animated feature film, *Animal Farm*,[54] based on the book of the same title written by George Orwell, the couple developed a personal style that in some animated shorts shares a similar aesthetic approach with UPA cartoons.

Among these shorts stand out *Hamilton the Musical Elephant*[55] and *Automania 2000*.[56] Hamilton is an elephant who is being trained in a circus and has the ability to play his trunk as a trumpet. He plays jazz music. Every day he learns a new trick, but unfortunately, he easily forgets it. The stylized character design resembles some UPA protagonists drawn by Bobe Cannon. Moreover, Hamilton is like Gerald: he produces (musical) sounds. Hamilton differs from Gerald in that Hamilton cannot remember what to play when he is being asked, but similar to Gerald, he finds both a man who supports his ability and a man (the owner of the circus) who treats him badly by exploiting him. The opening and closing credits remind the viewer of a visual music segment, since there are squares of different colors animated to the rhythm of a jazz score. Hamilton is animated mostly on a red-orange background.

UPA-like graphic modernism is also present in *Automania 2000*, where a stylized two-dimensional flat design characterizes both the character and the backgrounds. The film offers a humorous critique on the motorization and automation of the future.

Although *Hamilton the Musical Elephant* (1961) appears to pay homage to *Gerald McBoing Boing*, which won a British Academy Film Award in 1951, it is important to remember that the Halas & Batchelor studio was founded three years before Industrial Films and Poster Service, the forerunner of UPA. From the 1940s into the following decades, Halas and Batchelor sought a personal style in animation. It is possible that during the 1950s and 1960s, the British couple assimilated the UPA lesson and incorporated some UPA-like themes and stylistic elements, but it is also plausible that during the 1940s, they were experimenting innovative visual solutions without any influence from abroad.

More examples might better explain this apparent contradiction. William Larkins, the founder of W. M. Larkins studio, was another prominent figure in British animation. The studio opened during the 1940s and did not produce entertainment films but rather mainly industrial films and commercials for TV and theaters.[57] Directors Peter Sachs and Richard Taylor were among the creative minds. Sachs, for example, directed the animated short *River of Steel*[58] in 1951. The film was produced in collaboration with the British Iron and Steel Federation. It focuses on the manufacture of steel and shows the worldwide implications of living without steel. The audiovisual style resembles some UPA animated cartoons. There is an informational narrating voice that illustrates the story, thus reminding the viewer of the neutral narration of *Brotherhood of Man*; while the layout designs express Modern features such as backgrounds made of bright areas of colors, a constructivist composition of the frames and characters that resemble UPA figures.

During the 1950s, TV advertising exploded not only in the U.S. but also in Western Europe and especially in England. Many British animation studios were set up in this decade, such as Biographic Films, founded in 1954 by animator Bob Godfrey, in collaboration with Vera Linnecar, Keith Learner and Nancy Hanna. Godfrey had previously worked at Larkins' studio.[59] TV commercials were the perfect type of product to experiment with more graphic layouts and limited animation owing to economic restraints. Animation theorist Paul Wells thus comments on the stylistic innovations experimented at Biographic:

> One of the kind of interesting things about Biographic, particularly in the shape of Bob Godfrey, is Bob Godfrey's resistance to the

whole idea that animation has to be from the Disney style or from a modern art style. He wants it … to be much more simple, direct, straightforward, and actually not be full animation—you know, the figures can jump about a lot, they actually don't have to do fluid, lyrical movements, they can just jump from one thing to another.[60]

Godfrey confirms this: "You see, when commercial television came, we couldn't do traditional animation because it was too expensive and it took too long. So we would find quick, cut-out ways of doing things. We were very forward looking, avant gard."[61]

The same happened during the years of World War II, when artists at Halas & Batchelor and W. M. Larkins were working on commissioned works. Therefore, it is difficult to state a *direct* influence from UPA on the directors of these two studios. More plausibly, animators and directors at Halas & Batchelor and W. M. Larkins simultaneously and independently experimented with the medium and developed some of the same UPA stylistic innovations, especially the use of limited animation. Appearing in England few years later, UPA animated cartoons may have provided a good reinforcing example of an audiovisual style that was taking shape also in England and more generally in Europe.

TVC (Television Cartoons) London also was formed to satisfy the new demand for TV advertising; nevertheless, its founder, George Dunning, who worked in the New York and London UPA offices in the 1950s, was able to produce some independent films, too. Among them, *The Apple*[62] and *The Flying Man*[63] are much indebted to the UPA tradition. *The Apple*, from 1963, is about a man who tries in every possible way to grasp an apple from a tree. Interestingly, the character and the backgrounds are of the same nature: thin black lines drawn on a white paper. Only the apple is colored, specifically red. The apple tree is drawn in the left corner of the frame, thus emphasizing an asymmetrical layout. The soundtrack is minimalistic: a short musical score is used every time a new attempt at grasping the apple has failed. The sound effects are as informational as the visuals: we hear, for example, the sound of a car approaching, and a few frames later we see it. The movements of the character are also stylized. *The Flying Man*, made the year before, expresses a similar minimalistic approach with the difference that the layouts are made of watercolor figures painted directly on glass. The characters are defined by areas of colors on a white background.

5.2.4 Modern Animation in Italy: UPA Influences at Bruno Bozzetto Film

In Italy, animator Bruno Bozzetto made his debut with *Tapum! Weapons History*[64] in 1958 and, in the following decade, Bozzetto assured his popularity in animated cinema with the creation of Mr. Rossi, a short, brown, middle-aged, middle-class man. Mr. Rossi made his first of several appearances in *An Award for Mr. Rossi*.[65] In *Tapum! Weapons History*, we often see stylized characters that remind us of UPA experimentations. There are white silhouettes of men drawn on a black or red background, and there are men whose design consists of simple thin black lines on a red background. The face of the scientist, with his long nose, is reminiscent of Saul Steinberg's cartoons, a reference source for UPA artists in *Brotherhood of Man*. In another sequence, we see, for example, stylized half-profile Egyptians fighting with swords. The animation is stylized as well and emphasizes some relevant poses during the battle. The film illustrates the history of weapons with irony and without didacticism. A simplified audiovisual language is also used in Bozzetto's *Alpha Omega*,[66] where the character is drawn as if floating in the space. Minimalism characterizes also the sound effects.

As for Mr. Rossi, a visually similar character was developed in a segment of *The Boing-Boing Show* called *Uncle Sneaky*.[67] The nephew of Uncle Sneaky and Mr. Rossi look extremely alike, although the two stories are completely different. Still, it is interesting to highlight how two different studios operating in two different parts of the world developed similar visual stylistic solutions. And, although it is difficult to state a direct influence from *The Boing-Boing Show* on the creation of Mr. Rossi, since the American TV show was never broadcast in Italy, it is known, nevertheless, that Bozzetto corresponded with Bobe Cannon,[68] and this exchange might have influenced him to some extent.

Minimalism triumphs in *Two Castles*.[69] One single shot is kept for the duration of the entire film. We see two highly stylized flat castles, and we follow the adventures of a knight who exits from the castle on the left to attack the castle on the right (Figure 5.1). No colors are added to the background; there is only the black line on a white paper. No musical score is used, either, only sound effects. A medieval score is played at the very end for a few seconds. The film reminds us of a sequence in *The Juggler of Our Lady*, when two armies are attacking each other depicted with white lines on a blue background.

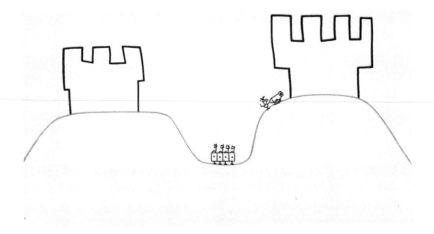

FIGURE 5.1   Still from *Two Castles*, Animated Film Directed by Bruno Bozzetto (1963). Reprinted with permission from Bruno Bozzetto Distribution S.N.C.

Comparisons aside, Bozzetto followed a path parallel to the UPA artists, albeit slightly later: he studied and assimilated the Disney lesson in order to depart from it and develop a personal style. As animation historian Giannalberto Bendazzi noted,

> Like the by now so famous UPA authors who left Disney drawing
> … Mickey Mouse and Minnie with segments and edges, Bozzetto
> innovated, re-created and modernized: he did not revolutionize.
> He was able to learn from Disney and McLaren (in this case, these
> two really are antithetical to the other) in equal measure.[70]

5.3 MODERN STYLES IN EASTERN EUROPEAN ANIMATION

5.3.1 Modern Animation in Yugoslavia: UPA Influences at Zagreb Film

Zagreb Film, today a Croatian film company, was founded in 1953 in the former Yugoslavia and by 1955 had already developed the limited animation technique,[71] the same technique that was developed by UPA artists just a few years before. Moreover, similar to but independent from UPA, Zagreb Film incorporated graphic design into animation, thereby producing films that departed from the Disney tradition. Among the directors, graphic designers and animators who worked at Zagreb Film in the early years were Dušan Vukotić, Nikola Kostelac, Aleksandar Marks,

Boris Kolar, Zlatko Bourek, Borivoj Dovniković, Vjekoslav Kostanjsek, Vladimir Jutrisa, Vatroslav Mimica, Vladislav "Vlado" Kristl and Zlatko Grgić. Although every director had a personal style, the so-called Zagreb school of animation shared a common sensibility and aesthetic. Director Dušan Vukotić is considered the master of the early stages of the Zagreb school.

Vukotić's production was still influenced by Disney both in its character design and background design in the early 1950s, as is evident in *How Kiko Was Born*,[72] made in 1951. In *The Playful Robot*[73] (1956), roundness defines the character design but not the backgrounds, which are more stylized and flat. There is also a difference in the score that indicates the filmic style of the director is evolving: in *How Kiko Was Born*, the character speaks, while in *The Playful Robot*, there is only a musical score. *Cowboy Jimmie*[74] (1957) presents a parody of the Western film genre, in which the popular film star Cowboy Jimmie is at first emulated by a group of children and later attacked and miserably captured by one of them. At the close of the film, he is kicked back to the cinema screen, thus putting an end to his mysterious legendary aura. *Abracadabra*,[75] of the same year, is the story of an evil magician who picks on a child with his malicious tricks. They eventually become friends. The magician, upon discovering how smart the little boy is, relinquishes his magic tools and clothes. The magician is highly stylized, and his skin is of the same color of the background, a visual solution already used in *Gerald McBoing Boing*. The backgrounds are often composed of different tonalities of yellow and orange. Yet, even more stylized and flat are the characters and the backgrounds of 1958's *Revenger*,[76] a story of betrayal with an existentialist reflection and a sad ending that is reminiscent of *Rooty Toot Toot* in its basic plot.

The Great Fear[77] belongs to the horror genre and has a dark atmosphere similar to the one evoked in UPA's *The-Tell Tale Heart*. It is the story of a man who becomes scared in his own house after reading a horror story. Sound effects are used to stress those objects or images that are scarily brought to life by the man's imagination. Similar to the scene in *The Tell-Tale Heart* where the pendulum is animated with its gearwheels, here we have an inner apparatus of the clock that is shown in multiple perspectives. Furthermore, in a moment of extreme fear, the body of the protagonist twists in the same way Nelly Bly was animated in *Rooty Toot Toot*.

Remarkable is the use of film space in *Concerto for Sub-Machine Gun*,[78] where in some sequences the backgrounds are made of only one color with the total absence of any drawn line. The film is a parody of the American gangster film. It tells the story of a bank robbery. At the beginning of the short, the subtitle appears on the cover of a sheet-music booklet: "Allegro con fuoco," which means literally "Allegro with fire." A gang of thieves is under the direction of an avaricious gangster, who disguises himself in a costume whose face resembles one of Steinberg's caricatures. One man in the gang instructs all the other thieves on how to shoot at the policemen. The film plays on the ambiguity of the actions performed by the thieves as if they were members of an orchestra. In the film there is the complete absence of voices; only sound effects are used to highlight the actions of the thieves. The characters, in fact, are animated according to the music and the sound effects, which mostly consist of the noises made by the firearms, although not exclusively. In one sequence, for example, one of the thieves has entered the bank, thus activating the alarm; he uses his hands to play with the sound waves until they are reduced to nothing, and then the alarm stops. Here, the sound effect finds a matching counterpart in the visual effect. About the film, animation historian Ralph Stephenson said: "*Concerto for Sub-Machine Gun* inherits generally from UPA, but the keen edge of the satire was the product of sharp outside observation, and could probably not have been made in America."[79]

The Cow on the Moon[80] was completed the same year that the first human-made object reached the surface of the Moon on the Soviet Union's *Luna 2* mission. The film portrays the funny adventures of a couple of children, a boy and a girl, who are playing in their courtyard. The little girl is designing a spaceship; the boy starts teasing her. She decides to have a little revenge: she constructs a small spaceship, gets the boy to climb in and fools him into believing that he is really going to the Moon. Next, in a more deserted area, she disguises herself as an alien and makes fun of the boy by scaring him. Simultaneously, a cow passes by and the adventure goes on. The opening credits of the film consist of a fixed image in which a spaceship is drawn on the left. It is designed as a drawing on a blackboard and reminds of both Émile Cohl's animations and a *Christopher Crumpet* sequence. The characters are as stylized and flat as the backgrounds in which areas of colors define the complexes of the houses and their gardens. Also, in this animated short, there is no narration or dialogue between the characters, only music and sound effects used to stress the actions of the two protagonists.

Piccolo,[81] meanwhile, reminds us of Norman McLaren's *Neighbours*[82] for its plot: two neighbors compete over who can make more noise by playing musical instruments, strictly for the pleasure of annoying the other. Yet, in *Substitute*,[83] the film that won Vukotić an Academy Award[84] for Short Subject, Cartoon, the stylization is carried even further. The film is about a tourist on a beach who inflates an air bed, a car, a costume and even a woman. Love ensues, together with jealousy and revenge. At the end, he punches holes in everything that surrounds him until the world that he has created disappears. The animated short harks back to the artificiality of the animated cartoon medium. The characters are drawn in a naive style, as if by children. The visual style is reminiscent of the artwork of Klee, both for the characters' design and the colors used. As in the majority of Vukotić's films, dialogue is absent; here there is only music, sound effects and the noise that the tourist makes singing a tune.

Vukotić independently arrived at the same synthesis that was typical of UPA films by developing a simplified audiovisual language for animated films that distanced itself from the Disney tradition. In his work he seemed to apply the Bauhaus principle of "form follows function," since every one of his films had a unique audiovisual style suitable to the story. Moreover, he carried the UPA experimentation even further by originally using the sound effects and musical score without any dialogue among the characters: his films are not talkative, whereas UPA animated shorts often are. Thus, Vukotić expressed an even more minimalistic approach that, in addition, was universal, as it was understandable to everyone.

How much were Vukotić and the artists of the Zagreb school *directly* influenced by UPA? It appears that the artists at Zagreb Film had no opportunity to see UPA animations, as confirmed by Zlatko Grgić in an interview:

> Even today it is thought that limited animation was invented by Zagreb Film. In some books it is written that two-dimensional characters were one of our inventions. However, I have seen retrospectives of the works of Bobe Cannon, the UPA series, *Gerald McBoing Boing*, which were created 10 years before us! This film was the first avant-gardist film vis-à-vis Disney. Hubley, Gene Deitch and the other designers who broke with Disney studio. At that time, we didn't have the chance to see these films. I have learned only now, by seeing the retrospective on Cannon, that

they had been doing the same things as us at Zagreb Film, with the difference that they had been doing them ten times better because they ... were animators with much more experience.[85]

Nikola Kostelac agreed with Zlatko Grgić: "The outcomes developed at Zagreb Film studio were not born under any direct influence from some particular production. They were developed by applying graphic design to animated cinema."[86]

Nevertheless, Boris Kolar asserted in the same interview that a combination of examples from Czech animated cinema, UPA films and Modern paintings helped the Zagreb Film studio escape the Disney formula and come up with a unique style.[87] Moreover, Vatroslav Mimica, who directed the two-dimensional and stylized *Alone*,[88] admitted a certain influence from UPA:

UPA applied the language of modern graphic on animated cinema, abandoning the soft and romantic drawing of Disney. Nevertheless, Bosustow's team wasn't able to make a certain break in animation. UPA subordinated a particular contemporary graphic form to the laws of Disney animation. With similar results, in Zagreb Film, Kostelac and Kostanjsek were able to make some commercial animated shorts. They worked by having in mind the outcomes of Bosustow's experience.[89]

5.3.2 Modern Animation in Romania: Ion Popescu-Gopo

Ion Popescu-Gopo can be considered the one person in Romanian animation who approached the medium with a Modern viewpoint, thus inaugurating a new trend in the country's animated cartoon history. Starting from 1956, he strove to differentiate his films from the classic Disney style, simplifying the characters, the backgrounds and the technique until reaching the bare essentials. For example, the little naked man he created was made of simple but indispensable black lines moving on a two-dimensional background.

The first film featuring this little man is *Short History*,[90] about the history of the Earth from the big bang to the 1950s. In a sequence, a tiger is animated moving from left to right: black outlines define its figure whose interior area is the same color as the background, a visual solution already exploited by UPA artists. *7 Arts*[91] offers a reflection on some of the seven arts as they are illustrated by the little man with a certain absurd humor.

The simplified audiovisual language developed by Popescu-Gopo was born from personal research on the animated cartoon medium. Like many animators and graphic designers who wanted to depart from the Disney approach, Popescu-Gopo's animations are the opposite of the three-dimensional redundant Disney style: they are minimalistic and essential. Considering the international political setting of Eastern European countries after World War II, it would have been difficult for UPA films from America to have reached Romania during the 1950s. For this reason, it is likely that Popescu-Gopo developed independently a simplified audiovisual language in animation, although sharing in common with UPA artists the desire to graphically express ideas different from Disney's approach.

5.3.3 Modern Animation in Czechoslovakia: Jiří Brdečka

Among those European films that anticipated some features of the UPA simplified audiovisual language there is *Love and the Zeppelin*,[92] directed by Jiří Brdečka in 1948. Made with the hand-drawn animation technique, the film tells a tender love story between a lady and a man who is inventing the dirigible. The woman runs away with the inventor on the zeppelin during the wedding ceremony in which she is supposed to marry a bearded man she does not love. The story is told with subtle irony and introduces the motif of a pair of lovers that Brdečka further developed in such later animated shorts as *Love*.[93]

Visually, the characters are animated as flat two-dimensional figures. Moreover, in a sequence, the hair of the young lady is of a slightly different red than the red of the background. In another sequence, where the engineer is designing the dirigible, we see thin black lines on a completely white background. The characters' personalities emerge from their gestures and actions and from the animation: the lady's father is smoking a cigar whose smoke "draws" rings in the air; the lady's mother is knitting a pair of white and red socks that are animated as rapidly growing longer and longer; the lady sticks her tongue out at the picture of the bearded man, expressing her discord in marrying him; the young inventor is animated as quickly walking backward and forward while he is thinking about the zeppelin he wants to design; and while he is designing it, sometimes he stops to think a little bit more by putting the pencil close to his mouth. These are just a few examples of the care that the director put into details, both in the characters' design and their animations.

The story is presumably set sometime during a period that spans from 1890 to 1915, as we can infer from the characters' clothes, the houses' interiors and exterior locations, and the fact that the zeppelin was a novelty of the times, patented in Germany in 1895. There are, in fact, several visual references to art nouveau expressions, and the musical score contributes to recall that historical period as well. In a sequence, for example, the inventor takes out of his pocket a picture of his beloved, which is shown a few frames later. Here there is a close-up of the picture, which is reminiscent of an art nouveau postcard with a detailed hot-air balloon in the background. There is also a sequence in which the lady is escaping from the wedding: she runs toward the inventor who is up in the air on the zeppelin he has built. An anchor is lowered, and she sits on it. Here, we see the two lovers blowing kisses to each other, while the bearded man runs after his fiancée. The backgrounds are flatly designed: we see the lady and the bearded man passing by a hotel, a group of lined buildings and a photographic store with a banner that reads "Foto Miracle Service."

Aurally, there is a richness of sounds. The music's rhythm has different paces according to the events portrayed, and its presentation changes throughout the film: for example, it is mostly composed of trumpet notes when the bearded man is introduced at the beginning as to suggest his personality, then only composed by a sad piano tune when we see the lady playing the piano and looking at the picture of the bearded man; there are metallic sounds when the lady is crying, huge teardrops falling down her eyes; then the lyrics turn triumphant when there is the wedding march in the middle of the film, and comic during the final chase, as in the slapstick comedy tradition. There are also well-balanced sound effects: knitting sounds, the sound of a glass picture breaking on the ground, church bells chiming the time (4 p.m.) of the rendezvous between the lady and the inventor, the lady exclaiming "Ha!" after she is stung by a rose, as well as whistles, cracks, explosions, bumps, gun shots and so on.

The film pays homage to the slapstick comedy tradition, especially with the comedy trick of the chase. Moreover, in some sequences, the characters are animated as in a Charlie Chaplin film: the bearded man walks emphatically; the gestures and movements of the lady's parents trying to separate the lady from the inventor are stressed by the animation;

and during the wedding march, people's steps are visually taken in time with the music.

Love and the Zeppelin exemplifies Brdečka's eclecticism in selecting diverse story subjects as well as audiovisual styles. Brdečka's fascination with history and popular science are also expressed, for example, in such shorts as *How Man Learned to Fly*,[94] a humorous take on the history of aviation, and *Man under Water*,[95] which focuses on deep-sea exploration. He mastered animation for children in *Our Little Red Riding Hood*,[96] his personal humorous response to the fable, and *The Television Fan*,[97] which features a child who enjoys watching TV instead of doing his homework but discovers the importance of responsibility after observing what happens when everyone in the world is watching TV instead of working. Other Brdečka films adopt a childlike perspective: his masterpiece, *Gallina Vogelbirdae*,[98] for example, is a tribute to creativity and free imagination. He also animated shorts based on American folk songs, such as *My Darling Clementine*[99] and *The Frozen Logger*[100] and addressed more adult and philosophical themes in *Reason and Emotion*,[101] *Plaisir d'Amour*[102] and *The Face*.[103] Finally, Brdečka's vast knowledge of Western ancient mythology and history, as well as popular tales and ballads, are expressed in films such as *Revenge*,[104] *Metamorpheus*,[105] *There was a Miller on a River*,[106] *What I Didn't Say to the Prince*[107] and the *Moravian Folk Ballads* series,[108] among others.

The same heterogeneity can be observed in the films' audiovisual styles. Brdečka is one of the few animators who combined a great variety of visual sources and materials in his entire filmic production, sometimes even in the same animated short: from cartoon-like drawings and cutout figures to live-action documentary footage, still images of old maps or illustrations, reproductions of Leonardo da Vinci's artwork, Gustave Doré's engravings, and so on. Similarly, he mastered sounds by combining lyrics, dialogue, songs and sound effects according to the needs of the story.

Similar to UPA artists, Brdečka experimented with different themes and audiovisual styles in order to distance himself from the Disney canon. Also, like UPA artists, he seemed to follow the principle "form follows function" in every animated short by matching the story with its style. He had a deep knowledge of art history—not just Modern art—and he knew how to use it by effectively making it part of the story without simply referencing it. Much more than UPA productions, Brdečka experimented with visuals, sounds and animation techniques in his attempt to express a unique style. Some Brdečka animated shorts made during the 1960s show similarities to UPA creations in the minimalism of the layout designs, hand-drawn animation or the animation itself. These include *Gallina Vogelbirdae, How to Keep Slim*,[109] *Minstrel's Song*,[110] *The Deserter*[111] and *The Power of Destiny*.[112] Nevertheless, Brdečka neither imitated UPA nor was he probably much influenced by UPA. His films were minimalist only when they needed to be and not because that was the major stylistic tendency during the 1960s. Brdečka animated shorts are so original that it is unlikely they can be compared to any other directors' or studio's style.

5.4 MODERN STYLES IN SOVIET UNION ANIMATION: FYODOR KHITRUK

After working 24 years as an animator at Soyuzmultfilm,[113] the Soviet state-founded company, Fyodor Khitruk started to direct animated films in the 1960s.[114] His directorial debut was *History of a Crime*,[115] the story of Vasily Vasilyevich Mamin, a quiet and modest accountant who commits homicide after being disturbed all night by loud noises. The film is remarkable for some visual stylistic solutions that are indebted to UPA productions.[116]

First and foremost, the backgrounds, as well as the characters, are two-dimensional and stylized. Areas of colors without outlines are used to define houses, cars, gardens, cats, people and every other possible object of the environment. The visual style is completely different from the classic Disney formula as well as the Russian tradition. The animation is used to stress the psychological reactions of some characters, such as, for example, when Vasily walks with little jumps toward two noisy ladies to kill them with a frying pan, suggesting his desperation and exhaustion. As soon as he kills them, people appear at the windows: their faces are just scribbled. A policeman arrives, and by trying to discover the reasons behind the murder, he reverses the story to one day before.

We see the man exiting the building at 8:30 a.m. and going to work. A crowd of people is passing by in the same manner as it was animated in *Gerald McBoing Boing's Symphony*. On the subway, people are reading the newspaper. Graphically, the newspaper is designed in the same way as it was in *Christopher Crumpet*. Interestingly, when Vasily is typing, buildings arise on the horizon, just outside his office building: the sound of the typewriter ironically defines the rhythm of the constructions. At 5 p.m., he finishes work and returns home. Here, he passes by other offices that are designed as huge squares defined by thick black lines.

Back home, neighbors start to make all possible sorts of noise: from a group of people playing dominoes to a man listening to the radio or watching the TV; from another group of people having a party upstairs to another neighbor getting in so late as to stir his wife's anger. Visual and sound effects are used to suggest loudness. The interior of the man's house is designed as a sky-blue rectangle in a totally black frame. The layout is asymmetrical. Vasily goes upstairs to ask a neighbor if he could be quieter: here, the words of the neighbor come out as unarticulated sounds, much in the way Gerald McBoing Boing expressed himself. When people are dancing upstairs, the frame is horizontally cut into two parts so that both environments are visible: we see what is happening upstairs and in Vasily's house, although we do not see the figures upstairs completely, only half of their bodies. This visual solution is unique and daringly carried a step further the experimentation started at UPA. When we see Vasily in his bedroom, there are only white lines on a black background to suggest the idea of the furniture, a bed and a small night table.

Boniface's Vacation[117] has a similar audiovisual style. Boniface is a circus lion that goes on vacation to his grandmother's in Africa to rest up but instead ends up entertaining a group of children. Characters and backgrounds are two-dimensionally designed, and different from classic Disney cartoons, black lines do not encircle the figures. Only colored areas are used to define the outlines of both the characters and the backgrounds. In some sequences, backgrounds are made of only a single color. The characters are highly stylized. Interestingly, the clowns, for example, are made of stylized geometrical figures that, in the case of the feet and the legs, are not attached to one another. This visual solution marks a detachment from UPA experimentations.

Khitruk, in fact, was able to develop a simplified audiovisual language of his own, possibly influenced by UPA but adding his personal touches. The crowd of people attending the circus show, for example, is drawn as if made of scribbled rounded faces almost overlapping each other, something that John Hubley had already experimented in *The Magic Fluke*. But daringly, here, in a sequence in which Boniface is performing at the circus, for example, only red lines express Boniface's outlines on a completely black background. A few frames later, the crowd of faces also appears as red as Boniface's on the black background. Khitruk seems to have pushed even further UPA's visual research.

Also, essentially and beautifully designed are the sequences in which Boniface is on the train headed toward the African jungle: here, the train, Boniface, the skyline and the surrounding environment are stylized. Colors are used majestically. The smoke that exits from the train is made of thick animated white lines. The shape of the boat on which Boniface later travels is also stylized. The layouts in the film are asymmetrically composed. As in *History of a Crime*, there is a voice narrating the story, but its presence is never too invasive, and the sound effects are used to accentuate some characters' movements.

Film, Film, Film[118] is a satire of filmmaking. It shows the tribulations a movie maker must go through, from the film's conception to its premiere. The script, for example, is reviewed by so many committees that the final product, the film, probably is something completely different from the original idea of the scriptwriter. *Film, Film, Film* can be considered a critique of censorship in the USSR. Differing from Khitruk's previous animated shorts, here there is no narrating voice; only the director sometimes emits some noises that sound like raspy screams. The backgrounds and the characters are stylized, as is the animation. The film uses the same aesthetic innovations of the director's preceding animated shorts. In some backgrounds, it is possible to note the influence of cubist and constructivist paintings in the composition of the frames, while a source of inspiration for the sequence where the cameraman is shooting, and the actors are acting might have been the paintings of Marc Chagall.

Khitruk's personal simplified audiovisual language enabled him to introduce little innovations. During the premiere of the film, while the crew, outside the cinema, is awaiting the response of the public, the director walks fast along the interior borders of the frame. This action thus suggests his uneasiness. At the same time, this is another reminder of the artificiality of the animated cartoon medium.

5.5 MODERN STYLES IN ASIAN ANIMATION: THREE JAPANESE DIRECTORS

5.5.1 Taiji Yabushita

Tōei Dōga (*dōga* means "animation" in Japanese) studio was founded in 1956 by Japanese businessman Hiroshi Okawa. Among its major objectives was the desire to produce animated feature films that could compete in popularity and in quality with Disney features. Japan was first exposed to American animation during the 1930s, when Paramount distributed, via its office in Tokyo, such popular American animated cartoons as Betty Boop, Mickey Mouse, Felix the Cat and Popeye the Sailor. Later, during the U.S. occupation of Japan after World War II (1945–1952), Japanese animation was heavily influenced by U.S. productions brought overseas. Then, starting in 1953, Japanese society underwent a series of transformations. That year, the Japanese public broadcasting corporation NHK branched out from radio into television; NHK's TV programs helped transmit values to a society looking for economic and political stability. Many of the TV programs were imported from the U.S., and the middle-class American way of life influenced Japanese people.[119]

Tōei's first anime feature is also Japan's first animated feature in color. *The White Snake Enchantress*[120] marked a pivotal point in the history of Japanese animation. The film represents the starting point of the personal stylistic search of Taiji Yabushita and the beginning of a search for a "Japanese" animation style that could express its cultural identity. Based on an ancient Hong Kong folktale, the film tells the story of the snake princess Bai-Niang and her young lover Xu-Xian. Bai-Niang is an immortal spiritual creature that has the power to turn itself into a beautiful woman. Originally, she was a white snake, the same white snake that Xu-Xian had had to abandon when he was a boy. Later, Xu-Xian and Bai-Niang (now in human form) fall happily in love until the Buddhist priest Fa-Hai, believing that Bai-Niang is an evil spirit, decides to separate them by sending Xu-Xian into exile as a slave laborer. After some adventures, Xu-Xian dies. Bai-Niang begs the Red Dragon God to save his life. In exchange, she must renounce her magic powers and her spiritual nature. Transformed forever into a human being, she is willing to bring the flower of life to Xu-Xian. With the help of Xu's little friends Panda and Mimi[121] and the princess' handmaiden Xiao Chin, love triumphs.

Yabushita's personal exploration of style follows close to the same artistic path walked by UPA artists. Yabushita's *The White Snake Enchantress* owes more than a debt to Disney tradition. For instance, it employed the use of the multiplane camera for a three-dimensional effect of the backgrounds, and it is fully animated. Characters' movements appear fluid and smooth, as is typical of the Disney visual style. Still, if the two animals Panda and Mimi resemble cute Disney creatures, the two main human characters appear Asian in their physical features and clothing. Here,

Chinese and Japanese traditions meet classic methods of animation as they were studied and interpreted by a Japanese director looking for a personal style. Chinese visual references can be seen in the backgrounds: some of them remind the viewer of classical Chinese paintings, especially when they portray natural landscapes; others are water-colored, thus paying homage to another ancient Chinese painting technique. Chinese calligraphy is referenced as well. The settings, therefore, faithfully represent ancient China with its pagodas, temples and gardens.

In 1959, Tōei produced its second animated feature, entitled *Magic Boy*[122] and distributed in the U.S. as *The Adventures of the Little Samurai*. The story is set in medieval Japan. It was the first Japanese animated feature released in Cinemascope. Next came *Alakazam the Great*,[123] in 1960, based again on a Chinese legend. More animated features followed during the 1960s.

Although Yabushita took inspiration from Disney, he was able to distinguish and separate himself from the Disney tradition by focusing on Asian folk tales and referring to Asian visual sources. Disney style, therefore, was not simply copied but rather studied and interpreted for the development of a personal style, much as UPA artists had done.

5.5.2 Osamu Tezuka

Widely known as the creator of Japan's first animated TV series, *Astro Boy*,[124] Osamu Tezuka was both a comic strip (manga) artist and an animation director. In Japan, he was referred to as the "God of comic-strips."[125] Tezuka joined Tōei studio in 1959 and later left to found Mushi Productions in 1962, first under the name Osamu Dōga Production for a short period of time.[126] Aside from working extensively on animated TV series and feature films, he also devoted himself to the production of experimental films in collaboration with promising young animators and artists.[127]

Tales of the Street Corner[128] is an impressionistic portrait of posters attached to the walls of a street corner. The animated short has no dialogues and is music-driven. The real dialogue in the cartoon is between the figures drawn on the posters, especially between a male violin player and a female piano player. Dealing with posters, the film is two-dimensional par excellence. The visual style is reminiscent of UPA attempts at rendering angular and flat characters and backgrounds. The stylization of the characters and the backgrounds here is brought to an extreme, as, for example, in the figure of the violinist. The backgrounds show a deep study of cinematographic compositional rules. Western art and animation are referenced: we see, for example, a Henri de Toulouse-Lautrec poster, another one with the image of Auguste Rodin's *The Thinker*[129] and others with more contemporary references, such as an American driver with a Cadillac. Posters of every type and content are animated on the street corner until a dictatorship and a war come. Now figures of a general multiplied over and over are animated as the famous marching cards in *Alice in Wonderland*. The film is visually rich in references and images taken from contemporary culture. Maria Roberta Novielli, historian of Japanese animated cinema, thus comments:

> *Tales of the Street Corner* is a personal work in addition to being a form of "study" intended to experiment with the potentialities of animation, as is demonstrated particularly by the visual and thematic richness, expressed from the posters, each of them drawn and animated with a different style.[130]

In *Male*,[131] produced by Tezuka and directed by Yamamoto, highly stylized male characters appear inside white circles or rectangles that pop up on totally black backgrounds. The protagonists of the short are a man and a cat, and the perspective adopted is the one of the cat. Sometimes only eyes are portrayed in the total darkness of the frame, which expresses the darkness of a room where the cat and the man are with their respective partners. In one sequence, the cat rips the black frame into two parts leaving a crack that resembles a torn piece of paper. This seems to be another reminder of the nature of the animated cartoon medium from an artist who developed a personal stylistic approach to animation.

In *Memory*,[132] there are few frames in which areas of color do not fill the outlines of the objects drawn on the background, a visual solution already exploited in *Gerald McBoing Boing*. The backgrounds are often drawn in a minimalistic style.

Mermaid,[133] "a minimalist homage to imagination and individualism,"[134] is a tender and touching story of a boy who daydreams of a mermaid on the beach. Alas, he lives in a country where it is forbidden to daydream and is therefore punished by local authorities. The visual style echoes UPA aesthetical innovations. The characters are angular and flat, but most important, they are animated as if they were transparent figures moving on colored backgrounds. Characters are drawn with thin essential black lines. In a sequence, the mermaid is emerging from a pond near the sea: her body is partially colored in blue that corresponds to the water, as to suggest the idea that she is a mermaid and she is living in the sea. When the characters are animated swimming under the sea, we only see thin white lines that define the outlines of the figures while they are moving on a blue background. Scant lines define also the interior of the jail cell in which the boy is confined. In another sequence, only quickly running legs are animated on the superior part of the frame: we see only the legs, not the rest of the body, an effect that Khitruk was experimenting with as well. *Mermaid* is another music-driven film. The score is *Prelude to the Afternoon of a Faun*[135] by Claude Debussy. There is no dialogue.

Pictures at an Exhibition[136] is a critique of the new "heroes" of the 1960s. Accompanied by Modest Mussorgsky's score,[137] the film illustrates nine contemporary professional figures with subtle irony: the Journalist, the Gardener of the artificial landscape, the Cosmetic Surgeon, the Big Factory Proprietor, the Beatnik, the Boxer, the TV Talent, the Zen Priest and the Soldiers. The film exemplifies the eclectic style of Tezuka, whose sources of inspirations ranged from the animated films of Disney to UPA and the Zagreb school. The Journalist, for example, is a highly stylized character drawn on a completely gray background. For the Cosmetic Surgeon, the visual style reminds the viewer of naive children's drawings and the art of Paul Klee. In the segment dedicated to the TV Talent, there are half-drawn figures on orange backgrounds that resemble characters from both the UPA and the Zagreb school traditions. Finally, in the allegorical conclusions, there are three men playing the horn; it seems a visual reference to a sequence of *Toot, Whistle, Plunk and Boom*.

Tezuka's eclectic style and deep knowledge of the history of animation are evident also in *Legend of the Forest*.[138] The animated film has an ecological message. Stylistically it can be seen as paying homage to the history of animated film: from Émile Cohl to the Fleischers' cartoons and from Disney up to UPA. The UPA dedication can be traced toward the end of the film in the characters' design. The score is Pyotr Ilyich Tchaikovsky's *Fourth Symphony, Op. 36*.[139]

5.5.3 Yōji Kuri

In 1958, animator Yōji Kuri, illustrator Ryōhei Yanagihara and painter Hiroshi Manabe formed the "Animation Group of Three." The core idea was to produce art films. In their manifesto the group declared it useful to be open to influences and styles from outside Japan but at the same time criticized those who have not been able to create something different from international productions.[140] Of the three, Yōji Kuri would become one of the most prominent independent Japanese animators of the following decades.

In his highly personal and original production, Kuri preferred a minimalistic approach both in the layouts and in the use of the sound effects. The contents and themes of his animations do not show any similarities with previous and contemporary productions. He favored a taste for the absurd with an often-misogynistic standpoint, reminiscent of James Thurber's themes in cartoons. His hand-drawn animations are highly stylized.

His productions are connoted by a common "surreal minimalism."[141] About his style, Novielli said: "An elementary graphism, combined from time to time with different techniques …, lends itself to becoming quintessence of a particular study on movement, explored in its microelements and bound with force to experimentations in sound and in color."[142]

In *Love*,[143] for example, there are two characters, a man and a woman, that look like Steinberg figures. The content of the short can be easily summarized: the woman is looking for love; therefore, she chases the man. The sound effects are disturbing: over and over, the woman repeats the word "*Ai*," which in Japanese means "love," in every possible intonation. The backgrounds consist of flat, two-dimensional hand-drawn black lines. Sometimes areas of colors appear in the backgrounds but sparingly. Being caricatures of the everyman and the everywoman, the two characters are dressed in blue and pink clothes to further underscore their genders. The animation is limited, and voluntary jerky movements emphasize the chase. In a sequence, for example, we see the two characters in a spacious area full of tables and chairs: the man and the woman are animated as appearing and disappearing seated continuously at different tables.

Kuri's personal approach to animation reminds the spectator of the UPA visual style in its attempt at using angular flat characters and backgrounds. Nevertheless, in the field of sound effects, Kuri experimented far more than UPA did, coming up with scores that are highly informational for his animated shorts. He demonstrated that it was possible to assimilate American or European influences while detaching himself from them in order to create something authentically original within the Japanese animation culture.

As evidenced from the examples discussed above, UPA's new attitude toward animation has been studied, interpreted, assimilated, disseminated and even expanded by international animators, designers and directors. In some cases, UPA's innovative stylistic features have been used for their aesthetic value (Disney and arguably NFB); other times they have been incorporated in personal films by independent animators (John and Faith Elliott Hubley, Ernest Pintoff, Friz Freleng and Hawley Pratt); and still other times, they have even been parodied (Tex Avery). There were directors who considered animation a mean to express themselves and, in their quest for a personal language, probably found UPA along the way and assimilated some of its stylistic features (Bruno Bozzetto, Dušan Vukotić, Fyodor Khitruk). There were also those who wanted to detach themselves from the Disney canon and thus experimented independently or even chronologically slightly before UPA became successful (John Halas and Joy Batchelor, George Dunning, Ion Popescu-Gopo) and even those who ended up using stylized layouts and animations for economic reasons (Peter Sachs and his colleagues at the W. M. Larkins studio), just as had happened to UPA artists. Other directors were so rooted in their cultures that UPA stylistic features could only be echoed or slightly recalled (Osamu Tezuka and Yōji Kuri). Finally, there is also the example of a director who developed such an original style that it could only be compared gently to the artistic path of UPA artists so as not to imply any daring influences from UPA (Jiří Brdečka).

Modern animation thus came to be better defined by all these artists who, voluntarily or involuntarily, directly or indirectly, through "contaminations" or assimilations, faced the challenge of their times and undertook a "dialogue" with what had in the meantime become known as the UPA "revolution."

ENDNOTES

1. Leslie, *Hollywood Flatlands*, 297.
2. *La Joie de vivre*, directed by Anthony Gross and Hector Hoppin (1934; Paris, FR: HG Productions). www.youtube.com/watch?v=oKpzTUyCtt0, accessed September 25, 2015.
3. *Melody*, directed by Charles A. Nichols and Ward Kimball (1953; DVD, *Walt Disney Treasures—Disney Rarities: Celebrated Shorts: 1920s–1960s*, Burbank, CA: Walt Disney Home Video, 2005).
4. *A Cowboy Needs a Horse*, directed by Bill Justice (1956; DVD, *Walt Disney Treasures—Disney Rarities: Celebrated Shorts: 1920s–1960s*, Burbank, CA: Walt Disney Home Video, 2005).

5. *Pigs Is Pigs*, directed by Jack Kinney (1954; DVD, *Walt Disney Treasures—Disney Rarities: Celebrated Shorts: 1920s–1960s*, Burbank, CA: Walt Disney Home Video, 2005).

6. The animated short was part of the animated feature film *Make Mine Music*, released by Disney in 1946. It was theatrically released as a single animated short in 1954. *Johnnie Fedora and Alice Bluebonnet*, directed by Jack Kinney (1946; DVD, *Make Mine Music*, Burbank, CA: Walt Disney Home Video, 2000). It is worth remembering that also in *Snow White and the Seven Dwarfs* there is a human being as the main character.

7. *One Hundred and One Dalmatians*, directed by Clyde Geronimi, Hamilton Luske and Wolfgang Reitherman (1961; DVD, Burbank, CA: Walt Disney Home Video, 1999).

8. *Symphony in Slang*, directed by Tex Avery (1951; DVD, *Tex Avery*, Burbank, CA: Turner Entertainment, 2003).

9. *Tex Avery*, DVD (Burbank, CA: Turner Entertainment, 2003).

10. *Sh-h-h-h-h*, directed by Tex Avery (1955; DVD, *Tex Avery*, Burbank, CA: Turner Entertainment, 2003).

11. *Crazy Mixed Up Pup*, directed by Tex Avery (1954; DVD, *Tex Avery*, Burbank, CA: Turner Entertainment, 2003).

12. *The Pink Phink*, directed by Friz Freleng and Hawley Pratt (1964; DVD, *The Pink Panther: Classic Cartoon Collection*, Burbank, CA: MGM Home Entertainment, 2005).

13. Maltin, *Of Mice and Magic: A History of American Animated Cartoons*.

14. Barrier, *Hollywood Cartoons: American Animation in Its Golden Age*.

15. Darrell Van Citters, *The Art of Jay Ward Productions* (Los Angeles, CA: Oxberry Press, 2013), 17.

16. Ibid.

17. Many former UPA employees worked at Format Films, including T. Hee, Leo Salkin, Alan Zaslove, Rudy Larriva, Joe Siracusa and secretary Hank Jordan.

18. Abraham, *When Magoo Flew: The Rise and Fall of Animation Studio UPA*.

19. Barrier, *Hollywood Cartoons: American Animation in Its Golden Age*.

20. *Flebus*, directed by Ernest Pintoff (1957; New Rochelle, NY: Terrytoons). www.youtube.com/watch?v=AdlMIE9egpE, accessed April 9, 2015.

21. *The Juggler of Our Lady*, directed by Al Kouzel (1959; New Rochelle, NY: Terrytoons). www.dailymotion.com/video/x8s7e2_juggler-of-our-lady_creation, accessed April 9, 2015.

22. Maltin, *Of Mice and Magic: A History of American Animated Cartoons*.

23. Abraham, *When Magoo Flew: The Rise and Fall of Animation Studio UPA*.

24. *The Violinist*, directed by Ernest Pintoff (1959; New York, NY: Pintoff Productions). www.youtube.com/watch?v=wlnuyZMRLr4, accessed April 9, 2015.

25. *The Critic*, directed by Ernest Pintoff (1963; New York, NY: Pintoff Productions). www.youtube.com/watch?v=PramR5oxn50, accessed April 9, 2015.

26. Van Citters, *The Art of Jay Ward Productions*, 13.

27. Ibid., 12.

28. The director is unknown.

29. Van Citters, *The Art of Jay Ward Productions*, 140.

30. Abraham, *When Magoo Flew: The Rise and Fall of Animation Studio UPA.*

31. Barrier, *Hollywood Cartoons: American Animation in Its Golden Age.*

32. *Adventure of An *, directed by John Hubley (1957; DVD, *Selected Films of John and Faith Hubley*, San Francisco, CA: McSweeney's *The Believer,* March–April 2014).

33. *The Tender Game*, directed by John Hubley (1958; DVD, *Selected Films of John and Faith Hubley*, San Francisco, CA: McSweeney's *The Believer,* March–April 2014).

34. *Moonbird*, directed by John Hubley (1959; DVD, *Selected Films of John and Faith Hubley*, San Francisco, CA: McSweeney's *The Believer*, March–April 2014).

35. Barrier, *Hollywood Cartoons: American Animation in Its Golden Age*, 564–565.

36. Opening credits of *Moonbird.*

37. *Windy Day*, directed by John Hubley and Faith E. Hubley (1968; DVD, *The Hubley Collection*, vol. 1, Los Angeles, CA: Image Entertainment, 1999).

38. John Hubley and Faith Hubley, "Animation: A Creative Challenge—by John and Faith Hubley," (interview).

39. Mike Barrier, "John and Faith Hubley: Traditional Animation Transformed," *Millimiter* (1977): 43.

40. Ibid.

41. John Hubley and Faith Hubley, "Animation: A Creative Challenge—by John and Faith Hubley (interview)".

42. *Begone Dull Care*, directed by Norman McLaren (1949; DVD, *Norman McLaren: The Master's Edition,* Ottawa, ON: National Film Board of Canada, 2006).

43. Vibeke Sorensen, interview by author, February 4, 2014.

44. Nichols, "A Star Is Drawn: Meet Gerald McBoing-Boing."

45. *My Financial Career*, directed by Gerald Potterton (1962; Ottawa, ON: National Film Board). www.nfb.ca/film/my_financial_career, accessed April 14, 2015.

46. *The House that Jack Built*, directed by Ron Tunis (1967; Ottawa, ON: National Film Board of Canada). www.nfb.ca/film/the_house_that_jack _built, accessed April 14, 2015.

47. The director is unknown.

48. After his collaboration on *The Boing-Boing Show*, Dunning worked at the UPA studio in London.

49. *Yellow Submarine*, directed by George Dunning (1968; DVD, Burbank, CA: MGM Home Entertainment, 1999).

50. Bendazzi, *Cartoons: 100 Years of Cinema Animation.*

51. *Three Blind Mice*, directed by George Dunning (1945; Ontario, ON: National Film Board of Canada). www.youtube.com/watch?v=OOTCVCR26Ko, accessed September 24, 2015.

52. *Cadet Rousselle*, directed by George Dunning (1947; Ontario, ON: National Film Board of Canada). www.nfb.ca/film/cadet_rousselle, accessed April 14, 2015.
53. Bendazzi, *Cartoons: 100 Years of Cinema Animation*.
54. *Animal Farm*, directed by John Halas and Joy Batchelor (1954; DVD, Chicago, IL: Home Vision Entertainment, 2004).
55. *Hamilton the Musical Elephant*, directed by John Halas (1961; DVD, *The Halas & Batchelor Short Film Collection*, London, UK: Network TV Home Entertainment, 2015).
56. *Automania 2000*, directed by John Halas (1963; DVD, *The Halas & Batchelor Short Film Collection*, London, UK: Network TV Home Entertainment, 2015).
57. Amidi, *Cartoon Modern: Style and Design in Fifties Animation*.
58. *River of Steel*, directed by Peter Sachs (1951; London, UK: Larkins studio). www.youtube.com/watch?v=4jejf5euwdw, accessed August 20, 2015.
59. Bendazzi, *Cartoons: 100 Years of Cinema Animation*.
60. Paul Wells, quoted in Neil Emmett, "Animation Nation: The Art of Persuasion Part 2," *The Lost Continent: Exploring the Art and History of British Animation* (blog), February 15, 2012 (12:23), http://ukanimation .blogspot.co.uk/2012/02/animation-nation-art-of-persuasion-part.html, accessed August 20, 2015.
61. Bob Godfrey, quoted in Neil Emmett, "Animation Nation: The Art of Persuasion Part 2."
62. *The Apple*, directed by George Dunning (1963; London, UK: TVC London). www.youtube.com/watch?v=0QFjJSG87es, accessed August 16, 2015.
63. *The Flying Man*, directed by George Dunning (1962; London, UK: TVC London). www.youtube.com/watch?v=zaJq4pcNk_w, accessed August 16, 2015.
64. *Tapum! Weapons History*, directed by Bruno Bozzetto (1958; DVD, *Tutto Bozzetto*, Rome, IT: Twentieth Century Fox Italy, 2012). Bozzetto established his Milan-based studio in 1960, according to Bendazzi, *Cartoons: 100 Years of Cinema Animation*.
65. *An Award for Mr. Rossi*, directed by Bruno Bozzetto (1960; DVD, *Il Signor Rossi—Una vita da cartone*, Milan, IT: San Paolo Multimedia, 2008).
66. *Alpha Omega*, directed by Bruno Bozzetto (1961; DVD, *Tutto Bozzetto*, Rome, IT: Twentieth Century Fox Italy, 2012).
67. The director is unknown.
68. As reported by Bruno Bozzetto to animation historian Giannalberto Bendazzi in 1961–1962. Bendazzi shared the information with the author when she took his graduate course "Guided Study in the History of Animation," at Nanyang Technological University, Singapore, from January to April 2014.
69. *Two Castles*, directed by Bruno Bozzetto (1963; DVD, *Tutto Bozzetto*, Roma, IT: Twentieth Century Fox Italy, 2012).

70. Giannalberto Bendazzi, *Bruno Bozzetto: Animazione Primo Amore* (Milan, IT: Isca, 1972), 25. "Come gli autori dell'ormai famosissima UPA, quelli che lasciarono la Disney corp. disegnando sui muri Topolino e Minni tutti a segmenti e spigoli, Bozzetto ha innovato, ha ricreato, ha rammodernato: non ha rivoluzionato. Ha saputo imparare da Disney e da McLaren (ecco, questi due sì, sono davvero l'antitesi l'uno dell'altro) in egual misura" (translated by author).

71. Bendazzi, *Cartoons: 100 Years of Cinema Animation.*

72. *How Kiko Was Born*, directed by Dušan Vukotić and Josip Sudar (1951; Zagreb, HR: Duga Film). http://film.nu/filmer/kako-se-rodio-kico/10240145.film, accessed April 19, 2015.

73. *The Playful Robot*, directed by Dušan Vukotić (1956; DVD, *Dušan Vukotić on DVD*, Chatsworth, CA: Rembrandt Films, 2007).

74. *Cowboy Jimmie*, directed by Dušan Vukotić (1957; DVD, *Dušan Vukotić on DVD*, Chatsworth, CA: Rembrandt Films, 2007).

75. *Abracadabra*, directed by Dušan Vukotić (1957; Zagreb, HR: Zagreb Film). www.youtube.com/watch?v=oMVORtqy3NM, accessed April 20, 2015.

76. *Revenger*, directed by Dušan Vukotić (1958; DVD, *Dušan Vukotić on DVD*, Chatsworth, CA: Rembrandt Films, 2007).

77. *The Great Fear*, directed by Dušan Vukotić (1958; DVD, *Dušan Vukotić on DVD*, Chatsworth, CA: Rembrandt Films, 2007).

78. *Concerto for Sub-Machine Gun*, directed by Dušan Vukotić (1958; DVD, *Dušan Vukotić on DVD*, Chatsworth, CA: Rembrandt Films, 2007).

79. Stephenson, *Animation in the Cinema*, 137.

80. *The Cow on the Moon*, directed by Dušan Vukotić (1959; DVD, *The Best of Zagreb Film: Be Careful What You Wish for and, the Classic Collection*, Chatsworth, CA: Rembrandt Films, 2000).

81. *Piccolo*, directed by Dušan Vukotić (1959; DVD, *Dušan Vukotić on DVD*, Chatsworth, CA: Rembrandt Films, 2007).

82. *Neighbours*, directed by Norman McLaren (1952; DVD, *Norman McLaren: The Master's Edition*, Ottawa, ON: National Film Board of Canada, 2006).

83. *Substitute*, directed by Dušan Vukotić (1961; Zagreb, HR: Zagreb Film). www.youtube.com/watch?v=xhfHXLuiTd8, accessed April 20, 2015.

84. In 1961 Dušan Vukotić became the first foreigner to win an Academy Award for Best Animated Short.

85. Zlatko Grgić, quoted in Srecko Jurdana, Nenad Polimac, Zoran Tadic, and Hrvoje Turkovic , "Redatelj bez poruke, Razgovor sa Zlatkom Grgicem," [The director without a message, an interview with Zlatko Grgić], in Zlatko Sudovic (editor), *Zagrebacki krug crtanog filma 4*, Zagreb, 1986, p. 412; Andrijana Ruzic's collection.
"I dan danas se limitirana animacija smatra izumom Zagreb filma. Cak pise i u knjigama da su dvodimenzionalni likovi, to crtanje trokutima, nas izum. No, ja sam vidio retrospektivu Boba Cannona, Gerald McBoing, Boing, seriju UPA, koja je nastala deset godina pre nas. To je bio prvi avangardni film vis-a-vis Disneya. Hubley, Gene Deitch I crtaci koji su se odvojili od

Disneyevog studija. Tada jos nismo bili videli te filmove. Shvatio sam tek na retrospektivama koje sam sada vidio da je to isto sto I Zagreb film, samo deset puta bolje. Jer oni su ipak bili animatori bogatijeg iskustva." (translated from Croatian to Italian by Andrijana Ruzic, and from Italian to English by the author)

86. Nikola Kostelac, quoted in Tomislav Butorac, "8 Autora I 15 Pitanja, Anketa O Domacem Crtanom Filmu," [8 authors and 15 questions, an inquiry on local animated cinema], in Zlatko Sudovic (editor), *Zagrebacki krug crtanog filma 3*, Zagreb, 1978, p. 102; Andrijana Ruzic's collection. "Danasnji rezultati naseg studija nisu nastali pod direktnim uticajem stila jedne odredjene produkcije, vec primenom moderne grafike u crtanom filmu" (translated from Croatian to Italian by Andrijana Ruzic, and from Italian to English by the author).

87 Boris Kolar, in Butorac, "8 Autora I 15 Pitanja, Anketa O Domacem Crtanom Filmu," [8 Authors and 15 Questions, Inquiry on Local Animated Cinema].

88. *Alone*, directed by Vatroslav Mimica (1958; Zagreb, HR: Zagreb Film). www .youtube.com/watch?v=ovLKKYIl1SY and www.youtube.com/watch?v =1bBiWxQmYes, accessed September 25, 2015.

89. Vatroslav Mimica, quoted in Nikola Stojanović, "Put ka sintezi, Razgovor sa Vatroslavom Mimicom," [The path toward synthesis, an interview with Vatroslav Mimica] in Sudovic (editor), *Zagrebacki krug crtanog filma 4*, Zagreb, 1986, p. 408; Andrijana Ruzic's collection.
"UPA je primijenila jezik moderne grafike, napustajuci onaj Disneyev slatki, mekano romanticarski crtez. Medjutim, Bosustowljeva grUPA nije uspijela da napravi odgovarajuci prodor i u animaciji. Ona je jednu suvremeniju graficku formu jos uvek podredjivala zakonima Disneyeve animacije. Kod nas su prve, najznacajnije prodore na tom polju napravili Kostelac i Kostanjsek sa jednom kratkom serijom reklamnih filmova. Oni su radili na iskustvu Bosustowljevih rezultata."
(translated from Croatian to Italian by Andrijana Ruzic, and from Italian to English by the author)

90. *Short History*, directed by Ion Popescu-Gopo (1956; Bucharest, RO: Cinematographic Studio Bucharest). www.youtube.com/watch?v=jI53-N6mGX8, accessed September 25, 2015.

91. *7 Arts*, directed by Ion Popescu-Gopo (1958; Bucharest, RO: Cinematographic Studio Bucharest). www.youtube.com/watch?v=Ic4xp6oQZAw, accessed September 25, 2015.

92. *Love and the Zeppelin*, directed by Jiří Brdečka (1948; DVD, *Jiří Brdečka— Animované filmy*, Prague, CZ: Anifilm and Limonádový Joe, 2015).

93. *Love*, directed by Jiří Brdečka (1978; DVD, *Jiří Brdečka—Animované filmy*, Prague, CZ: Anifilm and Limonádový Joe, 2015). The story is about the unusual love between a spider and a poet that live together in the same room. Their friendship will inevitably end after the poet falls in love with a woman who is repulsed by the spider.

94. *How Man Learned to Fly*, directed by Jiří Brdečka (1958; DVD, *Jiří Brdečka—Animované filmy*, Prague, CZ: Anifilm and Limonádový Joe, 2015).

95. *Man under Water*, directed by Jiří Brdečka (1961; DVD, *Jiří Brdečka—Animované filmy*, Prague, CZ: Anifilm and Limonádový Joe, 2015).

96. *Our Little Red Riding Hood*, directed by Jiří Brdečka (1960; DVD, *Jiří Brdečka—Animované filmy*, Prague, CZ: Anifilm and Limonádový Joe, 2015). Here the wolf falls sick after eating the little girl and her grandmother, who, in fact, have fun dancing in the wolf's belly. The wolf goes to the doctor, who cuts open his belly, removes the girl and grandmother, and then stuffs it with balloons.

97. *The Television Fan*, directed by Jiří Brdečka (1961; DVD, *Jiří Brdečka—Animované filmy*, Prague, CZ: Anifilm and Limonádový Joe, 2015).

98. *Gallina Vogelbirdae*, directed by Jiří Brdečka (1963; DVD, *Jiří Brdečka—Animované filmy*, Prague, CZ: Anifilm and Limonádový Joe, 2015). The plot revolves around a creative young boy who during an elementary school art lesson draws a non-realistic hen. The teacher dismisses his drawing as too far from the original hen that was supposed to be merely copied. Nevertheless, the boy's drawing is so imaginative that his creation comes to life. The hen is then captured by famous ornithologist Vogelbird, who names it after himself as if he has discovered a new species. Finally, the little boy's new drawing comes to life, although the teacher is still unable to recognize his creative powers.

99. *My Darling Clementine*, directed by Jiří Brdečka (1959; DVD, *Jiří Brdečka—Animované filmy*, Prague, CZ: Anifilm and Limonádový Joe, 2015). The film was commissioned by the American company Rembrandt Films. Information provided in the booklet that accompanies the *Jiří Brdečka—Animované filmy* 3 DVD set.

100. *The Frozen Logger*, directed by Jiří Brdečka (1962; DVD, *Jiří Brdečka—Animované filmy*, Prague, CZ: Anifilm and Limonádový Joe, 2015). This film was commissioned by an unknown American producer. Information provided in the booklet that accompanies the *Jiří Brdečka—Animované filmy* 3 DVD set. According to the opening credits, Gene Deitch was the supervising director.

101. *Reason and Emotion*, directed by Jiří Brdečka (1962; DVD, *Jiří Brdečka—Animované filmy*, Prague, CZ: Anifilm and Limonádový Joe, 2015). The film expresses the conflict between these two aspects of human life. They are represented as two gardeners who work following opposing stylistic canons and criteria but end up cooperating in a more balanced and harmonious way.

102. *Plaisir d'Amour (Joy of Love)*, directed by Jiří Brdečka (1966; DVD, *Jiří Brdečka—Animované filmy*, Prague, CZ: Anifilm and Limonádový Joe, 2015). This film illustrates the evolution of a couple, starting from their youth (the man courting the woman in a café), passing through their adult married life (the activities they do together in their living room) and finally ending in old age (their last years together).

103. *The Face*, directed by Jiří Brdečka (1973; DVD, *Jiří Brdečka—Animované filmy*, Prague, CZ: Anifilm and Limonádový Joe, 2015). The hand-drawn animation shows the metamorphosis of a man's face as he grows up and gets older and older. The film is a metaphor of the different stages of human life. It opens with a simple egg drawn on white paper and ends with the same egg. At the end of the film, there are sounds of chirping birds and, finally, a crying baby.

104. *Revenge*, directed by Jiří Brdečka (1968; DVD, *Jiří Brdečka—Animované filmy*, Prague, CZ: Anifilm and Limonádový Joe, 2015). The film is based on a short story written by Romantic French poet Gérard de Nerval. Information provided in the booklet that accompanies the *Jiří Brdečka— Animované filmy* 3 DVD set.

105. *Metamorpheus*, directed by Jiří Brdečka (1969; DVD, *Jiří Brdečka— Animované filmy*, Prague, CZ: Anifilm and Limonádový Joe, 2015). The original source is the Greek myth of Orpheus and Eurydice.

106. *There was a Miller on a River*, directed by Jiří Brdečka (1971; DVD, *Jiří Brdečka—Animované filmy*, Prague, CZ: Anifilm and Limonádový Joe, 2015). The film is based on a popular ballad that tells the story of a soldier who is accidentally killed by his parents after his return at home.

107. *What I Didn't Say to the Prince*, directed by Jiří Brdečka (1975; DVD, *Jiří Brdečka—Animované filmy*, Prague, CZ: Anifilm and Limonádový Joe, 2015). The film is an adaptation of Oscar Wilde's fairy tale *The Happy Prince* (1888). Information provided in the booklet that accompanies the *Jiří Brdečka—Animované filmy* 3 DVD set.

108. The series includes three animated shorts based on popular Moravian folk ballads.

109. *How to Keep Slim*, directed by Jiří Brdečka (1963; DVD, *Jiří Brdečka— Animované filmy*, Prague, CZ: Anifilm and Limonádový Joe, 2015). In this film there is a minimalist layout design, both in the characters and the backgrounds. Very few elements address the environments in which the protagonist lives, as in *Gerald McBoing Boing*. The film also resembles *Fudget's Budget* for the use of a sheet of graph paper as the background.

110. *Minstrel's Song*, directed by Jiří Brdečka (1964; DVD, *Jiří Brdečka— Animované filmy*, Prague, CZ: Anifilm and Limonádový Joe, 2015). Here the minimalism is solely in the animation, which is essential.

111. *The Deserter*, directed by Jiří Brdečka (1965; DVD, *Jiří Brdečka—Animované filmy*, Prague, CZ: Anifilm and Limonádový Joe, 2015). The film has a modern look and presents some stylization in the background design.

112. *The Power of Destiny*, directed by Jiří Brdečka (1968; DVD, *Jiří Brdečka— Animované filmy*, Prague, CZ: Anifilm and Limonádový Joe, 2015). The characters intentionally look like hand drawings on paper. Sometimes the frame is made of only thin black lines that define the characters and the environment. The film combines traditional two-dimensional animation with cutout animation.

113. The studio was founded in 1936.

114. Bendazzi, *Cartoons: 100 Years of Cinema Animation*.

115. *History of a Crime*, directed by Fyodor Khitruk (1962; DVD, *Masters of Russian Animation*, Los Angeles, CA: Image Entertainment and Jove Films, 2000).

116. The author could not find any document stating that UPA films were screened in the Soviet Union during the 1950s and 1960s, or in any other European country belonging to the Eastern Bloc. But, considering that after the Rencontres Internationales du Cinéma d'Animation (1956) other international meetings among the animation community, such as the Annecy International Animation Film Festival (1960), took place, it is highly possible that certain Soviet animators and directors like Fyodor Khitruk received information regarding foreign films, either in the form of screenings at these international events or in the form of catalogues, art magazines or personal letters that might have circulated among the international animation community.

117. *Boniface's Vacation*, directed by Fyodor Khitruk (1965; Moscow, RU: Soyuzmultfilm). www.dailymotion.com/video/xncpj7_boniface-s-vocation -1965-kanikuly-bonifaciya-eng-sp-subs-russian-animation-fedor-khitruk _shortfilms, accessed April 22, 2015.

118. *Film, Film, Film*, directed by Fyodor Khitruk (1968; DVD, *Masters of Russian Animation*, Los Angeles, CA: Image Entertainment and Jove Films, 2000).

119. For more information on the history of Japanese animated cinema, see: Maria Roberta Novielli, *Animerama: Storia del Cinema d'animazione giapponese* (Venice, IT: Marsilio, 2015); Guido Tavassi, *Storia dell'animazione giapponese: Autori, Arte, Industria, Successo dal 1917 a oggi* (Latina, IT: Tunué, 2012).

120. *The White Snake Enchantress*, directed by Taiji Yabushita (1958; DVD, *Le Serpent Blanc*, Paris, FR: Wild Side Video, 2012).

121. Panda and Mimi are a panda and a Japanese raccoon dog (tanuki, in Japanese), respectively. Therefore, they are symbols of China and Japan. Novielli, *Animerama: Storia del cinema d'animazione giapponese*.

122. *Magic Boy*, directed by Taiji Yabushita and Akira Daikubara (1959; DVD, Burbank, CA: Warner Home Video, 2014).

123. *Alakazam the Great*, directed by Taiji Yabushita, Daisaku Shirakawa and Osamu Tezuka (1960; Tokyo, JP: Tōei Animation).

124. Known in the West as *Astro Boy*, the original name of the TV series was *Tetsuwan Atomu* (Mighty atom). It was broadcast for the first time on January 1, 1963. Tavassi, *Storia dell'animazione giapponese: Autori, Arte, Industria, Successo dal 1917 a oggi*.

125. Bendazzi, *Cartoons: 100 Years of Cinema Animation*, 414.

126. Novielli, *Animerama: Storia del cinema d'animazione giapponese*.

127. During his long career, Osamu Tezuka produced and in the majority of the cases also directed 14 experimental films: *Tales of the Street Corner* (1962), *Male* (1962), *Memory* (1964), *Mermaid* (1964), *The Drop* (1965), *Cigarettes*

and Ashes (1965), *Pictures at an Exhibition* (1966), *The Genesis* (1968), *Jumping* (1984), *Broken Down Film* (1985), *Legend of the Forest* (1987), *Muramasa* (1987), *Push* (1987) and *Self-Portrait* (1988). Two more animated shorts were left unfinished at his death.

128. *Tales of the Street Corner*, directed by Yûsaku Sakamoto and Eiichi Yamamoto (1962; DVD, *The Astonishing Work of Tezuka Osamu*, New York, NY: Kimstim Films, 2013).

129. Auguste Rodin, *The Thinker*, 1880–1881. Bronze sculpture. Rodin Museum, Paris, FR.

130. Novielli, *Animerama: Storia del cinema d'animazione giapponese, 108.* "Storie all'angolo di una strada è un'opera personale oltre che una forma di 'studio,' intesa per sperimentare le potenzialità dell'animazione, come dimostra in particolare la ricchezza visuale e tematica espressa dai manifesti, ciascuno disegnato e animato con stile differente" (translated by author).

131. *Male*, directed by Eiichi Yamamoto (1962; DVD, *The Astonishing Work of Tezuka Osamu*, New York, NY: Kimstim Films, 2013).

132. *Memory*, directed by Osamu Tezuka (1964; DVD, *The Astonishing Work of Tezuka Osamu*, New York, NY: Kimstim Films, 2013).

133. *Mermaid*, directed by Osamu Tezuka (1964; DVD, *The Astonishing Work of Tezuka Osamu*, New York, NY: Kimstim Films, 2013).

134. Novielli, *Animerama: Storia del cinema d'animazione giapponese, 111.* "… un omaggio minimalista alla fantasia e all'individualismo" (translated by author).

135. Claude Debussy. *Prélude á l'après-midi d'un faune* (Paris, FR: Jean Jobert, 1922).

136. *Pictures at an Exhibition*, directed by Osamu Tezuka (1966; DVD, *The Astonishing Work of Tezuka Osamu*, New York, NY: Kimstim Films, 2013).

137. Modest Petrovich Mussorgsky, *Pictures at an Exhibition* (Saint Petersburg, RU: W. Bessel & Co., 1886).

138. *Legend of the Forest*, directed by Osamu Tezuka (1987; DVD, *The Astonishing Work of Tezuka Osamu*, New York, NY: Kimstim Films, 2013).

139. Pyotr Ilyich Tchaikovsky, *Symphony no. 4 in F Minor, Op. 36* (Moscow, RU: P. Jurgenson, 1888).

140. Novielli, *Animerama: Storia del cinema d'animazione giapponese.*

141. Ibid., 164. "Minimalismo surreale" (translated by author).

142. Ibid., 117. "… un grafismo elementare, combinato di volta in volta con tecniche differenti…, si presta a diventare quintessenza di un particolare studio sul movimento, esplorato nelle sue microcomponenti e legato con forza a sperimentazioni sul suono e sul colore" (translated by author).

143. *Love*, directed by Yōji Kuri (1964; Tokyo, JP: Kuri Jikken Kobo). www.youtube .com/watch?v=3fOeZFK7eg8, accessed April 29, 2015.

Conclusions

UPA: REDESIGNING ANIMATION

UPA films were among the first animated cartoons to express a Modern simplicity in animated cinema. Although independent animators had done this before worldwide, UPA artists were the first to conduct stylistic research and experimentation that incorporated Modern artistic expressions in films that were intended for the U.S. entertainment industry. UPA artists did not create art for art's sake but rather operated within the economic rules established by the market. Despite the difficulties and contractual restrictions imposed by the distribution company Columbia Pictures, UPA artists were able to develop personal audiovisual styles. According to Charles Solomon, this is the single most important contribution of UPA: "the idea that artists at one studio could employ disparate styles and use the animated film as a vehicle for personal expression."[1] Yet, to understand fully the UPA legacy, it is necessary to add to this comment that UPA artists accomplished this achievement having the entertainment business as their operative framework.

A similar freedom of expression was granted, for example, at Zagreb Film or Soyuzmultfilm. But, like all the successful animation studios operating in Eastern European countries, they were state-funded companies, although in different ways and to different degrees, and therefore conformed to other, controlled economic conditions and necessities. Artists and executive producers did not have to find clients to guarantee the survival of the studios, although they did have to communicate with state representatives and compromise with their requests. Nevertheless, although productions were funded and controlled by the state, censorship was mild, thus allowing artists to express their personal ideas and styles.

In Western countries, UPA studio was a pioneer. Eventually, most animation studios diversified their productions in animated TV commercials, educational films and personal animated films. After World War II, TV commercials and TV series came to represent the indispensable steady income necessary to produce personal films. Animated films intended as personal expressions are works of art, no matter what economic restrictions are imposed on them. UPA was one of the early studios to elevate the medium of animation to the level of art *within* the industry.

This was possible thanks to the changed historical and sociological context born out of World War II, which drove UPA artists to develop those innovative aesthetic features that implicitly consider animation as a form of art: the rise of labor unions in the animation industry culminating in the Disney strike; the HUAC hearings and general atmosphere of suspicion toward Hollywood and particularly the UPA studio; and the affirmation of Modernism in the visual arts, especially in painting, graphic design and advertising, operated as different and simultaneous cultural forces that ultimately determined the development of UPA's *simplified audiovisual language* in animation.

The UPA "revolution" in redesigning animation was also achieved thanks to a production system based on non-fixed units and its executive producer, Stephen Bosustow, who acted as a "catalyst" and a proselytizer among his employees. This is UPA's second legacy: a production system that allowed the formation of interchangeable teams of artists was proven to be successful in making films that are personal expressions. Although some of his employees did not consider Bosustow to be the artistic creator of UPA, he was one of the few executive producers in the history of U.S. animation who envisioned animation as an art form as much as Walt Disney did. Bosustow may not have managed to build a solid company as Walt Disney did, but he did produce animated films that entered the history of animation as Modern artworks. UPA history was short but intense. Considering the high quality of its one-shot animated cartoons and the popularity reached with the creation of Mr. Magoo, UPA studio stands out as a successful Western animation studio. It managed to balance personal *and* commercial productions for more than a decade within the American industry.

UPA's third legacy relates to its audiovisual styles. The UPA trademark was its simplicity in the design of the layouts *and* in the animation. UPA animated films did not express a unique audiovisual style but rather a multitude of audiovisual styles developed according to the stories. The UPA simplified audiovisual language is therefore more an *attitude* toward animation. This pioneering approach was so productive in allowing directors to experiment a personal style that it became emblematic of UPA and later inspired international productions. When John Hubley, for example, asserted that his personal films were born as experimentations on different techniques, he was applying the lesson he learned at UPA based on the principle "form follows function."

Regarding the two research questions of this book, we can conclude that the UPA attitude toward animation is the result of dual research: the first about the way the characters are drawn on the frame and the second about the way the characters are animated between the frames. The first reflects the influence of graphic Modernism on the visuals and originates from the combination of various elements, such as traditional compositional rules, asymmetrical layouts derived from Bauhaus design, angular and stylized characters and expressive colors. The second reflects the influence of graphic Modernism on the animation, which was limited rather than full for economic reasons and therefore accentuates the flatness and two-dimensionality of the layouts and some poses of the characters. The accommodation between these two focal points of research combined with an innovative use of sound effects allow that expression of Modern simplicity that characterizes UPA animated films.

In sum, UPA validated a type of simplified audiovisual language that had already been expressed in Europe by Gross and Hoppin with *La Joie de vivre* (1934), for example; showed that Disney's stylistic hegemony could be challenged; and reinforced the idea that animation could be used for personal expression as an independent form of art.

Looking at the studio's role from a historical viewpoint, UPA animated cartoons played an important role in the evolution of animation. UPA stood at a crucial point, and the animators and designers who internationally treasured the UPA lesson then pushed UPA experimentations even further, adding something more to the medium. At the end of the 1950s, UPA as a business was in full decline, but its example remained bountiful as other revolutionary animation studios and directors blossomed. Also, UPA filmmakers continued to expend the artfulness of animation after leaving the company.

Among the aims of this work is an examination of innovative UPA audiovisual styles by comparing them with those visual stylistic features that are present in Modern fine arts, graphic design and advertising. The work also investigates the main visual reference sources for UPA artists

and addresses how these influences were then assimilated in their animated cartoons.

Another aim is to present an analysis of the most qualitative relevant
UPA films in order to highlight Modern audiovisual characteristics in
hand-drawn animated cinema. Similarly, this study explores the UPA
production system and the role of its executive producer in relation to his
employees in order to point out those characteristics that can, and did,
lead to the creation of high-quality personal animated films within the
entertainment business.

The most significant findings of this study are especially related to the
figure of UPA executive producer Stephen Bosustow, since it outlines his
strengths, lapses and weaknesses in administering the company, meeting
outside demands, producing animated cartoons and mediating between
diverse UPA artists' personalities.

In relation to what has been written to date on UPA, this work focuses
on UPA studio and UPA animated cartoons as *case studies* for a Modern
animation company and Modern animated films. It also frames UPA
within its historical, sociological and cultural context in order to see it
as the product of a specific time period. Finally, this work also compares
UPA films with examples of 1950s and 1960s international productions
and attempts to trace direct and indirect UPA influences on these international films.

This study paves the way for possible future lines of research. As noted in
the introduction, one of them could be a specific exploration on the 1940s
and 1950s American musical scene, especially jazz music, in American
radio and TV programs and on the tradition of voice actors in American
animated cartoons in order to determine their influence on the scores and
sound effects of Modern animations, particularly at UPA.

A second line of research could be focused on UPA animated television
commercials. At the time this book was written, copies of UPA TV commercials were still scattered; some of them were available at the Margaret
Herrick Library in Los Angeles, others at the UCLA Film & Television
Archive. Nevertheless, they were still too limited in number to be taken as
case studies of a major production. None of the major distribution companies has released a compilation of UPA animated TV commercials to
date. Considering the interrelationships and cross-fertilization between
UPA animated films and all types of advertising art, as addressed in
Chapter 4, it could be argued that UPA TV commercials are peculiar in

their genre because they combine animation and advertising. A study on the aesthetic features of UPA TV commercials could therefore eventually be undertaken.

A third research topic could be centered on the filmography of Stephen Bosustow Productions, the company that Bosustow founded after he sold UPA to Henry G. Saperstein in 1960. Many of the animated and live-action films that he produced are available at the UCLA Film and Television Archive. They express a certain attention to social themes, and some of them are of good quality.

Finally, a fourth line of research could be dedicated to UPA and international Modern animated films. As stated earlier, the films and studios discussed in Chapter 5 are just some examples of an ample global trend. The research on international Modern animation could be broadened to include examples from South America and Oceania, and the examples proposed could also be linked to the history of animation of the specific country or continent in which they were made.

This current study is not strictly about UPA; it is more about Modern animation as it was expressed in UPA films. Therefore, it situates UPA within the greater history of U.S. and international Modern animation and connects Modern animation with Modern visual arts by tracing common stylistic features. Lastly, this study defines simplicity and minimalism as expressions of Modernism in hand-drawn animation, taking UPA animated cartoons as case studies.

ENDNOTE

1. Solomon, *Enchanted Drawings: The History of Animation,* 227.

Appendix

All the figures presented in this appendix are copies of materials belonging to Steve Bosustow's UPA collection, in the care of his son, Tee Bosustow. The pictures are photographs taken by the author with Tee Bosustow's consent.

The three scanned timelines were compiled by Stephen Bosustow and represent his most important professional stages from 1937 to 1960 (Timeline I), from 1950 to 1965 (Timeline II) and from 1920 to 1964 (Timeline III).

Timeline I

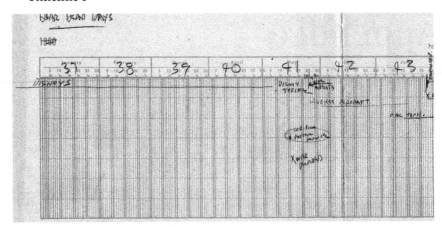

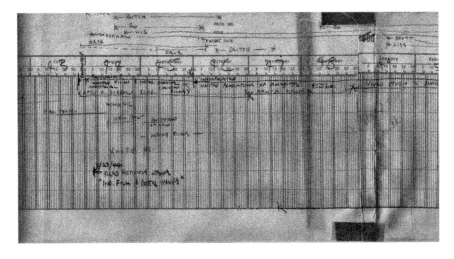

(Continued)

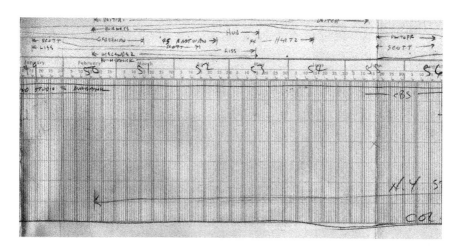

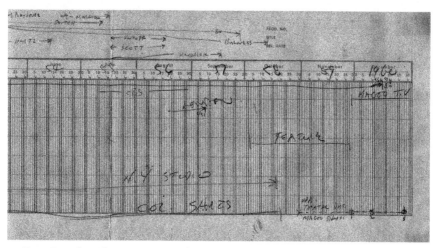

Reprinted with permission from Tee Bosustow (*Steve Bosustow's UPA collection, in the care of his son, Tee Bosustow*).

Timeline II

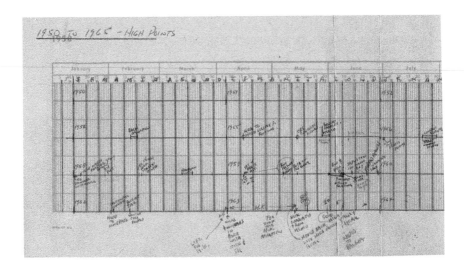

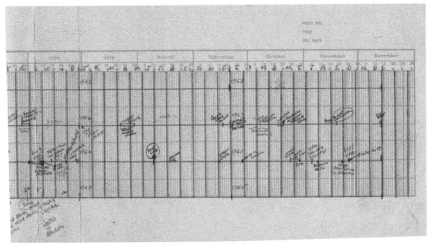

Reprinted with permission from Tee Bosustow (*Steve Bosustow's UPA collection, in the care of his son, Tee Bosustow*).

Timeline III

1920 | **1930** | **1935 to 1941** | **1942 to 1943**

- 10 YRS OLD
- WATER COLOR PAINTER
  VICTORIA COUNTY FAIR

- 17 YRS OLD
- HIGH SCHOOL
  COMMUNITY CHEST
  CONTEST

- 7 YRS AT DISNEYS
  · MICKEY MOUSE
  · SNOW WHITE
  · FANTASIA
  (ARTIST & WRITER)

- PROD. ILLUSTRATOR
  (HUGHES)
- PROD. CONTROL SUPERVISOR
- SAFETY POSTERS
  (NITRO?)

- CAL TECH.
  (E.S.M.W.T.)
- DESIGN SKETCHING
- SAFETY PIC.
  (NITRO?)

1944 | **1945** | **1946** | **1947** | **1948**

1944
- OWN CO.
- ? { (PARTNERSHIP SUCCEEDED ⅓·⅓·⅓ – BUT NO
  FINAL AGREEMENT)

- TAUGHT SCHOOL
- HUGHES POSTERS
- SAFETY PIX

- ROOSEVELT CAMPAIGN
  PIC. "THE BEST FOR EVERYBODY"
- BOEING PIX
- ARMY-NAVY
  TRAINING PICS.
- "DEAR SIR" SPEC. ENT. PIX.

1945
- CO. STARTED 12/20/45
  (NEEDED CAPITAL)
  (BOUGHT OUT PARTNERS)

- NAVY TRAINING PIX
- ENCYCLOPAEDIA
  ENCY. BRITANNICA
  ED. PIX.
- O.W.I. TRAINING
  PIX.
- "BROTHERHOOD OF MAN"

1946
- Col. Pix started
  SCALE

- BROTHERHOOD OF
  MAN (ED. PIX)
- DEAR SIR (SPEC)
  (1ST ENT. PIX.)
- NAVY TRAINING PIX

1947
- COL. PIX START
  TO 1938 (10 PIX)
  TO 1958
- STARTED DOING
  T.V. SPOTS

- NAVY PIX. CONT.

1948
- CONT. COL.
  SHORTS.
- CONTINUED FOR
  LIFE OF G.

- NAVY PIX.
  CONT.
- STARTED BUILDING
  NEW UPA BURBANK
  STUDIO BLDG.
  (MOVED IN DEC.)
- DID H. SAPERSTEIN
  CARTOON WORK
  ON NOVELTY.

(Continued)

1949 | 1950 | 1951 | 1952 | 1953

1954 | 1955 | 1956 | 1957 | 1958

(Continued)

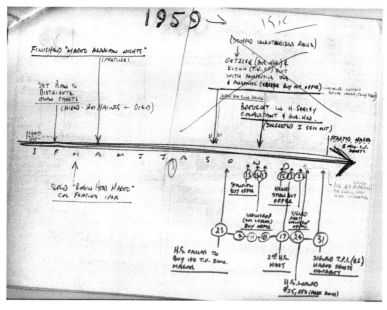

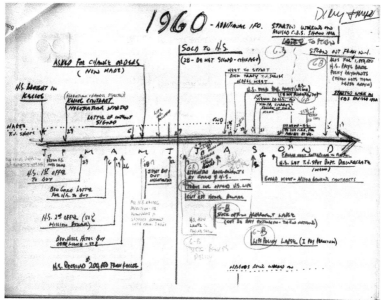

(Continued)

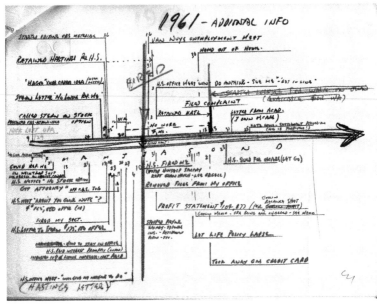

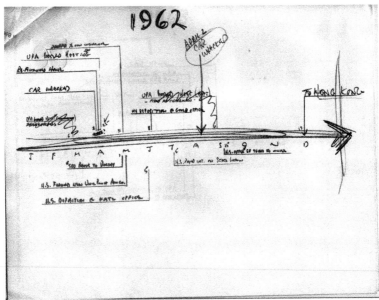

(Continued)

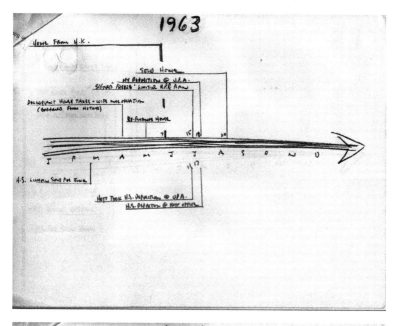

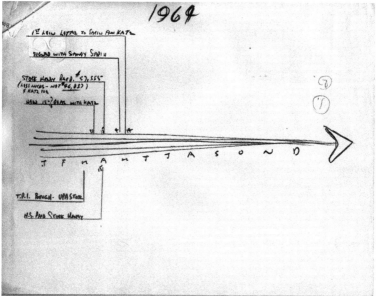

Reprinted with permission from Tee Bosustow (Steve Bosustow's UPA collection, in the care of his son, Tee Bosustow).

Primary Sources

ARCHIVES CONSULTED

John Canemaker Animation Collection; Fales Library and Special Collections, New York University Libraries; New York, NY

Audio and Video Tape:

Box 1; folder 40.0003; Art Babbitt interview by John Canemaker, New York City, June 4, 1975

Box 1; folder 40.0004; Art Babbitt interview by John Canemaker, New York City

Box 1; folder 40.0026; Art Babbitt on Don Graham and Disney art school, February 21, 1979

Box 1; folder 40.0028; Grim Natwick, NYC, May 19, 1974

Box 1; folder 40.0037; Willis Pyle, May 16, 1973

Box 1; folder 40.0038; June Foray, NYC, October 14, 1975

Box 1; folder 40.004; David Hilberman, Santa Cruz, CA

Box 1; folder 40.0041; Jules Engel, July 1, 1975

Box 1; folder 40.0045; Al Rezek and Tissa David, August 8, 1976

Box 1; folder 40.0047; R. O. Blechman, NYC, July 14, 1978

Box 2; folder 40.0064; Zack Schwartz, NYC, September 12, 1979

Box 2; folder 40.0066; Zack Schwartz, September 18, 1979

Box 2; folder 40.0075; William Pomerance (on the 1941 Disney strike), April 17, 1979

Box 2; folder 40.0078; Richard Williams on George Dunning, November 20, 1979

Box 2; folder 40.0079; Art Babbitt, NYC, July 12, 1979

Box 2; folder 40.008; Art Babbitt, NYC, July 12, 1979

Box 2; folder 40.0089 David Tissa, May 29, 1973; George Dunning recorded from CBS Camera Three, May 20, 1973

Documentary Material:

Box 5; folders 3–7; Babbitt, Art; undated

Box 11; folder 94; Engel, Jules; undated

Box 32; folder 289; Babbitt, Art; undated

Box 40; folder 358; Engel, Jules; undated

Accretions 2001—Series I: Documentary Material, Subseries A: Subjects:

Box 2; folders 5–7; United Productions of America

Accretions 2008—Series I: Documentary Material:

Box 3; folder 99; Hubley, John and Faith: Interview of Faith Hubley, 1996

Margaret Herrick Library, Academy of Motion Picture Arts and Sciences; Beverly Hills, CA—Special Collections

Paul Kohner Agency Records:

74.f-558 THE ARABIAN NIGHTS—script 1959

Abe and Charlotte Levitow Collection:

1.f-6 GAY PURR-EE—awards 1962

1.f-13 1001 ARABIAN NIGHTS—script 1958

3.f-37 THE BOING BOING SHOW [TV]—publicity 1956

8.f-109 Advertising —Benton & Bowles 1959

8.f-110 Advertising—Carling's Black Label Beer 1959, undated

8.f-111 Advertising—Global Van Lines 1960

8.f-112 Advertising—Kaiser Steel 1959

8.f-113 Advertising—storyboards circa 1960

9.f-122 UPA Pictures, Inc.—miscellaneous 1961–1962, undated

9.f-123 UPA Pictures, Inc.—Mr. Magoo (artwork) 1956–1961 and undated

9.f-124 UPA Pictures, Inc. —Mr. Magoo (exposure sheet) undated

9.f-125 UPA Pictures, Inc. —Mr. Magoo (publicity) 1962–1965, undated

9.f-126 UPA Pictures, Inc. —Mr. Magoo (storyboard) circa 1960

9.f-127 UPA Pictures, Inc. —publicity 1955–1956, undated

9.f-128 UPA Pictures, Inc. —storyboards circa 1960

10-OS.f-134 GERALD McBOING-BOING—artwork 1950

10-OS.f-139 1001 ARABIAN NIGHTS—artwork 1958

10-OS.f-145 THE BOING BOING SHOW [TV]—artwork 1956

10-OS.f-153 UPA Pictures, Inc.—storyboards undated

Andrew Marton Papers:

7.f–95 HANGMAN undated

Technicolor Collection:

4 BABY BOOGIE—shot-by-shot continuity 1955

5 BALLET-OOP—shot-by-shot continuity 1953

10 BRINGING UP MOTHER—shot-by-shot continuity 1953

50 THE POPCORN STORY—shot-by-shot continuity 1950, 1957

51 PROFESSOR SMALL AND MR. TALL—shot-by-shot continuity 1943, 1952

51 PUNCHY DE LEON—shot-by-shot continuity 1949

52 THE RAGTIME BEAR—shot-by-shot continuity 1949

53 THE RISE OF DUTON LANG—shot-by-shot continuity 1955

54 ROOTY TOOT TOOT—shot-by-shot continuity 1951, 1958

55 SAILING AND THE VILLAGE BAND—shot-by-shot continuity 1957

59 SPARE THE CHILD—shot-by-shot continuity 1954

60 SPRING AND SAGANAKI—shot-by-shot continuity 1958

63 THE TELL-TALE HEART—shot-by-shot continuity 1953

64 1001 ARABIAN NIGHTS—shot-by-shot continuity 1959

66 TREES AND JAMAICA DADDY—shot-by-shot continuity 1957

67 A UNICORN IN THE GARDEN—shot-by-shot continuity 1953, 1959

68 UPA 1949 FORD PLAYLETS—SERIES #2—shot-by-shot continuity 1950

68 UPA FORD MOTOR PLAYLETS 101-A-B-C—shot-by-shot continuity 1949

68 UPA FORD MOTOR PLAYLETS 101-D-E-F—shot-by-shot continuity 1949

71 WILLIE THE KID—shot-by-shot continuity 1952, 1958

71 THE WONDER GLOVES—shot-by-shot continuity 1951, 1958

Technicolor Negative Damage and Defect Reports:

9.f-115 Reports (Q–Z) 1946–1954

Theatre Vanguard Records:

6.f-34 Filmex project 1978 (animation) 1978

The Museum of Modern Art (MoMA) Archives; New York, NY

Manhattan Facility:

Alfred H. Barr, Jr. Papers—1.251 mf 2180:963

Early Museum History Administrative Records—III 26a, III 26b, III 26c, III 26d

Public Information Records—II.A.852

René d'Harnoncourt Papers—IV.222

Sound Recordings of Museum-Related Events—66.2, 66.2D

Queens Facility:

Department of Film Exhibition Files, 60

Department of Film Exhibition Files, 608

UCLA Film & Television Archive; Los Angeles, CA

DVD11670—GOOD GOODIES [1971] // MODERN LIFE: CHOICES AND CONFLICTS [1972] M73468

DVD12037—I TOLD 'EM EXACTLY HOW TO DO IT! [1974] M73389

DVD12038—EGO TRAP, OR, HOW TO SHOOT DOWN A NEW IDEA, THE [1977] M73484

DVD12039—BIRDS OF A FEATHER [1972] M73462

DVD12041—JANKO: IT'S ALL RELATIVE [1977] M73387

DVD12042—BEGINNING, THE [1972] M73474

DVD12043—WHO DO YOU THINK SHOULD BELONG TO THE CLUB? [1977] M73479

DVD12044—WHO'S AFRAID OF MURAKAMI-WOLF? [1959–1967] M200150

DVD30002—TEMPORARY DVD #3

[M195708] UPA Shorts Mister Magoo and Piel's Beer: When Magoo Flew // Barbecue Magoo // Kangaroo Courting // Ragtime Bear // Bungled Bungalow // Destination Magoo // Pink and Blue Blues // Piel's Beer

M73377 Title: Creole. 16 mm. safety print

M73391 Title: Just say hic. 16 mm. safety print

M73443 Title: A firefly named Torchy. 16 mm. safety print

M73458 Title: Noises in the night. 16 mm. safety print

M73624 Title: Gabrielle and Selena. 16 mm. safety print

VA816—AND NOW, AN ANIMATED WORD FROM OUR SPONSOR: 1948–1978

VA2187—FOUR POSTER, THE [1952]

VA20631—EVAN'S CORNER

VA21812—COMMERCIALS: UPA

VA23268—BLUES PATTERN

INTERVIEWS CITED

Bosustow, Stephen. By Tee Bosustow (December 11, 1976). Steve Bosustow's UPA collection.

Bosustow, Stephen. By Tee Bosustow (March 26, 1977). Steve Bosustow's UPA collection.

Bosustow, Stephen. By Tee Bosustow (June 1977). Steve Bosustow's UPA collection.

Goldberg, Eric. By author (May 28, 2014).

Griffin, George. By author (February 24, 2014).

Hilberman, David. By John Canemaker (June 16, 1979). John Canemaker Animation Collection; MSS 040; box 1; folder 40.0039; Fales Library and Special Collections, NYU.

Schwartz, Zachary. By John Canemaker (September 12, 1979). John Canemaker Animation Collection; MSS 040; box 2; folder 40.0065; Fales Library and Special Collections, NYU.

Schwartz, Zachary. By John Canemaker (September 18, 1979). John Canemaker Animation Collection; MSS 040; box 2; folder 40.0067; Fales Library and Special Collections, NYU.

Siracusa, Joe. By author (May 23, 2014).

Sorensen, Vibeke. By author (February 4, 2014).

PRIVATE COLLECTIONS

Andrijana Ruzic's collection

Giannalberto Bendazzi's collection

Steve Bosustow's UPA collection, in the care of his son, Tee Bosustow For inquiries, Tee Bosustow can be contacted via email: bosustow@ icloud.com

Secondary Sources

ARTWORKS REFERENCED

Debussy, Claude. *Prélude á l'après-midi d'un faune.* Paris, FR: Jean Jobert, 1922.

Dufy, Raoul. *Regatta at Cowes,* 1934. Oil painting. Washington D.C. National Gallery of Art.

Mussorgsky, Modest Petrovich. *Pictures at an Exhibition.* Saint Petersburg, RU: W. Bessel & Co., 1886.

Rand, Paul. Magazine cover of *Direction* 3, no. 6, 1940. Paul-Rand. www.paul-rand.com/foundation/editorial/#direction.

Rand, Paul. Magazine cover of *Direction,* Fall 1945. Paul-Rand. www.paul-rand.com/foundation/editorial/#direction.

Rand, Paul. Magazine cover of *Jazzways* 1, 1946. It's Nice That. www.itsnicethat.com/articles/paul-rand.

Rodin, Auguste. *The Thinker,* 1880–1881. Bronze sculpture. Rodin Museum, Paris.

Seurat, Georges. *Un dimanche après-midi à l'Île de la Grande Jatte,* 1884–1886. Oil on canvas. Art Institute of Chicago.

Tchaikovsky, Pyotr Ilyich. *Symphony no. 4 in F Minor, Op. 36.* Moscow, RU: P. Jurgenson, 1888.

AUDIOVISUAL MATERIALS REFERENCED

Abel Gance Lifetime Achievement Award Presented to Lester Novros. DVD. Directed by Ammiel G. Najar and Michael Bober. Los Angeles, CA: Graphic Films and Large Format Cinema Association, 1999.

Abracadabra. Directed by Dušan Vukotić. 1957; Zagreb, HR: Zagreb Film. www.youtube.com/watch?v=oMVORtqy3NM, accessed April 20, 2015.

Adventure of An *. Directed by John Hubley. 1957; DVD, *Selected Films of John and Faith Hubley,* San Francisco, CA: McSweeney's, *The Believer,* March/April 2014.

Alakazam the Great. Directed by Taiji Yabushita, Daisaku Shirakawa and Osamu Tezuka. 1960; Tokyo, JP: Tōei Animation.

Alice in Wonderland. Directed by Clyde Geronimi, Wilfred Jackson and Hamilton Luske. 1951; DVD, Burbank, CA: Buena Vista Home Entertainment and Walt Disney Studios Home Entertainment, 2010.

Alone. Directed by Vatroslav Mimica. 1958; Zagreb, HR: Zagreb Film. https://www.youtube.com/watch?v=ovLKKYIl1SY and https://www.youtube.com/watch?v=1bBiWxQmYes, accessed September 25, 2015.

Alpha Omega. Directed by Bruno Bozzetto. 1961; DVD, *Tutto Bozzetto*, Rome, IT: Twentieth Century Fox Italy, 2012.

Animal Farm. Directed by John Halas and Joy Batchelor. 1954; DVD, Chicago, IL: Home Vision Entertainment, 2004.

The Apple. Directed by George Dunning. 1963; London, UK: TVC London. https://www.youtube.com/watch?v=0QFjJSG87es, accessed August 16, 2015.

The Aristo-Cat. Directed by Chuck Jones. 1942; DVD, *Looney Tunes Golden Collection,* vol. 4, Burbank, CA: Warner Home Video, 2006.

Automania 2000. Directed by John Halas. 1963; DVD, *The Halas & Batchelor Short Film Collection,* London, UK: Network TV Home Entertainment, 2015.

An Award for Mr. Rossi. Directed by Bruno Bozzetto. 1960; DVD, *Il Signor Rossi— Una vita da cartone,* Milan, IT: San Paolo Multimedia, 2008.

Baby Boogie. Directed by Paul Julian. 1955; DVD, *UPA: The Jolly Frolics Collection,* Culver City, CA: Sony Pictures Home Entertainment, 2012.

Ballet-Oop. Directed by Robert Cannon. 1954; DVD, *UPA: The Jolly Frolics Collection,* Culver City, CA: Sony Pictures Home Entertainment, 2012.

Bambi. Directed by David Hand. 1942; DVD, Burbank, CA: Walt Disney Home Video, 2004.

Barefaced Flatfoot. Directed by John Hubley. 1951; DVD, *Mr. Magoo: The Theatrical Collection,* Culver City, CA: Sony Pictures Home Entertainment, 2014.

The Bear Scare. Director unknown. Circa 1955; Burbank, CA: United Productions of America, animated short of *The Boing-Boing Show.*

Begone Dull Care. Directed by Norman McLaren. 1949; DVD, *Norman McLaren: The Master's Edition,* Ottawa, ON: National Film Board of Canada, 2006.

Blues Pattern. Director unknown. Circa 1955; Burbank, CA: United Productions of America, animated short of *The Boing-Boing Show.*

Boniface's Vacation. Directed by Fyodor Khitruk. 1965; Moscow, RU: Soyuzmultfilm. http://www.dailymotion.com/video/xncpj7_boniface-s-vocation-1965-kanikuly-bonifaciya-eng-sp-subs-russian-animation-fedor-khitruk_shortfilms, accessed April 22, 2015.

Bringing up Mother. Directed by William T. Hurtz. 1954; DVD, *UPA: The Jolly Frolics Collection,* Culver City, CA: Sony Pictures Home Entertainment, 2012.

Brotherhood of Man. Directed by Robert Cannon. 1945; Los Angeles, CA: Industrial Film. www.youtube.com/watch?v=Fnrxbkajy9M, accessed May 11, 2015.

Bungled Bungalow. Directed by John Hubley and Pete Burness. 1950; DVD, *Mr. Magoo: The Theatrical Collection,* Culver City, CA: Sony Pictures Home Entertainment, 2014.

Cadet Rousselle. Directed by George Dunning. 1947; Ontario, ON: National Film Board of Canada. www.nfb.ca/film/cadet_rousselle, accessed April 14, 2015.

Calling Doctor Magoo. Directed by Pete Burness. 1956; DVD, *Mr. Magoo: The Theatrical Collection,* Culver City, CA: Sony Pictures Home Entertainment, 2014).

The Car of Tomorrow. Directed by Tex Avery. 1951; DVD, *Tex Avery,* Burbank, CA: Turner Entertainment, 2003.

The Case of the Missing Hare. Directed by Chuck Jones. 1942; DVD, *Looney Tunes Golden Collection,* vol. 3, Burbank, CA: Warner Home Video, 2005.

Christopher Crumpet. Directed by Robert Cannon. 1953; DVD, *UPA: The Jolly Frolics Collection,* Culver City, CA: Sony Pictures Home Entertainment, 2012.

Christopher Crumpet's Playmate. Directed by Robert Cannon. 1955; DVD, *UPA: The Jolly Frolics Collection,* Culver City, CA: Sony Pictures Home Entertainment, 2012.

Concerto for Sub-Machine Gun. Directed by Dušan Vukotić. 1958; DVD, *Dušan Vukotić on DVD,* Chatsworth, CA: Rembrandt Films, 2007.

Cowboy Jimmie. Directed by Dušan Vukotić. 1957; DVD, *Dušan Vukotić on DVD,* Chatsworth, CA: Rembrandt Films, 2007.

A Cowboy Needs a Horse. Directed by Bill Justice. 1956; DVD, *Walt Disney Treasures—Disney Rarities: Celebrated Shorts: 1920s–1960s,* Burbank, CA: Walt Disney Home Video, 2005.

The Cow on the Moon. Directed by Dušan Vukotić. 1959; DVD, *The Best of Zagreb Film: Be Careful What You Wish for And, The Classic Collection,* Chatsworth, CA: Rembrandt Films, 2000.

Crazy Mixed Up Pup. Directed by Tex Avery. 1954; DVD, *Tex Avery,* Burbank, CA: Turner Entertainment, 2003.

The Critic. Directed by Ernest Pintoff. 1963; New York, NY: Pintoff Productions. www.youtube.com/watch?v=PramR5oxn50, accessed April 9, 2015.

The Day of the Fox: A Legend of Sharaku. Directed by Alan Zaslove. 1955; Burbank, CA: United Productions of America, animated short of *The Boing-Boing Show.*

The Deserter. Directed by *Jiří Brdečka. 1965; DVD, Jiří Brdečka—Animované filmy,* Prague, CZ: Anifilm and *Limonádový Joe, 2015.*

Destination Magoo. Directed by Pete Burness. 1954; DVD, *Mr. Magoo: The Theatrical Collection,* Culver City, CA: Sony Pictures Home Entertainment, 2014.

Double Indemnity. Directed by Billy Wilder. 1944; DVD, Los Angeles, CA: Universal Pictures Home Entertainment, 2006.

The Dover Boys at Pimento University. Directed by Chuck Jones. 1942; Burbank, CA: Leon Schlesinger Studios. www.youtube.com/watch?v=dpOPyjmB8SI, accessed December 17, 2014.

Dumbo. Directed by Ben Sharpsteen. 1941; DVD, Burbank, CA: Walt Disney Home Video, 2006.

The Elephant Mystery. Director unknown. Circa 1955; Burbank, CA: United Productions of America, animated short of *The Boing-Boing Show*.

The Emperor's New Clothes. Directed by Ted Parmelee. 1953; DVD, *UPA: The Jolly Frolics Collection*, Culver City, CA: Sony Pictures Home Entertainment, 2012.

The Face. Directed by *Jiří Brdečka*. 1973; DVD, *Jiří Brdečka—Animované filmy*, Prague, CZ: Anifilm and *Limonádový Joe, 2015*.

Fantasia. Directed by Ben Sharpsteen. 1940; DVD, Burbank, CA: Walt Disney Home Video, 2010.

The Family Circus. Directed by Art Babbitt. 1951; DVD, *UPA: The Jolly Frolics Collection*, Culver City, CA: Sony Pictures Home Entertainment, 2012.

Fantasmagorie. Directed by Émile Cohl. 1908; Paris, FR: Société des Etablissements L. Gaumont. www.youtube.com/watch?v=aEAObel8yIE, accessed September 25, 2015.

The Farm of Tomorrow. Directed by Tex Avery. 1954; DVD, *Tex Avery*, Burbank, CA: Turner Entertainment, 2003.

Feline Follies. Directed by Pat Sullivan and Otto Messmer. 1919; DVD, *Felix!*; Burbank, CA: SlingShot Entertainment, 1999.

A Few Quick Facts. Directed by Osmond Evans. 1944; Burbank, CA: United Productions of America. www.youtube.com/watch?v=JYvembTqKKU, accessed December 18, 2014.

A Few Quick Facts about Fear. Directed by Zachary Schwartz. 1945; Burbank, CA: United Productions of America. www.youtube.com/watch?v=sjijPC0X9hM, accessed December 18, 2014.

The Fifty-First Dragon. Directed by Pete Burness. 1954; Burbank, CA: United Productions of America, animated short of *The Boing-Boing Show*.

Film, Film, Film. Directed by Fyodor Khitruk. 1968; DVD, *Masters of Russian Animation*, Los Angeles, CA: Image Entertainment and Jove Films, 2000.

The Five-Cent Nickel. Director unknown. Circa 1955; Burbank, CA: United Productions of America, animated short of *The Boing-Boing Show*.

Flat Hatting. Directed by John Hubley. 1946; Burbank, CA: United Productions of America. www.youtube.com/watch?v=bzIhwXKZdYc, accessed December 17, 2014.

Flebus. Directed by Ernest Pintoff. 1957; New Rochelle, NY: Terrytoons. www .youtube.com/watch?v=AdlMIE9egpE, accessed April 9, 2015.

Flowers and Trees. Directed by Burt Gillett. 1932; DVD, *Walt Disney Treasures: Silly Symphonies*, Burbank, CA: Walt Disney Home Video, 2001.

The Flying Man. Directed by George Dunning. 1962; London, UK: TVC London. www.youtube.com/watch?v=zaJq4pcNk_w, accessed August 16, 2015.

Four Wheels No Brakes. Directed by Ted Parmelee. 1955; DVD, *UPA: The Jolly Frolics Collection*, Culver City, CA: Sony Pictures Home Entertainment, 2012.

The Freeze Yum Story. Director unknown. Circa 1955; Burbank, CA: United Productions of America, animated short of *The Boing-Boing Show*.

The Frozen Logger. Directed by Jiří Brdečka. *1962;* DVD, *Jiří Brdečka—Animované filmy,* Prague, CZ: Anifilm and *Limonádový Joe, 2015.*

Fuddy-Duddy-Buddy. Directed by John Hubley. 1951; DVD, *Mr. Magoo: The Theatrical Collection,* Culver City, CA: Sony Pictures Home Entertainment, 2014.

Fudget's Budget. Directed by Robert Cannon. 1954; DVD, *UPA: The Jolly Frolics Collection,* Culver City; CA: Sony Pictures Home Entertainment, 2012.

Gallina Vogelbirdae. Directed by Jiří Brdečka. *1963;* DVD, *Jiří Brdečka— Animované filmy,* Prague, CZ: Anifilm and *Limonádový Joe, 2015.*

Georgie and the Dragon. Directed by Robert Cannon. 1951; DVD, *UPA: The Jolly Frolics Collection,* Culver City, CA: Sony Pictures Home Entertainment, 2012.

Gerald McBoing Boing. Directed by Robert Cannon. 1951; DVD, *UPA: The Jolly Frolics Collection,* Culver City; CA: Sony Pictures Home Entertainment, 2012.

Gerald McBoing! Boing! On Planet Moo. Directed by Robert Cannon. 1956; DVD, *UPA: The Jolly Frolics Collection,* Culver City, CA: Sony Pictures Home Entertainment, 2012.

Gerald McBoing Boing's Symphony. Directed by Robert Cannon. 1953; DVD, *UPA: The Jolly Frolics Collection,* Culver City, CA: Sony Pictures Home Entertainment, 2012.

Gertie the Dinosaur. Directed by Winsor McCay. 1914; New York, NY: Vitagraph Studios. www.youtube.com/watch?v=lmVra1mW7LU, accessed September 25, 2015.

Good Night, and Good Luck. Directed by George Clooney. 2005; DVD, Montreal, QC: TVA Films, 2006.

The Great Fear. Directed by Dušan Vukotić. 1958; DVD, *Dušan Vukotić on DVD,* Chatsworth, CA: Rembrandt Films, 2007.

Hamilton the Musical Elephant. Directed by John Halas. 1961; DVD, *The Halas & Batchelor Short Film Collection,* London, UK: Network TV Home Entertainment, 2015.

Hell-Bent for Election. Directed by Chuck Jones. 1944; Los Angeles, CA: Industrial Film. www.youtube.com/watch?v=2NLDih_5jAI, accessed May 11, 2015.

History of a Crime. Directed by Fyodor Khitruk. 1962; DVD, *Masters of Russian Animation,* Los Angeles, CA: Image Entertainment and Jove Films, 2000.

Hotsy Footsy. Directed by William T. Hurtz. 1952; DVD, *Mr. Magoo: The Theatrical Collection,* Culver City, CA: Sony Pictures Home Entertainment, 2014.

The House of Tomorrow. Directed by Tex Avery. 1949; DVD, *Tex Avery,* Burbank, CA: Turner Entertainment, 2003.

The House that Jack Built. Directed by Ron Tunis. 1967; Ottawa, ON: National Film Board of Canada. www.nfb.ca/film/the_house_that_jack_built, accessed April 14, 2015.

How Kiko Was Born. Directed by Dušan Vukotić and Josip Sudar. 1951; Zagreb, HR: Duga Film. http://film.nu/filmer/kako-se-rodio-kico/10240145.film, accessed April 19, 2015.

How Man Learned to Fly. Directed by Jiří Brdečka. 1958; DVD, *Jiří Brdečka—Animované filmy,* Prague, CZ: Anifilm and *Limonádový Joe,* 2015.

How Now Boing Boing. Directed by Robert Cannon. 1954; DVD, *UPA: The Jolly Frolics Collection,* Culver City, CA: Sony Pictures Home Entertainment, 2012.

How to Keep Slim. Directed by Jiří Brdečka. 1963; DVD, *Jiří Brdečka—Animované filmy,* Prague, CZ: Anifilm and *Limonádový Joe,* 2015.

The Invisible Moustache of Raoul Dufy. Directed by Aurelius Battaglia. 1955; Burbank, CA: United Productions of America, animated short of *The Boing-Boing Show.*

Is It Always Right to be Right? Directed by Lee Mishkin. 1970; Burbank, CA: Stephen Bosustow Productions. www.youtube.com/watch?v=LbWCjQ5L0ZY, accessed September 25, 2015.

The Jaywalker. Directed by Robert Cannon. 1956; DVD, *UPA: The Jolly Frolics Collection,* Culver City; CA: Sony Pictures Home Entertainment, 2012.

Johnnie Fedora and Alice Bluebonnet. Directed by Jack Kinney. 1946; DVD, *Make Mine Music,* Burbank, CA: Walt Disney Home Video, 2000.

La Joie de vivre. Directed by Anthony Gross and Hector Hoppin. 1934; Paris, FR: HG Productions. www.youtube.com/watch?v=oKpzTUyCtt0, accessed September 25, 2015.

The Juggler of Our Lady. Directed by Al Kouzel. 1959; New Rochelle, NY: Terrytoons. www.dailymotion.com/video/x8s7e2_juggler-of-our-lady_creation, accessed April 9, 2015.

Kangaroo Courting. Directed by Pete Burness. 1954; DVD, *Mr. Magoo: The Theatrical Collection,* Culver City, CA: Sony Pictures Home Entertainment, 2014.

The King and Joe. Director unknown. Circa 1955; Burbank, CA: United Productions of America, animated short of *The Boing-Boing Show.*

King-Size Canary. Directed by Tex Avery. 1947; DVD, *Tex Avery,* Burbank, CA: Turner Entertainment, 2003.

The Last Picture Show. Directed by Peter Bogdanovich. 1971; DVD, Culver City, CA: Sony Pictures Home Entertainment, 2009.

The Legend of John Henry. Directed by Sam Weiss. 1974; Burbank, CA: Stephen Bosustow Productions.

Legend of the Forest. Directed by Osamu Tezuka. 1987; DVD, *The Astonishing Work of Tezuka Osamu,* New York, NY: Kimstim Films, 2013.

Lion Hunt. Director unknown. Circa 1955; Burbank, CA: United Productions of America, animated short of *The Boing-Boing Show.*

Lion on the Loose. Director unknown. Circa 1955; Burbank, CA: United Productions of America, animated short of *The Boing-Boing Show.*

The Little Boy Who Ran Away. Director unknown. Circa 1955; Burbank, CA: United Productions of America, animated short of *The Boing-Boing Show.*

Little Boy with a Big Horn. Directed by Robert Cannon. 1953; DVD, *UPA: The Jolly Frolics Collection,* Culver City, CA: Sony Pictures Home Entertainment, 2012.

A Little Journey. Director unknown. Circa 1955; Burbank, CA: United Productions of America, animated short of *The Boing-Boing Show.*

Little Nemo. Directed by Winsor McCay. 1911; New York, NY: Vitagraph Studios. www.youtube.com/watch?v=kcSp2ej2S00, accessed September 25, 2015.

Love. Directed by *Jiří Brdečka. 1978; Jiří Brdečka—Animované filmy, Prague, CZ:* Anifilm and *Limonádový Joe, 2015.*

Love. Directed by Yōji Kuri. 1964; Tokyo, JP: Kuri Jikken Kobo. www.youtube .com/watch?v=3fOeZFK7eg8, accessed April 29, 2015.

Love and the Zeppelin. Directed by *Jiří Brdečka. 1948; DVD, Jiří Brdečka— Animované filmy, Prague, CZ:* Anifilm and *Limonádový Joe, 2015.*

Madeline. Directed by Robert Cannon. 1952; DVD, *UPA: The Jolly Frolics Collection,* Culver City; CA: Sony Pictures Home Entertainment, 2012.

Magic Boy. Directed by Taiji Yabushita and Akira Daikubara. 1959; DVD, Burbank, CA: Warner Home Video, 2014.

The Magic Fluke. Directed by John Hubley. 1949; DVD, *UPA: The Jolly Frolics Collection,* Culver City, CA: Sony Pictures Home Entertainment, 2012.

Magic Strength. Directed by Bob Wickersham. 1944; Culver City, CA: Screen Gems.

Magoo Express. Directed by Pete Burness. 1955; DVD, *Mr. Magoo: The Theatrical Collection,* Culver City, CA: Sony Pictures Home Entertainment, 2014.

Magoo Goes Skiing. Directed by Pete Burness. 1954; DVD, *Mr. Magoo: The Theatrical Collection,* Culver City, CA: Sony Pictures Home Entertainment, 2014.

Magoo Makes News. Directed by Pete Burness. 1955; DVD, *Mr. Magoo: The Theatrical Collection,* Culver City, CA: Sony Pictures Home Entertainment, 2014.

Magoo Saves the Bank. Directed by Pete Burness. 1957; DVD, *Mr. Magoo: The Theatrical Collection,* Culver City, CA: Sony Pictures Home Entertainment, 2014.

Magoo's Canine Mutiny. Directed by Pete Burness. 1956; DVD, *Mr. Magoo: The Theatrical Collection,* Culver City, CA: Sony Pictures Home Entertainment, 2014.

Magoo's Masterpiece. Directed by Pete Burness. 1953; DVD, *Mr. Magoo: The Theatrical Collection,* Culver City, CA: Sony Pictures Home Entertainment, 2014.

Magoo's Moose Hunt. Directed by Robert Cannon. 1957; DVD, *Mr. Magoo: The Theatrical Collection,* Culver City, CA: Sony Pictures Home Entertainment, 2014.

Magoo's Private War. Directed by Rudy Larriva. 1957; DVD, *Mr. Magoo: The Theatrical Collection,* Culver City, CA: Sony Pictures Home Entertainment, 2014.

Magoo's Puddle Jumper. Directed by Pete Burness. 1956; DVD, *Mr. Magoo: The Theatrical Collection,* Culver City, CA: Sony Pictures Home Entertainment, 2014.

Magoo's Three-Point Landing. Directed by Pete Burness. 1958; *Mr. Magoo: The Theatrical Collection*, Culver City, CA: Sony Pictures Home Entertainment, 2014.

Male. Directed by Eiichi Yamamoto. 1962; DVD, *The Astonishing Work of Tezuka Osamu*, New York, NY: Kimstim Films, 2013.

Man under Water. Directed by *Jiří Brdečka*. 1961; DVD *Jiří Brdečka—Animované filmy*, Prague, CZ: Anifilm and *Limonádový Joe*, 2015.

The Man with the Golden Arm. Directed by Otto Preminger. 1955; DVD, Los Angeles, CA: Passport International Entertainment, 2002.

Melody. Directed by Charles A. Nichols and Ward Kimball. 1953; DVD, *Walt Disney Treasures—Disney Rarities: Celebrated Shorts: 1920s–1960s*, Burbank, CA: Walt Disney Home Video, 2005.

Memory. Directed by Osamu Tezuka. 1964; DVD, *The Astonishing Work of Tezuka Osamu*, New York, NY: Kimstim Films, 2013.

Mermaid. Directed by Osamu Tezuka. 1964; DVD, *The Astonishing Work of Tezuka Osamu*, New York, NY: Kimstim Films, 2013.

The Merri-Go-Round in the Jungle. Director unknown. Circa 1955; Burbank, CA: United Productions of America, animated short of *The Boing-Boing Show*.

Metamorpheus. Directed by *Jiří Brdečka*. 1969; DVD, *Jiří Brdečka—Animované filmy*, Prague, CZ: Anifilm and *Limonádový Joe*, 2015.

Minstrel's Song. Directed by *Jiří Brdečka*. 1964; DVD, *Jiří Brdečka—Animované filmy*, Prague, CZ: Anifilm and *Limonádový Joe*, 2015.

Mr. Magoo: The Theatrical Collection. DVD. AA.VV. Culver City, CA: Sony Pictures Home Entertainment, 2014.

Mr. Tingley's Tangle. Directed by T. Hee. Circa 1955; Burbank, CA: United Productions of America, animated short of *The Boing-Boing Show*.

Moonbird. Directed by John Hubley. 1959; DVD, *Selected Films of John and Faith Hubley*, San Francisco, CA: McSweeney's, *The Believer*, March/April 2014.

My Darling Clementine. Directed by *Jiří Brdečka*. 1959; DVD, *Jiří Brdečka—Animované filmy*, Prague, CZ: Anifilm and *Limonádový Joe*, 2015.

My Financial Career. Directed by Gerald Potterton. 1962; Ottawa, ON: National Film Board. www.nfb.ca/film/my_financial_career, accessed April 14, 2015.

Neighbours. Directed by Norman McLaren. 1952; DVD, *Norman McLaren: The Master's Edition*, Ottawa, ON: National Film Board of Canada, 2006.

Northwest Hounded Police. Directed by Tex Avery. 1946; DVD, *Tex Avery*, Burbank, CA: Turner Entertainment, 2003.

Once upon a Winter Time. Directed by Hamilton Luske. 1948; DVD, *Melody Time*, Burbank, CA: Buena Vista Home Entertainment, 2000.

One Hundred and One Dalmatians. Directed by Clyde Geronimi, Hamilton Luske and Wolfgang Reitherman. 1961; DVD, Burbank, CA: Walt Disney Home Video, 1999.

1001 Arabian Nights. Directed by Jack Kinney. 1959; DVD, *Mr. Magoo: The Theatrical Collection*, Culver City, CA: Sony Pictures Home Entertainment, 2014.

One Wonderful Girl. Director unknown. Circa 1955; Burbank, CA: United Productions of America, animated short of *The Boing-Boing Show*.

On the Waterfront. Directed by Elia Kazan. 1954; DVD, Culver City, CA: Columbia Tristar Home Entertainment, 2001.

The Oompahs. Directed by Robert Cannon. 1952; DVD, *UPA: The Jolly Frolics Collection*, Culver City, CA: Sony Pictures Home Entertainment, 2012.

Our Little Red Riding Hood. Directed by Jiří Brdečka. 1960; DVD, *Jiří Brdečka— Animované filmy*, Prague, CZ: Anifilm and *Limonádový Joe*, 2015.

Pas de Deux. Directed by Norman McLaren. 1968; DVD, *Norman McLaren: The Master's Edition*, Ottawa, ON: National Film Board of Canada, 2006.

Payday. Directed by Friz Freleng. 1944; DVD, *Private Snafu Golden Classics*, Ann Arbor, MI: Thunderbean Animation, 2010.

Pee-Wee the Kiwi Bird. Director unknown. Circa 1955; Burbank, CA: United Productions of America, animated short of *The Boing-Boing Show*.

The Performing Painter. Director unknown. Circa 1955; Burbank, CA: United Productions of America, animated short of *The Boing-Boing Show*.

A Personal Journey with Martin Scorsese through American Movies. DVD. Directed by Martin Scorsese and Michael Henry Wilson. Santa Monica, CA: Voyager Co. and Buena Vista Home Entertainment, 1995.

Pete Hothead. Directed by Pete Burness. 1952; DVD, *UPA: The Jolly Frolics Collection*, Culver City, CA: Sony Pictures Home Entertainment, 2012.

Piccolo. Directed by Dušan Vukotić. 1959; DVD, *Dušan Vukotić on DVD*, Chatsworth, CA: Rembrandt Films, 2007.

Picnics are Fun and Dino's Serenade. Directed by Lew Keller and Fred Crippen. 1959; DVD, *UPA: The Jolly Frolics Collection*, Culver City, CA: Sony Pictures Home Entertainment, 2012.

Pictures at an Exhibition. Directed by Osamu Tezuka. 1966; DVD, *The Astonishing Work of Tezuka Osamu*, New York, NY: Kimstim Films, 2013.

Pigs Is Pigs. Directed by Jack Kinney. 1954; DVD, *Walt Disney Treasures—Disney Rarities: Celebrated Shorts: 1920s–1960s*, Burbank, CA: Walt Disney Home Video, 2005.

Pink and Blue Blues. Directed by Pete Burness. 1952; DVD, *Mr. Magoo: The Theatrical Collection*, Culver City, CA: Sony Pictures Home Entertainment, 2014.

The Pink Phink. Directed by Friz Freleng and Hawley Pratt. 1964; DVD, *The Pink Panther: Classic Cartoon Collection*, Burbank, CA: MGM Home Entertainment, 2005.

Pinocchio. Directed by Ben Sharpsteen and Hamilton Luske. 1940; DVD, Burbank, CA: Walt Disney Home Video, 2009.

Plaisir d'Amour (Joy of Love). Directed by Jiří Brdečka. 1966; DVD, *Jiří Brdečka— Animované filmy*, Prague, CZ: Anifilm and *Limonádový Joe*, 2015.

The Playful Robot. Directed by Dušan Vukotić. 1956; DVD, *Dušan Vukotić on DVD*, Chatsworth, CA: Rembrandt Films, 2007.

Pleasantville. Directed by Gary Ross. 1998; DVD, Los Angeles, CA: New Line Home Video, 1999.

The Popcorn Story. Directed by Art Babbitt. 1950; DVD, *UPA: The Jolly Frolics Collection*, Culver City, CA: Sony Pictures Home Entertainment, 2012.

The Power of Destiny. Directed by Jiří Brdečka. 1968; DVD, *Jiří Brdečka— Animované filmy*, Prague, CZ: Anifilm and *Limonádový Joe*, 2015.

Punchy de Leon. Directed by John Hubley. 1950; DVD, *UPA: The Jolly Frolics Collection*, Culver City, CA: Sony Pictures Home Entertainment, 2012.

The Ragtime Bear. Directed by John Hubley. 1949; DVD, *UPA: The Jolly Frolics Collection*, Culver City; CA: Sony Pictures Home Entertainment, 2012.

Reason and Emotion. Directed by Jiří Brdečka. 1962; DVD, *Jiří Brdečka— Animované filmy*, Prague, CZ: Anifilm and *Limonádový Joe*, 2015.

Rebel without a Cause. Directed by Nicholas Ray. 1955; DVD, Burbank, CA: Warner Home Video, 1999.

Red Hot Riding Hood. Directed by Tex Avery. 1943; DVD, *Tex Avery*, Burbank, CA: Turner Entertainment, 2003.

Revenge. Directed by Jiří Brdečka. 1968; DVD, *Jiří Brdečka—Animované filmy*, Prague, CZ: Anifilm and *Limonádový Joe*, 2015.

Revenger. Directed by Dušan Vukotić. 1958; DVD, *Dušan Vukotić on DVD*, Chatsworth, CA: Rembrandt Films, 2007.

River of Steel. Directed by Peter Sachs. 1951; London, UK: W. M. Larkins studio. www.youtube.com/watch?v=4jejf5euwdw, accessed August 20, 2015.

Robin Hoodlum. Directed by John Hubley. 1948; DVD, *UPA: The Jolly Frolics Collection*, Culver City, CA: Sony Pictures Home Entertainment, 2012.

Rooty Toot Toot. Directed by John Hubley. 1952; *UPA*: DVD, *The Jolly Frolics Collection*, Culver City, CA: Sony Pictures Home Entertainment, 2012.

The Sad Lion. Director unknown. Circa 1955; Burbank, CA: United Productions of America, animated short of *The Boing-Boing Show*.

Sailing and Village Band. Directed by Lew Keller and Fred Crippen. 1958; DVD, *UPA: The Jolly Frolics Collection*, Culver City, CA: Sony Pictures Home Entertainment, 2012.

Saludos Amigos. Directed by Wilfred Jackson, Jack Kinney, Hamilton Luske and William Roberts. 1942; DVD, Burbank, CA: Walt Disney Studios Home Entertainment, 2000.

Scoutmaster Magoo. Directed by Robert Cannon. 1958; DVD, *Mr. Magoo: The Theatrical Collection*, Culver City, CA: Sony Pictures Home Entertainment, 2014.

Señor Droopy. Directed by Tex Avery. 1949; *Tex Avery*, DVD, Burbank, CA: Turner Entertainment, 2003.

7 Arts. Directed by Ion Popescu-Gopo. 1958; Bucharest, RO: Cinematographic Studio Bucharest. www.youtube.com/watch?v=Ic4xp6oQZAw, accessed September 25, 2015.

Sh-h-h-h-h. Directed by Tex Avery. 1955; DVD, *Tex Avery*, Burbank, CA: Turner Entertainment, 2003.

Short History. Directed by Ion Popescu-Gopo. 1956; Bucharest, RO: Cinematographic Studio Bucharest. www.youtube.com/watch?v=jI53 -N6mGX8, accessed September 25, 2015.

Snow White and the Seven Dwarfs. Directed by David Hand. 1937; DVD, Burbank, CA: Walt Disney Home Video, 2009.

Song of Victory. Directed by Bob Wickersham. 1942; Culver City, CA: Screen Gems. ww.youtube.com/watch?v=Bmd-UuP0-H8, accessed September 25, 2015.

Sparks and Chips Get the Blitz. Director unknown. 1943; Los Angeles, CA: Industrial Film.

Spellbound Hound. Directed by John Hubley and Pete Burness. 1949; DVD, *Mr. Magoo: The Theatrical Collection,* Culver City, CA: Sony Pictures Home Entertainment, 2014.

Spring and Saganaki. Directed by Lew Keller and Fred Crippen. 1958; DVD, *UPA: The Jolly Frolics Collection,* Culver City, CA: Sony Pictures Home Entertainment, 2012.

Steamboat Willie. Directed by Ub Iwerks and Walt Disney. 1928; DVD, *Mickey Mouse in Black and White,* Burbank, CA: Walt Disney Home Video, 2002.

A Streetcar Named Desire. DVD. Directed by Elia Kazan. 1951; Burbank, CA: Warner Home Video, 2006.

Substitute. Directed by Dušan Vukotić. 1961; Zagreb, HR: Zagreb Film. www.youtube.com/watch?v=xhfHXLuiTd8, accessed April 20, 2015.

Swab Your Choppers. Director unknown. 1947; Burbank, CA: United Productions of America.

Sweet Smell of Success. Directed by Alexander Mackendrick. 1957; DVD, New York, NY: The Criterion Collection, 2011.

Symphony in Slang. Directed by Tex Avery. 1951; DVD, *Tex Avery,* Burbank, CA: Turner Entertainment, 2003.

Tales of the Street Corner. Directed by Yûsaku Sakamoto and Eiichi Yamamoto. 1962; DVD, *The Astonishing Work of Tezuka Osamu,* New York, NY: Kimstim Films, 2013.

Tapum! Weapons History. Directed by Bruno Bozzetto. 1958; DVD, *Tutto Bozzetto,* Rome, IT: Twentieth Century Fox Italy, 2012.

The Television Fan. Directed by Jiří Brdečka. 1961; DVD, *Jiří Brdečka—Animované filmy,* Prague, CZ: Anifilm and *Limonádový Joe,* 2015.

The Tell-Tale Heart. Directed by Ted Parmelee. 1953; DVD, *UPA: The Jolly Frolics Collection,* Culver City, CA: Sony Pictures Home Entertainment, 2012.

The Tender Game. Directed by John Hubley. 1958; DVD, *Selected Films of John and Faith Hubley,* San Francisco, CA: McSweeney's, *The Believer,* March/April 2014.

Terror Faces Magoo. Directed by Chris Ishii and Jack Goodford. 1959; DVD, *Mr. Magoo: The Theatrical Collection,* Culver City, CA: Sony Pictures Home Entertainment, 2014.

There Was a Miller on a River. Directed by Jiří Brdečka. 1971; DVD, *Jiří Brdečka—Animované filmy,* Prague, CZ: Anifilm and *Limonádový Joe,* 2015.

Three Blind Mice. Directed by George Dunning. 1945; Ontario, ON: National Film Board of Canada. www.youtube.com/watch?v=OOTCVCR26Ko, accessed September 24, 2015.

The Three Caballeros. Directed by Norman Ferguson. 1944; DVD, Burbank, CA: Buena Vista Home Video, 2000.

Three Little Pigs. Directed by Burt Gillett. 1933; DVD, *Walt Disney Treasures: Silly Symphonies*, Burbank, CA: Walt Disney Home Video, 2005.

Throne of Blood. Directed by Akira Kurosawa. 1957; DVD, New York, NY: The Criterion Collection, 2003.

Toot, Whistle, Plunk and Boom. Directed by Charles A. Nichols and Ward Kimball. 1953; DVD, *Walt Disney Treasures—Disney Rarities: Celebrated Shorts: 1920s–1960s*, Burbank, CA: Walt Disney Home Video, 2005.

Trees and Jamaica Daddy. Directed by Lew Keller and Fred Crippen. 1958; DVD, *UPA: The Jolly Frolics Collection*, Culver City, CA: Sony Pictures Home Entertainment, 2012.

The Trojan Horse. Director unknown. Circa 1956; Burbank, CA: United Productions of America, animated short of *The Boing-Boing Show*.

Trouble Indemnity. Directed by John Hubley and Pete Burness. 1950; DVD, *Mr. Magoo: The Theatrical Collection*, Culver City, CA: Sony Pictures Home Entertainment, 2014.

Turned around Clown. Director unknown. Circa 1955; Burbank, CA: United Productions of America, animated short of *The Boing-Boing Show*.

TV of Tomorrow. Directed by Tex Avery. 1953; DVD, *Tex Avery*, Burbank, CA: Turner Entertainment, 2003.

Two by Two. Directed by George Dunning. Circa 1955; Burbank, CA: United Productions of America, animated short of *The Boing-Boing Show*.

Two Castles. Directed by Bruno Bozzetto. 1963; DVD, *Tutto Bozzetto*, Rome, IT: Twentieth Century Fox Italy, 2012.

The Unbearable Bear. Directed by Chuck Jones. 1943; DVD, *Looney Tunes Mouse Chronicles: The Chuck Jones Collection*, Burbank, CA: Warner Home Video, 2012.

Uncle Sneaky. Director unknown. Circa 1955; Burbank, CA: United Productions of America, animated short of *The Boing-Boing Show*.

Uncle Tom's Cabaña. Directed by Tex Avery. 1947; DVD, *Tex Avery*, Burbank, CA: Turner Entertainment, 2003.

The Unenchanted Princess. Director unknown. Circa 1955; Burbank, CA: United Productions of America, animated short of *The Boing-Boing Show*.

The Unicorn in the Garden. Directed by William T. Hurtz. 1953; DVD, *UPA: The Jolly Frolics Collection*, Culver City, CA: Sony Pictures Home Entertainment, 2012.

UPA: The Jolly Frolics Collection. DVD. AA.VV. Culver City, CA: Sony Pictures Home Entertainment, 2012.

The Violinist. Directed by Ernest Pintoff. 1959; New York, NY: Pintoff Productions. www.youtube.com/watch?v=wlnuyZMRLr4, accessed April 9, 2015.

Wackiki Wabbit. Directed by Chuck Jones. 1943; DVD, *Looney Tunes Golden Collection*, vol. 3, Burbank, CA: Warner Home Video, 2005.

Walt & El Grupo: The Untold Adventures. Directed by Theodore Thomas. 2008; DVD, Burbank, CA: Walt Disney Studios Home Entertainment, 2010.

What I Didn't Say to the Prince. Directed by *Jiří Brdečka. 1975; DVD, Jiří Brdečka—Animované filmy, Prague, CZ:* Anifilm and *Limonádový Joe, 2015.*

When Magoo Flew. Directed by Pete Burness. 1955; DVD, *Mr. Magoo: The Theatrical Collection,* Culver City, CA: Sony Pictures Home Entertainment, 2014.

The White Snake Enchantress. Directed by Taiji Yabushita. 1958; DVD, *Le Serpent Blanc,* Paris, FR: Wild Side Video, 2012.

Willie the Kid. Directed by Robert Cannon. 1952; DVD, *UPA: The Jolly Frolics Collection,* Culver City, CA: Sony Pictures Home Entertainment, 2012.

Willoughby's Magic Hat. Directed by Bob Wickersham. 1943; Culver City, CA: Screen Gems. www.youtube.com/watch?v=-vb5QTQSj5Y, accessed September 25, 2015.

Windy Day. Directed by John Hubley and Faith E. Hubley. 1968; DVD, *The Hubley Collection,* vol. 1, Los Angeles, CA: Image Entertainment, 1999.

The Wonder Gloves. Directed by Robert Cannon. 1951; DVD, *UPA: The Jolly Frolics Collection,* Culver City, CA: Sony Pictures Home Entertainment, 2012.

Yellow Submarine. Directed by George Dunning. 1968; DVD, Burbank, CA: MGM Home Entertainment, 1999.

WORKS REFERENCED

Abraham, Adam. *When Magoo Flew: The Rise and Fall of Animation Studio UPA.* Middletown, CT: Wesleyan University Press, 2012.

Alberti, Walter. *Il Cinema di Animazione 1832–1956.* Turin, IT: Edizioni Radio Italiana, 1957.

Amidi, Amid. *Cartoon Modern: Style and Design in Fifties Animation.* San Francisco, CA: Chronicle Books, 2006.

———. *Inside UPA.* New York, NY: Cartoon Brew Books, 2007.

Barrier, J. Michael. *Hollywood Cartoons: American Animation in Its Golden Age.* Oxford, UK: Oxford University Press, 1999.

Barrier, Mike. "John and Faith Hubley: Traditional Animation Transformed." *Millimiter* (February 1977): 42–43.

Bartram, Alan. *Bauhaus Modernism and the Illustrated Book.* London, UK: British Library, 2004.

Bass, Jennifer, and Pat Kirkham. *Saul Bass: A Life in Film & Design.* London, UK: Laurence King Publishing, 2011.

Benayoun, Robert. *Le Dessin Animé après Walt Disney.* Paris, FR: Jean-Jacques Pauvert, 1961.

Bendazzi, Giannalberto. *Bruno Bozzetto: Animazione Primo Amore.* Milan, IT: Isca, 1972.

———. *Cartoons: 100 Years of Cinema Animation.* London, UK: John Libbey Cinema and Animation; Bloomington, IN: Indiana University Press, 1994.

Bogart, Michele Helene. *Artists, Advertising, and the Borders of Art.* Chicago, IL: University of Chicago Press, 1995.

Bongard, David. "Animated Cartoons Find Higher Purpose: Film Cartoonists Try to Be More Than Just Quaint." *Los Angeles Daily News*, February 2, 1953, 20–22.

"Bright-Toned Fantasy." *Newsweek*, December 21, 1959. *1001 Arabian Nights* file, Core collection production files, Margaret Herrick Library, Academy of Motion Picture Arts and Sciences.

Chalais, François. "Le fil à couper Disney." *Cahiers du Cinéma*, no. 6 (1951): 49–51.

Chevalier, Denys. *J'aime le Dessin Animé*. Lausanne, CH: Editions Rencontre, 1962.

Clarens, Bernard, ed. *André Martin 1925–1994. Écrits Sur L'animation*, vol. 1. Paris, FR: Dreamland, 2000.

Cohen, Karl F. *Forbidden Animation: Censored Cartoons and Blacklisted Animators in America*. Jefferson, NC: McFarland, 1997.

Coursodon, Jean Pierre. *Keaton et Cie: Les Burlesques Américains du "Muet."* Cinéma d'aujourd'hui. Paris, FR: Éditions Seghers, 1964.

"Creativity Basic." *Television Age*, December 1, 1958, 46–47, 60–62. Steve Bosustow's UPA collection.

Crowther, Bosley. "McBoing Boing, Magoo and Bosustow." *New York Times Magazine*, December 21, 1952, 14–15, 23.

Daggett, Charles. Production Notes, "Gerald McBoing Boing," Early Museum History: Administrative Records, III.26.a; The Museum of Modern Art Archives, New York.

———. Production Notes, "The Unicorn in the Garden," Early Museum History: Administrative Records, III.26.a; The Museum of Modern Art Archives, New York.

———. Production Notes, "The Tell-Tale Heart," Early Museum History: Administrative Records, III.26.a; The Museum of Modern Art Archives, New York.

"Declaration of Independence." National Archives and Records Administration. www.archives.gov/exhibits/charters/declaration_transcript.html, accessed November 27, 2014.

Deitch, Gene. "10. Steve Bosustow." In *genedeitchcredits: The 65 Greats behind the Scenes!* (blog), 9 April 2012. http://genedeitchcredits.com /roll-the-credits/10-steve-bosustow/.

———. "19. Saul Steinberg meets Margaret Hamilton!" In *genedeitchcredits: The 65 Greats behind the Scenes!* (blog). http://genedeitchcredits.com /roll-the-credits/10-steve-bosustow/.

———. "Chapter 12: The Upa Experience." In *How to Succeed in Animation: Don't Let a Little Thing Like Failure Stop You!* Van Nuys, CA: Animation World Network, 2013. www.awn.com/genedeitch/chapter-twelve-the-UPA -experience, accessed January 20, 2015.

Droste, Magdalena. *Bauhaus*. Cologne, DE: Taschen, 2014.

"Edward R. Murrow: A Report on Senator Joseph R. McCarthy. See it Now (CBS-TV, March 9, 1954)." Media Resources Center, Moffitt Library, University of California, Berkeley, CA. www.lib.berkeley.edu/MRC/murrow mccarthy.html, accessed October 9, 2015.

Eisenstein, Sergei M. *Eisenstein on Disney.* Calcutta, IN: Seagull Books, 1986.

Emmett, Neil. "Animation Nation: The Art of Persuasion Part 2," *The Lost Continent: Exploring the Art and History of British Animation* (blog), February 15, 2012 (12:23), http://ukanimation.blogspot.co.uk/2012/02/animation-nation-art-of -persuasion-part.html.

F. H. "Oh for a Magic Lamp Like Magoo in '1001 Nights'!" *Hollywood Citizen News,* December 21, 1959. *1001 Arabian Nights* file, Core collection production files, Margaret Herrick Library, Academy of Motion Picture Arts and Sciences.

Fisher, David. "U.P.A. in England." *Sight and Sound,* 45. Abe and Charlotte Levitow papers, Margaret Herrick Library, Academy of Motion Picture Arts and Sciences.

Fry, Roger Edward. "Line as a Means of Expression in Modern Art." *Burlington Magazine for Connoisseurs* 33, no. 189 (1918): 201–208. http://www.jstor .org/stable/860829?Search=yes&resultItemClick=true&searchText=Line& searchText=as&searchText=a&searchText=Means&searchText=of&search Text=Expression&searchUri=%2Faction%2FdoBasicSearch%3FQuery%3 DLine%2Bas%2Ba%2BMeans%2Bof%2BExpression%26amp%3Bacc%3D off%26amp%3Bwc%3Don%26amp%3Bfc%3Doff%26amp%3Bgroup%3D none&seq=1#page_scan_tab_contents, accessed February 17, 2015.

Furniss, Maureen. *Art in Motion: Animation Aesthetics.* Sydney, AU: John Libbey Publishing, 1998.

———.*The Animation Bible: A Practical Guide to the Art of Animating, from Flipbooks to Flash.* London, UK: Laurence King Publishing; New York, NY: Harry N. Abrams, 2008.

Genter, Robert. *Late Modernism: Art, Culture, and Politics in Cold War America.* Philadelphia, PA: University of Pennsylvania Press, 2010.

Gerber, Anna. *Graphic Design: The 50 Most Influential Graphic Designers in The World.* London, UK: A&C Black Publishers, 2010.

Goldman, Eric Frederick. *The Crucial Decade—and After. America, 1945–1960.* New York, NY: Random House, 1969.

Goldwater, Robert J. *Primitivism in Modern Painting.* New York, NY: Harper and Brothers Publishers, 1938.

Graham, Donald W. *Composing Pictures: Donald W. Graham.* Beverly Hills, CA: Silman-James Press, 2009. Originally published: New York, NY: Van Nostrand Reinhold Co., 1970.

Gropius, Walter. "Reorientation." In *The New Landscape in Art and Science,* ed. György Kepes. Chicago, IL: Paul Theobald and Company, 1956.

Guernsey, Otis L. Jr. "The Movie Cartoon Is Coming of Age." *New York Herald Tribune,* November 29, 1953.

Harris, Neil, and Martina R. Norelli. "Art, Design, and the Modern Corporation." Ed. National Museum of American Art. Washington, DC: Smithsonian Institution Press, 1985.

Heller, Steven. *Design Literacy: Understanding Graphic Design*. New York, NY: Allworth Press, 2014.

Hift, Fred. "'McBoing' to 'Rooty Toot.'" *New York Times*, March 16, 1952.

"How Does UPA Do It?" *Television Magazine*, December 1955, 44–45, 75–76. Steve Bosustow's UPA collection.

Hubley, John, and Faith Hubley. "Animation: A Creative Challenge—by John and Faith Hubley (interview)," interview by John D. Ford, September 24–25, 1973. Kansas City, MO: Kansas City Art Institute, Book-Periodical Annex, Margaret Herrick Library, Academy of Motion Picture Arts and Sciences.

Hubley, John, and Zachary Schwartz. "Animation Learns a New Language." *Hollywood Quarterly* 1, no. 4 (1946): 360–363. www.jstor.org/stable/1209495? seq=1#page_scan_tab_contents, accessed November 4, 2012.

Jezer, Marty. *The Dark Ages: Life in the United States, 1945–1960*. Boston, MA: South End Press, 1982.

Jin, Lei. "Silence and Sound in Kurosawa's *Throne of Blood*." CLCWeb: *Comparative Literature and Culture* 6, no. 1 (2004). http://docs.lib.purdue .edu/cgi/viewcontent.cgi?article=1206&context=clcweb, accessed June 16, 2016.

Kazan, Elia. *A Life*. London, UK; Sydney, AU; and Auckland, NZ: Pan Books, 1988.

Kennedy, John F. *Profiles in Courage*. 1955, 1st ed. New York, NY: HarperCollins Publishers, 2004.

Kepes, György. *Language of Vision*. 2nd ed. New York, NY: Dover, 1995.

Klee, Paul. *Pedagogical Sketchbook*. 7th ed. New York, NY, and Washington, DC: Praeger Publishers, 1972.

Klein, Norman M. *Seven Minutes: The Life and Death of the American Animated Cartoon*. London, UK; and New York, NY: Verso, 1997.

Knight, Arthur. "The New Look in Cartooning." *Saturday Review of Literature*, April 21, 1951, 30.

———. "Up from Disney." *Theatre Arts*, August 1951, 32–33, 92.

———. "UPA, Magoo & McBoing-Boing." *Art Digest*, February 1, 1952, 22.

———. "U.P.A. Goes Boing-Boing." *Esquire*, February 1953, 49, 112.

Langsner, Jules. "UPA." *Arts and Architecture*, December 1954.

Leslie, Esther. *Hollywood Flatlands*. London, UK, and New York, NY: Verso, 2002.

"Life and Work." Saul Steinberg Foundation. www.saulsteinbergfoundation.org /life_work.html, accessed June 18, 2015.

Lo Duca, Giuseppe Maria. *Le Dessin Animé: Histoire, Esthétique, Technique*. Paris, FR: Prisma, 1948.

Maltin, Leonard. *Of Mice and Magic: A History of American Animated Cartoons*. New York, NY: New American Library, 1987.

McCandlish, Phillips. "Without Lisping Pigs: UPA Cartoons Penetrate TV's Culture Barrier with Esthetic Appeal." *New York Times,* March 17, 1957.

Meggs, Philip B. *Meggs' History of Graphic Design.* Hoboken, NJ: John Wiley & Sons, 2006.

Miller, Arthur. *Death of a Salesman.* 1949, 1st ed. New York, NY: Penguin Books, 1998.

Moholy-Nagy, László. *The New Vision and Abstract of an Artist.* 4th ed. New York, NY: Wittenborn Schultz, 1949.

———. *Vision in Motion.* Chicago, IL: Paul Theobald and Company, 1956.

"The Monroe Doctrine: Also, Jefferson's Letter to Monroe." University of California. www.archive.org/stream/monroedoctrineal00unit/monroedoc trineal00unit_djvu.txt, accessed November 27, 2014.

Moon, Barbara. "The Silly, Splendid World of Stephen Bosustow." *Maclean's,* December 7, 1957.

Moritz, William. "UPA, Reminiscing 30 Years Later." *ASIFA Canada* 12, no. 3 (1984): 14–22. John Canemaker Animation Collection; MSS 040; box 2; folder 5; Fales Library and Special Collections, NYU.

Newman, Barnett. "The First Man Was an Artist." *Tiger's Eye* 1, no. 1 (October 1947): 57–60.

Newsom, Jon. "'A Sound Idea' Music for Animated Films." *Quarterly Journal of the Library of Congress* 37, nos. 3–4 (1980): 279–309. www.jstor.org /stable/29781862?seq=1#page_scan_tab_contents, accessed April 8, 2015.

New Yorker magazine. *The 40s: The Story of a Decade.* New York, NY: Random House, 2014.

Nichols, Luther. "A Star Is Drawn: Meet Gerald McBoing-Boing." *San Francisco Chronicle,* January 21, 1951.

Novielli, Maria Roberta. *Animerama: Storia del cinema d'animazione giapponese.* Venice, IT: Marsilio, 2015.

Oeri, Georgine. "UPA: A New Dimension for the Comic Strip." *Graphis: International Journal of Graphic Art and Applied Art* 9, no. 50 (1953): 470–479.

Parker, Becki Lee. "UPA Animation: No Animals, No Violence, Just Good Stories." Unpublished paper, University of Oregon, Eugene, OR, 1993. Giannalberto Bendazzi's collection.

Penney, Ed. "U.P.A. Animated Art." *The Arts,* March 1953, 12–13.

Pikkov, Ülo. *Animasophy: Theoretical Writings on the Animated Film.* Tallinn, EE: Estonian Academy of Arts, 2010.

Rand, Paul. *Thoughts on Design.* 4th ed. San Francisco, CA: Chronicle Books, 2014. Originally published: New York, NY: Wittenborn Schultz, 1947.

Remington, Roger and Lisa Bodenstedt. *American Modernism: Graphic Design, 1920 to 1960.* London, UK: Laurence King Publishing, 2003.

Rieder, Howard Edward. "The Development of the Satire of Mr. Magoo." Master's thesis, Graduate School, University of Southern California, August 1961.

Rondolino, Gianni. *Storia Del Cinema D'animazione.* 2nd ed. Torino, IT: UTET, 2003. Rosenberg, Milton J. "Mr. Magoo as Public Dream." *Quarterly of Film Radio and Television* 11, no. 4 (Summer 1957): 337–342.

Savas, Minae Yamamoto. "The Art of Japanese Noh Theatre in Akira Kurosawa's *Throne of Blood*." *Bridgewater Review* 30, no. 2 (2011): 19–23. http://vc.bridgew.edu/cgi/viewcontent.cgi?article=1279&context=br_rev, accessed June 16, 2016.

Schatz, Thomas. *The Genius of the System: Hollywood Filmmaking in the Studio Era*. New York, NY: Pantheon Books, 1988.

Schwartz, Zachary. "Notes from Zack Schwartz Appearance at UCLA." Zach Schwartz animation conference, UCLA, Los Angeles, California, July 7, 1977. John Canemaker Animation Collection; MSS 040; box 2; folder 5; Fales Library and Special Collections, NYU.

Seldes, George. "Delight in Seven Minutes." *Saturday Review*, May 31, 1952, 27.

Shull, Michael S. and David E. Wilt. *Doing Their Bit: Wartime American Animated Short Films, 1939-1945*. Jefferson, NC: McFarland, 2004.

Sito, Tom. *Drawing the Line: The Untold Story of the Animation Unions from Bosko to Bart Simpson*. Lexington, KY: University Press of Kentucky, 2006.

Solomon, Charles. *Enchanted Drawings: The History of Animation*. New York, NY: Alfred A. Knopf, 1989.

Spigel, Lynn. *TV by Design: Modern Art and the Rise of Network Television*. Chicago, IL: University of Chicago Press, 2008.

Stephenson, Ralph. *Animation in the Cinema*. London, UK: A. Zwemmer Limited, 1967.

Stinson, Charles. "Mr. Magoo Triumphs over Arabian Foes." *Los Angeles Times*, December18, 1959. *1001 Arabian Nights* file, Core collection production files, Margaret Herrick Library, Academy of Motion Picture Arts and Sciences.

Sudovic, Zlatko (editor) *Zagrebacki krug crtanog filma 3*, Zagreb, 1978. Andrijana Ruzic's collection.

Sudovic, Zlatko (editor), *Zagrebacki krug crtanog filma 4*, Zagreb, 1986. Andrijana Ruzic's collection.

Tavassi, Guido. *Storia dell'animazione Giapponese: Autori, Arte, Industria, Successo dal 1917 a oggi*. Latina, IT: Tunué, 2012.

Taylor, Nick. *American-Made—The Enduring Legacy of the WPA: When FDR Put the Nation to Work*. New York, NY: Bantam Dell, 2008.

The Museum of Modern Art, New York. "Bauhaus 1919–1928." Ed. Walter Gropius, Herbert Bayer and Ise Gropius. New York, NY, 1938.

"United Films." *Direction*, 1945, 2–3. Steve Bosustow's UPA collection.

Van Citters, Darrell. *The Art of Jay Ward Productions*. Los Angeles, CA: Oxberry Press, 2013.

Wells, Paul. *Understanding Animation*. London, UK: Routledge, 2008.

Winsten, Archer. "The Problem of Quality." *New York Post*, August 23, 1955. Steve Bosustow's UPA collection.

Wong, Dick. "Search for the Magic Pen." *frameafterframe* (2006): 42–46.

Zanotto, Piero. "Petite histoire du cinéma d'animation: Stephen Bosustow et l'U.P.A." *Séquences: la revue du cinéma*, no. 44 (1966): 43–50.

Index

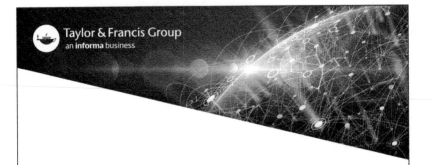

Printed and bound by CPI Group (UK) Ltd, Croydon, CR0 4YY

17/10/2024

01775705-0001